Adding English: ESL Teacher's Guide

Scott Foresman

Editorial Offices: Glenview, Illinois • Parsippany, New Jersey • New York, New York
Sales Offices: Parsippany, New Jersey • Duluth, Georgia • Glenview, Illinois
Carrollton, Texas • Ontario, California

Authors

Anna Uhl Chamot is an associate professor in the area of ESL teacher preparation at George Washington University. She also serves as associate director of the Georgetown University/George Washington University/Center for Applied Linguistics National Capital Language Resource Center, which conducts research, training, and materials development for language learning strategies, immersion programs, and portfolio assessment. Books she has co-authored include *Learning Strategies in Second Language Acquisition, The CALLA Handbook: How to Implement the Cognitive Academic Language Learning Approach,* and *The Learning Strategies Handbook*. Dr. Chamot holds a Ph.D. in English as a Second Language and Applied Linguistics from the University of Texas at Austin.

Carolyn Kessler is Professor Emerita of English as a Second Language and Applied Linguistics at the University of Texas at San Antonio. She has worked extensively in ESL/bilingual staff development for school districts and other agencies throughout Texas and other parts of the U. S. Among her recent books are *Literacy con Cariño: A Story of Migrant Children's Success* and *Teaching Science to English Learners, Grades 4–8.* Her research interests include second language acquisition for children and adults, accelerating academic language learning, and processes for building learning communities. She is recipient of the President's Distinguished Achievement Award for Teaching Excellence at the University of Texas at San Antonio. Dr. Kessler received her Ph.D. from Georgetown University.

Jim Cummins is a professor in the Modern Language Centre and Curriculum Department of the Ontario Institute for Studies in Education. He has published several books related to bilingual education and ESL student achievement including *Bilingualism and Special Education: Issues in Assessment and Pedagogy* and *Bilingualism in Education: Aspects of Theory, Research and Policy* (with Merrill Swain). Among other works by Dr. Cummins is the highly acclaimed *Brave New Schools: Challenging Cultural Illiteracy Through Global Learning Networks* (with Dennis Sayers). His current research focuses on the challenges educators face in adjusting to classrooms where cultural and linguistic diversity is the norm. Dr. Cummins received his Ph.D. from the University of Alberta, Canada.

Lily Wong Fillmore is a professor in the Graduate School of Education at the University of California, Berkeley. Her specializations are in the areas of second language learning and teaching, the education of language minority students, and socialization for learning across cultures. She is project director and principal investigator for the Family, Community, and the University Partnership, which prepares professionals to work in educational institutions in American Indian communities in the Southwest. Dr. Wong Fillmore received her Ph.D. in linguistics from Stanford University.

Table of Contents

The Philosophy of *Adding English*

Adding English: ESL Teacher's Guide, a companion to *Scott Foresman Reading,* accelerates reading instruction for English language learners. The lessons and strategies in *Adding English* follow the overarching principle that English language learners come to the classroom with a wealth of experiences, language, and knowledge and that teachers will "add English" to this rich base. *Adding English* helps students as they read the same literature as students whose home language is English, while teaching the strategies they need to become independent, lifelong readers.

The Cognitive Academic Language Learning Approach (CALLA)

Adding English lessons follow the Cognitive Academic Language Learning Approach (CALLA) model for meeting the academic needs of English language learners in classrooms in the United States. The CALLA approach, which is also the basis of *Scott Foresman ESL,* has been successful in accelerating ESL students' academic achievement in school districts nationwide. The model includes three instructional objectives:

- the teaching of topics from academic subjects
- the development of academic language skills
- explicit instruction in learning strategies for both content and language acquisition

Adding English applies the CALLA model to reading instruction by providing additional support for teaching reading vocabulary and the vocabulary needed to learn and use reading strategies; by using the CALLA lesson plan (Preview, Present, Practice, Connect, and Assess); by providing support for students to access authentic literature; and by making connections, wherever possible, to students' home languages and cultures.

The Lesson Plan

Each *Adding English* lesson uses the five-part CALLA lesson plan.

Preview— to integrate prior knowledge and experience and provide a foundation for new information

Present— to present new information, using a variety of appropriate teaching and learning strategies

Practice— to have students use new information through scaffolded activities that call for the use of oral and written language

Connect— to have students attain a deeper understanding of reading concepts

Assess— to monitor students' progress through appropriate tools and apply fix-up strategies when needed

Learning Strategies

Learning strategies are actions or thoughts that students can apply on their own to a challenging task. *Adding English* lessons explicitly teach students learning strategies, how to apply them, and how to monitor their use of the strategies. Among strategies students learn are using picture clues, classifying, summarizing, note-taking, and using context clues. Accompanying *Adding English* are activities and posters for teaching learning and comprehension strategies. These posters depict strategies using situations familiar to all students. Once students understand the strategy within the familiar, visual context, they can more easily apply the strategy to the literature.

Proficiency Levels

Second-language learners often demonstrate a fluent understanding of English even though their speech may contain grammatical errors. Since these students may move quickly from one proficiency level to another, proficiency labels may be of limited use. Activities in each lesson are scaffolded to insure success for English language learners. Proficiency labels (**B**-beginning, **I**-intermediate, **A**-advanced) are assigned to activities in the Comprehension Strategies section, pages 10–15.

Crossing Cultures

Adding English helps teachers get to know their students as individuals with unique personal histories. Each lesson begins with Crossing Cultures, a note that alerts the teacher to connections between the literature and students' home cultures and languages. These suggestions let teachers know when students can be the experts by teaching others words in their home language, when to validate English language learners as people who know more than one language and culture, and when other opportunities exist for cultural awareness.

Teaching Strategies

Activities in *Adding English* lessons incorporate teaching strategies used in English as a Second Language instruction. Among these strategies is Total Physical Response (TPR) by which teachers model language and then confirm students' understanding by having them respond physically to directions. Other strategies include the use of graphic organizers, real objects, pantomime, demonstrating, and modeling. Each lesson is followed by Adding English Grammar and Phonics Practice Masters for additional practice. For visual aids, teachers can use the Adding English Posters that show illustrated selection vocabulary. To teach Comprehension Strategies, *Adding English* provides a teaching routine, activities, and posters.

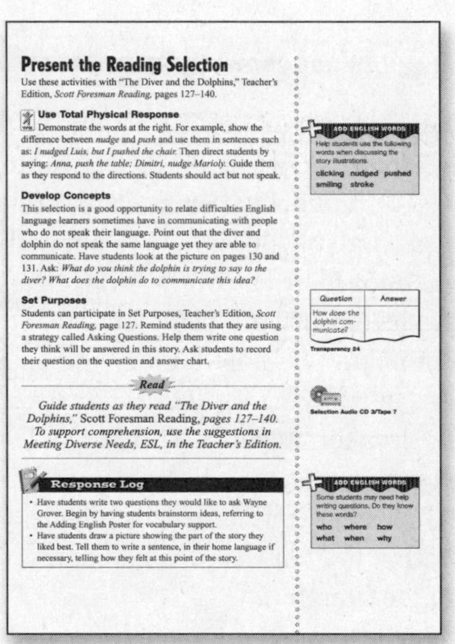

Present the Reading Selection

Use these activities with "The Diver and the Dolphins," Teacher's Edition, *Scott Foresman Reading,* pages 127–140.

Use Total Physical Response

Demonstrate the words at the right. For example, show the difference between *nudge* and *push* and use them in sentences such as: *I nudged Luis, but I pushed the chair.* Then direct students by saying: *Anna, push the table; Dimitri, nudge Marioly.* Guide them as they respond to the directions. Students should act but not speak.

Develop Concepts

This selection is a good opportunity to relate difficulties English language learners sometimes have in communicating with people who do not speak their language. Point out that the diver and dolphin do not speak the same language yet they are able to communicate. Have students look at the picture on pages 130 and 131. Ask: *What do you think the dolphin is trying to say to the diver? What does the dolphin do to communicate this idea?*

Set Purposes

Students can participate in Set Purposes, Teacher's Edition, *Scott Foresman Reading,* page 127. Remind students that they are using a strategy called Asking Questions. Help them write one question they think will be answered in this story. Ask students to record their question on the question and answer chart.

Read

Guide students as they read "The Diver and the Dolphins," Scott Foresman Reading, *pages 127–140. To support comprehension, use the suggestions in Meeting Diverse Needs, ESL, in the Teacher's Edition.*

Response Log

- Have students write two questions they would like to ask Wayne Grover. Begin by having students brainstorm ideas, referring to the Adding English Poster for vocabulary support.
- Have students draw a picture showing the part of the story they liked best. Tell them to write a sentence, in their home language if necessary, telling how they felt at this point of the story.

ADD ENGLISH WORDS

Help students use the following words when discussing the story illustrations.

clicking nudged pushed smiling stroke

Question	Answer
How does the dolphin communicate?	

Transparency 24

Selection Audio CD 3/Tape 7

ADD ENGLISH WORDS

Some students may need help writing questions. Do they know these words?

who where how what when why

Assessment

In each lesson, *Adding English* provides If . . . Then . . . scenarios for assessing English language learners' knowledge of comprehension strategies as well as supported reader response activities for assessing students' understanding of the selections. Activities for *Ten Important Sentences*, blackline masters that accompany *Adding English,* can be used for assessment. Students are also asked to self-assess their understanding of learning strategies, following the model of *The CALLA Handbook.* Finally, each lesson has assessment checklists for the reading and language arts objectives, as well as for learning strategies.

Lesson Features

Adding English lessons support English language learners as they read selections in *Scott Foresman Reading.* Each *Adding English* lesson uses the Cognitive Academic Language Learning Approach (CALLA) sequence of instruction to meet the academic needs of ESL students: Preview, Present, Practice, Connect, Assess.

Crossing Cultures
Alerts the teacher to make connections between the literature and students' cultural knowledge

Part 1: The Skill Lesson

Activate Prior Knowledge
Develops vocabulary and builds a foundation for new information

Read-alouds
Provide a context for the vocabulary

Graphic Organizers
Help students classify, organize, and analyze

Comprehension Strategies
A link to a teaching routine, activities, and posters that support the Skill Lesson instruction.

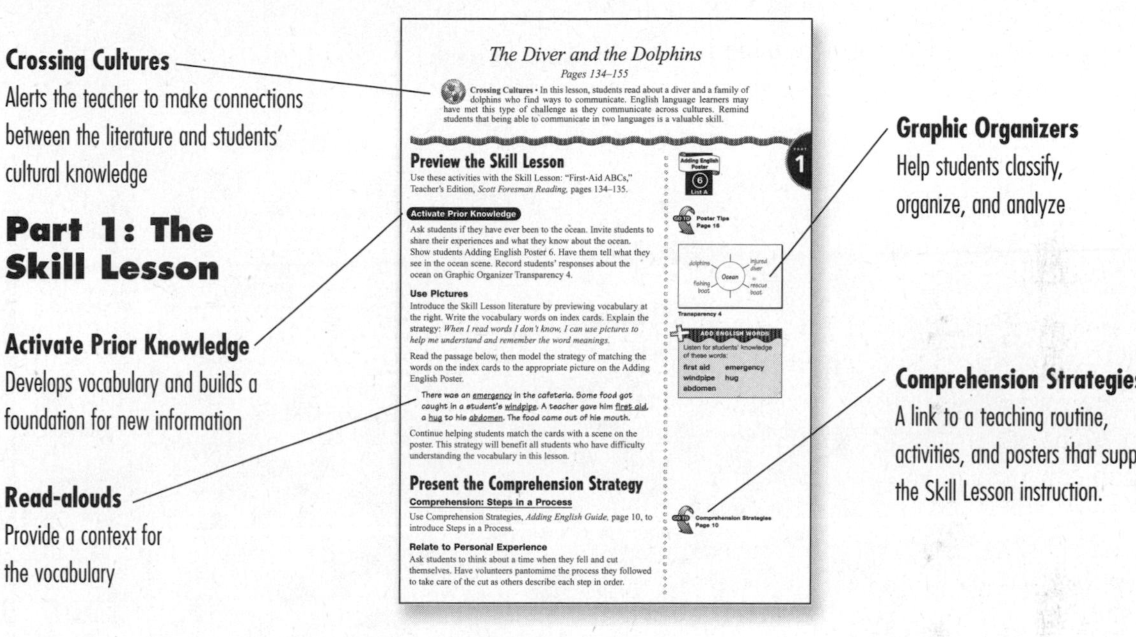

The Diver and the Dolphins

Pages 134–155

Crossing Cultures • In this lesson, students read about a diver and a family of dolphins who find ways to communicate. English language learners may have met this type of challenge as they communicate across cultures. Remind students that being able to communicate in two languages is a valuable skill.

PART 1

Preview the Skill Lesson

Use these activities with the Skill Lesson: "First-Aid ABCs," Teacher's Edition, *Scott Foresman Reading,* pages 134–135.

Activate Prior Knowledge

Ask students if they have ever been to the ocean. Invite students to share their experiences and what they know about the ocean. Show students Adding English Poster 6. Have them tell what they see in the ocean scene. Record students' responses about the ocean on Graphic Organizer Transparency 4.

Use Pictures

Introduce the Skill Lesson literature by previewing vocabulary at the right. Write the vocabulary words on index cards. Explain the strategy: *When I read words I don't know, I can use pictures to help me understand and remember the word meanings.*

Read the passage below, then model the strategy of matching the words on the index cards to the appropriate picture on the Adding English Poster.

There was an emergency in the cafeteria. Some food got caught in a student's windpipe. A teacher gave him first aid, a hug to his abdomen. The food came out of his mouth.

Continue helping students match the cards with a scene on the poster. This strategy will benefit all students who have difficulty understanding the vocabulary in this lesson.

Present the Comprehension Strategy

Comprehension: Steps in a Process

Use Comprehension Strategies, *Adding English Guide,* page 10, to introduce Steps in a Process.

Relate to Personal Experience

Ask students to think about a time when they fell and cut themselves. Have volunteers pantomime the process they followed to take care of the cut as others describe each step in order.

Adding English Poster 6 List A

GO TO Poster Tips Page 16

Transparency 4

ADD ENGLISH WORDS
Listen for students' knowledge of these words:
first aid, emergency, windpipe, hug, abdomen

GO TO Comprehension Strategies Page 10

Part 2: The Reading Selection

Practice
Frequent pantomime and oral response opportunities

Assess
Specific assessment and fix-up strategies

Learning Strategies
Strategies that are explicitly named, modeled, practiced

Resources
Suggestions for using related Scott Foresman ESL materials and videos

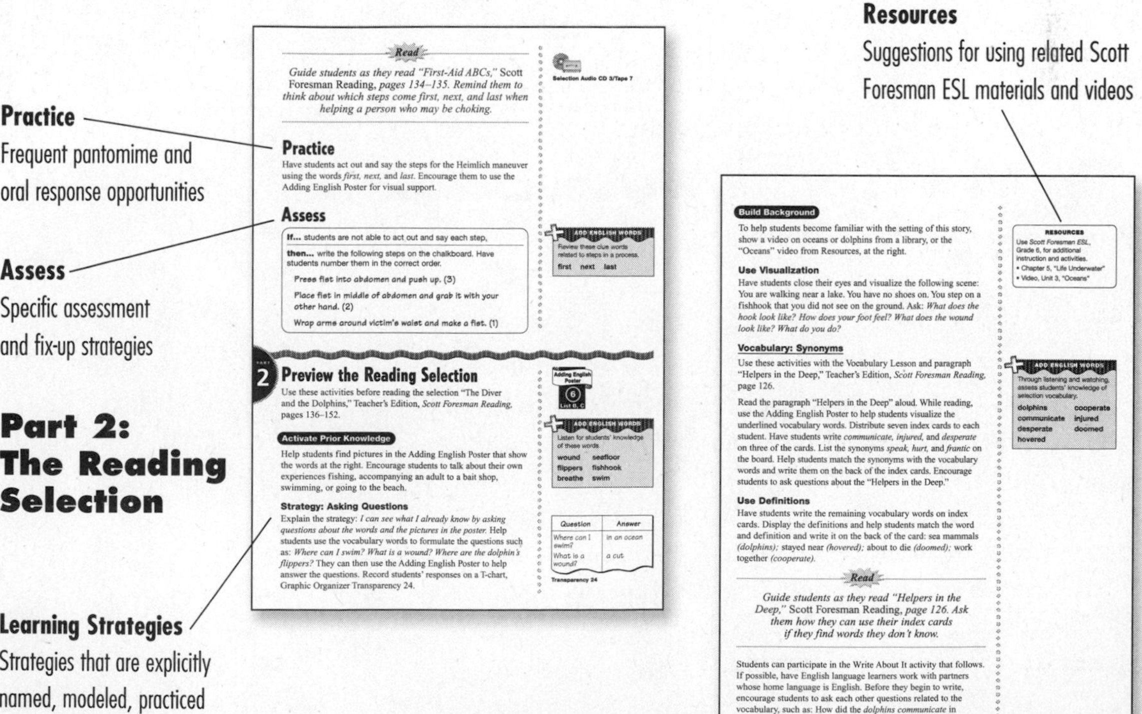

Read

Guide students as they read "First-Aid ABCs," Scott Foresman Reading, *pages 134–135. Remind them to think about which steps come first, next, and last when helping a person who may be choking.*

Practice

Have students act out and say the steps for the Heimlich maneuver using the words *first, next,* and *last*. Encourage them to use the Adding English Poster for visual support.

Assess

If... students are not able to act out and say each step,

then... write the following steps on the chalkboard. Have students number them in the correct order.

Press fist into abdomen and push up. (3)

Place fist in middle of abdomen and grab it with your other hand. (2)

Wrap arms around victim's waist and make a fist. (1)

Selection Audio CD 3/Tape 7

ADD ENGLISH WORDS
Review these clue words related to steps in a process.
first, next, last

PART 2

Preview the Reading Selection

Use these activities before reading the selection "The Diver and the Dolphins," Teacher's Edition, *Scott Foresman Reading,* pages 136–152.

Activate Prior Knowledge

Help students find pictures in the Adding English Poster that show the words at the right. Encourage students to talk about their own experiences fishing, accompanying an adult to a bait shop, swimming, or going to the beach.

Strategy: Asking Questions

Explain the strategy: *I can see what I already know by asking questions about the words and the pictures in the poster.* Help students use the vocabulary words to formulate the questions such as: *Where can I swim? What is a wound? Where are the dolphin's flippers?* They can then use the Adding English Poster to help answer the questions. Record students' responses on a T-chart, Graphic Organizer Transparency 24.

Adding English Poster 6 List B, C

ADD ENGLISH WORDS
Listen for students' knowledge of these words.
wound, seafloor, flippers, fishhook, breathe, swim

Question	Answer
Where can I swim?	in an ocean
What is a wound?	a cut

Transparency 24

Build Background

To help students become familiar with the setting of this story, show a video on oceans or dolphins from a library, or the "Oceans" video from Resources, at the right.

Use Visualization

Have students close their eyes and visualize the following scene: You are walking near a lake. You have no shoes on. You step on a fishhook that you did not see on the ground. Ask: *What does the hook look like? How does your foot feel? What does the wound look like? What do you do?*

Vocabulary: Synonyms

Use these activities with the Vocabulary Lesson and paragraph "Helpers in the Deep," Teacher's Edition, *Scott Foresman Reading,* page 126.

Read the paragraph "Helpers in the Deep" aloud. While reading, use the Adding English Poster to help students visualize the underlined vocabulary words. Distribute seven index cards to each student. Have students write *communicate, injured,* and *desperate* on three of the cards. List the synonyms *speak, hurt,* and *frantic* on the board. Help students match the synonyms with the vocabulary words and write them on the back of the index cards. Encourage students to ask questions about the "Helpers in the Deep."

Use Definitions

Have students write the remaining vocabulary words on index cards. Display the definitions and help students match the word and definition and write it on the back of the card: sea mammals *(dolphins);* stayed near *(hovered);* about to die *(doomed);* work together *(cooperate).*

Read

Guide students as they read "Helpers in the Deep," Scott Foresman Reading, *page 126. Ask them how they can use their index cards if they find words they don't know.*

Students can participate in the Write About It activity that follows. If possible, have English language learners work with partners whose home language is English. Before they begin to write, encourage students to ask each other questions related to the vocabulary, such as: How did the *dolphins communicate* in the show?

RESOURCES
Use *Scott Foresman ESL,* Grade 6, for additional instruction and activities.
• Chapter 5, "Life Underwater"
• Video, Unit 3, "Oceans"

ADD ENGLISH WORDS
Through listening and watching, assess students' knowledge of selection vocabulary.
dolphins, cooperate, communicate, injured, desperate, doomed, hovered

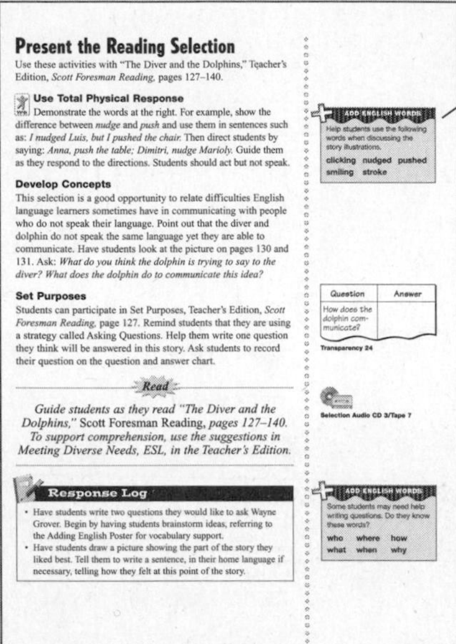

Present the Reading Selection

Use these activities with "The Diver and the Dolphins," Teacher's Edition, *Scott Foresman Reading*, pages 127–140.

Use Total Physical Response
Demonstrate the words at the right. For example, show the difference between *nudge* and *push* and use them in sentences such as: *I nudged Luis, but I pushed the chair.* Then direct students by saying: *Anna, push the table; Dimitri, nudge Mariola.* Guide them as they respond to the directions. Students should act but not speak.

Develop Concepts
This selection is a good opportunity to relate difficulties English language learners sometimes have in communicating with people who do not speak their language. Point out that the diver and dolphin do not speak the same language yet they are able to communicate. Have students look at the picture on pages 130 and 131. Ask: *What do you think the dolphin is trying to say to the diver? What does the dolphin do to communicate this idea?*

Set Purposes
Students can participate in Set Purposes, Teacher's Edition, *Scott Foresman Reading*, page 127. Remind students that they are using a strategy called Asking Questions. Help them write one question they think will be answered in this story. Ask students to record their question on the question and answer chart.

Read

Guide students as they read "The Diver and the Dolphins," Scott Foresman Reading, pages 127–140. To support comprehension, use the suggestions in Meeting Diverse Needs, ESL, in the Teacher's Edition.

Response Log
- Have students write two questions they would like to ask Wayne Grover. Begin by having students brainstorm ideas, referring to the Adding English Poster for vocabulary support.
- Have students draw a picture showing the part of the story they liked best. Tell them to write a sentence, in their home language if necessary, telling how they felt at this point of the story.

ADD ENGLISH WORDS
Help students use the following words when discussing the story illustrations.
clicking nudged pushed smiling stroke

Question	Answer
How does the dolphin communicate?	

Transparency 24

Selection Audio CD 3/Tape 7

ADD ENGLISH WORDS
Some students may need help writing questions. Do they know these words?
who where how what when why

Add English Words

Lists extra vocabulary English language learners need to understand literature and strategies

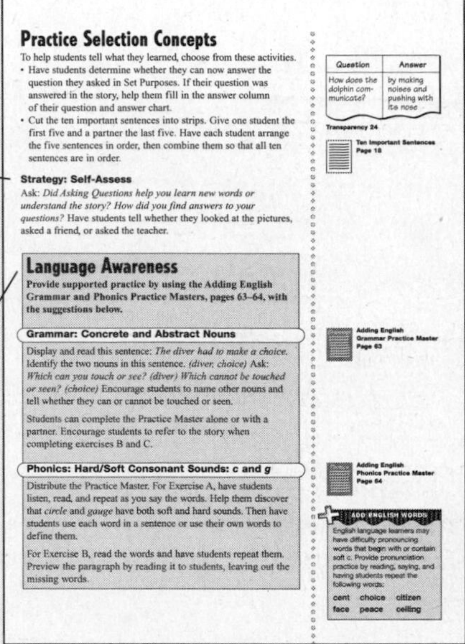

Practice Selection Concepts

To help students tell what they learned, choose from these activities.
- Have students determine whether they can now answer the question they asked in Set Purposes. If their question was answered in the story, help them fill in the answer column of their question and answer chart.
- Cut the ten important sentences into strips. Give one student the first five and a partner the last five. Have each student arrange the five sentences in order, then combine them so that all ten sentences are in order.

Strategy: Self-Assess
Ask: *Did Asking Questions help you learn new words or understand the story? How did you find answers to your questions?* Have students tell whether they looked at the pictures, asked a friend, or asked the teacher.

Language Awareness
Provide supported practice by using the Adding English Grammar and Phonics Practice Masters, pages 63–64, with the suggestions below.

Grammar: Concrete and Abstract Nouns
Display and read this sentence: *The diver had to make a choice.* Identify the two nouns in this sentence. *(diver, choice)* Ask: *Which can you touch or see? (diver) Which cannot be touched or seen? (choice)* Encourage students to name other nouns and tell whether they can or cannot be touched or seen.

Students can complete the Practice Master alone or with a partner. Encourage students to refer to the story when completing exercises B and C.

Phonics: Hard/Soft Consonant Sounds: c and g
Distribute the Practice Master. For Exercise A, have students listen, read, and repeat as you say the words. Help them discover that *circle* and *gauge* have both soft and hard sounds. Then have students use each word in a sentence or use their own words to define them.

For Exercise B, read the words and have students repeat them. Preview the paragraph by reading it to students, leaving out the missing words.

Question	Answer
How does the dolphin communicate?	by making noises and pushing with its nose

Transparency 24

Ten Important Sentences Page 18

Adding English Grammar Practice Master Page 63

Adding English Phonics Practice Master Page 64

ADD ENGLISH WORDS
English language learners may have difficulty pronouncing words that begin with or contain soft c. Provide pronunciation practice by reading, saying, and having students repeat the following words:
cent choice citizen face peace ceiling

Self-Assess

Students talk about how and when they used a learning strategy, and self-assess whether it helped them.

Language Awareness

Instruction for grammar and phonics skills taught with the selection leads to supported practice in the Adding English Grammar and Phonics Practice Masters.

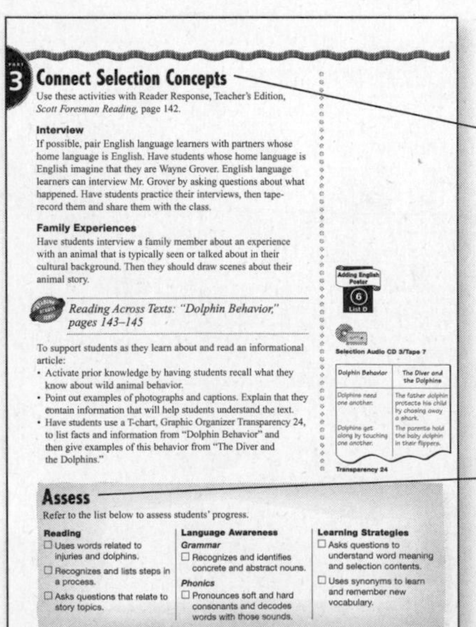

3 Connect Selection Concepts

Use these activities with Reader Response, Teacher's Edition, *Scott Foresman Reading*, page 142.

Interview
If possible, pair English language learners with partners whose home language is English. Have students whose home language is English imagine that they are Wayne Grover. English language learners can interview Mr. Grover by asking questions about what happened. Have students practice their interviews, then tape-record them and share them with the class.

Family Experiences
Have students interview a family member about an experience with an animal that is typically seen or talked about in their cultural background. Then they should draw scenes about their animal story.

Reading Across Texts: "Dolphin Behavior," pages 143–145

To support students as they learn about and read an informational article:
- Activate prior knowledge by having students recall what they know about wild animal behavior.
- Point out examples of photographs and captions. Explain that they contain information that will help students understand the text.
- Have students use a T-chart, Graphic Organizer Transparency 24, to list facts and information from "Dolphin Behavior" and then give examples of this behavior from "The Diver and the Dolphins."

Adding English Poster 6 Unit 6

Selection Audio CD 3/Tape 7

Dolphin Behavior	The Diver and the Dolphins
Dolphins need one another.	The father dolphin protects his child by chasing away a shark.
Dolphins get along by touching one another.	The parents hold the baby dolphin in their flippers.

Transparency 24

Assess
Refer to the list below to assess students' progress.

Reading
- ☐ Uses words related to injuries and dolphins.
- ☐ Recognizes and lists steps in a process.
- ☐ Asks questions that relate to story topics.

Language Awareness
Grammar
- ☐ Recognizes and identifies concrete and abstract nouns.

Phonics
- ☐ Pronounces soft and hard consonants and decodes words with those sounds.

Learning Strategies
- ☐ Asks questions to understand word meaning and selection contents.
- ☐ Uses synonyms to learn and remember new vocabulary.

Part 3: Connect and Assess

Connect

A variety of response activities to create a deeper understanding of the selection and relate to students' own experiences.

Assess

Checklists guide assessment for the reading and language arts objectives as well as for learning strategies.

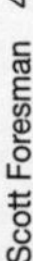

Practice Masters for Grammar and Phonics

Adding English Practice Masters for Grammar and Phonics teach the same grammar and phonics skills in the same sequence as they are taught in *Scott Foresman Reading*. The practice extends from grammar and phonics instruction in the Language Awareness section in the *Adding English* lesson.

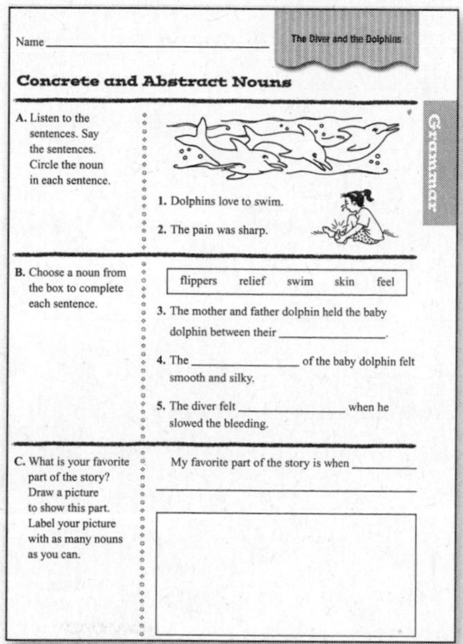

Name ______________________ The Diver and the Dolphins

Concrete and Abstract Nouns

Grammar

A. Listen to the sentences. Say the sentences. Circle the noun in each sentence.

1. Dolphins love to swim.
2. The pain was sharp.

B. Choose a noun from the box to complete each sentence.

flippers	relief	swim	skin	feel

3. The mother and father dolphin held the baby dolphin between their ______________.
4. The ______________ of the baby dolphin felt smooth and silky.
5. The diver felt ______________ when he slowed the bleeding.

C. What is your favorite part of the story? Draw a picture to show this part. Label your picture with as many nouns as you can.

My favorite part of the story is when ______________

Name ______________________ The Diver and the Dolphins

Hard and Soft Consonant Sounds: *c* and *g*

Phonics

A. Listen to the sounds the letters *c* and *g* make in the words. Then say the words.

circle coat pencil gauge

B. Choose a word from the box to complete each sentence. When you are done, read the paragraph to a partner. Then listen as your partner reads it to you.

careful	cut	gentle	peace	struggled

The diver had to ______________ the hook out of the baby dolphin's back. The baby dolphin ______________. The diver tried to be very ______________ and ______________. Finally, he got the hook out. Saving the baby dolphin made the diver feel at ______________.

C. Talk with a partner about the part of the story in which the sharks tried to attack the dolphins. Write a sentence to go with the picture. Use some of the words in the box.

raced
bigger
fierce
became
enraged
again

Posters for Vocabulary

The Adding English Poster illustrates selection vocabulary in colorful and high-interest contexts. Since students learn the pictured vocabulary quickly, teachers can use the visual context to teach high-frequency and abstract words that are not picturable. Students are encouraged to refer to the Adding English Poster whenever they need language support—as they activate prior knowledge, use selection vocabulary, describe scenes, or brainstorm before writing. More information about using the posters is in Poster Tips, page 16.

Comprehension Strategies

The Comprehension Routine

To support students' understanding of comprehension strategies, use the following routine.

Step 1: Present

Explain the strategy directly, using examples that children are familiar with, along with simple diagrams, objects, demonstration, or modeling. Follow the instruction in the *Adding English* lessons in Present the Comprehension Strategy. Throughout, watch for students' understanding of vocabulary. Model the strategy using the clue words.

Step 2: Practice

Students can demonstrate knowledge of the strategy by using examples from their experience. As students read, remind them to use the strategy. Pause to ask them how it is going. After students read, have them reflect on how and when they used the strategy. Encourage students to use the strategy when reading in other curriculum areas. Intermediate or advanced second-language learners can model the strategy for beginners.

Below are examples of how to use the routine for specific strategies. As a general guide, use the following key for the activities below: **B**-beginning, **I**-intermediate, **A**-advanced. You may wish to use **B** activities as warm-ups and proceed to **I** and **A** activities with older or more fluent students.

Full-sized Comprehension Strategies Posters are also available.

Cause and Effect

Clue words: what happened, why, cause, effect

Present

As you read or listen, think about things that happen and why those things happen. The effect is the thing that happened. The cause is why it happened. What happened to the glass in the picture? (It fell.) Why? (The cat pushed it.) The cat is the cause of the glass falling.

Practice

Have students act out one event causing another, while others tell which is the cause and which is the effect. **(B)** Students can tell about an event that may cause something else to happen, while the others suggest possible results of the event. **(I)** Students identify cause and effect in a brief paragraph they read. **(A)**

Compare and Contrast

Clue words: alike, different, compare, contrast

Present

Think about what is alike between two things. This is called comparing. Think about what is different between two things. This is called contrasting. Look at the picture. How are the two animals alike? How are they different?

Continue by discussing the two balls and the two people.

Practice

Have students draw a picture of two similar objects, people, or animals, and then ask a partner to describe their similarities and differences. **(B)** Have students write about two similar objects, people, or animals, and then ask a partner to describe similarities and differences. **(I)** Have students read about two characters and use a Venn diagram to tell how they are alike and different. **(A)**

Main Idea/Supporting Details

Clue words: What is ____ about?, main idea, details

Present

When you read, ask yourself "What is this about?" The answer is the main idea. Look for details to support your answer. Students should tell what the picture is about. (Possible response: It takes a lot of people to build a house.) Have them talk about details that support their answer.

Practice

After students look at a picture, have them explain the main idea and provide support for their answers. **(B)** Students can listen to a story and describe the main idea, providing support for answers. **(I)** After reading a story, students can write the main idea and supporting details. **(A)**

Predicting Outcomes

Clue words: happen, next, predict, prediction

Present

When you read, think about what you have heard or read and what you already know about the subject. As you listen or read, pay attention to clues that may help you decide what might happen next. Then make a guess or prediction about what you think will happen. What is the girl in the picture thinking? What do you think will happen next?

Practice

Have students draw a series of pictures of familiar actions, and then ask someone to predict what will happen next. **(B)** They can act out a series of familiar actions (getting ready for school, getting ready for bed) while others predict what will happen next. **(I)** Students can write a short description or story, leaving out the ending, and then ask someone to predict what will happen next. **(A)**

Fact and Opinion

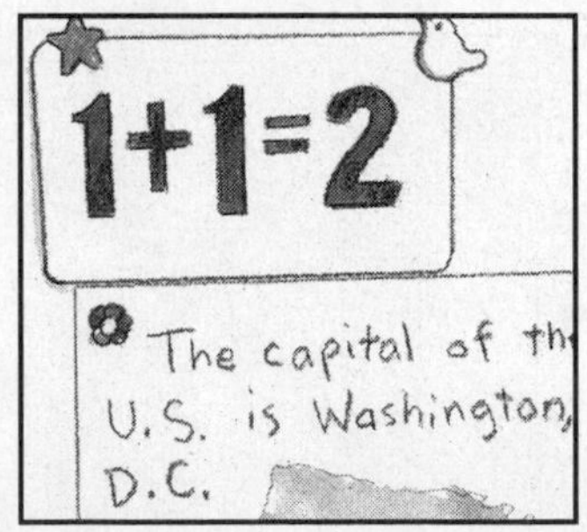

Clue words: statement of fact, statement of opinion

Present

When you read, you can decide whether the author is writing a statement that can be proved true or false. If it can, it is a statement of fact. If it cannot, it is a statement of opinion. Which statements in the picture can you prove? (1+1=2; The capital of the U.S. is Washington, D.C.) *Are the boy and girl stating facts or opinions?* (opinions)

Practice

Have students listen to several statements and say whether they are statements of fact or opinion. **(B)** Have students read a series of statements, determine whether they are statements of fact or opinion, and explain why. **(I)** Have students write a series of statements and ask someone to label them fact or opinion. **(A)**

Classifying

Clue words: belong, group

Present

When you want to understand what things belong together, you can put them in groups. It will help you understand what you hear and read. Look at the pictures. Where will the boy put the grapes? Why do they belong in that group? Where will he put the monkey? Why?

Practice

Have students draw pictures of objects that belong together. **(B)** Students draw pictures, put them in groups, and name each picture and each group. **(I)** Students write the names of familiar objects on index cards and put the cards in groups. They make duplicate cards for objects that belong in more than one group. Then they write a heading for each group. **(A)**

Sequence

Clue words: first, next, then, last

Present

When you read, notice how some things happen in a certain order. If you keep track of the order, it will be easier to understand what you read. Look at the picture. It shows the sequence of a baby chick hatching. What happens first? What happens next? Then what happens? What happens last?

Practice

Have students tell, draw, or write what happens first, next, then, and last in the following: when they get ready for bed **(B)**; during a school day **(I)**; in a story they know **(A)**.

Drawing Conclusions

Clue words: fact, detail, decide, draw conclusions

Present

You can think about facts or details that you know to decide about people and events. Look at the picture. One fact is that the father is pointing at his watch. What is another fact? (only one plate is clean) What conclusion can you draw about the girl? (She is late for dinner.)

Practice

Pantomime putting on a coat and hat and have students draw conclusions.(Possible response: You are going out.) **(B)** Show a brief narrative video and have students draw conclusions about the characters. **(I)** Have students read a short story and draw conclusions from the pictures, text, and prior knowledge. **(A)**

Steps in a Process

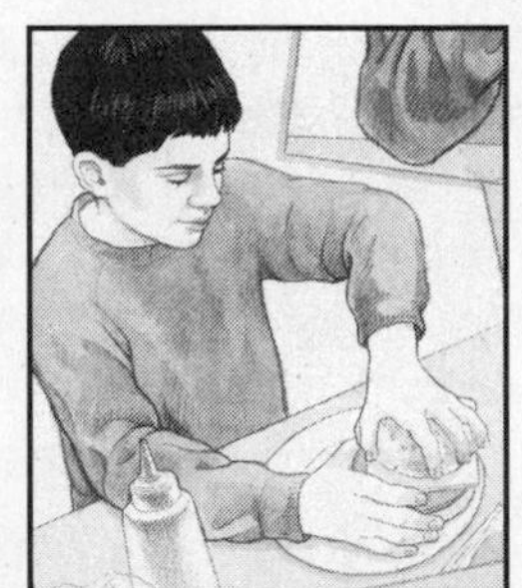

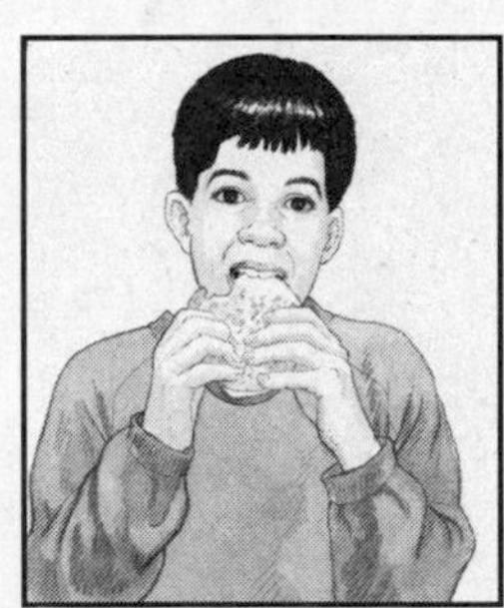

Clue words: step 1, step 2, step 3, step 4

Present

When you read about making something, you can follow steps in order. The steps are called directions or instructions. What is happening in the picture? What is the order of the steps?

Practice

Demonstrate making a paper plate mask and have students describe each step of the process. **(B)** Have students read simple directions and follow them. **(I)** Have students write and illustrate directions for making a food or simple craft. **(A)**

Generalizing

Clue words: all, none, most, many, always, sometimes, generally

Present

When you read, you are given ideas about how several things are alike or different. Think about what you know and decide if the statements are true (valid) or false (faulty).

Discuss the picture, encouraging students to make generalizations such as *All bikes have two wheels, All birds have wings,* or *Most children go to school.* Ask students to decide if the statements are true or false.

Practice

Have students draw shapes that are alike or slightly different and make a statement about them using *some* or *all*. **(B)** Students can make generalizations about their school or foods they eat. In groups they can discuss whether they are true or false. **(I)** Students can find generalizations in their reading and decide if they are valid or faulty. **(A)**

Character

Clue words: people, animals, real, make-believe, actions, feelings

Present

Characters are the people and animals in a story. Some are real and some are make-believe. You can learn about a character by reading about what the character says and does, and by how other characters treat him or her. Which character in the pictures is make-believe? (the mouse) How do you know? What kind of person do you think the diver is? (kind, helpful) How do you know?

Practice

Students can look at a picture of a character in a story they have read and tell whether the character is real or make-believe, giving reasons for their answers. **(B)** Students can view part of a narrative video, and then tell what they know about a character from what the character said or did. **(I)** Students can read a short story and create a character web describing a character. **(A)**

Poster Tips

Adding English Posters are valuable tools for introducing and reinforcing vocabulary for every selection in *Scott Foresman Reading.* The posters show selection vocabulary and high frequency words, as well as words that appear in Phonics Stories (Grades 1–2) and Skill Lessons and Reading Across Texts (Grades 3–6).

Use the Adding English Poster as needed to support your instructional needs. You might introduce vocabulary by pointing to objects that are illustrated, such as *basket* and *apple.*

With the poster, you can help students use words such as *of* or *instead* in meaningful contexts, such as *This is a basket. What is it full of?* or *This boy didn't plant flowers like the other children. What did he do instead?* When students answer, they can point to the corresponding pictures on the poster or label them. Throughout a lesson, the Adding English Poster is a familiar context that teachers and students can refer to often for clarifying, questioning, and elaborating. More ideas are provided in each Adding English lesson and in the tips below.

Independently, students can

- label parts of the poster with words or phrases.
- make a small frame out of paper and hold the frame up to focus on parts of the poster for describing, finding, and naming words.
- play I Spy to find vocabulary words.
- answer yes and no to questions, such as *Is the man working in the garden?*
- answer questions, such as *What are the children doing?*
- describe scenes that are familiar to them and relate them to their own experience.
- ask questions about what they see that is not familiar.
- use their home language to name pictures in the poster.
- create webs or charts of related words based on the poster.
- point to words that reflect a particular phonics skill, such as initial consonants.
- pantomime actions shown on the poster for other students to guess.
- draw themselves into the poster.

With support, students can

- compare and contrast in contexts such as *This is a picture of a school and a classroom. Is it like your classroom? Here the sky is dark, but here it is ___. (light) Here it is night. Here it is ___. (day)*
- discuss parts of the poster that are similar to a selection.
- practice comprehension strategies, such as predicting what a pictured figure will do next, drawing conclusions about a scene or person based on details, making statements about the main idea of a poster and identifying supporting details.
- describe a setting.
- write sentences using vocabulary words shown in the poster.
- make up a new story or extend the plot of a story by using vocabulary pictured in the poster.
- practice pronouncing pictured words and using them in sentences.
- practice present, past, and future tenses as they invent stories about the poster.
- create a dialogue for people shown in the poster.

A Visit with Grandpa

Pages 20–43

Crossing Cultures • In this lesson, when a boy visits his grandfather's ranch in Missouri, he changes his mind about what is "men's work" and "women's work." Some students may feel their ideas are being challenged. Allow students time before asking them to share opinions and experiences about this topic.

PART 1

Preview the Skill Lesson

Use these activities with the Skill Lesson: "The Red Fox," Teacher's Edition, *Scott Foresman Reading,* pages 20–21.

Activate Prior Knowledge

Invite volunteers to share what they know about Adding English Poster 1. Introduce the unit theme, Focus on Family, by talking about the different types of families, including a family of foxes, a herd of cattle, and a human family. Let students use their home language as necessary. Use a web, Graphic Organizer Transparency 5, to generate words about fox families.

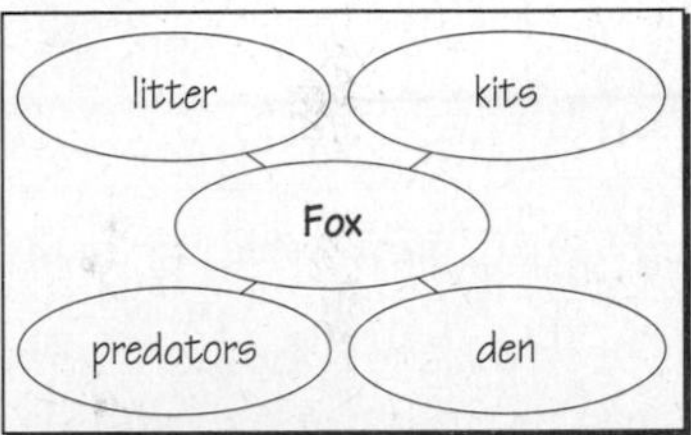

Transparency 5

Use Total Physical Response

Introduce the Skill Lesson literature by previewing vocabulary at the right. Write the vocabulary words on the board. As you read the passage that follows, have students follow the directions and act out each word. Model the strategy by pantomiming how a *predator* stalks it prey.

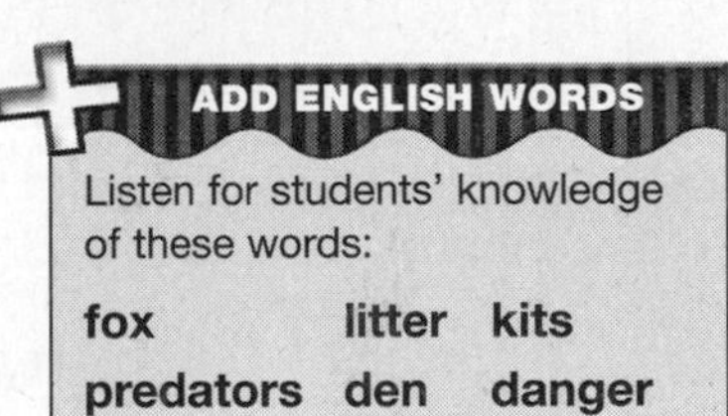

> There is danger! Let's put our heads down and hide! Now, the danger is over. The fox is safe in its house, called a den. Show me how a fox hides in its den. Baby foxes are called kits. Kits look like kittens. Form a small group so we can act like a litter of kits. The mother fox must protect her litter from predators. Predators are animals that hunt and eat other animals. Act like a mountain lion hunting for a kit.

Guide students to show the meaning of each word, using TPR. As a reinforcement, have students point out illustrations of these words on the Adding English Poster. Other students in the class may also benefit from reviewing this vocabulary.

Present the Comprehension Strategy

Comprehension: Setting

Use Comprehension Strategies, *Adding English Guide,* page 10, to introduce Setting.

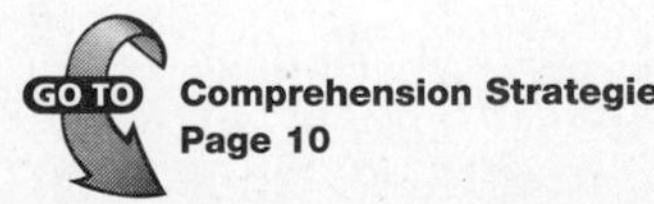

Relate to Personal Experience

Ask students to imagine that they are writing a story about their family. Have them draw a picture of the setting of their story. Then they can use the picture to describe the setting to a partner.

Guide students as they read "The Red Fox," Scott Foresman Reading, *pages 20–21. Remind them to think about when and where the story takes place.*

Selection Audio CD 1/Tape 1

Practice

Have students identify the setting in "The Red Fox." Students can draw a picture to show the setting. Encourage students to use the Adding English Poster for support.

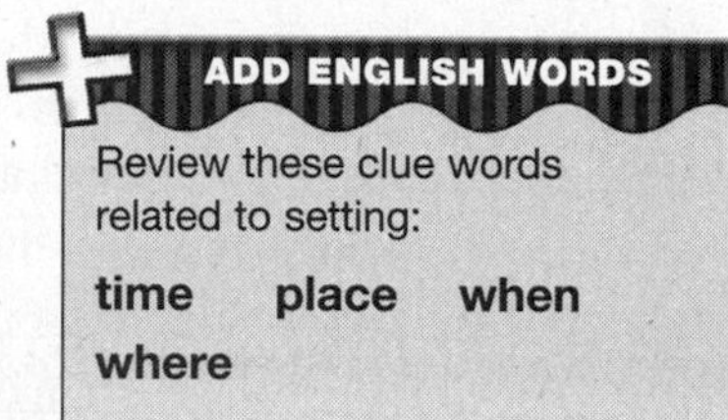

Assess

If... students are not able to identify the setting,

then... use a two-column chart and have students use the following story clues to describe the time and place.

- March wind
- cold in the forest

Time	Place
March	the forest

Transparency 24

PART 2 Preview the Reading Selection

Use these activities before reading the selection: "A Visit with Grandpa," Teacher's Edition, *Scott Foresman Reading,* pages 22–40.

Activate Prior Knowledge

Invite students to identify the parts of the Adding English Poster that picture the words at the right. Ask students what chores they have to do at home and which ones they think are "men's work" and which ones are "women's work." Begin a story prediction from previewing chart, Graphic Organizer Transparency 1.

ADD ENGLISH WORDS

Listen for students' knowledge of words related to life on a ranch.

housework **easy**
fence **cook**
cry

Strategy: Story Predicting from Previewing

Explain the strategy: *When I want to predict what a story will be about, I can use a chart. It is a strategy called Story Predicting from Previewing.* Model writing the selection title on the chart. Then have students look at the illustration on pages 22–23. Ask: Why does this room look this way? What might the man be thinking? Continue previewing illustrations.

Title A Visit with Grandpa

Read the title and look at the pictures in the story. What do you think a problem in the story might be?

I think a problem might be ___________

Transparency 1

Build Background

Explain to students that people who work on ranches sometimes bring food with them instead of returning to the ranch house to eat. Tell students that in the story, a boy and his grandfather bring ingredients for biscuits with them on the trail and bake the biscuits for lunch. Ask students why this solution might be better than going back to the ranch house to have lunch.

Practice New Words

Ask students to brainstorm ways they can learn new words. Possibilities include listening to the word, looking at the word, saying the word silently, saying it out loud, and writing it. Pairs of students can use these methods to learn the words *housework, easy, fence, cook,* and *cry.*

Vocabulary: Context Clues

Use these activities with the Vocabulary Lesson and paragraph "A Day with Grandpa," Teacher's Edition, *Scott Foresman Reading,* page 22.

Create a question-and-answer dialogue that uses each word at the right in context. For example:

> **The paper got wrinkled when I folded it. What does *wrinkled* mean?**
>
> **I put butter and jam on these biscuits. What are *biscuits*?**

Demonstrate meanings when needed, or use the Adding English Poster for support. Students can point to an illustration of each word on the poster as they answer the questions.

Use Pictures

Write these words on the board: *prairie, raisins, biscuits, dough.* Then have students draw a picture to illustrate each word, using the Adding English Poster for vocabulary support.

Guide students as they read "A Day with Grandpa," Scott Foresman Reading, *page 22. Ask them how they can use context clues to define unfamiliar words.*

Students can participate in the Write About It activity that follows. Prepare students by having them draw pictures to show what they think they might see at a ranch. If possible, have English language learners work with partners whose home language is English to label each part of the picture.

RESOURCES

Use *Scott Foresman ESL,* Grade 4, for additional instruction and activities.

- Chapter 1, "The American West Today"
- Video, Unit 1, "The Wonderful West"

ADD ENGLISH WORDS

Observe students and listen to their responses to assess their comprehension of selection vocabulary.

rumpled	**prairie**
wrinkled	**biscuits**
teasing	**raisins**
dough	

Present the Reading Selection

Use these activities with "A Visit with Grandpa," Teacher's Edition, *Scott Foresman Reading,* pages 23–40.

Preview the Title

Explain the strategy: *Before I start to read, I look at the title to get an idea of what the story will be about.* Have students read the selection title and the book title on page 23. Ask: *Who will Justin visit? What food do you think Grandpa will make for Justin?* Invite volunteers to discuss what they do when they visit their grandparents or other relatives and what foods they make and eat during their visit. Have students copy the selection title onto their story prediction from previewing charts. Then help students fill in the problem on their charts. Remind students that they are using the strategy called Making Predictions from Previewing.

Title A Visit with Grandpa

Read the title and look at the pictures in the story. What do you think a problem in the story might be?

I think a problem might be A boy does not want to do housework.

After reading ______________, draw a picture of one of the problems in the story.

Transparency 1

Develop Concepts

For this selection, students may need support in understanding a cowboy's responsibilities on a ranch. To prepare students, have them look at the pictures on pages 28–29 and 30–31. Ask: *What does Grandpa do on the ranch?* Help students understand that cowboys repair equipment and care for animals. Point out that cowboys also cook and clean. Students can list some chores they have in the classroom and at home and decide whether cowboys must do these same chores.

Set Purposes

Students can participate in Set Purposes, Teacher's Edition, *Scott Foresman Reading,* page 23. Let volunteers read aloud their predictions from their story prediction from vocabulary charts.

Selection Audio CD 1/Tape 1

Guide students as they read "A Visit with Grandpa," Scott Foresman Reading, *pages 23–40. To support comprehension, use the suggestions in Meeting Individual Needs, ESL, in the Teacher's Edition.*

Response Log

- Have students tell what part of ranching they might like best. Encourage them to refer to the Adding English Poster for support and to draw pictures to help express their ideas.
- Ask students to write about how chores are divided in their families. Do they feel certain jobs are "men's work" or "women's work"? Why or why not?

Practice Selection Concepts

To help students tell what they learned, choose from these activities.

- Have students illustrate a problem in the story on their story prediction from previewing charts.
- Have students read the ten important sentences and find words that identify and describe the setting. Remind students to look for words that tell time and place.

Strategy: Self-Assess

Ask: *Did making predictions from previewing help you understand the story?* Have students tell how closely their predictions matched the outcome of the story.

Language Awareness

Provide supported practice by using the Adding English Grammar and Phonics Practice Masters, pages 23–24, with the suggestions below.

Grammar: Sentences

Write the following fragment on the board: *Went to visit Grandpa.* Read the fragment aloud. Then say: *This is a sentence fragment. It does not express a complete thought. What part is missing?* Guide students to see that we don't know who went to visit Grandpa. Invite volunteers to supply the missing subject. Continue using examples of fragments based on the Adding English Poster. Point out that a capital letter and a period are not enough to make a group of words a sentence.

Students can complete the Practice Master alone or with a partner.

Phonics: Vowel Digraphs *ai, ay, ea, ee, ei, oa, oe, ow*

Distribute the Practice Master. Have students listen, read, and repeat as you use the words in Exercise A in sentences. Pair students to ask and answer questions with the words, such as *What is a stream? A stream is a small river.*

For Exercise B, have students read each sentence aloud before choosing the answer.

Title A Visit with Grandpa

Read the title and look at the pictures in the story. What do you think a problem in the story might be?

I think a problem might be A boy does not want to do housework.

After reading A Visit with Grandpa, draw a picture of one of the problems in the story.

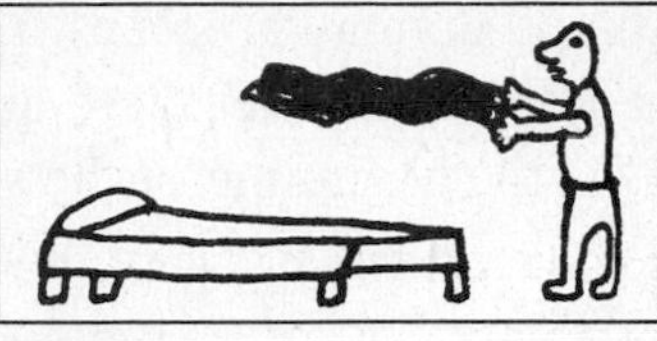

Transparency 1

Ten Important Sentences Page 13

Adding English Grammar Practice Master Page 23

Adding English Phonics Practice Master Page 24

PART 3

Connect Selection Concepts

Use these activities with Reader Response, Teacher's Edition, *Scott Foresman Reading,* page 40.

Dramatize

If possible, have English language learners work in small groups with students whose home language is English. Together they should dramatize scenes from "A Visit with Grandpa," focusing on scenes that answer these questions:

- At the beginning of the story, how did Justin feel about chores?
- What did Justin learn about ranching from Grandpa?
- What advice did Grandpa give Justin about chores?

Foods from Other Cultures

Students can describe and name kinds of bread they like to eat at home. Encourage them to describe the ingredients.

Reading Across Texts: "Understanding Horses," pages 41–43

To support students as they read an informational article:

- Have students preview the article, looking at the pictures and reading the captions. What kind of information about horses do they think this article will provide? Read the article and captions together.
- Ask: What is this article mostly about? How do horses express the way they feel? (Review the five senses, if necessary, pointing out that most animals take in information about their surroundings through their senses. Their reactions to this information are often shown in their behaviors.)
- Compare "Understanding Horses" to "A Visit with Grandpa." How could the information in "Understanding Horses" be useful to Justin? In which selection do you learn the most about horses?

Assess

Refer to the list below to assess students' progress.

Reading

- ☐ Uses words related to household chores and cowboys and the West.
- ☐ Describes a story's setting.
- ☐ Uses title to predict events.

Language Awareness

Grammar

- ☐ Identifies and writes complete sentences.

Phonics

- ☐ Pronounces and decodes words with vowel digraphs *ai, ay, ea, ee, ei, oa, oe, ow*.

Learning Strategies

- ☐ Uses a story prediction from previewing chart.
- ☐ Uses context clues to learn unfamiliar words.

Name ____________________

Sentences

A. Listen to the words. Underline the complete sentence.

1. Grandpa made biscuits for lunch.

2. Ate the biscuits.

B. Make each sentence complete by adding the word or words in parentheses.

3. The cowboys running. (are)

____

4. The pasture big. (is)

____

5. was going very fast. (The cowboy)

____

6. cook biscuits with raisins. (I)

____

7. Who the fence? (will fix)

____

C. What would you do on a vacation? Talk to a partner. Then write about the vacation.

On my vacation I would like to ____________________

____

____

____

____

Name ______________________________

Phonics

Vowel Digraphs *ai, ay, ea, ee, ei, oa, oe, ow*

A. Listen to the words. Read the words. Say the words.

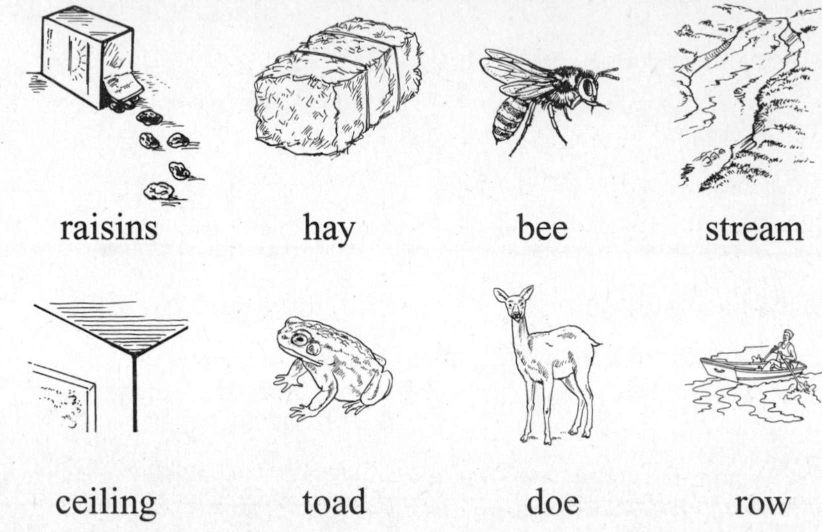

raisins hay bee stream

ceiling toad doe row

B. Write a word from the box to complete each sentence.

blow	ceiling	road	tail

1. I will ___________ out the birthday candles.

2. There are cars on the ___________.

3. When it rains, the ___________ leaks.

4. My dog wags his ___________.

C. Say the underlined words. Read the paragraph to a partner. Then listen as your partner reads it to you.

It is lunchtime on the prairie. The deer eats nuts and leaves. The fox feeds her kits. The doe drinks at the stream. Grandpa takes a load of hay to the cattle. We feed raisins to the birds. Then we eat biscuits.

Train to Somewhere

Pages 44–69

Crossing Cultures • As you provide background for the historical period in "Train to Somewhere," encourage students to ask questions frequently. To convey high expectations of English language learners, wait for their responses as long as needed.

PART 1

Preview the Skill Lesson

Use these activities with the Skill Lesson: "Will Sarah Return?," Teacher's Edition, *Scott Foresman Reading,* pages 44–45.

Activate Prior Knowledge

Invite children to define *family,* using Adding English Poster 2 for visual support. Have students brainstorm a list of words that name family members, such as *cousins, parents*. Draw a simple family tree and ask students to describe the relationship between various family members. (*Todd is Dana's uncle. Dana is Todd's niece.*) You may want to include step parents, half-siblings, and other nontraditional family members in your discussion.

Poster Tips
Page 16

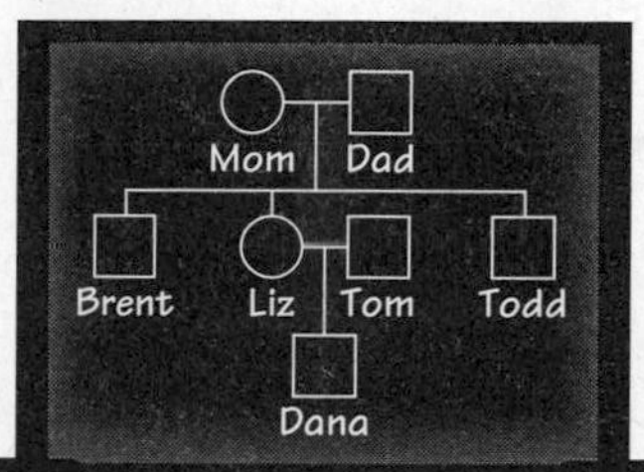

Use Synonyms

Introduce the Skill Lesson literature by previewing the vocabulary at the right. Write the vocabulary words on the board. Have students listen for the words as you read the following paragraph. Encourage them to listen for synonyms, such as *deck* and *patio*.

> On warm nights, we sit on the <u>porch</u>. My father calls the porch a deck or a patio. First I <u>sweep</u> the porch, pushing away dirt with a broom. Then we play games like checkers. My sister plays with her favorite stuffed animal, a fuzzy <u>sheep</u>. My brother pushes his <u>wagon</u> on the porch. His wagon is a little cart. Sometimes we have a cold drink like <u>lemonade</u>.

Write the synonyms from the paragraph on the board. Have students match them with the vocabulary words. Then have students point to the poster to show that they have figured out the meaning of each vocabulary word. Other students may also benefit from reviewing this vocabulary.

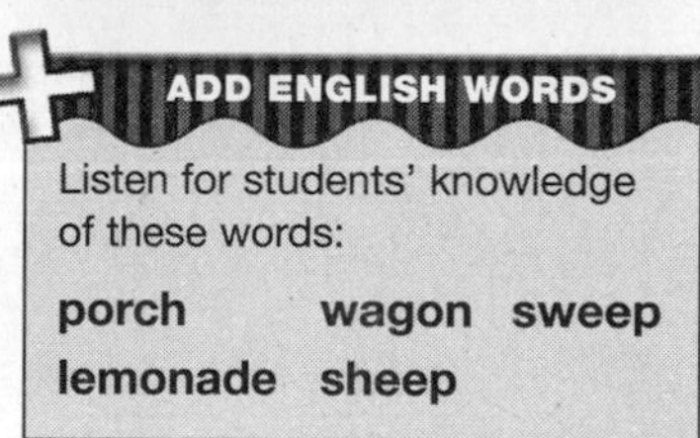

Listen for students' knowledge of these words:

porch **wagon** **sweep**
lemonade **sheep**

Present the Comprehension Strategy

Comprehension: Sequence

Use Comprehension Strategies, *Adding English Guide,* page 10, to introduce Sequence.

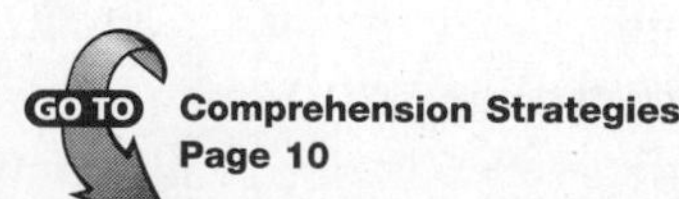

Comprehension Strategies
Page 10

Relate to Personal Experience

Have students think about how they get ready for school in the morning. In groups, students can list the things they do at home, such as brush their teeth, eat breakfast, and get dressed. Then have students dramatize the steps they follow in chronological order, from the time they get up to the time they leave for school.

Guide students as they read "Will Sarah Return?," Scott Foresman Reading, *pages 44–45. Remind them to think about what happens first, next, and last.*

Selection Audio CD 1/Tape 2

Practice

Have students retell the events in "Will Sarah Return?" in the order in which they occurred. Encourage students to use the Adding English poster for help in expressing actions and ideas.

Assess

If... students are not able to retell the story in sequence,

then... write the following sentences on strips of paper. Guide students to arrange the strips in sequence.

First, Caleb and Anna watched Sarah leave.

Next, the kids did their chores.

Then they talked to Papa about Sarah.

Last, Anna set the dinner table with four plates.

ADD ENGLISH WORDS

Review these clue words related to sequence.

first next then last

PART 2

Preview the Reading Selection

Use these activities before reading the selection: *Train to Somewhere,* Teacher's Edition, *Scott Foresman Reading,* pages 46–67.

Activate Prior Knowledge

Ask students to point out parts of the Adding English Poster that picture the words at the right. Ask students why the family would be welcoming the young boy at the train station. Encourage students to talk about adoption and the different ways that families are created. Begin a K-W-L chart, Graphic Organizer Transparency 7, about adoption.

ADD ENGLISH WORDS

Observe whether students understand the following words related to families and adoption.

families conductor
orphans pretty
feather ready

Strategy: Using a K-W-L Chart

Explain the strategy: *When I want to learn new facts, I can use a chart. It is a strategy called Using a K-W-L Chart.* Point out what each letter means and model filling out the K column. Have students begin their own charts by completing the first column.

K What I Know	W What I Want to Know	L What I Learned
Families can adopt orphans.		

Transparency 7

RESOURCES

Use *Scott Foresman ESL,* Grade 4, for additional instruction and activities.

- Chapter 2, "Setting the West"
- Video, Unit 1, "The Wonderful West"

Build Background

Display a feather, a railroad ticket, a suitcase, a whistle, and a hat. Have the class study the Adding English Poster and explain how they could use these items to copy the actions shown there. Then have students act out scenes from the poster, using some or all of the props. Encourage students to use the vocabulary words as they act out the scenes.

Ask Questions

Draw students' attention to the poster. Have volunteers describe what they see and name some of the items that relate to families and adoption. Have students generate a list of questions about the poster, using the vocabulary words. Write the questions on chart paper. Have students work in pairs to try to answer the questions.

Vocabulary: Antonyms

Use these activities with the Vocabulary Lesson and paragraph "Diary Entry: May 25, 1880," Teacher's Edition, *Scott Foresman Reading,* page 46.

Write *pretty* on an index card. On the back of the card, write its antonym, *ugly*. Display the card and explain that we can sometimes figure out what a word means by knowing its opposite. Write the selection vocabulary words on the chalkboard. Then write *give away* and *happiness*. Explain that these are antonyms for two of the vocabulary words. Have students match the antonym pairs, using dictionaries and the poster for help as needed.

ADD ENGLISH WORDS

Observe students and listen to their responses to assess their comprehension of selection vocabulary.

misery **couple**
adopt **atlas**
carriage **platform**

Read

Guide students as they read "Diary Entry: May 25, 1880," Scott Foresman Reading, *page 46. Ask them how they can use antonyms to define unfamiliar words.*

Students can participate in the Write About It activity that follows. If possible, have English language learners work in groups with students whose home language is English to discuss what might happen when the writer and her husband arrive at the train. Have students draw a picture of the scene and write a sentence to explain it.

Present the Reading Selection

Use these activities with *Train to Somewhere,* Teacher's Edition, *Scott Foresman Reading,* pages 46–67.

Preview the Illustrations

Explain the strategy: *Before I start to read, I look at the pictures to get an idea of what the story will be about.* Have students study the picture on pages 46–47. Ask: *How do you know the story takes place in the past? What do you think the children are doing? What are they waiting for?* Continue previewing the illustrations.

Develop Concepts

For this selection, students may need support in understanding that the story is historical fiction: fiction based on historical fact. To prepare students, read the head note on page 48 aloud. Then ask: *What parts of the story will be real? What parts of the story will be made-up?*

Set Purposes

Students can participate in Set Purposes, Teacher's Edition, *Scott Foresman Reading,* page 47. Then help students fill in the W column on their K-W-L charts. Remind students that they are using the strategy called Using a K-W-L Chart.

Guide students as they read Train to Somewhere, Scott Foresman Reading, *pages 46–67. To support comprehension, use the suggestions in Meeting Individual Needs, ESL, in the Teacher's Edition.*

Response Log

- Have students write some advice for Marianne about fitting in with her new parents. Encourage students to think about experiences they had fitting into a new culture or a new neighborhood. They can refer to the poster for support and draw pictures to help express their ideas.
- Have students finish this sentence: *A good parent is* ______. Then have students discuss whether the couples waiting at the stations in the story would be good parents for the orphans. What supporting clues can they find?

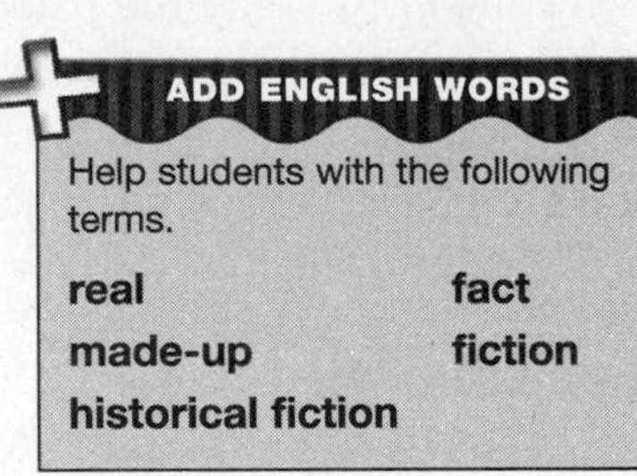

ADD ENGLISH WORDS

Help students with the following terms.

real **fact**
made-up **fiction**
historical fiction

K What I Know	W What I Want to Know	L What I Learned
Families can adopt orphans.	What was the orphan train like?	

Transparency 7

Selection Audio CD 1/Tape 2

Practice Selection Concepts

To help students tell what they learned, choose from these activities.

- Help students complete the L column in their K-W-L charts.
- Have students read the ten important sentences and choose one to illustrate. Let students show their pictures and have classmates guess which sentences were illustrated.

Strategy: Self-Assess

Ask: *Did Using a K-W-L Chart help you learn more about adoption?* Have students tell what they liked and disliked about the strategy and which parts they found especially useful.

K What I Know	W What I Want to Know	L What I Learned
Families can adopt orphans.	What was the orphan train like?	People went to the train station to pick orphans to adopt.

Transparency 7

Ten Important Sentences Page 14

Language Awareness

Provide supported practice by using the Adding English Grammar and Phonics Practice Masters, pages 31–32, with the suggestions below.

Grammar: Subjects and Predicates

Write the following sentence on the board: *Marianne ran fast.* Read the sentence aloud. Ask: *Who does something? What is she doing?* Explain that sentences have two parts: a subject who does something and a predicate that tells what the subject is doing. Help students understand that *ran fast* is the predicate. Invite a volunteer to come to the board and label the subject and predicate. Continue with other examples.

Students can complete the Practice Master alone or with a partner. Encourage students to refer to the selection as they complete the exercises.

Adding English Grammar Practice Master Page 31

Phonics: Vowel digraphs *ea, ou*

Distribute the Practice Master. Use each word in Exercise A in a sentence and have students repeat each word. Have students read the words aloud.

Let students read the words in Exercise B aloud to a partner. Listen for correct pronunciation, giving help as needed. Then introduce the rhyming sentences. Review rhyming words and same ending sounds. Have students work in pairs to complete the page.

Adding English Phonics Practice Master Page 32

PART 3

Connect Selection Concepts

Use these activities with Reader Response, Teacher's Edition, *Scott Foresman Reading,* page 67.

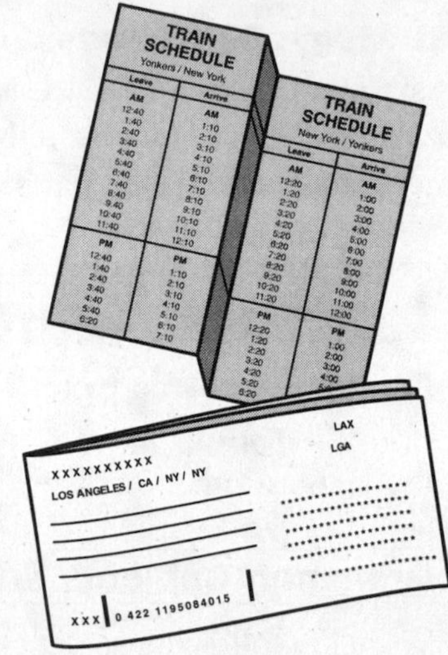

Dramatize

If possible, place English language learners in groups with students whose home language is English. Then invite groups to act out one of the following scenes from *Train to Somewhere:*

- the orphans getting on the train
- the orphan train's stop at Porterville, Illinois
- Miss Randolph and Marianne meeting Mr. and Mrs. Book

It's a Small World

Students who have been on a train, airplane, or bus can bring in their tickets, schedules, boarding passes, and other mementos to share with the class. Display the items and invite students to identify each piece and explain how it is used.

Sharing Music

In the story, Miss Randolph sings a song to lift the children's spirits. Invite students to share songs from their cultural backgrounds that they associate with happy times. Possibilities include holiday songs, traditional tunes, and family favorites.

Reading Across Texts: "The American Railroad," pages 68–69

To support students as they read a picture encyclopedia:

- Have students preview "The American Railroad" by looking at the pictures and reading a few words from each caption. Explain that this selection can be read in any order. Read the introduction with students. After reading, ask: *How does this kind of article help you understand* Train to Somewhere?

Assess

Refer to the list below to assess students' progress.

Reading

- ☐ Uses words related to families and adoption.
- ☐ Describes the sequence of events in a story.
- ☐ Uses illustrations to preview a story.
- ☐ Distinguishes between fact and fiction.

Language Awareness

Grammar

- ☐ Recognizes subjects and predicates.

Phonics

- ☐ Pronounces and decodes words with the vowel digraphs *ea* and *ou*.

Learning Strategies

- ☐ Uses a K-W-L chart.
- ☐ Uses antonyms to learn unfamiliar vocabulary.

Name ___________________________________

Subjects and Predicates

A. Listen to the sentences. Underline the complete subject. Circle the complete predicate.

1. Nora had a hat.

2. The conductor took the ticket.

B. Read the subject with each group of words. Find the words that tell what the subject is doing. Circle them.

Subject: The boys and the girls

3. go on a train.

4. a new home.

5. buy new clothes.

6. eat cookies and drink milk.

7. rich people.

8. sit on a stage.

C. Talk to a partner about a time you took a trip. Then write about what you saw, heard, and did.

On my trip, ______________________________

____

____

____

____

Name ________________________________

Phonics

Vowel Digraphs *ea, ou*

A. Listen to the words. Read the words. Say the words.

feather sweater couple touch

B. Write a word from the box to complete each rhyme.

ready	head	trouble

1. Today it was late when I jumped out of bed. I ran out of the house with no hat on my ____________.

2. I see soapy water! I see a bubble! Don't walk on the floor, or you'll be in ____________.

3. Good runners are fast and steady. When the whistle blows, they are ____________.

C. Pretend you are Marianne and your partner is Nora. You are meeting a week after being with your new family. Talk to each other. Use the words in the box.

ready	head	couple	trouble

Yingtao's New Friend

Pages 70–95

Crossing Cultures • In this lesson, students read about a Chinese boy and the friends he makes after coming to the United States. Have English language learners vote on what they think is important in a friendship. Is it sharing a language or an interest? Is it the ability to get along? Or is it something else?

PART 1

Preview the Skill Lesson

Use these activities with the Skill Lesson: "Anna's New School," Teacher's Edition, *Scott Foresman Reading,* pages 70–71.

Activate Prior Knowledge

Invite volunteers to describe what school is like. Explain that schools are similar and different all over the world. Let students share information about different schools they have attended. Then show Adding English Poster 3. Have students brainstorm a list of words that describe the school activities and classroom objects they see in the poster. Let students use their home languages as necessary. Write the English words on index cards and have students tape the cards to the corresponding objects in the classroom.

ADD ENGLISH WORDS

Listen for students' knowledge of these words:

cry	**desk**
different	**blackboards**
chalk	**glasses**

Use Context Clues

Introduce the Skill Lesson literature by previewing the vocabulary at the right. Write the vocabulary words on the board. Explain the strategy: *When I hear a word I don't know, I listen to the words around it to help me understand the unfamiliar word.* Emphasize context clues and point to items on the Adding English Poster as you read the passage.

> Jane was sad on her first day of school. "Don't cry," the teacher said, as she wiped away her tears.
>
> "I don't want to be different," Jane cried.
>
> "All people are not the same. We are all unique," the teacher said. Jane sat at her desk. She liked the little table and chair. Jane put on her glasses. They had round lenses and a brown frame.
>
> "Please go to the blackboards," the teacher said. Jane and the other children walked to the big chalkboards at the front of the room. Jane picked up a piece of chalk. The chalk was soft and white, like a big pencil.

Check understanding by having students match a poster item with its corresponding vocabulary word. All students may benefit from reviewing this vocabulary before they read the selection.

Present the Comprehension Strategy

Comprehension: Compare and Contrast

Use Comprehension Strategies, *Adding English Guide,* page 10, to introduce Compare and Contrast.

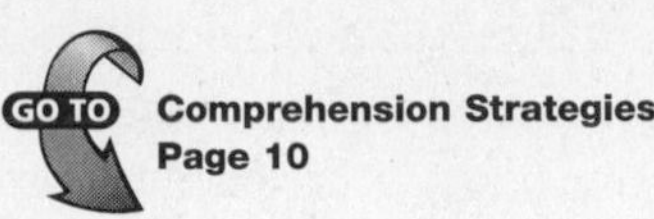

Relate to Personal Experience

Ask students to think about their favorite food from their home culture and their favorite American food. Ask: *How are these foods the same? How are they different?* Have students describe the similarities and differences to a partner. Students can then draw pictures of the two foods side by side.

Guide students as they read "Anna's New School," Scott Foresman Reading, *pages 70–71. Remind them to compare and contrast Anna's new school with her old school.*

Selection Audio CD 1/Tape 3

Practice

Have students tell how Anna's new school is like her old school and how it is different. Encourage students to refer to objects in the classroom and the Adding English Poster as vocabulary aids.

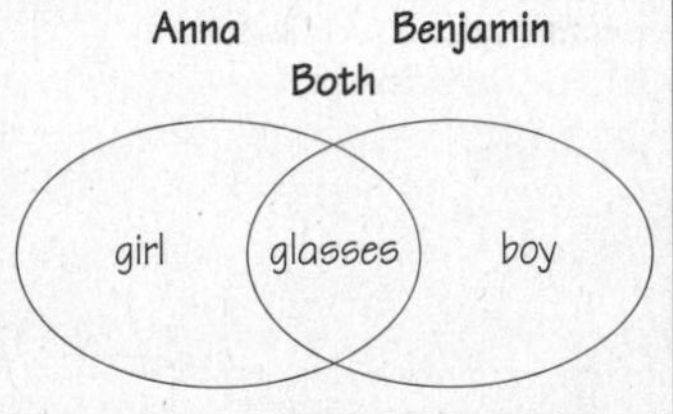

Transparency 21

Assess

If... students are not able to compare and contrast the schools,

then... create a Venn diagram, Graphic Organizer Transparency 21, and have students arrange the following items from the story on it: *girl, boy, glasses.*

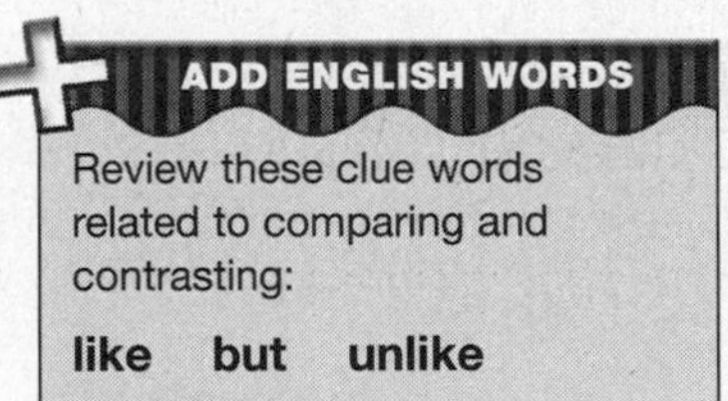

Review these clue words related to comparing and contrasting:

like **but** **unlike**

PART 2

Preview the Reading Selection

Use these activities before reading "Yingtao's New Friend," Teacher's Edition, *Scott Foresman Reading,* pages 72–93.

Activate Prior Knowledge

Invite students to identify parts of the Adding English Poster that picture the words at the right. Encourage students to discuss some of the activities that are valued in their homes, such as music, sports, and community service.

ADD ENGLISH WORDS

Watch for students' understanding of words related to music:

conductor	**audition**
cello	**violin**
lessons	**guest**

Build Background

Arrange students in small groups and draw their attention to the list of vocabulary words. Have one student in each group pantomime playing a violin. Have the others guess what the student is doing. Students can switch parts and continue the activity for the words *cello* and *conductor*. Encourage them to use the Adding English Poster for pantomiming ideas.

Strategy: Using a Vocabulary Frame

Use a vocabulary frame, Graphic Organizer Transparency 8, to help students master more difficult or abstract words, such as *audition, lessons,* and *guest*. Explain the strategy: *When I want to learn new vocabulary words, I can use a special type of chart. It is a strategy called Using a Vocabulary Frame.* Model how to fill out the vocabulary frame for the word *audition.* Have students work with partners to fill out a vocabulary frame for *lessons* and *guest*.

Vocabulary: Multiple-Meaning Words

Use these activities with the Vocabulary Lesson and paragraph "Right Place, Wrong Page!," Teacher's Edition, *Scott Foresman Reading,* page 72.

Write the word *measures* on the board. Explain that English has many words that have more than one meaning. Point out that *measures* means "bars of music," but *measures* also can mean "finds the size of something." Have students identify the meaning illustrated on the poster. Then use each word in a sentence. Demonstrate the use of context clues to decide which meaning is appropriate. Repeat this process with *triangle* and *instruments*.

Use Vocabulary Frames

Have partners make a vocabulary frame, Graphic Organizer Transparency 8, for the words at the right. Remind students that they are using a strategy called Using a Vocabulary Frame.

Guide students as they read "Right Place, Wrong Page!," Scott Foresman Reading, *page 72. Ask them how they will choose the correct meaning of multiple-meaning words.*

Students can participate in the Talk About It activity that follows. If possible, have English language learners work with partners whose home language is English to discuss what they might have heard at the concert.

RESOURCES

Use *Scott Foresman ESL,* Grade 5, for additional instruction and activities.

- Chapter 2, "Uses of Sound"
- Video, Unit 1, "Music to Your Ears"

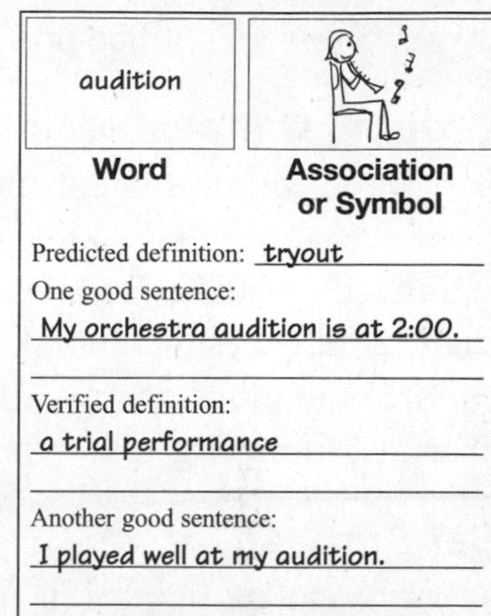

Transparency 8

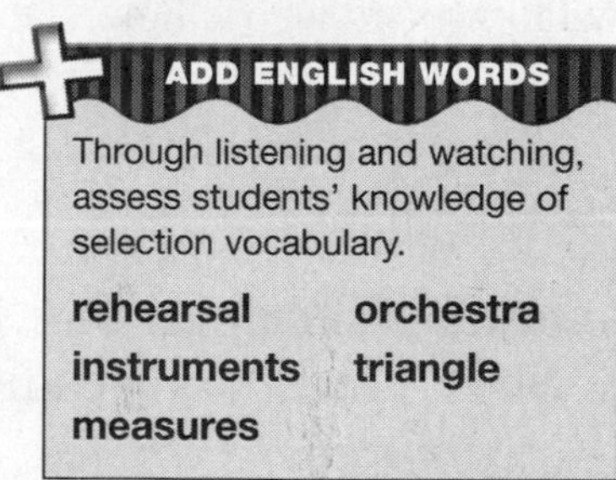

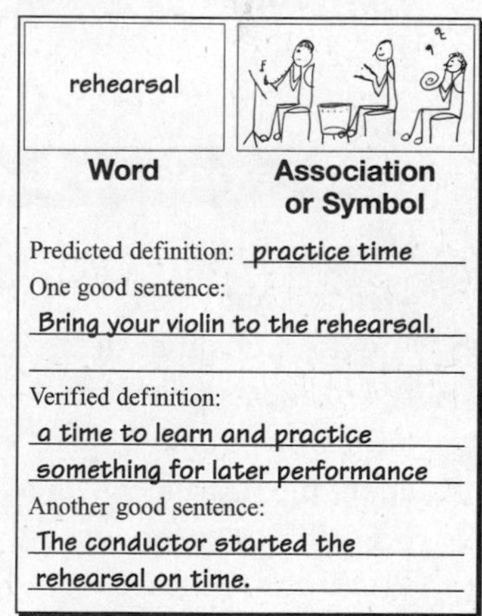

Transparency 8

Present the Reading Selection

Use these activities with "Yingtao's New Friend," Teacher's Edition, *Scott Foresman Reading,* pages 72–93.

Preview Illustrations

Explain the strategy: *Before I read, I look at the pictures in the story to get an idea of what the story will be about.* Have students study the pictures. Ask: *How do you know there will be music in this story? How are the children in the pictures the same? How are they different?* Continue previewing the illustrations.

Develop Concepts

For this selection, students may need support in understanding certain aspects of Chinese culture, such as naming traditions, eating habits, and educational styles. As students read, they can share differences they notice among American culture, Yingtao's culture, and other cultures. Students can record their ideas on a chart, Graphic Organizer Transparency 25.

Yingtao's Culture	American Culture	Other Culture
eat fresh fish	eat hamburger	eat curry

Transparency 25

Set Purposes

Students can participate in Set Purposes, Teacher's Edition, *Scott Foresman Reading,* page 73. English language learners can work with partners whose home language is English to list two or three things they hope to find out by reading the story.

Guide students as they read "Yingtao's New Friend," Scott Foresman Reading, *pages 72–93. To support comprehension, use the suggestions in Meeting Individual Needs, ESL, in the Teacher's Edition.*

Selection Audio CD 1/Tape 3

Response Log

- Have students list qualities they feel are important in a friend, such as kindness, trust, and honesty. Encourage students to think about the qualities demonstrated by Matthew and Yingtao.
- Ask students to answer this question: *If you could play any musical instrument, what would it be, and why?* Partners can talk about the instruments they like. They can refer to the Adding English Poster for support and draw pictures to help express their ideas.

Practice Selection Concepts

To help students tell what they learned, choose from these activities.

- Have students use a Venn diagram, Graphic Organizer Transparency 21, to compare and contrast Matthew and Yingtao.
- Give pairs of students one of the ten important sentences. Have each pair make a vocabulary frame, Graphic Organizer Transparency 8, for one of the words in their sentence. Then let the pairs share their vocabulary knowledge with the class.

Strategy: Self-Assess

Ask: *Did making a vocabulary frame help you learn the meanings of new vocabulary words?* Have students tell which parts of the strategy they found especially useful.

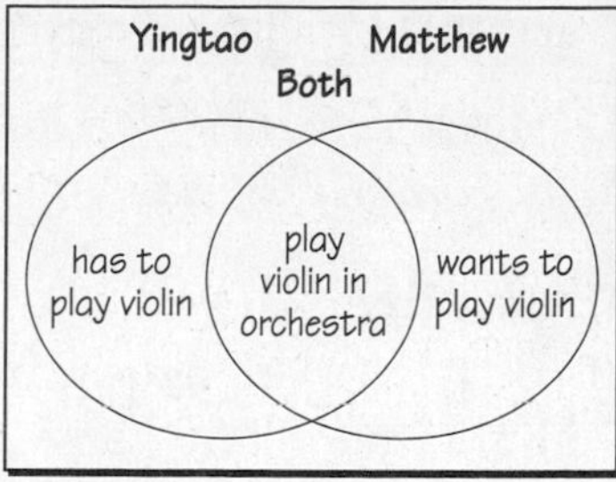

Transparency 21

Ten Important Sentences Page 15

Language Awareness

Provide supported practice by using the Adding English Grammar and Phonics Practice Masters, pages 39–40, with the suggestions below.

Grammar: Declarative and Interrogative Sentences

Write the following sentences on the board: *I play the violin. Do you play the violin?* Read each sentence aloud. Ask: *How are these sentences the same? How are they different?* Guide students to see that both sentences deal with the same topic, but that the first sentence is a statement and the second sentence is a question. Explain that statements are also called *declarative sentences,* and questions are also called *interrogative sentences.* Point out that interrogative sentences always end with a question mark, and declarative sentences always end with a period. Using the story illustrations or the Adding English Poster for ideas, write other declarative and interrogative sentences on the board. Have volunteers label the sentences as declarative or interrogative.

Students can complete the Practice Master alone or with a partner.

Adding English Grammar Practice Master Page 39

Phonics: Vowel Digraphs *oo* and *ui*

Distribute the Practice Master. Have students listen to the words in Exercise A and repeat them. Point out that *oo* and *ui* each make two different sounds. Have students practice the sounds. Then have students practice saying the words to a partner.

For Exercise B, complete the first riddle with the class. Then have students read the riddles aloud before writing their answers.

Adding English Phonics Practice Master Page 40

PART 3

Connect Selection Concepts

Use these activities with Reader Response, Teacher's Edition, *Scott Foresman Reading,* page 93.

Dramatize

If possible, have English language learners work in small groups with students whose home language is English to act out these scenes from "Yingtao's New Friend":

- Yingtao meeting Matthew in the orchestra
- Second Sister cutting tea bags
- Eldest Brother seeing how well Matthew plays the violin
- Matthew eating dinner with the Yang family

My World and Welcome to It

Partners can discuss what they would tell a friend about their family before the friend comes to visit. Students should focus on ways their family is special. They might discuss the music, art, food, and activities enjoyed by family members.

Reading Across Texts: "Making Music," pages 94–95

To support students as they read a nonfiction article:

- Build prior knowledge by asking students to look at the pictures and identify the instruments and the kind of group shown.
- Use the Adding English Poster to review vocabulary related to orchestras.
- After students read the information, ask: *What are the three kinds of instruments in an orchestra? What is the connection between this information and "Yingtao's New Friend?"*

Assess

Refer to the list below to assess students' progress.

Reading

- ☐ Uses words related to school.
- ☐ Uses words related to music.
- ☐ Compares and contrasts two or more things.
- ☐ Uses illustrations to predict story events.

Language Awareness

Grammar

- ☐ Identifies and writes declarative and interrogative sentences.

Phonics

- ☐ Decodes and pronounces words with the vowel digraphs *oo* and *ui*.

Learning Strategies

- ☐ Uses a vocabulary frame.
- ☐ Uses context clues to identify the correct meaning of multiple-meaning words.

Name ____________________________________

Declarative and Interrogative Sentences

A. Underline the statement. Circle the question.

1. I have a violin.

2. Can you play the cello?

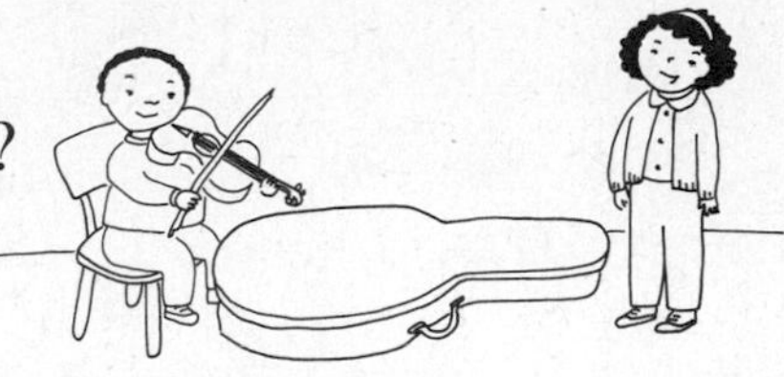

B. Add a period (.) or question mark (?). Read the statements and questions to a partner.

3. Sit at the desk ___

4. Do you like to write with chalk ___

5. Do you play the violin in the school orchestra ___

6. I take music lessons after school ___

7. A guest is watching our rehearsal ___

8. How many instruments do you play ___

C. Imagine that a new student came to your class. What would you tell the student? What would you ask him or her? Talk with a partner. Then write statements and questions.

____

____

____

____

____

____

Name ________________________________

Vowel Digraphs *oo* and *ui*

Phonics

A. Listen to the words. Read the words. Say the words.

moon

book

fruit

building

B. Write the word that answers each riddle. Take turns reading the riddles with a partner.

1. I can tell a story.
Sometimes I have pictures.
I sound like *look.*

What am I? ___________ (took/book)

2. I shine at night.
I can be round like a circle.
I sound like *soon.*

What am I? ___________ (moon/spoon)

3. I am good for you.
I sound like *boot.*

What am I? ___________ (suit/fruit)

4. I am in your mouth.
I help you chew your food.
I sound like *youth.*

What am I? ___________ (tooth/booth)

C. Say the underlined words. Read the paragraph to a partner. Then listen as your partner reads it to you.

It is Juan's first day at <u>school</u>. He is wearing a new <u>suit</u>. He <u>looks</u> around the <u>building</u>. He finds his <u>room</u>. At <u>noon</u>, Juan eats with a new friend. He has <u>fruit</u> and cheese. <u>Soon</u>, Juan will get a new reading <u>book</u>. He likes to read. He is a <u>good</u> student.

Family Pictures

Pages 96–115

Crossing Cultures • In this lesson, students read about the author's memories of growing up in Kingsville, Texas, near the Mexican border. The bilingual text mirrors the author's childhood experiences as she grew up Hispanic American, a member of two cultures. Before and after English language learners read, let them share their ideas about knowing two cultures and speaking two languages.

PART 1

Preview the Skill Lesson

Use these activities with the Skill Lesson: "Painting Mist and Fog," Teacher's Edition, *Scott Foresman Reading,* pages 96–97.

Activate Prior Knowledge

Ask students to find examples of artwork they see in Adding English Poster 4. Explain that what they already know about artwork can help them learn more about the topic. Use a web, Graphic Organizer Transparency 5, to generate words about art and artists.

Poster Tips Page 16

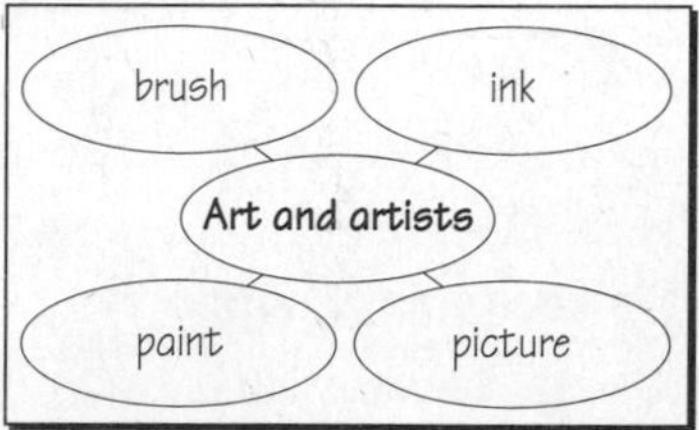

Transparency 5

Use Total Physical Response

Introduce the Skill Lesson literature by previewing the vocabulary at the right. Write the vocabulary words on the board. As you read the passage that follows, have students follow the directions and act out each word. Model the strategy by pantomiming how an artist paints a picture.

> First, I pick up my brush. Pick up your brush so we can get ready to paint. Then I dip the brush into water so it gets wet. Show me how you make your brush wet. Now pat your brush into the ink, like this. Move close to the paper and draw a line. Make your line long and straight! Use more water on your brush to show mist and fog.

Check understanding by asking students to point out illustrations of the vocabulary words on the Adding English Poster. Then direct students' attention to the mist and fog shown on the poster.

Present the Comprehension Strategy

Comprehension: Author's Purpose

Use Comprehension Strategies, *Adding English Guide,* page 10, to introduce Author's Purpose.

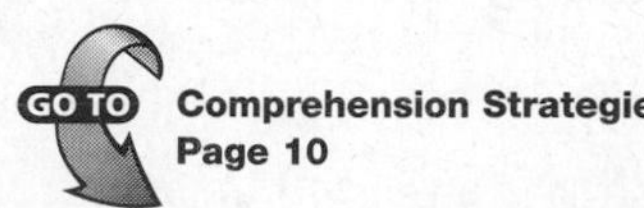

Comprehension Strategies Page 10

Relate to Personal Experience

Ask students to think about what they read at home. In groups, students can talk about why they read each thing. For example, students may read comics to be entertained; they may read instructional books and notes from family members to be informed. Explain that we read different materials for different reasons, just as authors write for different reasons. Introduce two other possible purposes for writing—to express and to persuade—by sharing a poem or journal entry (expression) and a magazine ad (persuasion).

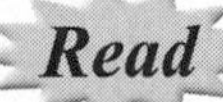

Guide students as they read "Painting Mist and Fog," Scott Foresman Reading, *pages 96–97. Remind them to think about why the author wrote this piece.*

Selection Audio CD 2/Tape 4

Practice

Have students explain the author's purpose for writing "Painting Mist and Fog." Encourage them to use the Adding English Poster for vocabulary support.

Assess

If... students are not able to identify the author's purpose,

then... help them summarize the article and select the author's purpose from the following possibilities and explain the reason for their choice.

- *To persuade students to paint a picture of mist and fog*
- *To explain how to paint a picture of mist and fog*

ADD ENGLISH WORDS

Review these clue words related to author's purpose.

inform	**entertain**
express	**persuade**

PART **2**

Preview the Reading Selection

Use these activities before reading *Family Pictures,* Teacher's Edition, *Scott Foresman Reading,* pages 100–113.

Activate Prior Knowledge

Ask students to point to the parts of the Adding English Poster that picture the words at the right. Ask students what the family is doing. Invite volunteers to list some of the fun things their families do. Begin a K-W-L chart, Graphic Organizer Transparency 7, about family life.

ADD ENGLISH WORDS

Listen for students' comprehension of the following words related to the author's family:

family	**artist**
grandparents	**pick**
birthday party	**leaves**

Strategy: Using a K-W-L Chart

Explain the strategy: *When I want to learn new facts, I can use a chart. It is a strategy called Using a K-W-L Chart.* Point out what each letter means and model filling out the K column. Have students begin their own charts.

K What I Know	W What I Want to Know	L What I Learned
Families can have fun together.		

Transparency 7

RESOURCES

Use *Scott Foresman ESL,* Grade 4, for additional instruction and activities.

- Chapter 11, "Regions of our Country"
- Video, Unit 6, "Regions and States"

Build Background

Direct students' attention to activities shown in the Adding English Poster. Have students use vocabulary words to generate a list of questions about the people and what they are doing. Students can work with partners to answer the questions, referring to the poster as they talk.

Use Freeze Frame

Display leaves, a birthday card, paper napkins and plates, an apron, and art materials. Invite students to explain how they could use these items to create live scenes from the Adding English Poster. Have students pretend to be people in the poster and use the props to stage "frozen scenes." Have students "unfreeze" one by one and describe the scene they are showing.

Vocabulary: Synonyms

Use these activities with the Vocabulary Lesson and paragraph "A Story from the Past," Teacher's Edition, *Scott Foresman Reading,* page 98.

While reading the paragraph aloud, point to the Adding English Poster to demonstrate the words *edge/border, cloth/handkerchief,* and *wash/laundry.* Then write the first of each pair on the board. Have students match each word to its synonym.

ADD ENGLISH WORDS

Through listening and watching, assess students' knowledge of selection vocabulary.

handkerchief	**laundry**
inspired	**scene**
involved	**memories**
border	**future**

Use Personalization

To teach *future* and *memories,* relate them to familiar situations. For example:

- Write *future* on the board and show a calendar marked with holidays and school events. Have a volunteer point to today. Then indicate some holidays and events coming in the future.
- Point out a past holiday or event on your calendar. Write *memories* on the board and sketch a thought bubble with things you remember about the day or event.

Guide students as they read "A Story from the Past," Scott Foresman Reading, *page 98. Ask them how they can use synonyms to define unfamiliar words.*

Students can participate in the Write About It activity that follows. If possible, have English language learners work in groups with students whose home language is English to discuss what happened to Lucinda in the past and predict what might happen to Lucinda in the future. Students can work together to draw storyboards to predict the rest of her story.

Present the Reading Selection

Use these activities with *Family Pictures,* Teacher's Edition, *Scott Foresman Reading,* pages 100–113.

Preview Headings and Illustrations

Explain the strategy: *Before I start to read, I first look at the headings and pictures to get an idea of what the story will be about.* Have students talk about the selection title and the picture on page 101, and then picture and heading on pages 102–103. Ask: *Why might oranges be important in this selection? What are the people in the picture doing?* Continue previewing the headings and illustrations.

Develop Concepts

Have students look at the English and Spanish words. Ask: *Which part of the page is written in English? Which part is written in Spanish? Why do you think the writer told the same story in both English and Spanish?* Help students understand the writer's dual ties to Mexico and the United States. Encourage Hispanic students to share information about their culture and to read aloud portions of the Spanish text. Students can use a T-chart, Graphic Organizer Transparency 24, to list benefits of their two cultures.

Set Purposes

Students can participate in Set Purposes, Teacher's Edition, *Scott Foresman Reading,* page 101. Then help students fill in the W column on their K-W-L charts about family life. Remind students that they are using a strategy called Using a K-W-L Chart.

Guide students as they read Family Pictures, Scott Foresman Reading, *pages 100–113. To support comprehension, use the suggestions in Meeting Individual Needs, ESL, in the Teacher's Edition.*

Home Culture	American Culture
home language	English
home foods	hamburgers and french fries
traditional holidays	Fourth of July, Thanksgiving

Transparency 24

K What I Know	W What I Want to Know	L What I Learned
Families can have fun together.	What fun things do families enjoy?	

Transparency 7

Selection Audio CD 2/Tape 4

Response Log

- Have students draw a "family picture," showing a fun time they had with their family, and write a caption describing the event. Encourage students to refer to the poster for support.
- Ask students to list three things they like to do with their families. Students can look at the poster for ideas.

K What I Know	W What I Want to Know	L What I Learned
Families can have fun together.	What fun things do families enjoy?	Some families pick fruit, have parties, cook special foods, go on trips, and make plans together.

Transparency 7

Practice Selection Concepts

To help students tell what they learned, choose from these activities.

- Help students complete the L column in their K-W-L charts.
- Have students read the ten important sentences and pick one they like. Students can then rewrite the sentence to tell about their own family.

Ten Important Sentences Page 16

Strategy: Self-Assess

Ask: *Did Using a K-W-L Chart help you learn more about families?*

Language Awareness

Provide supported practice by using the Adding English Grammar and Phonics Practice Masters, pages 47–48, with the suggestions below.

Grammar: Imperative and Exclamatory Sentences

Adding English Grammar Practice Master Page 47

Write the following sentences on the board: *Pick up the leaves. What pretty leaves!* Read each sentence aloud. Ask: *How are these sentences the same? How are they different?* Guide students to see that both sentences tell about the same topic, but the first sentence is a command, or an *imperative sentence* (tells what to do), and the second sentence is an *exclamatory sentence* (expresses strong feeling). Imperative sentences usually end with a period, while exclamatory sentences often end with an exclamation mark. Write other imperative and exclamatory sentences on the board. Have volunteers label the sentences as imperative or exclamatory.

Students can complete the Practice Master alone or with a partner.

ADD ENGLISH WORDS

Students may need extra practice to remember that the final *e* is silent and a long vowel sound is used in CVCe words. Have students read aloud these word pairs:

kit/kite **tap/tape**
plum/plume **not/note**

Phonics: Common Word Patterns CVCe, VCCV

Adding English Phonics Practice Master Page 48

Distribute the Practice Master. Say each word in Exercise A as students listen, read, and repeat the words as a group. Help students to see which words have the CVCe pattern and which have the VCCV pattern.

For Exercise B, have students name things in the picture before they read aloud and choose the answers.

PART 3

Connect Selection Concepts

Use these activities with Reader Response, Teacher's Edition, *Scott Foresman Reading,* page 113.

Literature Discussion Groups

If possible, have English language learners work in small groups with students whose home language is English. Together they should talk about *Family Pictures,* focusing on the following questions:

- Who is telling the story?
- What family activities does the author describe?
- Why is the story in Spanish and English?
- What questions would you like to ask Carmen Lomas Garza?

Color My World

Have students create their own "family pictures" page by first drawing a scene from their own lives and writing several English sentences to describe each scene. Students can add sentences in their home language and compile the pages to create a class book.

READING ACROSS TEXTS

Reading Across Texts: "Family Photo" and "New Baby," pages 114–115

Guide students as they read these poems. To support comprehension and make connections to Family Pictures, *see the suggestions in the Teacher's Edition,* Scott Foresman Reading.

Assess

Refer to the list below to assess students' progress.

Reading

- ☐ Uses words related to painting.
- ☐ Uses words related to family life.
- ☐ Identifies an author's purpose.
- ☐ Previews headings and illustrations to predict a story's events.

Language Awareness

Grammar

- ☐ Identifies imperative and exclamatory sentences.

Phonics

- ☐ Pronounces and decodes words with the patterns CVCe and VCCV.

Learning Strategies

- ☐ Uses a K-W-L chart.
- ☐ Uses synonyms to learn unfamiliar vocabulary.

Name ______________________________

Imperative and Exclamatory Sentences

A. Listen to the sentences. How are they different?

1. The fog is rolling in!

2. Put away your laundry.

B. Write a period (.) or an exclamation mark (!) to complete each sentence. Explain to a partner why you chose each ending.

3. Don't pick the leaves ___

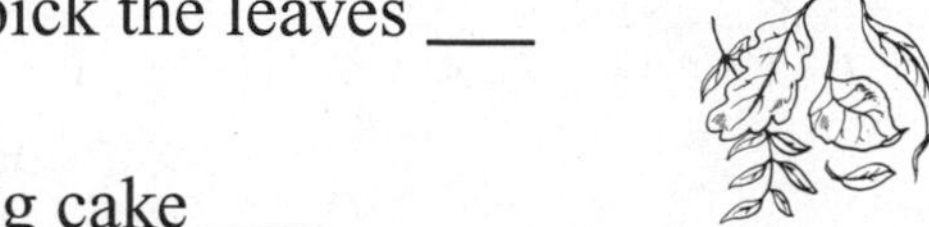

4. It's a big cake ___

5. Please be nice to my family ___

6. Make plans now for your future ___

7. What a pretty scene ___

8. Please fold the handkerchief ___

C. What are your best memories? Talk with a partner. Then finish the sentence.

I remember ______________________________

____

____

____

____

____

____

Grammar

Name ________________________________

Phonics

Common Word Patterns CVCe, VCCV

A. Listen to the words. Read the words. Say the words.

rope cave lake apron basket cactus

B. Each word has the pattern CVCe or VCCV. Listen and repeat the words. Write each word under its pattern.

artist	make	scene
summer	pine	after

CVCe	VCCV
____________	____________
____________	____________
____________	____________

C. Say the underlined words. Read the paragraph to a partner. Then listen as your partner reads it to you. Write a title.

Title: ________________________________

Jane is an artist. She will paint a scene. She takes a brush and ink. The picture has pine trees and a lake. How will the scene look after summer is over?

Addie in Charge

Pages 116–135

Crossing Cultures • In this lesson, students read about the differences of pioneer life in America. Some children in the selections have extra responsibilities due to family circumstances. What do English language learners think of these responsibilities? What are they expected to do for their families?

PART 1

Preview the Skill Lesson

Use these activities with the Skill Lesson: "Ma on the Prairie," Teacher's Edition, *Scott Foresman Reading,* pages 116–117.

Activate Prior Knowledge

Invite students to share what they know about the prairie. Show Adding English Poster 5 and discuss what it would be like to be a pioneer on the prairie. Then have students list five things they would take with them if their family was going to live on the prairie. Let students discuss their choices in small groups.

Things to Take
1. food
2. clothes
3. toys
4. books
5. family pictures

Use Context Clues

Introduce the Skill Lesson literature by previewing the vocabulary at the right. Write the vocabulary words on the board and have students listen for the words as you read the following paragraph. Direct them to listen for context clues, such as *big, flat grassland.*

> We live on the prairie, a big, flat grassland with no trees, just small plants and grass. Because we are very far from our relatives, I don't see my grandparents very often. I send letters when we have stamps and envelopes. When we first came to the prairie, I was very lonesome. I missed my friends. Then I met a new friend, and now I am happy. I smile a lot.

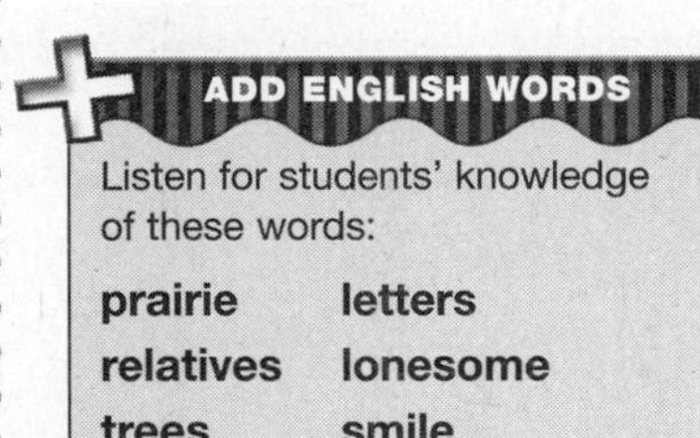

Guide students to match each vocabulary word with its corresponding context clue. Check understanding by asking students to point to the illustrations of the vocabulary words on the poster.

Present the Comprehension Strategy

Comprehension: Character

Use Comprehension Strategies, *Adding English Guide,* page 10, to introduce Character.

Relate to Personal Experience

In groups, have students talk about what a person's actions and words tell about him or her. Pairs of students can act out a meeting between two people. The class can watch and then describe the characters they saw.

Guide students as they read "Ma on the Prairie," Scott Foresman Reading, *pages 116–117. Remind them to think about what Ma is like.*

Selection Audio CD 2/Tape 5

Practice

Have students describe Ma's character in "Ma on the Prairie." Encourage students to use the Adding English Poster for vocabulary support.

Assess

If... students are not able to describe Ma's character,

then... have them underline the word that best matches each description from the story.

Story Clue	Ma's Character	
• It was awfully lonesome inside the house.	talkative	quiet
• She'd hardly stepped foot outside in weeks, now.	apart	with others
• that lonesomeness of hers	happy	unhappy
• Ma never laughed anymore, hardly spoke, seldom smiled.	cheerful	sad

ADD ENGLISH WORDS

Review these clue words related to character:

think do say

PART 2

Preview the Reading Selection

Use these activities before reading the selection "Addie in Charge," Teacher's Edition, *Scott Foresman Reading,* pages 118–132.

Activate Prior Knowledge

Ask students to point out the parts of the Adding English Poster that picture the words at the right. Direct their attention to the grass and fire. Ask students why a fire can be dangerous. Begin a story prediction from vocabulary chart, Graphic Organizer Transparency 3, about the story.

ADD ENGLISH WORDS

Review the following words related to life on the prairie.

grass fire hide
burn well ladder

Strategy: Making Predictions from Vocabulary

Explain the strategy: *When I want to use vocabulary words to predict what a story will be about, I can use a chart. It is a strategy called Making Predictions from Vocabulary.* Model how to fill out the chart. Have students begin their own charts.

Build Background

Have students brainstorm a list of jobs involved in caring for a home and family, such as cooking, cleaning, watching children, and washing clothes. Let pairs of students pantomime each job for the class to guess. Have students raise their hands to show which jobs they have done at home. Discuss which jobs are most important and which are the most difficult.

Practice New Words

Ask students to brainstorm ways they can learn new words. Possibilities include listening to the word, looking at the word, saying it silently and out loud, drawing a simple picture, and writing it in English and their home language. Pairs of students can use these methods to learn the vocabulary words.

Vocabulary: Context Clues

Use these activities with the Vocabulary Lesson and paragraph "Bravery Under Fire!," Teacher's Edition, *Scott Foresman Reading,* page 118.

Create a dialogue that uses each word at the right along with a context clue. For example:

> **We crouched low in the grass; we bent over to stay out of the smoke. What does crouched mean?**
>
> **The billows of smoke looked like puffy white clouds. What does billows mean?**

Students can point to a picture of each word on the Adding English Poster as they answer the questions.

Use Antonyms

Explain that we can sometimes figure out what a word means by knowing its opposite. Write the word *up* and ask students for its opposite. Invite volunteers to name opposites for *hard* (soft), *night* (day), *white* (black), and *smarted* (soothed). Use pictures, objects, and pantomime to clarify meanings as needed. Continue with other words from the list at the right that have clear antonyms.

Title "Addie in Charge"

Look at the selection title above and the list of words and phrases below. Write sentences that predict who and what this story might be about.

Words and Phrases

grass, fire, hide, burn, well, ladder

Characters: ______

Problem: A house is on fire, and people are looking for a place to hide.

Events: Someone is rescued with a ladder. People use water from a well to put out the fire.

Transparency 3

RESOURCES

Use *Scott Foresman ESL,* Grade 4, for additional instruction and activities.

- Chapter 2, "Settling the West"
- Video, Unit 1, "The Wonderful West"

ADD ENGLISH WORDS

Through listening and watching, assess students' knowledge of selection vocabulary.

billows **tufts**
bellows **smarted**
crouched

Guide students as they read "Bravery Under Fire!," Scott Foresman Reading, *page 118. Ask them what they will do if they find words they don't know.*

Students can participate in the Write About It activity that follows. First have students draw pictures of the scene described in the paragraph. If possible, English language learners can then work in pairs with students whose home language is English to label their pictures and create certificates for Pedro.

Present the Reading Selection

Use these activities with "Addie in Charge," Teacher's Edition, *Scott Foresman Reading,* pages 118–132.

Preview Title and Illustrations

Explain the strategy: *Before I start to read, I look at the title and the pictures to get an idea of what the story will be about.* Have students read the story title on page 119 and copy it onto the top line of their Story Prediction from Vocabulary charts. Then help students add information to their charts. Remind students that they are using a strategy called Making Predictions from Vocabulary. Continue previewing the pictures.

Title "Addie in Charge"

Look at the selection title above and the list of words and phrases below. Write sentences that predict who and what this story might be about.

Words and Phrases

grass, fire, hide, burn, well, ladder

Characters: Addie, brothers

Problem: A house is on fire, and people are looking for a place to hide.

Events: Someone is rescued with a ladder. People use water from a well to put out the fire.

Transparency 3

Develop Concepts

For this selection, students may need support in understanding that the story is historical fiction, or fiction based on historical fact. Read aloud "About the Author" on page 131. Then ask: *What parts of the story will be real? What parts of the story will be made-up?* Help students understand the concepts *real* and *made-up* by posing real and fictitious situations. Students can identify them as fact or fiction and then suggest additional situations of their own.

Fire is hot. (real, fact)   Fire can talk. (made-up, fiction)

ADD ENGLISH WORDS

Help students with the following terms:

made-up **real**
fiction **fact**
historical fiction

Set Purposes

Students can participate in Set Purposes, Teacher's Edition, *Scott Foresman Reading,* page 119. Let volunteers read aloud their predictions from their story prediction from vocabulary charts.

Guide students as they read "Addie in Charge," Scott Foresman Reading, *pages 118–132. To support comprehension, use the suggestions in Meeting Individual Needs, ESL, in the Teacher's Edition.*

Selection Audio CD 2/Tape 5

Response Log

- Have students write how Addie could fight the fire saving herself and Burt. They can refer to the Adding English Poster for support.
- Ask students to list other forces of nature that can cause great destruction, such as floods, hurricanes, typhoons, and blizzards. Have students draw a picture of one of these fierce natural disasters and label each part to show what is happening.

Practice Selection Concepts

To help students tell what they learned, choose from these activities.

- Help students complete the "Outcome" section of their story prediction from vocabulary charts.
- Have groups of students illustrate the ten important sentences. Then guide them to arrange their pictures in order to tell the story, using the sentences as captions.

Strategy: Self-Assess

Ask: *Did Making Predictions from Vocabulary help you understand the story? How?*

Language Awareness

Provide supported practice by using the Adding English Grammar and Phonics Practice Masters, pages 55–56, with the suggestions below.

Grammar: Compound and Complex Sentences

Write the following sentence on the board: *There is a fire, and the grass will burn.* Explain that, in a *compound sentence*, two simple sentences are linked with a comma and a connecting word such as *and, but,* or *or.* Then write this sentence: *Addie was in charge of Burt while her parents were away.* Explain that this is a complex sentence because it has one simple sentence and one group of words that cannot stand on its own. Using the Adding English Poster for ideas, ask students to suggest other compound and complex sentences.

Help students complete Exercise B. Remind them to delete the first period when combining phrases and/or sentences.

Phonics: Initial Three-Letter Blends *thr, scr, str, squ*

Distribute the Practice Master. Have students listen, read, and repeat as you say the words in exercises A and B. Pair students to ask and answer questions with the words, such as *What is a strawberry? A strawberry is a small, red fruit.*

Title "Addie in Charge"

Look at the selection title above and the list of words and phrases below. Write sentences that predict who and what this story might be about.

Words and Phrases
grass, fire, hide, burn, well, ladder

Characters: Addie, brothers

Problem: A house is on fire, and people are looking for a place to hide.

Events: Someone is rescued with a ladder. People use water from a well to put out the fire.

Outcome: Addie saved her brother Burt and herself from a prairie fire.

Transparency 3

Ten Important Sentences Page 17

Adding English Grammar Practice Master Page 55

Consonant Blends, Digraphs

Adding English Phonics Practice Master Page 56

PART 3

Connect Selection Concepts

Use these activities with Reader Response, Teacher's Edition, *Scott Foresman Reading,* page 132.

Dramatize

If possible, have English language learners work in small groups with students whose home language is English to act out scenes from "Addie in Charge," focusing on these parts of the text:

- the chores Addie does before she sees the fire
- Addie and Burt hiding in the well
- George and Addie talking about the fire near the end of the story

Home on the Range

Have students think of a challenge they have faced, such as learning English or adjusting to a new school. Have them write a brief letter explaining the specific challenge they faced and offering advice to someone dealing with a similar situation.

Reading Across Texts: "Merle Builds a Sod House," pages 133–135

To support students as they learn about and read an Internet article:

- Activate prior knowledge by inviting students to tell what they already know about using the Internet. If possible, let pairs demonstrate techniques for pointing, clicking, and scrolling.
- Use the Adding English Poster to teach the vocabulary words. Ask students to list and describe other types of homes they know about.
- Ask: *How is "Merle Builds a Sod House" like "Addie in Charge"? How is it different?* Record their responses in a Venn diagram, Graphic Organizer Transparency 21.

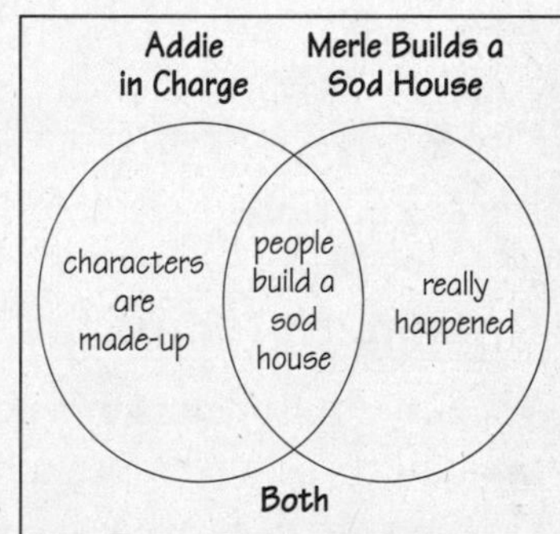

Transparency 21

Assess

Refer to the list below to assess students' progress.

Reading

- ☐ Uses words related to the prairie and pioneer life.
- ☐ Uses words related to fire.
- ☐ Describes a character in a story.
- ☐ Previews title and illustrations to predict a story's events.

Language Awareness

Grammar

- ☐ Identifies and writes compound and complex sentences.

Phonics

- ☐ Pronounces and decodes words with the initial blends *thr, scr, str,* and *squ*.

Learning Strategies

- ☐ Uses a story prediction from vocabulary chart.
- ☐ Uses context clues to learn unfamiliar vocabulary.

Name ____________________

Compound and Complex Sentences

A. Underline the sentence with the connecting word. Circle the connecting word.

1. The fire was hot, but we were safe.

2. Although the fire was hot, we were safe.

B. Add the punctuation and words from the parentheses to make one sentence.

3. When the wind blows. Ma stays inside. (,)

____

____

4. While Burt napped. Addie worked on her sampler. (,)

____

____

5. Addie's legs shook. Her legs hurt. (, and)

____

____

6. Addie was afraid. She did something brave. (, but)

____

____

C. Imagine that you saw a house on fire. Talk with a partner. Then write what you would do.

If I saw a fire, ____________________

____

____

____

____

Name ________________________________

Initial Three-Letter Blends *thr, scr, str, squ*

A. Listen to the words. Read the words. Say the words.

three

screw

strawberry

squirrel

B. Listen and say the name of each picture. Find the word in the box. Write it on the line under the picture. Then find another word with the same beginning sound. Write it on the second line.

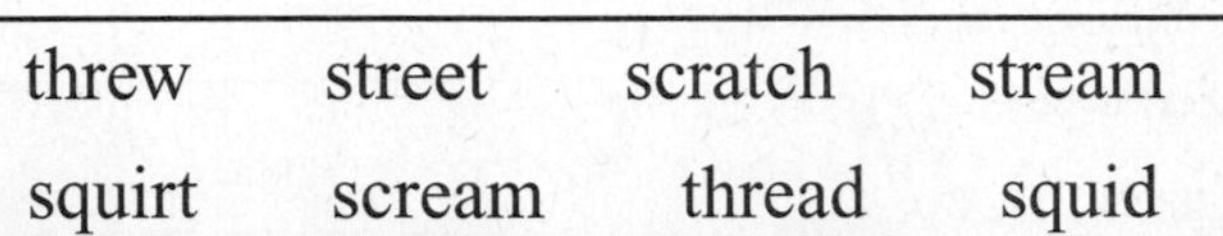

threw	street	scratch	stream
squirt	scream	thread	squid

1. ________ **2.** ________ **3.** ________ **4.** ________

________ ________ ________ ________

C. Read the letter to a partner. Then listen as your partner reads it. Underline the words that begin with *thr*, *scr*, *str*, and *squ*. Say the words to your partner.

Dear Sally,

I'm getting used to being a pioneer, but it's still strange. Ma and I washed clothes and rinsed them in our stream. I felt a squirt of water, and it was so cold that I let out a scream. Ma and I made thread. I wish I could buy it in a shop on a street!

The Cricket in Times Square

Pages 146–167

Crossing Cultures • In this lesson, students read fanciful selections about animals with human characteristics. The contrast between country and city life is a major theme of the stories. Ask students to describe and compare city and country areas of their home countries.

PART 1

Preview the Skill Lesson

Use these activities with the Skill Lesson: "Caught in the Kitchen," Teacher's Edition, *Scott Foresman Reading,* pages 146–147.

Activate Prior Knowledge

Ask students what they see in Adding English Poster 6. Encourage them to tell how parts of the picture are like or different from their experiences. Allow students to use their home language when needed. Tell students to imagine that they are in the picture. Ask: *What can you see, hear, smell, taste, and feel?* Use a five-column chart, Graphic Organizer Transparency 27, to record students' responses.

Hear	Smell	Taste
traffic whir train		sugar cream cakes

Transparency 27

Use Context Clues

Introduce the Skill Lesson literature by previewing vocabulary at the right. List the vocabulary words on the board. Explain the strategy: *When I hear a word I don't know, I listen to words before and after it. They help me understand it.*

As you read the following passage, direct students to listen for context clues, such as the clue for *spilled* (making the grass white), to help them figure out meaning.

> The picnic basket, containing food, fell off the table. A bowl of sugar rolled out of the picnic basket. A box of cream spilled onto the ground, making the grass white. Three young gray mice scampered toward the upset picnic basket.

Have students demonstrate their understanding of words like *picnic basket* and *mice* by completing sentence stems such as, *I see the* ______, and pointing to the correct items in the Adding English Poster. All students in the class may benefit from reviewing this vocabulary before reading the selection.

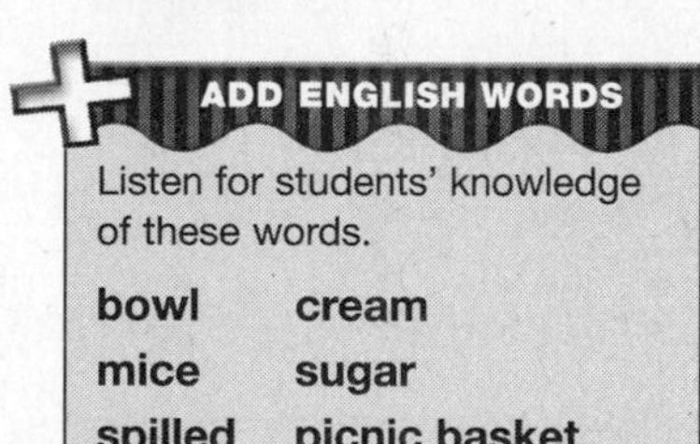

Present the Comprehension Strategy

Comprehension: Visualizing

Use Comprehension Strategies, *Adding English Guide,* page 10, to introduce Visualizing.

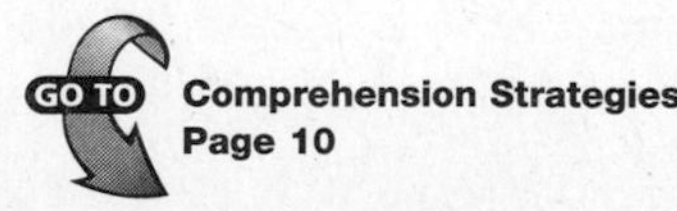

Relate to Personal Experience

Have students think about an outing such as a picnic, a visit to a fair, or a trip to a beach. Have them list things they saw, heard, smelled, tasted, and felt. Then have volunteers share their lists while other students try to picture the place in their minds.

Guide students as they read "Caught in the Kitchen," Scott Foresman Reading, *pages 146–147. Remind them to visualize what they read.*

Selection Audio CD 3/Tape 7

Practice

Have students describe or draw scene(s) they visualized while reading "Caught in the Kitchen."

Assess

If... students are not able to visualize the story,

then... have them read the following passage and tell what they think of when they read *splashed, dribbled,* and *streams.*

> "The cream splashed over the countertop, covering Gertrude and Omeletta, then dribbled down in several streams to the floor."

ADD ENGLISH WORDS

Review these clue words related to visualizing.

see **hear** **smell**
taste **feel** **details**

PART 2

Preview the Reading Selection

Use these activities with the selection *The Cricket in Times Square,* Teacher's Edition, *Scott Foresman Reading,* pages 148–164.

ADD ENGLISH WORDS

Listen for students' knowledge of words related to the city and country.

cricket **country**
newsstand **stump**
train **city**

Activate Prior Knowledge

Involve students in talking about parts of the Adding English Poster that picture the words at the right. Direct their attention to things that are related to the country, the city, and both country and city. Begin a Venn diagram, Graphic Organizer Transparency 21, to record students' responses.

Strategy: Using a Venn Diagram

Explain the strategy: *When I want to compare things that are alike as well as different, I can use a diagram. It is a strategy called Using a Venn Diagram.* Model writing entries on the diagram. Have students begin their own diagrams.

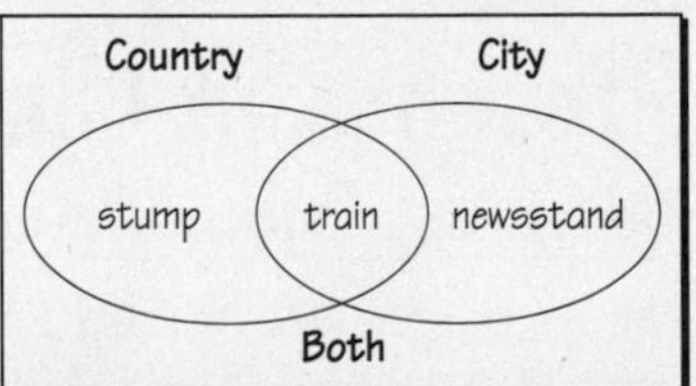

Transparency 21

Build Background

Show students a picture of a cricket. Explain that crickets are insects about 1 inch long (show 1 inch on a ruler). Point to the antennae for feeling, long back legs for jumping, and wings for flying. Explain that crickets live in the country. They make a chirping sound.

Vocabulary: Synonyms

Use these activities with the Vocabulary Lesson and paragraph "A Special Birthday," Teacher's Edition, *Scott Foresman Reading,* page 148.

Write these selection vocabulary words on the board: *venturing, occasion, melody,* and *furiously*. Then write these sentences:

The band played a lively tune.

The mouse is going too far from its nest.

Visiting the park is a special event.

The frightened dog wagged its tail wildly.

Ask students to read each sentence and find a vocabulary word that means the same as the underlined word.

Use Flash Cards

Write the selection vocabulary words on index cards and have students match them with pictures on the Adding English Poster. Then have students make their own cards with the words on one side and a drawing on the other side. Partners can use the cards to test each other.

Guide students as they read "A Special Birthday," Scott Foresman Reading, *page 148. Ask them how thinking of synonyms might help them understand an unfamiliar word.*

Students can participate in the Write About It activity that follows. Before they begin writing, have English language learners work with partners whose home language is English to list how life in a park would be different from life in a subway for a cricket.

Present the Reading Selection

Use these activities with *The Cricket in Times Square,* Teacher's Edition, *Scott Foresman Reading,* pages 148–164.

RESOURCES

Use *Scott Foresman ESL,* Grade 3, for additional instruction and activities.

- Chapter 2, "Life in the City"
- Video, Unit 1, "The Farm and the City"

ADD ENGLISH WORDS

Through listening and watching, assess students' knowledge of selection vocabulary.

subway	**traffic**
railroad	**venturing**
occasion	**chirp**
melody	**furiously**

Preview Title and Illustrations

Explain the strategy: *Before I begin to read a story, I read the title and look at the pictures to see what the story is about.* Explain that Times Square is in New York City. Discuss the picture on page 149. Make sure students see the cricket in the small matchbox up on the shelf. Continue previewing the pictures. Then have students add new ideas prompted by the pictures to their Venn diagrams about country and city life. Remind students that they are using a strategy called Using a Venn Diagram.

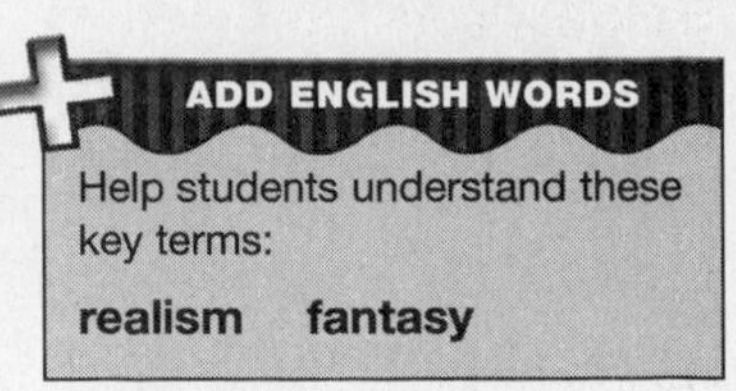

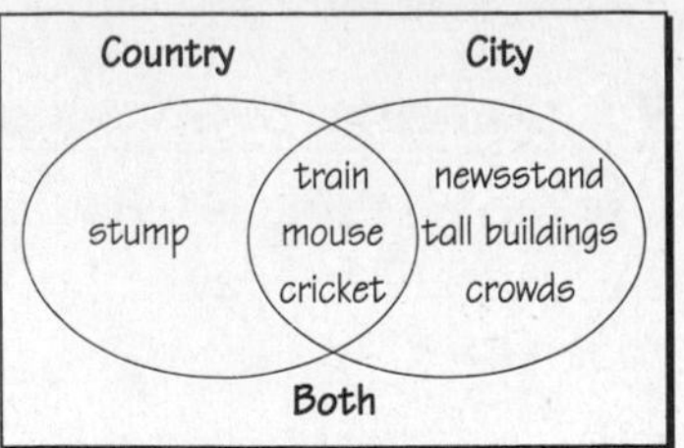

Transparency 21

Develop Concepts

Students may need support in distinguishing between realism and fantasy in this selection, since the settings are realistic. As students look at a picture, ask: *What things might be real? What things are fantasy, or could be only in a make-believe story?* Have students give reasons for their answers.

Set Purposes

Students can participate in Set Purposes, Teacher's Edition, *Scott Foresman Reading,* page 149. Encourage students to visualize the story as they read by looking for details that help them see, hear, smell, taste, and feel things described in the story.

Guide students as they read The Cricket in Times Square, Scott Foresman Reading, *pages 148–164. To support comprehension, use the suggestions in Meeting Individual Needs, ESL, in the Teacher's Edition.*

Selection Audio CD 3/Tape 7

Response Log

- Have students write about the part of the story they liked best and tell why they liked it.
- Ask students to imagine that one of the characters in the story is their friend. Which character would they choose, and why? Have them draw a picture and write about how they would have fun with the friend. Students can refer to the Adding English Poster for ideas.

Practice Selection Concepts

To help students tell what they learned, choose from these activities.

- Help students add information from the story to their Venn diagrams about country and city life.
- Distribute the ten important sentences. Have students work in groups to underline details that helped them visualize the story.

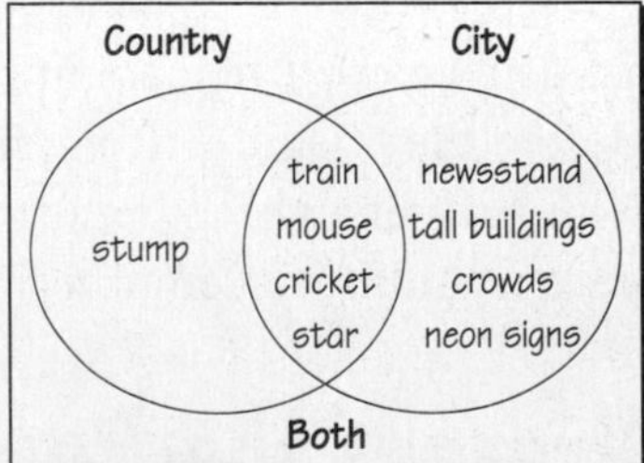

Transparency 21

Ten Important Sentences Page 20

Strategy: Self-Assess

Ask: *Did Using a Venn Diagram help you compare country life and city life? How?*

Language Awareness

Provide supported practice by using the Adding English Grammar and Phonics Practice Masters, pages 63–64, with the suggestions below.

Grammar: Nouns

Adding English Grammar Practice Master Page 63

Write the following on the board: *The mouse lived near the newsstand.* Read the sentence aloud. Then point to the word *mouse* and say: Mouse *is a noun. A noun is a word that names a person, place, or thing.* Invite a volunteer to circle *mouse.* Continue: *There is another noun in this sentence.* Point to *newsstand.* Invite a volunteer to circle *newsstand.* Have students brainstorm a list of nouns using the book illustrations and the Adding English Poster. Then let volunteers dictate sentences with those nouns as you write them on the board. Other students can circle the nouns in the sentences.

Students can complete the Practice Master alone or with a partner.

Phonics: Diphthongs

Adding English Phonics Practice Master Page 64

Distribute the Practice Master. Have students listen as you say the words, read, and then repeat the words in Exercise A. Prompt students to use the words in sentences. Ask questions such as: *What does a mouse look like?*

For Exercise B, have students read the sentences aloud before they choose their answers.

PART 3

Connect Selection Concepts

Use these activities with Reader Response, Teacher's Edition, *Scott Foresman Reading,* page 164.

Literature Discussion Group

Have English language learners work in groups with students whose home language is English. Together they should talk about *The Cricket in Times Square,* focusing on these questions:

- What were some things that scared Chester Cricket?
- What were some of your favorite parts of the story?
- What does Tucker Mouse do that makes him seem more like a person than an ordinary mouse?

Travel "Firsts"

Groups of students can compare their travel "firsts," for example, their first ride on a train, bus, plane, subway, boat, or cable car. Suggest that students bring photographs, tickets, maps, or other souvenirs for a class display.

Reading Across Texts: "The Country Mouse and the City Mouse," pages 165–167

To support students as they learn about and read a fable:

- Remind students that a fable teaches a lesson. Have students name some fables they have read, such as "The Tortoise and the Hare." Have them find the *moral* at the end of "The Country Mouse and the City Mouse." See if they recall morals of other fables they know.
- Discuss how students can figure out the lesson in a fable. First they should think about the characters and what happens to them. Then they should ask themselves what it all means. Ask students if they agree with the moral of "The Country Mouse and the City Mouse." Have them tell why or why not.
- Ask: *How is "The Country Mouse and the City Mouse" like* The Cricket in Times Square*? How is it different?* Have students use the Adding English Poster and the illustrations for the selections as they respond.

ADD ENGLISH WORDS

Use the Adding English Poster to help students with the following words.

travel **crust** **feast**
cakes **fear** **peace**

Assess

Refer to the list below to assess students' progress.

Reading

- ☐ Uses words related to the country and the city.
- ☐ Uses words related to the five senses.
- ☐ Visualizes scenes and events.
- ☐ Distinguishes between realism and fantasy.

Language Awareness

Grammar

- ☐ Identifies and uses nouns.

Phonics

- ☐ Pronounces diphthongs *oi, oy, ou, ow* and decodes words with those sounds.

Learning Strategies

- ☐ Uses a Venn diagram.
- ☐ Uses synonyms to find the meanings of unfamiliar words.

Name ______________________________

Nouns

A. Read the sentences. Circle the nouns.

1. The cricket was hungry.

2. The mouse made a sandwich for the cricket.

3. He put liverwurst on some bread.

4. The cricket had a good feast.

B. Circle the noun that completes each sentence.

5. A (spilled/subway) runs under the ground.

6. The (newsstand/enjoying) was near the stairway.

7. Many newspapers were on the (through/shelf).

8. A (cricket/furiously) slept there in a matchbox.

C. Think of a city or town that you like. Talk with a partner. Then write sentences that describe your city or town.

I like ______________________________

____

____

because ______________________________

____

____

____

Grammar

Name ____________________________________

Phonics

Diphthongs

A. Listen to the words. Read the words. Then say the words.

coin

boy

mouse

clown

B. Write a word from the box to complete each sentence.

brown	down	house	mouse	now

1. The cat and the ____________ are friends.

2. They live in a big ____________ box.

3. Their ____________ is warm and cozy.

4. Today the wind blew it ____________.

5. They need a new home ____________.

C. Say the underlined words. Read the sentences to a partner. Then listen as your partner reads them to you.

Chester Cricket was amazed by the sights and sounds of Times Square. The crowd was so noisy! Nearby, a boy dropped a coin. It landed on the ground about an inch from Chester. The boy shouted and pointed down. Chester hid behind Tucker Mouse. He wasn't enjoying his visit to New York City.

A Big-City Dream

Pages 168–193

Crossing Cultures • In this lesson, students read about urban community cleanup projects led by young people. Since not all students are familiar with urban landscapes, point out that even in large cities, gardens grow, animals live, and streams flow. Discuss how people who live in cities can clean up and protect their environment. While the class reads "A Big-City Dream," invite students whose home language is Spanish to read aloud and explain Spanish phrases.

PART 1

Preview the Skill Lesson

Use these activities with the Skill Lesson: "Super Cooper Scoopers," Teacher's Edition, *Scott Foresman Reading,* pages 168–169.

Activate Prior Knowledge

Ask students to tell what looks familiar on Adding English Poster 7. Encourage discussion of the environments pictured. Have students compare elements such as the creek with those they've seen. Allow students to use their home language when needed. Use a T-chart, Graphic Organizer Transparency 24, to record students' responses.

Poster Tips
Page 16

Poster World	Student's World
creek	neighborhood

Transparency 24

Group Words Together

Introduce the Skill Lesson literature by previewing vocabulary at the right. List the vocabulary words on the board. Explain the strategy: *To understand and remember a new word, I look for other words that will help remind me of what it means.*

As you read the following paragraph, urge students to think about how words go together.

> **Sometimes people are careless and throw their garbage on the ground. This trash can end up in creeks and rivers. It can hurt fish and other animals that live in the water. Cleanup crews volunteer to use shovels and other tools to get rid of cans, bottles, and other trash.**

ADD ENGLISH WORDS

Listen for students' knowledge of these words:

creek **fish**
cleanup **garbage**
shovels **trash**

Have students make connections among words, using the poster as support. Students should explain their groups of words. Record the word groups on the board. Prompt students to supply the missing words in sentences such as: *We used ___ for the playground cleanup.* Ensure that all students understand the less-familiar vocabulary in the passage.

Present the Comprehension Strategy

Comprehension: Cause and Effect

Use Comprehension Strategies, *Adding English Guide,* page 10, to introduce Cause and Effect.

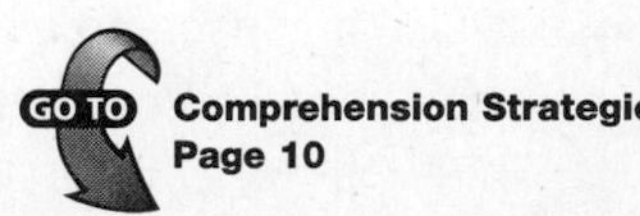

Comprehension Strategies
Page 10

Relate to Personal Experience

Have students recall something they did before they came to school this morning and why they did it (for example, *I ran for the bus* because *I was late*). Explain that the reason for their action is called the *cause,* and their action is the *effect*. Pairs can take turns describing morning experiences. Then have students brainstorm a list of other familiar causes and effects (*cause: pushing the power button, effect: the computer turns on*).

Guide students as they read "Super Cooper Scoopers," Scott Foresman Reading, *pages 168–169. Remind them to look for causes and effects.*

Selection Audio CD 3/Tape 8

Practice

Put students in pairs. Have one student list two effects in "Super Cooper Scoopers." Have the partner list two causes from the article. Partners can exchange papers and complete each other's work.

Assess

If... students are not able to find causes and effects in the article,

then... write the following effects and causes on strips of paper. Help them match the causes with the effects.

Effect: The salmon stopped coming to the creek.

Effect: The salmon are swimming in the creek again.

Cause: The kids made the creek clean.

Cause: The creek was too dirty for the salmon.

ADD ENGLISH WORDS

Review these words related to cause and effect.

cause **effect** **why**
what **because**

PART 2

Preview the Reading Selection

Use these activities before reading the selection "A Big-City Dream," Teacher's Edition, *Scott Foresman Reading,* pages 170–189.

Activate Prior Knowledge

Involve students in talking about parts of the Adding English Poster that picture the words at the right. Have them use the words to propose hypothetical cause and effect situations prompted by the poster. Use a cause and effect chart, Graphic Organizer Transparency 18, to record students' responses.

ADD ENGLISH WORDS

Listen for students' knowledge of words related to a community cleanup.

lot **neighborhood**
garden **corner**
fence **soil**
proud

Strategy: Using a Cause and Effect Chart

Explain the strategy: *When I want to understand what happens and why, I can use a chart. It is a strategy called Using a Cause and Effect Chart.* Point out the headings and the boxes on the chart. Model writing a cause and an effect from your poster discussion on the chart. Remind students to ask the question *What happened?* to find an effect and to ask *Why did it happen?* to find the cause. Have students record other causes and effects related to the Adding English Poster on their own charts.

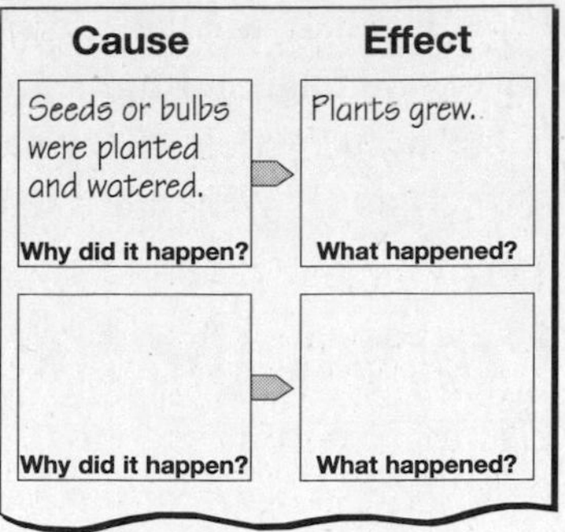

Transparency 18

Build Background

Bring in seeds or small plants. Plant seeds and plants in a few small flowerpots. Throughout the unit, discuss causes and effects of sunlight, water, and plant growth.

RESOURCES

Use *Scott Foresman ESL,* Grade 3, for additional instruction and activities.

- Chapter 11, "Changing the Earth"
- Video, Unit 6, "Protecting Our Earth"

Brainstorm a Topic

Have students brainstorm names of things that grow in a garden. Using seed catalogs, encyclopedias, and other sources, play a game: One student says, "I'll plant apples in my garden." The next student might offer, "I'll plant apples and carrots in my garden," and so on, each student repeating what was said and adding something new. Students can refer to the Adding English Poster for ideas.

Vocabulary: Context Clues

Use these activities with the Vocabulary Lesson and paragraph "Teamwork," Teacher's Edition, *Scott Foresman Reading,* page 170.

Write sentences using the selection vocabulary on the board. Include context clues, for example: *Jamie used a key to unlock the padlock on the door of the shed. He opened the door and went inside.* Have students read the sentences and then tell what context clues helped them know the meanings of the underlined words.

ADD ENGLISH WORDS

Through listening and watching, assess students' knowledge of selection vocabulary.

padlock **catalog**
blisters **celebrate**
impressed

Use Personalization

Model the use of the word *impressed: When I use the word* impressed, *I think about something that has a strong effect on my feelings and that I don't forget for a long time. For example, I am impressed by the lovely flower beds in our city park—how colorful and well-cared-for they are.* Have students relate the meaning of *impressed* to their experiences by completing this sentence stem: *I am impressed by _____.*

Guide students as they read "Teamwork!" Scott Foresman Reading, *page 170. Ask how they can learn the meanings of words they do not know.*

Students can participate in the Talk About It activity that follows. Have English language learners work in pairs with students whose home language is English to talk about the causes and effects told about in the article. They can take turns asking, "What happened?" (effect) and, "Why did it happen?" (cause).

Present the Reading Selection

Use these activities with "A Big-City Dream," Teacher's Edition, *Scott Foresman Reading,* pages 170–189.

Preview Title and Illustrations

Explain the strategy: *Before I begin to read a story, I read the title and look at the pictures to see what the story is about.* Discuss the picture on pages 170–171. Ask whether the students have seen anything similar to it. Point out the tulip at the right. Ask students how the scene is related to the title of the story.

Develop Concepts

Students may need support in identifying and keeping track of the many characters in the story. Suggest that they write down the names of the characters and make notes about them as they read. For example, students might write: *Luz—the girl telling the story; Mami—Luz's mother; Ms. Kline—a member of the Green Giants.*

Set Purposes

Students can participate in Set Purposes, Teacher's Edition, *Scott Foresman Reading,* page 171. Encourage students to look for cause and effect relationships as they read and to record the causes and effects on a chart. Remind students that they are using the strategy called Using a Cause and Effect Chart. Distribute additional copies of Graphic Organizer Transparency 18 as needed.

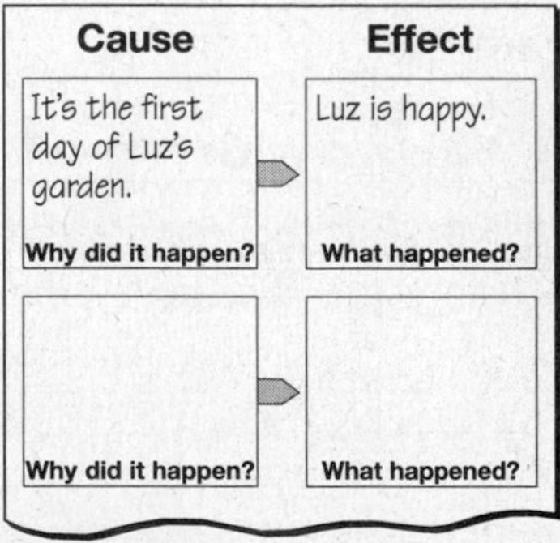

Transparency 18

Guide students as they read "A Big-City Dream," Scott Foresman Reading, *pages 170–189. To support comprehension, use the suggestions in Meeting Individual Needs, ESL, in the Teacher's Edition.*

Selection Audio CD 3/Tape 8

Response Log

- Have students write about what they would do if they could help plant Luz's Dream Garden.
- Ask students to draw a picture to show how Luz's garden might look three months after it was planted. Have them use the Adding English Poster for ideas. Tell them to write sentences or add labels to explain their pictures.

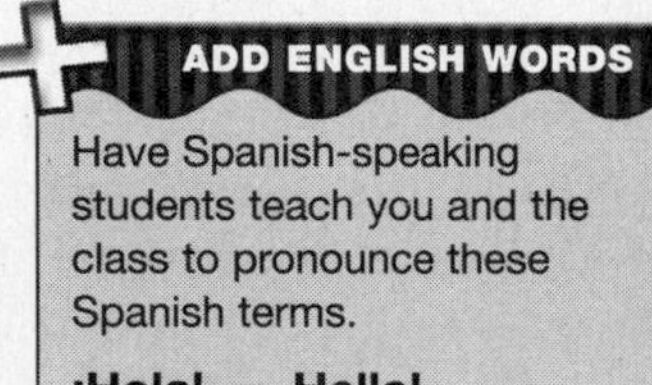

ADD ENGLISH WORDS

Have Spanish-speaking students teach you and the class to pronounce these Spanish terms.

¡Hola! = Hello!
Muchas gracias = Thank you very much.

Practice Selection Concepts

To help students tell what they learned, choose from these activities.

- Help students complete their cause and effect charts for the story. Supply them with additional copies of the chart if needed. Then let volunteers read a cause from their charts so other students can guess the effect. Repeat with students reading an effect for others to guess the cause.
- Have students read the ten important sentences and select one that tells an effect from the story. Remind students that an effect is *what happened.* Have pairs of students write causes *(why it happened)* for the effect they chose.

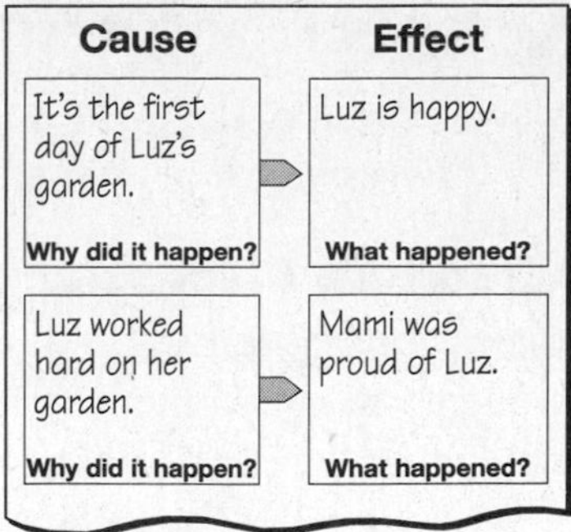

Transparency 18

Ten Important Sentences Page 21

Strategy: Self-Assess

Ask: *Did Using a Cause and Effect Chart help you understand the story? Did it help you enjoy the story? How?*

Language Awareness

Provide supported practice by using the Adding English Grammar and Phonics Practice Masters, pages 71–72, with the suggestions below.

Grammar: Proper Nouns

Adding English Grammar Practice Master Page 71

Write the following on the board: *Rosie is moving away in July.* Read the sentence aloud and point to the word *Rosie*. Say: *The name* Rosie *is a proper noun. You know that a noun is a word that names a person, place, or thing. A proper noun is a noun that names a particular person, place, or thing. Proper nouns begin with a capital letter.* Invite a volunteer to circle *Rosie.* Continue: *There is another proper noun in the sentence.* Point to *July* and say that it is a proper noun because it names a specific month. Invite a volunteer to circle *July.* Let volunteers dictate sentences using those proper nouns for you to write on the board. Other students can circle the proper nouns in the sentences.

Students can complete the Practice Master alone or with a partner.

Phonics: Hard and Soft Consonant Sounds *c* /k/, /s/ and *g* /g/, /j/

Adding English Phonics Practice Master Page 72

Distribute the Practice Master. Have students listen, read, and repeat as you say the words in Exercise A. Then students should say the words aloud. Watch for students' pronunciations of hard and soft sounds. Prompt students to use the words in sentences. Ask questions such as: *What does a cat look like?*

For Exercise B, have students read the words aloud before they choose answers.

Spanish-speaking students may have trouble with /j/ because the sound doesn't occur in Spanish words. Provide practice with these words.

gem January
gym jump

PART 3

Connect Selection Concepts

Use these activities with Reader Response, Teacher's Edition, *Scott Foresman Reading,* page 189.

Literature Discussion Group

If possible, have English language learners work in groups with students whose home language is English. Together they should talk about "A Big-City Dream," focusing on these questions:

- Who were the Green Giants? How did they help Luz?
- How did members of Luz's family feel toward her? How do you know?
- Did you think Luz's plan for a dream garden would work? Why or why not?
- How do the illustrations add to the story?

Cleanup Projects

Groups of students can discuss outdoor cleanup projects they have taken part in or that they know about. Students may also talk about areas that they would like to see cleaned up. Have them set up a display of newspaper articles, photographs, their own reports, and other related items to share with the class.

Reading Across Texts: "River of Grass," pages 190–193

To support students as they read a magazine article:

- Talk about the images students have for the word *river.* Can they visualize what a *river of grass* might look like?
- Preview the article, paying special attention to the photographs. Ask English language learners to identify the animals in their home language.
- Read the article with students. Then complete the Think and Connect with students.

Assess

Refer to the list below to assess students' progress.

Reading

- ☐ Uses words related to plants and gardens.
- ☐ Understands cause and effect relationships.

Language Awareness

Grammar

- ☐ Recognizes and uses proper nouns.

Phonics

- ☐ Pronounces the hard and soft *c* and *g* sounds and decodes words with those sounds.

Learning Strategies

- ☐ Uses a cause and effect chart.
- ☐ Uses context clues to identify the meanings of unfamiliar words.

Name ______________________________

Proper Nouns

A. Read the sentences. Circle the proper nouns.

1. Ms. Kline helps Luz clean the garden.
2. DeVonn plays baseball for the Tornados.
3. Luz orders garden supplies, flower seeds, and trees from the Green Giants catalog.
4. Mami is very proud of Luz.

B. Circle the proper noun that completes each sentence.

5. On (one day/Saturday) workers will finish the garden.
6. (A girl/Luz) is planning a party to celebrate.
7. At the party, Luz will thank (a woman/Ms. Kline).
8. Luz invites (a police officer/Officer Ramirez) to come.

C. Talk with a partner about your neighborhood. Then write sentences that describe it. Use at least two proper nouns.

My neighborhood ______________________________

____

____

____

____

____

____

Name ________________________________

Phonics

Hard and Soft Consonant Sounds c /k/, /s/ and g /g/, /j/

A. Listen to the words. Read the words. Then say the words.

cat cent gate giant

B. Say the words. Then write them in the correct bowls.

corn	garden	cake	cent
gentle	circle	gate	giant

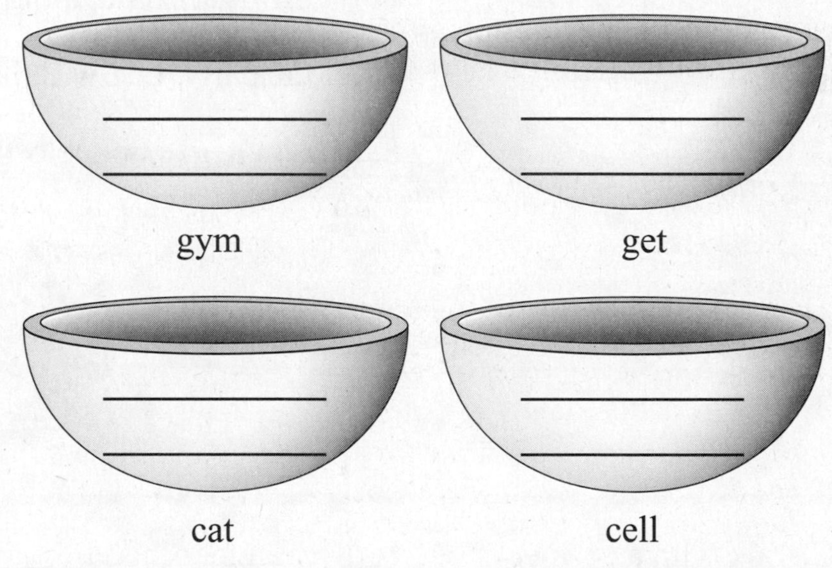

gym get cat cell

C. Say the underlined words. Read the sentences to a partner. Then listen as your partner reads them to you.

Gina and Cindy were going on a picnic. They put a bag of grapes, some cold cuts, and a container of juice in a large basket. "I can't wait to feel the sun on my face," said Cindy. Gina agreed. "Yes, it will be great!"

I Love Guinea Pigs

Pages 194–211

Crossing Cultures • In this lesson, students read about two kinds of pets: dogs and guinea pigs. Invite students to share stories about their own pets. How do they care for their pets? What are the most common pets in various cultures? Not all cultures sentimentalize domestic animals, so students' views on pets may vary.

PART 1

Preview the Skill Lesson

Use these activities with the Skill Lesson: "Your Best Friend," Teacher's Edition, *Scott Foresman Reading,* pages 194–195.

Activate Prior Knowledge

Ask students to tell what they see in Adding English Poster 8. Ask: *What do you know about taking care of dogs? Have you ever seen a wolf? What is similar between wolves and dogs? What is different?* Allow them to use their home language. Use a T-chart, Graphic Organizer Transparency 24, to record students' responses.

Poster Tips Page 16

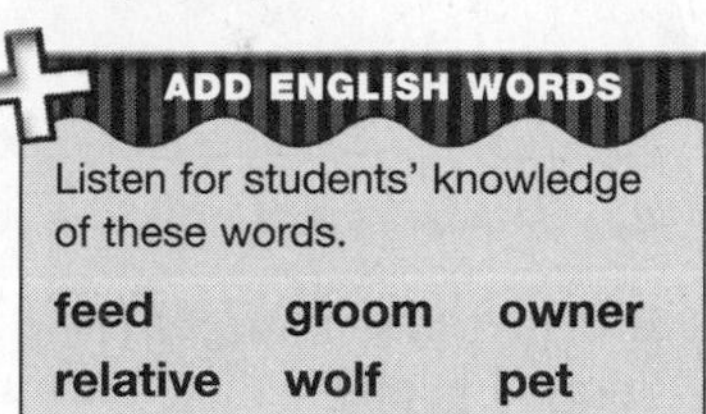

Wolves	Dogs
live in the wild	live with people

Transparency 24

Use Context Clues

Introduce the Skill Lesson literature by previewing vocabulary at the right. List the vocabulary words on the board. Explain the strategy: *When I hear a word I don't know, I listen to the words before and after it. They help me understand it.*

ADD ENGLISH WORDS

Listen for students' knowledge of these words.

feed	groom	owner
relative	wolf	pet

Have students listen for vocabulary words as you read the passage that follows. Direct them to listen for context clues.

> On his birthday, Leon became the owner of a new pet. It is a puppy. A relative, his aunt Susi, gave it to him. She also gave him a bag of pet food to feed the puppy and a brush to groom its fur. Leon thinks he will name the puppy "Wolf," because it has soft gray fur, a long bushy tail, and a pointed face. It looks like a baby wolf. Maybe it will even howl like a wolf!

Ask students to find pictures for all the vocabulary words on the Adding English Poster. Brainstorm different kinds of relatives. Help the class understand that some animals are related. For example, a lion is a relative of a house cat. Elicit other related animals. All students may benefit from reviewing this vocabulary before reading the selection.

Present the Comprehension Strategy

Comprehension: Text Structure

Use Comprehension Strategies, *Adding English Guide,* page 10, to introduce Text Structure.

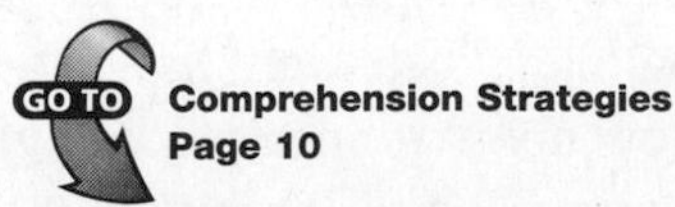

Comprehension Strategies Page 10

Relate to Personal Experience

Write *time order* on the board. Have students tell, in order, the first three things they would do in each situation:

- You go to a pet store to decide which new pet to buy.
- You think your goldfish may be sad.
- You want to train a pet dog to roll over.

Guide students as they read "Your Best Friend," Scott Foresman Reading, *pages 194–195. Remind students to think about how the text is organized. Point out that the headings offer important clues.*

Selection Audio CD 3/Tape 9

Practice

Have groups of students discuss the text structure of "Your Best Friend," and then take a class vote on the method of organization (main ideas and details). Have each group choose a paragraph from the article and list its main idea and details.

Assess

If... students are not able to identify how a text is organized,

then... have them arrange these main ideas from "Your Best Friend" in order. Help them find two details in the article to support each main idea.

- Dogs are related to wolves.
- Dogs still behave like wolves in some ways.
- If you take care of your dog, it will become your friend.
- Owning a dog can be a lot of fun.

ADD ENGLISH WORDS

Review these words related to text structure.

main idea	**details**
cause	**effect**
fact	**opinion**
comparison	**contrast**
chronological order	

PART 2

Preview the Reading Selection

Use these activities before reading the selection *I Love Guinea Pigs,* Teacher's Edition, *Scott Foresman Reading,* pages 196–209.

Activate Prior Knowledge

Have volunteers tell how to care for pets. Ask them how they take care of their pets, including feeding and playing with them, and how they keep them healthy. Encourage students to tell what they know about guinea pigs. Begin a K-W-L chart, Graphic Organizer Transparency 7, about guinea pigs.

ADD ENGLISH WORDS

Listen for students' knowledge of words related to guinea pigs.

guinea pigs	**teeth**
hutch	**pen**
handle	

Strategy: Using a K-W-L Chart

Explain the strategy: *When I want to learn new things that are facts, I can use a chart. It is a strategy called Using a K-W-L Chart.* Point out what each letter means and model filling out the K column based on the class discussion. Have students begin their own charts.

K What I Know	W What I Want to Know	L What I Learned
Guinea pigs can be pets. Guinea pigs have fun.		

Transparency 7

RESOURCES

Use *Scott Foresman ESL,* Grade 3, for additional instruction and activities.

- Chapter 7, "Plants, Animals, and Climate"
- Video, Unit 4, "Living Things Adapt"

Build Background

Show students a live guinea pig or several pictures of one. Briefly describe the guinea pig as a rodent, related to mice and rabbits. Have students make observations about what they see. What do they notice about guinea pigs that they never knew before?

Recognize Fiction and Nonfiction

Review with students that in fiction, writers tell a made-up story, and that in nonfiction, writers tell facts and information. Have students recall "Your Best Friend." Ask: *Is it fiction or nonfiction?* Write the vocabulary words at the right on the board. Have students point to a picture of each one on the Adding English Poster. Then write this question on the board: *Is it okay to hold a newborn puppy?* Ask: *Where would you look for the answer to this question—in a fictional story or in a nonfiction article?* Discuss with students why they would look in a nonfiction article.

Vocabulary: Homographs

Use these activities with the Vocabulary Lesson and paragraph "Guinea Pigs: Popular Pets," Teacher's Edition, *Scott Foresman Reading,* page 196.

Write the following sentences on the board and invite volunteers to read them aloud.

- Sow rhymes with go and means "to plant seeds."
- Sow rhymes with now and means "a female pig."

Have students decide which word is pictured on the Adding English Poster. Then have students make a word card for each homograph, drawing a picture showing its meaning on the back. Have students work in groups, with one student saying a sentence using one of the words and the others holding up a card to show which word was used in the sentence.

ADD ENGLISH WORDS

Through listening and watching, assess students' knowledge of selection vocabulary.

varieties **fond**
gnawing **sow**
boars

Use Synonyms

Write the selection vocabulary on the board and help students find a picture of each word on the poster. Then have small groups brainstorm synonyms for *gnawing, varieties,* and *fond*. Groups can share their lists.

Guide students as they read "Guinea Pigs: Popular Pets," Scott Foresman Reading, *page 196. Ask them what they can do to understand the correct meanings of homographs.*

Students can participate in the Write About It activity that follows. Before they begin writing, English language learners can work in groups with students whose home language is English to list reasons why guinea pigs would make good pets. Students can add items from their lists to the K column of their K-W-L charts.

K What I Know	W What I Want to Know	L What I Learned
Guinea pigs can be pets. Guinea pigs have fun. They aren't very big.		

Transparency 7

Present the Reading Selection

Use these activities with *I Love Guinea Pigs,* Teacher's Edition, *Scott Foresman Reading,* pages 196–209.

Preview Captions and Illustrations

Explain the strategy: *Before I begin to read, I look at the pictures and captions to see what the story is about.* Discuss the illustrations on pages 200–201. Point out that the dark type tells about the pictures. Continue previewing the pictures and captions.

ADD ENGLISH WORDS

Help students understand this key term:

point of view

Develop Concepts

Students may need support in understanding that the selection is written from the point of view of the author. Have them look at page 197. Make sure they understand that the illustration shows the author, Dick King-Smith, holding a guinea pig. Say: *The author wrote the article from his point of view. The word* I *in the title is a clue. Do you think that someone who loves guinea pigs would be a good person to write about them? Why or why not?*

Set Purposes

Students can participate in Set Purposes, Teacher's Edition, *Scott Foresman Reading,* page 197. Help students fill in the W column of their K-W-L charts with what they want to learn about guinea pigs. Remind students that they are using a strategy called Using a K-W-L Chart.

K What I Know	W What I Want to Know	L What I Learned
Guinea pigs can be pets. Guinea pigs have fun. They aren't very big.	What sounds do guinea pigs make? Do they bite?	

Transparency 7

Selection Audio CD 3/Tape 9

Guide students as they read I Love Guinea Pigs, Scott Foresman Reading, *pages 196–209. To support comprehension, use the suggestions in Meeting Individual Needs, ESL, in the Teacher's Edition.*

Response Log

- Point out that Dick King-Smith has had hundreds of guinea pig pets, and so he must know many things about them. Have students write two questions they would like to ask him about guinea pigs that were not answered in *I Love Guinea Pigs.*
- Have students imagine that they are a guinea pig looking for a home. Tell them to write a list of things they are looking for in an owner. They may also draw what kind of hutch they would like to live in.

K What I Know	W What I Want to Know	L What I Learned
Guinea pigs can be pets. Guinea pigs have fun. They aren't very big.	What sounds do guinea pigs make? Do they bite?	They whistle and say chutter, putt, chut, tweet, drr, and purr. Guinea pigs are rodents.

Transparency 7

Practice Selection Concepts

To help students tell what they learned, choose from these activities.

- Help students fill in the L column of their K-W-L Charts.
- Distribute the ten important sentences. Write the following main idea statement on the board: Guinea pigs make good pets. Have students tell which sentences give details to support this statement.

Ten Important Sentences Page 22

Strategy: Self-Assess

Ask: *Did Using a K-W-L Chart help you learn information? How?*

Language Awareness

Provide supported practice by using the Adding English Grammar and Phonics Practice Masters, pages 79–80, with the suggestions below.

Grammar: Regular Plural Nouns

Write the following on the board: *The girl will use two dishes to feed her pets.* Read the sentence aloud. Point to the word *girl* and say: Girl *is a singular noun. It names one.* Point to the words *pets* and *dishes* and say: Pets *and* dishes *are plural nouns. They name more than one.* Explain that most nouns are made plural by adding *-s* or *-es.* Have students brainstorm a list of plural nouns, referring to the poster for ideas. Let volunteers write sentences using those plural nouns on the board. Other students can circle the plural nouns.

Students can complete the Practice Master alone or with a partner.

Adding English Grammar Practice Master Page 79

Compound Words

Phonics: Compound Words

Distribute the Practice Master. Have students listen, read, and repeat as you say the compound words in Exercise A. Point to the two words that make up each compound word. Explain: *The meanings of the two smaller words help you figure out the meaning of the compound word.*

For Exercise B, have students read the compound words aloud after they choose their answers.

Adding English Phonics Practice Master Page 80

PART 3

Connect Selection Concepts

Use these activities with Reader Response, Teacher's Edition, *Scott Foresman Reading,* page 209.

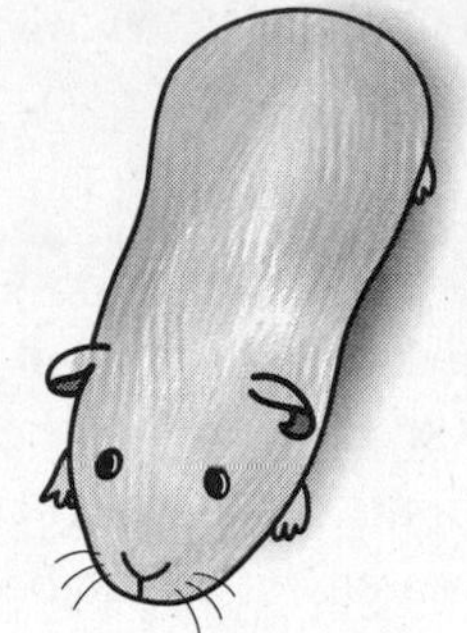

Literature Discussion Group

Have English language learners work in groups with students whose home language is English. Together they should talk about *I Love Guinea Pigs,* focusing on these questions:

- What did you learn about guinea pigs?
- How does the author use illustrations to explain information?
- What other animals are discussed in this selection?

Pet Anecdotes

Groups of students can compare anecdotes about their pets, or about pets they know or have read about or seen on TV. They might talk about funny experiences, sad ones, frightening ones, unusual ones, or incredible ones. Have them set up a display of written accounts, photographs, newspaper clippings, and drawings to share with the whole class.

Reading Across Texts: "What You Always Wanted to Know About Pets," pages 210–211

To support students as they read an informational article:

- Have students preview the article. How is the article organized? What three questions will students read to have answered?
- Activate prior knowledge by talking about how students might answer the three questions. Read the text together and discuss the answers. What other questions do students have about animal behavior?
- Compare "What You Always Wanted to Know" to *I Love Guinea Pigs.* Ask: *How are these two selections alike? How are they different?*

Assess

Refer to the list below to assess students' progress.

Reading

- ☐ Uses words related to pets and pet care.
- ☐ Uses words related to guinea pigs.
- ☐ Recognizes different kinds of text structure.
- ☐ Distinguishes between fiction and nonfiction.
- ☐ Understands first-person point of view.

Language Awareness

Grammar

- ☐ Identifies and correctly forms regular plural nouns.

Phonics

- ☐ Pronounces and decodes compound words.

Learning Strategies

- ☐ Uses a K-W-L chart.
- ☐ Uses context clues to identify the meanings of homographs.

Name ______________________________

Regular Plural Nouns

A. Read the sentences. Circle the plural nouns.

1. Some owners make hutches for their pets.

2. The hutches can be made out of wire and boards.

3. Pens must have covers to keep out other pets and rodents.

4. Put rocks in the pens for the animals to hide behind.

B. Write the plural of the word in parentheses to complete each sentence.

5. A guinea pig has two small __________ (ear) and four short __________ (leg).

6. The fur of a guinea pig can be many __________ (color).

7. Guinea pigs are happy in big, roomy __________ (hutch).

8. Be sure to clean their water __________ (bottle) every day.

C. Imagine that you have a guinea pig. What would it look, feel, and sound like? Talk with a partner. Then write sentences that describe the guinea pig.

My guinea pig ______________________________

____

____

____

____

____

Name ________________________________

Phonics

Compound Words

A. Listen to the words. Read the words. Then say the words.

doghouse

newborn

flowerpot

mealtime

B. Draw lines from words in the first column to words in the second column to make compound words.

1. dog	**a.** mother
2. home	**b.** house
3. flower	**c.** room
4. grand	**d.** times
5. bed	**e.** pot
6. some	**f.** work

C. Say the underlined words. Read the sentences to a partner. Then listen as your partner reads them.

My guinea pig, Ralph, likes to play while I do my homework. He climbs on the desk in my bedroom and jumps on the lampshade. I catch him before he falls off! Sometimes he tries to dig in the flowerpot. His fur keeps him warm in wintertime. I love Ralph.

The Swimming Hole

Pages 212–231

Crossing Cultures • In this lesson, students read about life in a pioneer family on the Midwest prairie. Since the story takes place more than a century ago, talk with students about what life might have been like so long ago in any rural area. Encourage students to tell what they know about members of their own families who lived on farms.

PART 1

Preview the Skill Lesson

Use these activities with the Skill Lesson: "Ant and Dove," Teacher's Edition, *Scott Foresman Reading,* pages 212–213.

Poster Tips
Page 16

Activate Prior Knowledge

Ask if students have ever been in a situation where someone helped them and they helped that person in return. Remind them that sharing responsibilities at home is a form of helping. Encourage students to look at Adding English Poster 9 for support. Use a T-chart, Graphic Organizer Transparency 24, to record students' responses.

How Someone Helped Me	How I Helped Someone
My brother taught me basketball.	I helped him with math.

Transparency 24

Use Context Clues

Introduce the Skill Lesson literature by previewing vocabulary at the right. List the vocabulary words on the board. Explain the strategy: *When I hear a word I don't know, I listen to the words before and after it. They help me understand it.*

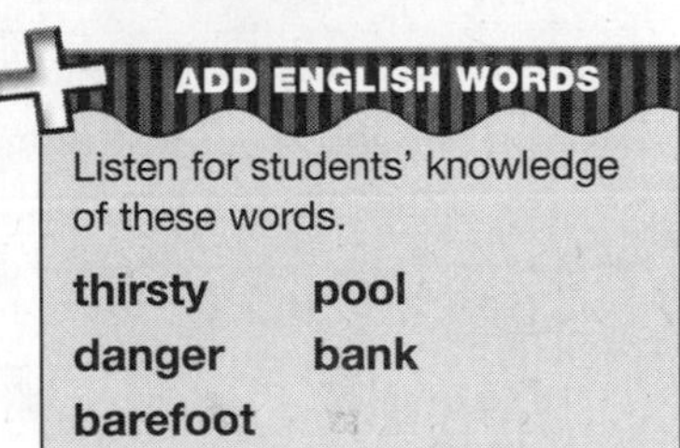

Have students listen for vocabulary words as you read the passage that follows. Direct them to listen for context clues for help figuring out what each vocabulary word means.

> Henry and Lucy were walking along the bank of the creek. They were barefoot, having taken off their shoes and socks to wade in the water. Here in the woods the creek formed a deep pool of clear water. Henry was thirsty and knelt down to get a drink. Suddenly, lightning flashed across the sky, and they heard thunder. They were scared. They knew the danger of being in the woods in a thunderstorm.

Have students demonstrate that they have inferred the meanings of the vocabulary words by pointing to appropriate pictures on the Adding English Poster. All students may benefit from reviewing this vocabulary before reading the selection.

Present the Comprehension Strategy

Comprehension: Theme

Use Comprehension Strategies, *Adding English Guide,* page 10, to introduce Theme.

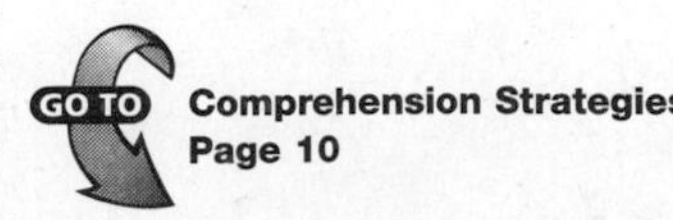

Relate to Personal Experience

Write several proverbs on the board, such as *Haste makes waste* and *Practice makes perfect.* Have students tell what each means, then draw a picture of a personal experience that demonstrates one of the proverbs. Ask students to write the appropriate proverb as a caption for their picture. Explain how it expresses the theme.

Guide students as they read "Ant and Dove," Scott Foresman Reading, *pages 212–213. Remind them to think about the theme, or underlying idea, of the fable.*

Selection Audio CD 4/Tape 10

Practice

Have students tell the theme of the story, for example: If someone helps you, then you should help that person. Ask: *What did Dove do to help Ant? What did Ant do to help Dove?*

Assess

If... students are not able to tell the theme of the fable,

then... write the following events from the story on slips of paper. Have partners arrange the sentences in order and place the captions beside the appropriate sentences.

- Ant falls in the pool.
- Dove drops a leaf in the pool for Ant to climb on.
- A birdcatcher tries to catch Dove.
- Ant bites the birdcatcher's heel, and Dove escapes.
- One good turn:
- Another good turn:

ADD ENGLISH WORDS

Review these clue words related to theme.

theme **big idea**

PART 2

Preview the Reading Selection

Use these activities before reading the selection "The Swimming Hole," Teacher's Edition, *Scott Foresman Reading,* pages 214–229.

Activate Prior Knowledge

Have students talk about how they spend their free time. Say: *Imagine that you live in the country far from neighbors and stores. How would your after-school and weekend activities change? What would you do for fun?*

ADD ENGLISH WORDS

Listen for students' knowledge of words related to the prairie:

swimming hole **splashed**
path **badger**
watch

Strategy: Using a Visualizing Chart

Explain the strategy: *When I really want to enjoy a story, I can use my five senses and look for details that help me see, hear, smell, taste, and feel the things described in the story. I can use a chart to write down the things I visualize, or picture, in my mind. This strategy is called Using a Visualizing Chart.* To provide practice using the chart, reread the paragraph about Henry and Lucy on page 81. Ask students to use a five-column chart, Graphic Organizer Transparency 27, to list sensory observations. Model writing entries on your own chart.

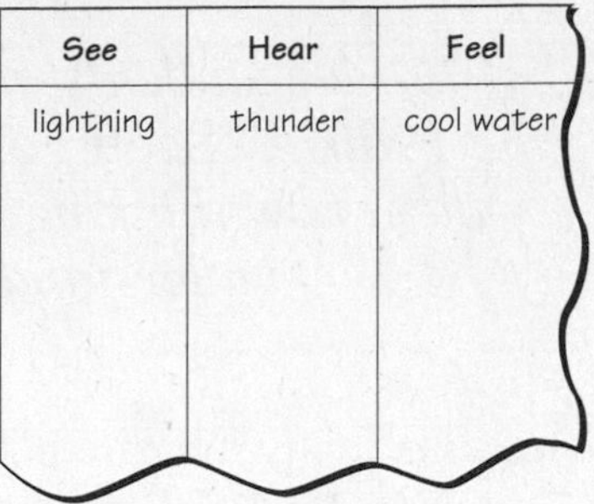

Transparency 27

Build Background

Display pictures of a prairie and a creek and have students tell what they see. Discuss plants and animals found in those environments. Show a map of the United States and explain that much of the Midwest was once covered by prairies. If possible, show a picture of a dugout. Tell students that many of the first settlers on the prairie lived in dugout homes. Discuss the features of a dugout and ask students to imagine what it must have been like to live in one.

RESOURCES

Use *Scott Foresman ESL,* Grade 3, for additional instruction and activities.

- Chapter 9, "What Shelters Are Made Of"
- Video, Unit 5, "Shelters"

Vocabulary: Antonyms

Use these activities with the Vocabulary Lesson and paragraph "An Evening on the Prairie," Teacher's Edition, *Scott Foresman Reading,* page 214.

Review with students that words with opposite meanings are called antonyms and have students give examples. Write *shallow, naughty,* and *punish* on the board. Then write these sentences: *At this time of year, the water in the creek is deep. The collie was a good dog and ran toward the open gate. Would you reward someone for what he did?*. Read aloud each sentence. Then have students find a vocabulary word that means the opposite of the underlined word. Read the sentence again, substituting the antonym. Discuss with students how the new word changes the meaning of the sentence.

ADD ENGLISH WORDS

Through listening and watching, assess students' knowledge of selection vocabulary.

bristled	**shallow**
rushes	**jointed**
naughty	**dugout**
punish	

Use Word Cards

Have students work with a partner and write each vocabulary word at right on a card. Then have them take turns matching the words with pictures on the Adding English Poster. Afterward, they can illustrate each word on the back of its card and then take turns matching their illustrations with those on the poster. Help students understand that *rushes* is shown as a noun instead of a verb by pointing out this item on the poster.

Guide students as they read "An Evening on the Prairie," Scott Foresman Reading, *page 214. Ask them how thinking of antonyms might help them understand an unfamiliar word.*

Students can participate in the Talk About It activity that follows. First, have English language learners work with partners whose home language is English to make a list of things they know about the prairie and about pioneer life on the prairie.

Present the Reading Selection

Use these activities with "The Swimming Hole," Teacher's Edition, *Scott Foresman Reading,* pages 214–229.

Preview Title and Illustrations

Explain the strategy: *Before I begin to read a story, I read the title and look at the pictures to see what the story is about.* Discuss the title and the picture on pages 214–215. Make sure students understand that the girl is running along on top of a dugout house. Ask: *What kind of person do you think she is? What makes you think so?* Continue previewing the pictures. Ask students which picture seems to illustrate the title of the story.

Develop Concepts

Students may need support in understanding that the selection is historical fiction. Explain that historical fiction is based on real historical events and sometimes on real people but that parts of the story, including many details and conversations, are make-believe. Have students look at the picture on pages 214–215 and point out details that show something that happened in the past.

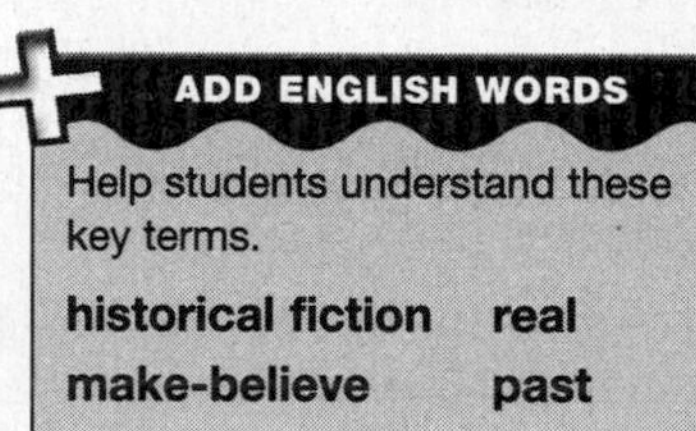

See	Hear	Feel
swimming hole	birds talking and singing	splash

Transparency 27

Set Purposes

Students can participate in Set Purposes, Teacher's Edition, *Scott Foresman Reading,* page 215. Encourage students to visualize the story as they read by looking for details that help them see, hear, smell, taste, and feel the things described. Ask students to write these details on their charts. Remind students that they are using a strategy called Using a Visualizing Chart.

Guide students as they read "The Swimming Hole," Scott Foresman Reading, *pages 214–229. To support comprehension, use the suggestions in Meeting Individual Needs, ESL, in the Teacher's Edition.*

Selection Audio CD 4/Tape 10

Response Log

- Have students write about the part of the story they liked best and tell why they liked it.
- Have students imagine that they are visiting the story family. Have them draw a picture and write about what they would do.

See	Hear	Smell	Feel
swimming hole	birds talking and singing	prairie flowers	splash warm, soft mud

Transparency 27

Practice Selection Concepts

To help students tell what they learned, choose from these activities.

- Help students complete their visualizing charts for the story.
- Cut the ten important sentences into strips and have students work in groups to arrange them in order. Ask students to explain which sentence best tells the theme of the story.

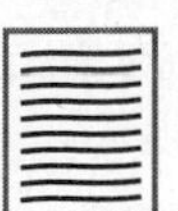

Ten Important Sentences Page 23

Strategy: Self-Assess

Ask: *Did Using a Visualizing Chart help you understand and enjoy the story? How?*

Language Awareness

Provide supported practice by using the Adding English Grammar and Phonics Practice Masters, pages 87–88, with the suggestions below.

Grammar: Irregular Plural Nouns

Adding English Grammar Practice Master Page 87

Write the following on the board: *I read a story about a wolf. I like stories about wolves.* Read the first sentence aloud. Point out that *story* and *wolf* are singular nouns because each names one thing. Read the second sentence aloud. Point out that *stories* is a plural noun. It names more than one. *Stories* is made plural by changing *y* to *i* and adding *-es*. Point to *wolves* and explain that some nouns ending in *f* or *fe* are made plural by changing *f* or *fe* to *v* and adding *-es*. Use the following sentences to explain that some nouns change spelling in the plural while others do not: *The goose walked past a sheep. Six geese ate with two sheep.* Have students brainstorm a list of irregular plural nouns. Write them on the board.

Students can complete the Practice Master alone or with a partner.

Compound Review Words

Phonics: Vowel Digraphs

Adding English Phonics Practice Master Page 88

Distribute the Practice Master. Have students listen and read as you say the words in Exercise A. Then students say the words aloud. Point out the four spellings of /o/: *au, aw, ough,* and *augh*.

For Exercise B, have students read the sentences aloud before they choose their answers.

PART 3

Connect Selection Concepts

Use these activities with Reader Response, Teacher's Edition, *Scott Foresman Reading,* page 229.

Literature Discussion Group

Have English language learners work in groups with students whose home language is English. Together they should talk about "The Swimming Hole," focusing on these questions:

- What was the story about?
- Where and when did the story take place?
- What did Laura and Mary do for fun?

Rules for Swimmers

Groups of students can talk about places they have gone swimming or places they would like to go swimming. Have them make lists of rules that swimmers should follow. Arrange for students to share the lists with other classmates in a bulletin-board display.

Reading Across Texts: "Badger Toes and Rabbit Feet," pages 230–231

To support students as they read a picture encyclopedia:

- Have students preview "Badger Toes and Rabbit Feet" by looking at the pictures and reading the labels and a few words from each caption. Explain that this selection can be read in any order. Read the introduction with students.
- Ask: *What is this article mostly about? How is the information in this article related to one of the events in "The Swimming Hole?"*

Assess

Refer to the list below to assess students' progress.

Reading

- ☐ Uses words related to pioneer life on the prairie.
- ☐ Uses words related to the senses.
- ☐ Recognizes the theme of a story.
- ☐ Understands historical fiction.

Language Awareness

Grammar

- ☐ Identifies and forms irregular plural nouns.

Phonics

- ☐ Pronounces and decodes words containing digraphs *au, aw, augh,* and *ough*.

Learning Strategies

- ☐ Uses a visualizing chart.
- ☐ Uses antonyms to find the meanings of unfamiliar words.

Name ________________________________

Grammar

Irregular Plural Nouns

A. Read the sentences. Circle the plural noun in each sentence.

1. The leaves had turned a beautiful golden color.

2. Some bunnies scampered around a stump.

3. Two deer disappeared behind a large tree.

4. Three tiny field mice ran toward the creek.

B. Circle the word that completes each sentence.

5. Both (child/children) helped Ma with the work.

6. Laura put straw down for the two (calves/calf).

7. Mary helped her mother bake four (loaves/loaf) of bread.

8. The girls filled their pails with (berry/berries).

C. Imagine that you live on a prairie in pioneer times. Talk with a partner. Then write sentences that describe your home.

My home on the prairie ____________________

____

____

____

____

____

____

Name ______________________________

Vowel Digraphs

A. Listen to the words. Read the words. Then say the words.

caught

paw

cough

author

B. Circle the word that completes each sentence.

1. A badger was (catch/caught) in a hole.

2. It began to (claw/clue) at the sides of the hole.

3. A man (sow/saw) the trapped animal.

4. He (bring/brought) a shovel to make the hole bigger.

5. The badger jumped out and hid behind a pile of (straw/stream).

C. Say the underlined words. Read the sentences to a partner. Then listen as your partner reads them to you.

One day Ma took her daughters to town. Mary saw a pretty straw bonnet. Ma thought Mary needed a new hat, so she bought the straw bonnet for Mary. Laura felt awful. She wanted a new hat too. She kicked the water trough outside the store. That was very naughty. Laura's temper was her worst fault.

Komodo Dragons

Pages 232–249

Crossing Cultures • In this lesson, students read about Komodo dragons, lizards that are more than ten feet long. Encourage students to tell about dragons in stories from their home cultures, or any dragon stories they know.

PART 1

Preview the Skill Lesson

Use these activities with the Skill Lesson: "Crocodilians," Teacher's Edition, *Scott Foresman Reading,* pages 232–233.

Activate Prior Knowledge

Ask students to tell what kinds of animals they see in Adding English Poster 10. Encourage students to discuss the appearance and behavior of reptiles they have seen. Also have students describe the environments and climates in which they saw the reptiles. Use a T-chart, Graphic Organizer Transparency 24, to record students' responses.

Poster Tips Page 16

Reptiles I Have Seen	What They Were Doing
alligator	sleeping near a river
python	swallowing a whole mouse

Transparency 24

Recognize Vocabulary Words

Introduce the Skill Lesson literature by previewing vocabulary at the right. List the vocabulary words on the board. Have students listen for them as you read the passage that follows.

> Reptiles avoid their enemies in different ways. For example, crocodiles are hard to see when they are hiding in a swamp with just their nostrils sticking out of the water. They lie there quietly, not making the water ripple. Lizards are another kind of reptile. They are hard to see when they sun themselves on a rock because the color of the scales covering their bodies is like the color of the rock.

Reread the passage, having students point to parts of the Adding English Poster that relate to the vocabulary words. All students in the class may benefit from reviewing this vocabulary before reading "Crocodilians."

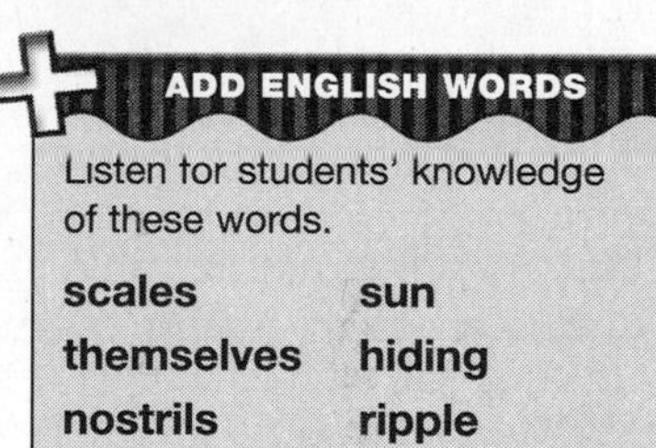

Present the Comprehension Strategy

Comprehension: Context Clues

Use Comprehension Strategies, *Adding English Guide,* page 10, to introduce Context Clues.

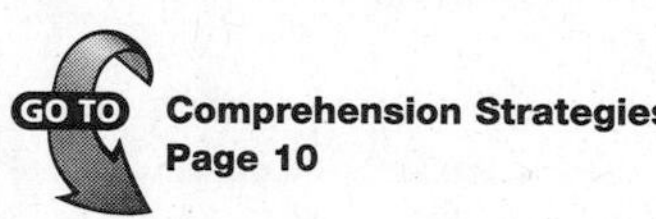

Comprehension Strategies Page 10

Relate to Personal Experience

Tell students to imagine they are at a zoo. They hear a boy say, "It's *fascinating* to see these lizards slithering about and climbing things. It's interesting to watch them." Ask: *What does the word* fascinating *mean?* (interesting) *What clues in what the boy said helped you figure out the meaning of the word* fascinating*?* Invite students to tell about a time when they figured out the meaning of an unfamiliar word that someone else used. How did they do it?

Guide students as they read "Crocodilians," Scott Foresman Reading, *pages 232–233. Remind them to use context clues when they come to an unfamiliar word.*

Selection Audio CD 4/Tape 11

If possible, have English language learners work with students whose home language is English. Have them find phrases in the text that tell what *osteoderms* and *amphibious* mean. Then have them use the words in sentences and write definitions.

Assess

If... students are not able to understand unfamiliar words in the article by using context clues,

then... write this sentence on the board: *Students read about reptiles.* Remind students that context clues are words that tell about another word. Have students create a context clue for *students*. (Possible answer: girls and boys who go to school) Then have students read the first sentence of the article and find a context clue for *crocodilians*. (like other reptiles)

ADD ENGLISH WORDS

Review these words related to context clues.

synonyms **definition**
explanation

PART 2

Preview the Reading Selection

Use these activities before reading *Komodo Dragons,* Teacher's Edition, *Scott Foresman Reading,* pages 234–247.

Activate Prior Knowledge

Have students tell what they know about snakes, turtles, lizards, alligators, and crocodiles from books, magazines, movies, zoos, science museums, or firsthand experiences. Suggest that students bring in pictures and literature about reptiles, add captions, and prepare a bulletin-board display.

ADD ENGLISH WORDS

Listen for students' knowledge of these words.

Komodo dragons
islands **burrows**
claws **tongues**
eggs

Strategy: Using a K-W-L Chart

Explain the strategy: *When I want to learn new facts, I can use a chart. It is a strategy called Using a K-W-L Chart.* Point out what each letter means and model filling out the K column based on your Adding English Poster discussion. Have students begin their own charts with what they know about Komodo dragons.

K What I Know	W What I Want to Know	L What I Learned
They are reptiles. They are very big.		

Transparency 7

Build Background

Show students Komodo Island on a map. Tell students that the island is very hot, and some animals that live there have to change to fit their environment by lowering or raising their body temperature. Show students pictures of Komodo dragons in their natural settings and discuss what students notice.

Use Word Riddles

Have students work with a partner to write a riddle for each vocabulary word, using the Adding English Poster for ideas. For example: *We are large and fierce-looking lizards.* (Komodo dragons) or *We are land and have ocean all around us.* (islands) Have students take turns reading their riddles while classmates try to guess the answer. The student who guesses the answer points out the answer on the Adding English Poster.

RESOURCES

Use *Scott Foresman ESL,* Grade 3, for additional instruction and activities.

- Chapter 7, "Plants, Animals, and Climate"
- Video, Unit 4, "Living Things Adapt"

Vocabulary: Context Clues

Use these activities with the Vocabulary Lesson and paragraph "Komodo Dragons—Not for Pets!," Teacher's Edition, *Scott Foresman Reading,* page 234.

Review with students that when they read an unfamiliar word they should look for words around it that provide information about its meaning. Write this sentence on the board: *The lizards roam among the hills and wander along the beach.* Have students read the sentence and tell what the underlined word means and what context clues helped them. Continue with sentences that use context clues to illustrate the other vocabulary words.

ADD ENGLISH WORDS

Through listening and watching, assess students' knowledge of selection vocabulary.

lizards **reptiles**
roam **harshest**
armor **fierce**
prey

Use Total Physical Response

Help students understand *roam* and *fierce*. Say, *I roam about the room,* as you walk casually around. Then tell a student to roam. Demonstrate a fierce look as you say, *I am fierce; you should be afraid of me.* Tell students to look fierce, as if they are powerful and might scare others.

Guide students as they read "Komodo Dragons—Not for Pets!" Scott Foresman Reading, *page 234. Ask them how using context clues can help them understand an unfamiliar word.*

Students can participate in the Write About It activity that follows. If possible, have English language learners work with partners whose home language is English to study the photo of a Komodo dragon on pages 234–235. Students can describe the creature to each other.

Present the Reading Selection

Use these activities with *Komodo Dragons,* Teacher's Edition, *Scott Foresman Reading,* pages 234–247.

Preview Headings and Illustrations

Explain the strategy: *Before I begin to read a story, I look at the pictures and headings to see what the story is about.* Point out the illustration on page 236 and have students identify the area under the magnifying glass. Continue previewing the pictures. Call attention to the headings throughout the article. What information do they provide?

Develop Concepts

Students may need support in understanding that the selection is an informational article. Ask: *What kind of illustrations are used in this selection?* Discuss why students think photographs were used instead of an artist's drawings. Then have students select a photograph they like and write about it, telling why they like it and what facts it shows about Komodo dragons. Have pairs of students share what they have written.

K What I Know	W What I Want to Know	L What I Learned
They are reptiles. They are very big.	What do they eat? Why are they called dragons?	

Transparency 7

Set Purposes

Students can participate in Set Purposes, Teacher's Edition, *Scott Foresman Reading,* page 235. Then have students continue their K-W-L charts by filling in the W column with what they want to know about Komodo dragons. Remind students that they are using a strategy called Using a K-W-L Chart.

Selection Audio CD 4/Tape 10

Guide students as they read Komodo Dragons, Scott Foresman Reading, *pages 234–247. To support comprehension, use the suggestions in Meeting Individual Needs, ESL, in the Teacher's Edition.*

Response Log

- Have students write about the two most interesting things they learned about Komodo dragons.
- Have students draw a picture to show what a baby Komodo dragon looks like and what it might do. Have them use the article and the Adding English Poster for ideas. Tell them to write captions to explain their pictures.

Practice Selection Concepts

To help students tell what they learned, choose from these activities.

- Help students fill in the L column of their K-W-L charts.
- Distribute the ten important sentences. Have groups of students write the headings "Facts About Komodo Dragons," "What Komodo Dragons Look Like," and "What Komodo Dragons Do" on separate pieces of paper, then cut the sentences apart and arrange them below the appropriate headings. (Facts About Komodo Dragons: 1, 2, 9, 10; What Komodo Dragons Look Like: 4, 5; What Komodo Dragons Do: 3, 6, 7, 8)

Strategy: Self-Assess

Ask: *Did Using a K-W-L Chart help you learn new information? How?*

K What I Know	W What I Want to Know	L What I Learned
They are reptiles. They are very big.	What do they eat? Why are they called dragons?	They eat rats, goats, water buffalo, and other animals. They are called dragons because they are the biggest lizards in the world, and they look like dragons.

Transparency 7

Ten Important Sentences Page 24

Language Awareness

Provide supported practice by using the Adding English Grammar and Phonics Practice Masters, pages 95–96, with the suggestions below.

Grammar: Possessive Nouns

Write the following on the board: *The book belongs to the boy. It is the boy's book.* Read the sentences aloud. Point to the word *boy's* and say: Boy's *is a singular possessive noun. A possessive noun tells who owns, or possesses, something.* Write the following on the board: *The book belongs to the boys. It is the boys' book.* Read the sentences aloud. Invite a volunteer to circle the possessive noun. Say: Boys' *is a plural possessive noun.* Explain that when a plural noun ends in *s,* we add only an apostrophe to make it possessive. When a plural noun does not end in *s,* we add *'s (women's, children's).*

Students can complete the Practice Master alone or with a partner.

Adding English Grammar Practice Master Page 95

Phonics: *R*-Controlled Vowels

Distribute the Practice Master. Have students listen to and read as you say the words in Exercise A. Then students should say the words aloud. Prompt students to use the words in sentences.

For Exercise B, have students read the sentences aloud before they write their answers.

Adding English Phonics Practice Master Page 96

PART 3

Connect Selection Concepts

Use these activities with Reader Response, Teacher's Edition, *Scott Foresman Reading,* page 247.

Literature Discussion Group

If possible, have English language learners work in groups with students whose home language is English to discuss the following questions:

- What kind of environment do Komodo dragons need?
- How can areas where Komodo dragons live be preserved?
- Do you think it's important to protect Komodo dragons? Why?

Radio Advertisements

Have partners write a script for a radio advertisement for a program about Komodo dragons. What information will make people interested in the program? Volunteers can pretend to use a microphone as they read their advertisements.

Reading Across Texts: "Two Uncommon Lizards," pages 248–249

To support students as they learn about and read a CD-ROM encyclopedia article:

- Remind students that headings tell what they will read about in the paragraphs that follow. Photographs show what the paragraphs are about. Captions give information about the photographs.
- Have students tell what they already know about the two kinds of lizards. Ask what they expect to learn from the articles.
- Ask: *How is "Two Uncommon Lizards" like* Komodo Dragons*? How is it different?* Record their responses on a Venn diagram, Graphic Organizer Transparency 21.

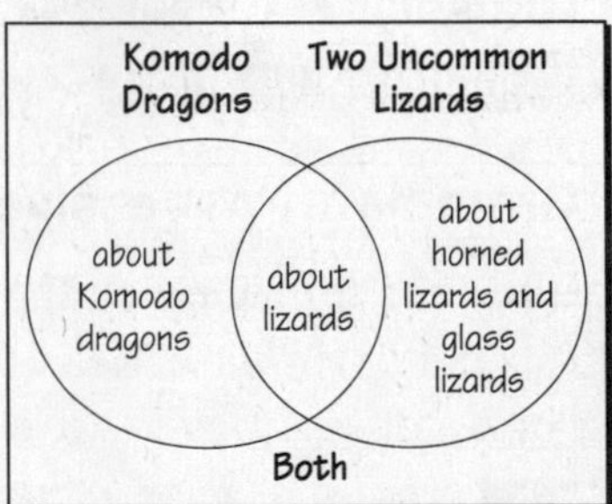

Transparency 21

Assess

Refer to the list below to assess students' progress.

Reading

- ☐ Uses words related to Komodo dragons and other reptiles.
- ☐ Uses context clues to identify the meanings of unfamiliar words.

Language Awareness

Grammar

- ☐ Recognizes and uses possessive nouns.

Phonics

- ☐ Pronounces and decodes words with *r*-controlled vowels.

Learning Strategies

- ☐ Uses a K-W-L chart.
- ☐ Applies context clues to learn unfamiliar vocabulary.

Name ______________________________

Possessive Nouns

Grammar

A. Read the sentences. Circle the possessive nouns.

1. A Komodo dragon's teeth are very sharp.

2. These lizards' tongues stick out all the time.

3. A goat cannot escape a dragon's claws.

4. The author has written many children's books about animals.

B. Choose the correct possessive noun to complete each sentence.

5. On cool days, the sun warms a __________ body. (dragon's/dragons')

6. Several __________ burrows are on the hillside. (dragon's/dragons')

7. Most adult __________ scales are dark. (dragon's/dragons')

8. A baby __________ food is made up of insects and rodents. (dragon's/dragons')

C. Talk with a partner about Komodo dragons and other reptiles. Then choose a reptile and write sentences that describe it.

____

____

____

____

____

____

Name ______________________________

r-Controlled Vowels

A. Listen to the words. Read the words. Then say the words.

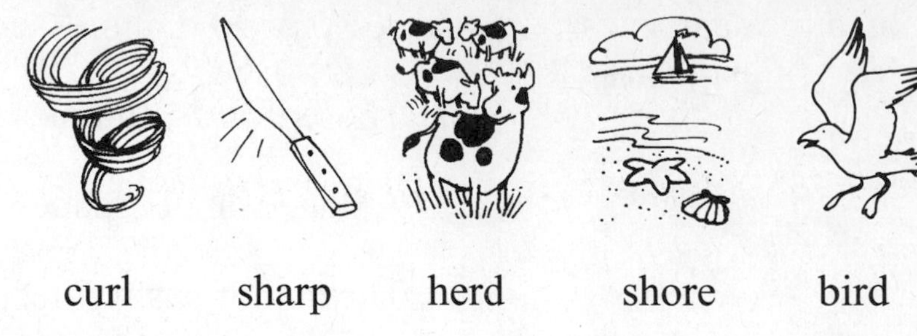

curl sharp herd shore bird

B. Read the sentences. Write a word from the box to complete each sentence.

armor	dinner	hurt	warm

1. Lizards' scales are like suits of ___________.

2. The weather is ___________ where Komodo dragons live.

3. Dragons eat animals for ___________.

4. If you try to pet one, you will get ___________!

C. Say the underlined words. Read the sentences to a partner. Then listen as your partner reads them to you.

Some reptiles are very large. Some move slowly, and others dart swiftly about. Reptiles live in many parts of the world, in warm climates and in cold. They have various ways of fighting and can easily harm with a blow from their tail or a bite from their sharp teeth.

John Henry

Pages 260–281

Crossing Cultures • In this lesson, students read about a legendary hero of American folklore. Tell students that this tale is not meant to teach a lesson, but to make people laugh and enjoy a good story. Invite students to share funny tales from their cultural backgrounds.

Preview the Skill Lesson

Use these activities with the Skill Lesson: "Welcome to McBroom's Farm," Teacher's Edition, *Scott Foresman Reading,* pages 260–261.

Activate Prior Knowledge

Show Adding English Poster 11 and ask students to describe what they see. Point out the barn, the silo, and other things found on a farm. List new farm vocabulary on the board. Ask students how the farm in the poster is similar to or different from farms they have seen. They can use a web, Graphic Organizer Transparency 4, to name things on a farm.

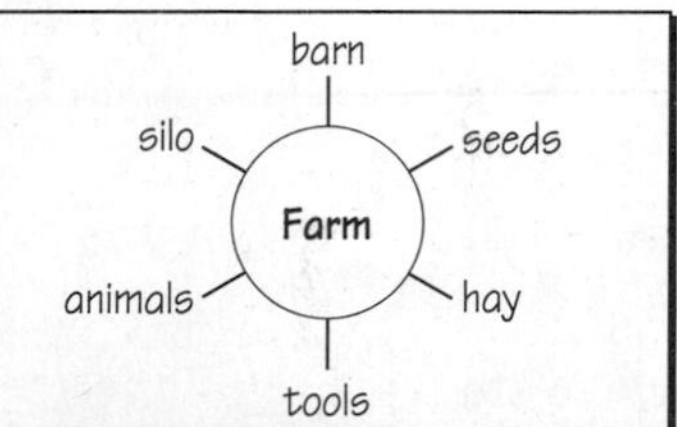

Transparency 4

Use Pantomime

Use the words at the right to preview the Skill Lesson literature. Write them on the board and read each one aloud. Then read aloud the following paragraph, pausing to let students pantomime the actions.

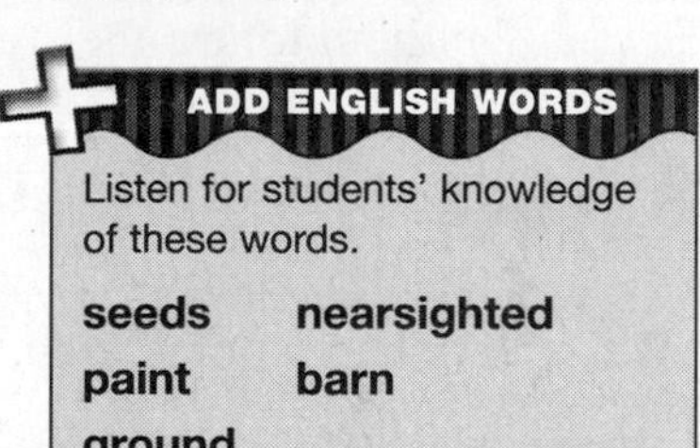

> My grandmother has trouble seeing things that are far away. She is very nearsighted. She can barely see the barn from her house. One day I used red paint to make the barn bright red. Then I planted seeds in the ground around the barn. By springtime, brightly colored flowers grew around the red barn. Now grandmother sees it! Her new glasses help too.

To reinforce comprehension, have students use the words in sentences. All students can benefit from reviewing this vocabulary.

Present the Comprehension Strategy

Comprehension: Making Judgments

Use Comprehension Strategies, *Adding English Guide,* page 10, to introduce Making Judgments.

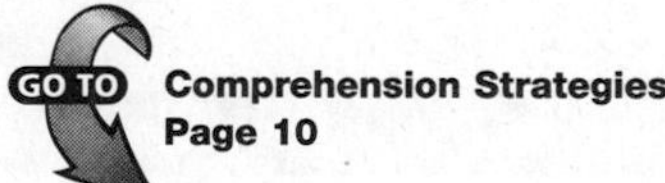

Relate to Personal Experience

Show students a picture of a bicycle in a magazine or store catalogue. Provide time for them to closely examine the bicycle to decide whether or not they like it. Then on a T-chart, Graphic Organizer Transparency 24, have students list what they like and don't like about the bicycle. Invite volunteers to share their lists and their judgments about the bike. Then extend this activity to a concept, such as *Working with a partner is better than working alone.* Help students realize that they use personal beliefs, knowledge, and experience to evaluate objects and ideas.

What I Like	What I Don't Like
12 speeds	the color

Transparency 24

Guide students as they read "Welcome to McBroom's Farm," Scott Foresman Reading, *pages 260–261. Tell them to think about how they would react if someone told them a similar story. Would they believe it?*

Selection Audio CD 5/Tape 13

Practice

Have students retell the story and tell how they feel about it. Ask them to identify parts of the story they feel couldn't be true. Encourage them to use the Adding English Poster as an aid.

Story Details	Could Be True	Could Not Be True
Crops shoot up before your eyes.		✔

Transparency 25

Assess

If... students are not able to make judgments about the story,

then... have them list several details from the story on a three-column chart, Graphic Organizer Transparency 25. Decide together whether each detail could be true and then put a check mark in the appropriate column. Calculate together which column has more check marks.

ADD ENGLISH WORDS

Review these clue words related to making judgments.

decide **influence**
opinion

PART 2

Preview the Reading Selection

Use these activities before reading *John Henry,* Teacher's Edition, *Scott Foresman Reading,* pages 262–279.

Activate Prior Knowledge

Have students look at the Adding English Poster and point to the pictures showing the words at the right. Ask students to point out other actions they see in the poster. List new words on the board. Ask students to act out several words, such as *paint, dig, bury, wash, holler.*

ADD ENGLISH WORDS

Listen for students' knowledge of these words.

jumped **race**
rainbow **buried**

Build Background

Show pictures of legendary heroes students might recognize. Discuss qualities that each is famous for, such as courage, skill, and strength. Encourage students to share stories about heroes from their home cultures.

Explain to students that they will read a story about a character who helps build roads and railroads. Have students talk about what it would be like to be a road worker or a railroad builder. Have them answer questions like the following: *What would you wear? What tools would you use?* Begin a K-W-L chart, Graphic Organizer Transparency 7, about building roads and railroads.

Strategy: Using a K-W-L Chart

Explain the strategy: *When I want to learn new facts, I can use a chart. It is a strategy called Using a K-W-L Chart.* Point out what each letter means and model filling out the K column. Have students begin their own charts with what they know about building roads and railroads.

Vocabulary: Multiple-Meaning Words

Use these activities with the Vocabulary Lesson and paragraph "Digging Out!," Teacher's Edition, *Scott Foresman Reading,* page 262.

Write the Words to Know on the board. Have pairs of students copy each word on an index card and define or illustrate it on the back. Point out that two of the words have more than one meaning. Have students use their dictionaries to write the second meaning of *tunnel* and *glimpse* on the back of the appropriate index cards. Then ask students to determine which meaning of those words (noun or verb) is illustrated on the Adding English Poster.

Use Total Physical Response

For *glimpse,* have one student act out looking for a classmate, who shows his or her face for a second before hiding. Explain that the first student had a glimpse of the second student. Invite students to act out other words on the list.

Guide students as they read "Digging Out!," Scott Foresman Reading, *page 262. Ask them what they will do when they find a word that has more than one meaning.*

RESOURCES

Use *Scott Foresman ESL,* Grade 5, for additional instruction and activities.

- Chapter 10, "What Makes a Good Story?"
- Video, Unit 5, "Reading Fun"

K What I Know	W What I Want to Know	L What I Learned
People who build roads are strong.		

Transparency 7

ADD ENGLISH WORDS

Through listening and watching, assess students' knowledge of selection vocabulary.

shivered	**tunnel**
boulder	**hollered**
rhythm	**glimpse**
horizon	

Students can participate in the Write About It activity that follows. If possible, have English language learners write their letters with partners whose home language is English, first brainstorming a list of vocabulary related to job application letters and construction work.

Present the Reading Selection

Use these activities with *John Henry,* Teacher's Edition, *Scott Foresman Reading,* pages 262–279.

Preview Illustrations

Explain the strategy: *Before I read a story, I can look at the pictures to get an idea of what the story is about.* Have students look at the illustration on pages 262–263. Then ask them questions about John Henry, such as *Does he look strong? What is he wearing? What type of work do you think he does? What tools does he have?* Continue previewing the pictures.

Develop Concepts

Students may need help understanding that *John Henry* uses exaggeration, or descriptions and events that are amazing and unbelievable. Give an example of exaggeration in everyday speech, such as *Mr. Jones is as tall as a skyscraper.* Have students think of their own examples. Then they can find other examples in "Welcome to McBroom's Farm."

Set Purposes

Students can participate in Set Purposes, Teacher's Edition, *Scott Foresman Reading,* page 263. Ask students to tell you what they want to find out about road and railroad building. Have them write their responses in the W column of their K-W-L charts. Remind students that they are using a strategy called Using a K-W-L Chart.

Guide students as they read John Henry, Scott Foresman Reading, *pages 262–279. To support comprehension, use the suggestions in Meeting Individual Needs, ESL, in the Teacher's Edition.*

Response Log

- Have students make a list of things they like about John Henry. Begin by having students brainstorm ideas, referring to the Adding English Poster for support.
- Have students draw a rainbow and write words to describe John Henry in each of the colored arches.

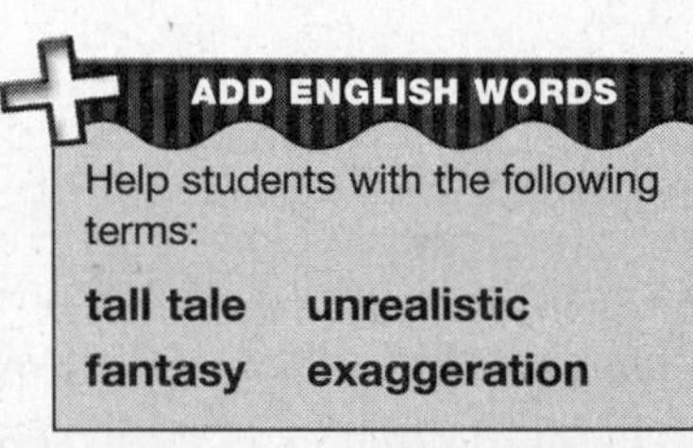

K What I Know	W What I Want to Know	L What I Learned
People who build roads are strong.	How are roads built?	

Transparency 7

Selection Audio CD 5/Tape 13

Practice Selection Concepts

To help students tell what they learned, choose from these activities.

- Help students fill in the L column of their K-W-L charts with information they learned about building roads and railroads. Help them make judgments about reality and fantasy as they decide what to write.
- Divide the class into five groups. Distribute two of the Ten Important Sentences to each group. Have the groups explain where in the story their sentences belong.

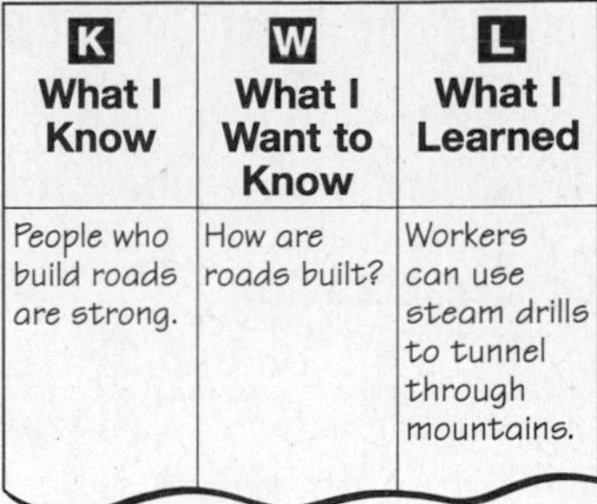

Transparency 7

Strategy: Self-Assess

Ask: *Did Using a K-W-L Chart help you learn new information about building roads and railroads? How?*

Ten Important Sentences
Page 23

Language Awareness

Provide supported practice by using the Adding English Grammar and Phonics Practice Masters, pages 103–104, with the suggestions below.

Grammar: Verbs

Write the following sentence on the board: *John Henry hollered louder than any child and jumped higher than any person.* Read the sentence aloud. Point out that the sentence has two action words (verbs). Invite volunteers to circle the verbs. Then ask them what the words mean. Encourage students to make up other sentences about John Henry as you write them on the board. Invite others to circle the verbs and tell what they mean.

Students can complete the Practice Master alone or with a partner.

Adding English
Grammar Practice Master
Page 103

Phonics: Inflected Forms with *-er* and *-est*

Distribute the Practice Master. Have students listen, read, and repeat as you say the words in Exercise A. Then draw two stick figures on the board. Point out that one is *tall*, but the other is *taller.* Explain that we add *-er* to some adjectives when we compare two things. Now add a third stick figure that is *tallest.* Explain that the *-est* ending is used to compare three or more things. Point out that other spelling changes sometimes occur when *-er* or *-est* is added to adjectives: the final consonant may be doubled, a final *e* may be dropped, or a *y* may be changed to *i.*

For Exercise B, have students read the sentences aloud before writing their answers.

Adding English
Phonics Practice Master
Page 104

PART 3

Connect Selection Concepts

Use these activities with Reader Response, Teacher's Edition, *Scott Foresman Reading,* page 279.

Dramatization

Divide the class into four groups. If possible, have English language learners work with students whose home language is English to dramatize *John Henry.* Assign the beginning of the story to the first group, the middle of the story to the second group, the ending to the third group, and the roles of the people who mourn the death of John Henry to the fourth group. Give each group time to practice before presenting their dramatizations.

Telling Tales

Ask students to think of tales they have heard from family members or friends. Then have them use exaggeration to transform their stories into tall tales. Students can tape-record these stories and play them back later for the class to hear and enjoy.

Reading Across Texts: "John Henry" pages 280–281

Guide students as they read this poem. To support comprehension and make connections to John Henry, *see the suggestions in the Teacher's Edition,* Scott Foresman Reading.

Assess

Refer to the list below to assess students' progress.

Reading

- ☐ Uses words related to road and railroad building.
- ☐ Make judgments about characters and events in a story.
- ☐ Distinguishes between real and fantasy events.
- ☐ Recognizes elements of a tall tale.

Language Awareness

Grammar

- ☐ Identifies and uses verbs in sentences.

Phonics

- ☐ Decodes and pronounces words with inflected endings *-er* and *-est.*
- ☐ Uses adjectives with endings *-er* and *-est* to make comparisions.

Learning Strategies

- ☐ Uses a K-W-L chart to learn and organize facts.
- ☐ Recognizes multiple-meaning words and uses context clues to decide their meaning.

Name ____________________

Verbs

A. Circle the verbs in each sentence.

1. John Henry grew and grew and grew.

2. He grew so tall that his head and shoulders burst through the roof.

3. He laughed and scared the sun away.

B. Write a verb from the box to complete each sentence.

fell	met	raised	sang	walked

4. John Henry ____________ quickly down the road.

5. He ____________ the hammer to hit the nail.

6. John Henry slowly ____________ to the ground.

7. He ____________ a man named Freddy.

8. John Henry ____________ a song as he worked.

C. Talk with a partner about John Henry. Then write sentences comparing him to a steam drill.

____

____

____

____

Name ___________________________________

Phonics

Inflected Forms with *-er* and *-est*

A. Listen to the words. Read the words. Then say the words.

tall	taller	tallest
big	bigger	biggest

nice	nicer	nicest
funny	funnier	funniest

B. Choose the word in parentheses that best completes each sentence.

1. Ferret-Faced Freddy was the ____________ man in the state. (meaner/meanest)

2. John Henry was ____________ than the other railroad worker. (stronger/strongest)

3. He was the ____________ man you've ever seen! (bigger/biggest)

C. Say the underlined words. Read the paragraph to a partner. Then listen as your partner reads it to you.

When John Henry was a baby, he grew bigger each day until he was the tallest man in the area. He thought being big was one of the funniest things in the world. One day he met Ferret-Faced Freddy. Freddy was the meanest man in the state. John Henry played a trick on him, and Freddy changed into a much nicer person.

Marven of the Great North Woods

Pages 282–303

Crossing Cultures • In this selection, a young boy becomes friends with a burly lumberjack—someone the boy thought was too different to be his friend. Have children tell about a friendship they have had with someone older. Do they think people who seem very different can be friends?

PART 1

Preview the Skill Lesson

Use these activities with the Skill Lesson: "Winter of the Snowshoe Hare," Teacher's Edition, *Scott Foresman Reading,* pages 282–283.

Activate Prior Knowledge

Show students Adding English Poster 12. Ask them if anything in the poster is familiar to them. Point out and discuss images of the woods in wintertime. Together, name some of the things pictured. Students can also brainstorm other things they might expect to see or hear in the woods. Use a web, Graphic Organizer Transparency 4, to record students' responses

Poster Tips
Page 16

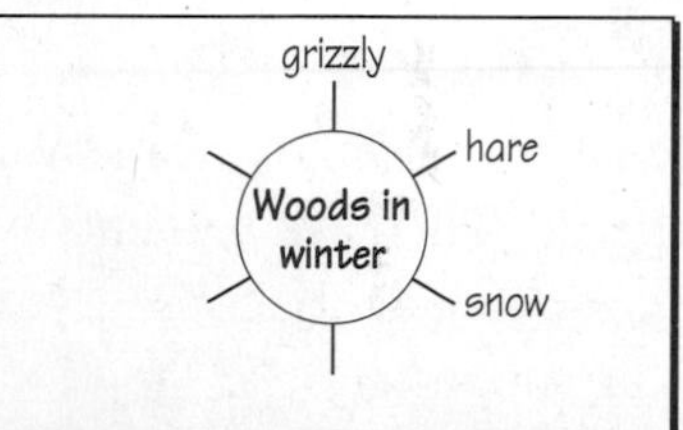

Transparency 4

Use Paraphrasing

Introduce the Skill Lesson literature by previewing vocabulary at the right. List the vocabulary words on the board. Explain the strategy: *When I have trouble remembering a word, I think of a way to say the same thing using other words that I know.*

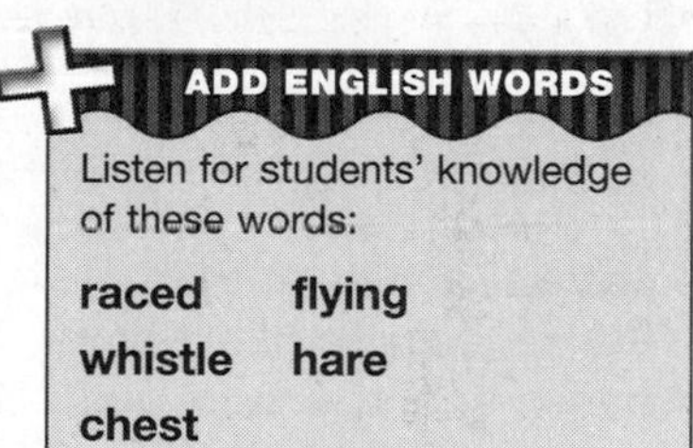

Have students point to parts of the Adding English Poster and practice describing it in their own words. Read aloud the following paragraph.

> The hare raced through the snowy woods on its large feet. It wanted to return to its snug burrow. It ran so fast that it was almost flying. With its long ears it heard the whistle of birds in the trees. When the hare got home, its chest was pounding.

Model paraphrasing the first sentence: *The rabbit with big feet ran through the snowy woods.* Then help students paraphrase the other sentences.

Present the Comprehension Strategy

Comprehension: Drawing Conclusions

Use Comprehension Strategies, *Adding English Guide,* page 10, to introduce Drawing Conclusions.

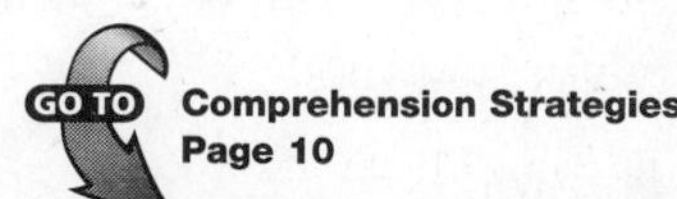

Comprehension Strategies
Page 10

Relate to Personal Experience

Ask students what they would think if they visited a friend or relative and found the home filled with packed boxes, suitcases by the door, and bare walls and shelves. Would they think their friend or relative was moving out of that home? If so, they would be drawing conclusions based on facts, details, and their own knowledge. Show students how to list facts and details and record their conclusions on a T-chart, Graphic Organizer Transparency 24.

Facts/Details	Conclusions
packed boxes suitcases bare walls and shelves	moving out of the home

Transparency 24

Guide students as they read "Winter of the Snowshoe Hare," Scott Foresman Reading, *pages 282–283. Remind them to use the details and facts to make a decision or draw a conclusion.*

Selection Audio CD 5/Tape 14

Practice

List some details from "Winter of the Snowshoe Hare" on the board. Then ask students what conclusions they can draw from these details. Encourage students to use the Adding English Poster for support.

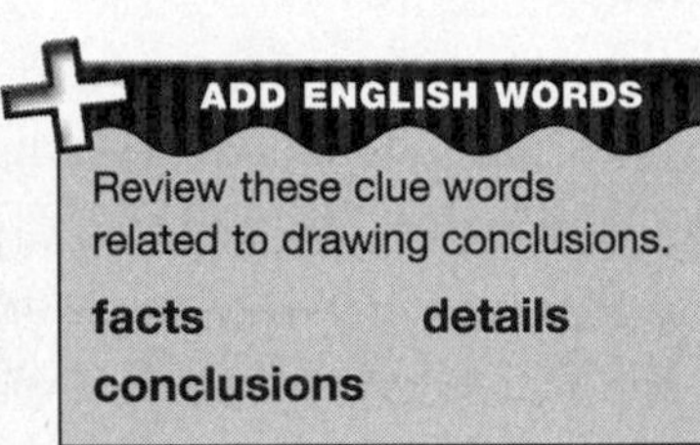

ADD ENGLISH WORDS

Review these clue words related to drawing conclusions.

facts **details**
conclusions

Assess

If... students are not able to draw conclusions from the story,

then... ask them to list several facts and details from the story in the left column of a T-chart. Then help students draw conclusions based on these facts and details as well as on their own personal experience.

Facts/Details	Conclusions
The hare was running so fast he was almost flying.	The hare was scared.
The hare heard the sound of the dog's paws grow louder and louder.	The dog chasing him was getting closer.

Transparency 24

PART 2

Preview the Reading Selection

Use these activities before reading *Marven of the Great North Woods,* Teacher's Edition, *Scott Foresman Reading,* pages 284–306.

Activate Prior Knowledge

Direct students' attention to the Adding English Poster. Point to the lumberjack. Ask students to tell what work he does and where he does it. Use the poster to illustrate the meanings of other vocabulary words.

ADD ENGLISH WORDS

Listen for students' knowledge of these words.

bookkeeper
lumberjacks (jacks)
beards **in the sack**
skis **flu**

Build Background

Ask students if they have ever seen a movie or television show about logging or about life in the north woods. Ask them to tell what they know about logging camps. Begin a K-W-L chart, Graphic Organizer Transparency 7, about life in a logging camp. Encourage them to use the vocabulary words.

Strategy: Using a K-W-L Chart

Explain the strategy: *When I want to learn new facts, I can use a chart. It is a strategy called Using a K-W-L Chart.* Point out what each letter means. Model filling out the K column and have students complete the K column of their own charts.

Vocabulary: Multiple-Meaning Words

Use these activities with the Vocabulary Lesson and paragraph "From an Idaho Logging Camp, 1902," Teacher's Edition, *Scott Foresman Reading,* page 284.

Explain to students that many words in English have more than one meaning. Use some examples students know, such as *bat* (baseball) and *bat* (rodent). Write the word *cord* on the board. Explain that students may know the word as meaning a string or a rope, but that in the context of the story, the word *cord* means a unit for measuring. Have students make a chart of multiple-meaning words they know such as *duck, slide,* and *fly.*

Use Paraphrasing

Write the selection vocabulary on the board. Have students explain in their own words what each vocabulary word means. For example, *snowshoes are shoes to wear in the snow; a grizzly is a large bear.* Students can use the Adding English Poster for support.

Guide students as they read "From an Idaho Logging Camp, 1902," Scott Foresman Reading, *page 284. Ask what they will do if they find words that have more than one meaning.*

Students can participate in the Talk About It activity that follows. If possible, have English language learners work in groups with students whose home language is English to discuss what it would be like to spend a month at a logging camp. What would they most like to do there? What jobs would they have?

RESOURCES

Use *Scott Foresman ESL,* Grade 4, for additional instruction and activities.

- Chapter 8, "Weather and People"
- Video, Unit 4, "Living Things Adapt"

K What I Know	W What I Want to Know	L What I Learned
It's in the woods. Lumberjacks work there. They cut trees.		

Transparency 7

ADD ENGLISH WORDS

Through listening and watching, assess students' knowledge of selection vocabulary.

flapjacks **snowshoes**
depot **grizzly**
cord

Present the Reading Selection

Use these activities with *Marven of the Great North Woods,* Teacher's Edition, *Scott Foresman Reading,* pages 284–301.

Preview Illustrations

Explain the strategy: *Before I begin to read, I look at the pictures in the story to get an idea of what the story is about.* Have students look at the picture on pages 284–285. Ask: *What are these people doing?* Show students the Adding English Poster. Ask: *What place do you see in the poster that you also see on page 287?* Have students study each illustration and try to match what they see there with the poster.

Develop Concepts

For this selection, students may need support in understanding vocabulary that reflects a setting and a period of time with which they may not be familiar. Use a T-chart, Graphic Organizer Transparency 24, to write some words from the story that are not commonly used today. Help students brainstorm a modern alternative for each word.

Words Used in Story	Words Used Today
woodstove	gas or electric stove; furnace
flapjacks	pancakes
inkwell, fountain pen	ballpoint pen

Transparency 24

Set Purposes

Students can participate in Set Purposes, Teacher's Edition, *Scott Foresman Reading,* page 285. Ask students to think about what they might be able to learn about logging camps from the story. Help them fill in the W column in their K-W-L charts about life in a logging camp. Remind students they are using the strategy called Using a K-W-L Chart.

K What I Know	W What I Want to Know	L What I Learned
It's in the woods. Lumberjacks work there. They cut trees.	What do lumberjacks do for fun? Who else works there?	

Transparency 7

Guide students as they read Marven of the Great North Woods, Scott Foresman Reading, *pages 284–306. To support comprehension, use the suggestions in Meeting Individual Needs, ESL, in the Teacher's Edition.*

Response Log

- Have students write a paragraph comparing their typical day with a typical day at the logging camp for Marven. They can include details about what time they get up in the morning, their chores, and so on. Begin by having students brainstorm ideas, referring to the Adding English Poster for support.
- Ask students to make a list of words that describe Marven and a separate list of words that describe themselves. Encourage them to share their lists with a partner. In what ways are they like or not like Marven?

Practice Selection Concepts

To help students tell what they learned, choose from these activities.

- Have students fill in the L column of their K-W-L charts with what they learned about life in a logging camp.
- Have pairs of students choose one of the ten important sentences, discuss, and write about a conclusion they drew from the sentence. For example: *Marven took a deep breath, walked bravely over to the bed, reached out, and tapped the jack's shoulder.* (Possible conclusion: Jean Louis woke up.)

Strategy: Self-Assess

Ask: *Did Using a K-W-L Chart help you learn new information about life in a logging camp? How?* Show students how to add an H column to the K-W-L charts and explain that H stands for "how they learned." Have students fill it in.

Language Awareness

Provide supported practice by using the Adding English Grammar and Phonics Practice Masters, pages 111–112, with the suggestions below.

Grammar: Subject-Verb Agreement

Write the following sentences on the board: *Marven works in the logging camp. He loves the woods. The lumberjacks sing and dance.* Have students identify and circle the subject and verb of each sentence. Next, replace the subject in each sentence, changing singular subjects to plural, and vice versa. Ask: *Should the verbs change too?* Explain that the subject and the verb must agree. Elicit the necessary verb changes. Invite volunteers to come to the board to write a sentence. Students can complete the Practice Master alone or with a partner.

Phonics: Regular Plurals

Distribute the Practice Master. Have students listen, read, and repeat as you say the words in Exercise A. Then students should say the words aloud and use them in sentences. On the board, create a chart with the headings Add *-s*, Add *-es,* and Change *y* to *i* and add *-es*. Ask volunteers to write the plural of words such as *tree, box,* and *pony* in the appropriate column.

For Exercise B, have students read each word aloud before they choose an answer.

K What I Know	W What I Want to Know	L What I Learned
It's in the woods. Lumberjacks work there. They cut trees.	What do lumberjacks do for fun? Who else works there?	Lumberjacks dance and sing. Bookkeepers and cooks work there.

Transparency 7

Ten Important Sentences Page 24

Adding English Grammar Practice Master Page 111

Adding English Phonics Practice Master Page 112

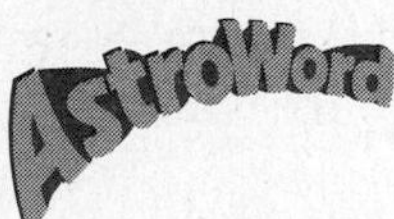

Base Words, Endings

PART 3

Connect Selection Concepts

Use these activities with Reader Response, Teacher's Edition, *Scott Foresman Reading,* page 301.

Literature Discussion Group

Have students work in groups to talk about the story, focusing on these questions:

- What were Marven's duties at the lumber camp?
- Why did Marven have with a problem with the food?
- Draw conclusions about Jean Louis. What kind of person is he? What details support your conclusion?

Connect with the Story

Ask students if they have ever had a similar experience of being away from home for a long period of time. Encourage them to share their experiences. Compare and contrast students' experiences with Marven's.

Reading Across Texts: "Counting Money," pages 302–303

To support students as they read an excerpt from a math textbook:

- Activate prior knowledge by asking how students read a math textbook. Ask: *What parts do you pay special attention to?*
- Ask students if they have experience in using different currencies. Is the decimal point always used?
- Give groups of students play money. Make up story problems based on *Marven of the Great North Woods.* For example: *Jean Louis earned $20 cutting cords of lumber. Did he earn more money than you have?* Ask a student to write the problem and answer on the board, using >, <, and =.

ADD ENGLISH WORDS

Use the Adding English Poster to help students with the following words:

bills	**coins**	**digits**
dollar	**quarter**	**penny**
dime	**nickel**	

Assess

Refer to the list below to assess students' progress.

Reading

- ☐ Uses words related to logging and the north woods.
- ☐ Draws conclusions based on personal experiences, facts, and details.

Language Awareness

Grammar

- ☐ Identifies and uses verbs in sentences with plural and singular subjects.

Phonics

- ☐ Changes singular nouns to plural nouns by adding *-s,* or *-es.*

Learning Strategies

- ☐ Uses a K-W-L chart.
- ☐ Recognizes multiple-meaning words and decides which meaning is being used.

Name ____

Subject-Verb Agreement

A. Underline the verb in each sentence. Then circle the complete subject in each sentence.

1. Marven runs to the bunkhouse.

2. Two lumberjacks climb a mountain.

3. Marven and Jean Louis arrive late for breakfast.

B. Choose a verb in parentheses to complete each sentence.

4. Marven and Jean Louis __________ breakfast together. (eat/eats)

5. Marven __________ the lumberjacks' songs and games. (learn/learns)

6. Jean Louis __________ Marven a new ax. (give/gives)

7. Mama and Papa __________ Marven at the train. (meet/meets)

C. Imagine that you are Marven, writing a letter home. What is it like in the north woods? How is it different from home? Talk with a partner. Then write what Marven might say.

Dear Mama and Papa,

____

____

____

____

Your son,

Marven

Name ______________________________

Regular Plurals

Phonics

A. Listen to the words. Read the words. Then say the words.

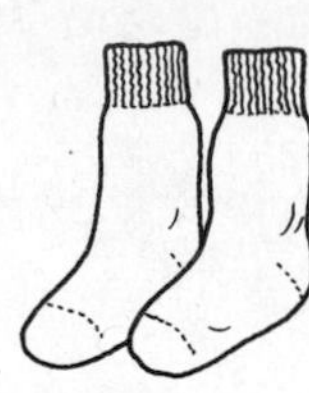
sock/socks

game/games

family/families

ax/axes

face/faces

kiss/kisses

B. Circle each plural noun. Write its singular form.

1. boxes desk ______________

2. dime pennies ______________

3. quarter nickels ______________

4. trees lake ______________

C. Say the underlined words. Read the paragraph to a partner. Then listen as your partner reads it to you.

Marven was happy to see his parents and sisters. After many hugs and kisses, he told them all about the lumber camp, especially the grizzlies and the lumberjacks. He told them how the lumberjacks cut down trees with axes. Marven explained how he organized the chits to show how many cords each lumberjack cut. Marven felt proud of his work.

On the Pampas

Pages 304–323

Crossing Cultures • *On the Pampas* contains references and vocabulary specific to ranch life in Argentina. Students who speak Spanish may not know these words, but may be able to pronounce them for others. Encourage students to find similarities and differences between life on this ranch and their lives.

PART 1

Preview the Skill Lesson

Use these activities with the Skill Lesson: "Salmon for All," Teacher's Edition, *Scott Foresman Reading,* pages 304–305.

Poster Tips
Page 16

Activate Prior Knowledge

Show students Adding English Poster 13. Have them point out other parts of the poster that are familiar to them. Elicit from students what they know about fishing. Have students pantomime various aspects of fishing, from baiting a hook to casting a line or net to cleaning and cooking the fish. List fishing words on a web, Graphic Organizer Transparency 4.

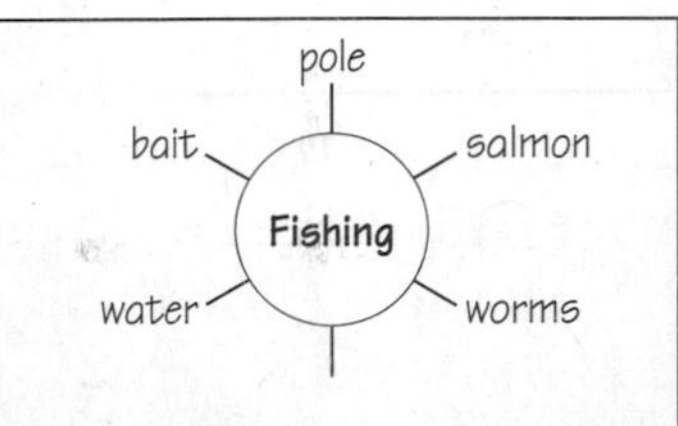

Transparency 4

Use Pantomime

Use the vocabulary at the right to introduce the Skill Lesson literature. Write the words on the board. Then explain that one way to understand and remember a new word is to act it out.

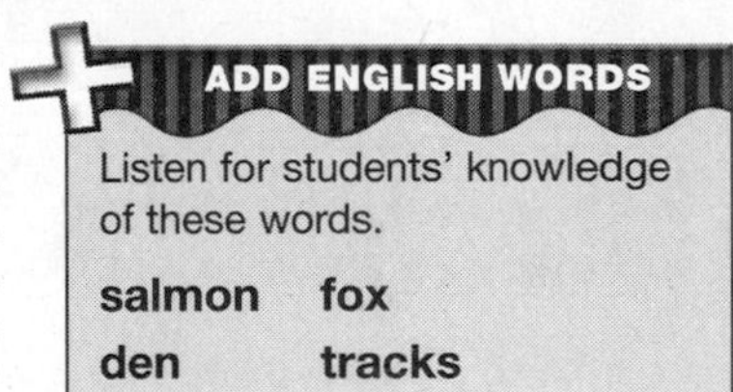

ADD ENGLISH WORDS

Listen for students' knowledge of these words.

salmon	**fox**
den	**tracks**

Read the following passage aloud and act it out. Invite students to follow along and pantomime the actions described.

> We are in the woods. Shhhh. Be quiet, so the animals won't hear us. Let's follow these <u>tracks</u> in the snow. I see pawprints, like tracks a dog would make. I think a <u>fox</u> made them. I wonder where the fox lives. Its <u>den</u> can't be far from here. Look! The tracks stop here, by the river. Look at all the <u>salmon</u> swimming through the water. We can go fishing! I'll use my knife to cut some fishing line. Cast your lines. When you feel a pull, reel in your line. There's one! Look at the size of that salmon! There will be plenty of fish to eat for lunch.

Volunteers can pantomime selected words, such as *salmon* or *tracks*. Others can guess which word is being pantomimed and point out where each word is pictured on the poster. All students could benefit from this vocabulary review.

Present the Comprehension Strategy

Comprehension: Generalizing

Use Comprehension Strategies, *Adding English Guide,* page 10, to introduce Generalizing.

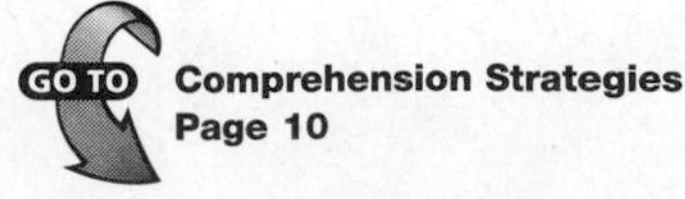

Comprehension Strategies
Page 10

Relate to Personal Experience

Ask students a yes or no question on a topic of interest. For example, *Do you like hot weather?* Have students raise their hands to answer and record the yes and no votes on the board. Make a general statement based on the answer to the question: *Most of us like hot weather.* Explain that this is a *generalization,* a broad statement that applies to many examples. Point out that generalizations frequently include clue words such as *all, most, some, usually, often.*

Read

Guide students as they read "Salmon for All," Scott Foresman Reading, *pages 304–305. Tell them to look for generalizations as they read.*

Selection Audio CD 5/Tape 15

Practice

Have students reread one paragraph from "Salmon for All," then write a generalization about the paragraph. Encourage them to use the Adding English Poster as a vocabulary aid.

Assess

If... students are not able to generalize about the story,

then... have them read the generalizations below and decide whether they are valid. Have students identify the clue words.

> Many birds come to eat fish scraps. (valid/Many)
>
> All people in town fish. (faulty/All)
>
> Mother animals usually find food for their babies. (valid/usually)

ADD ENGLISH WORDS

Review these clue words related to generalizing.

examples **facts** **details**
valid **faulty** **most**
usually **some**

PART 2

Preview the Reading Selection

Use these activities before reading *On the Pampas,* Teacher's Edition, *Scott Foresman Reading,* pages 306–321.

Activate Prior Knowledge

Show students the Adding English Poster and ask them to share what they know about horses and ranching. Have they ever ridden or cared for a horse? Have they ever been on a ranch?

ADD ENGLISH WORDS

Listen for students' knowledge of words from the story.

cattle **mare** **belt**
buckle **saddles** **nest**
foal

Strategy: Using a Word Web

List the vocabulary at right on the board. Explain the strategy: *When I want to see how vocabulary words are connected, I can use a chart. It is a strategy called Using a Word Web.* Model beginning a web, Graphic Organizer Transparency 4, about a ranch. Have students begin their own word webs.

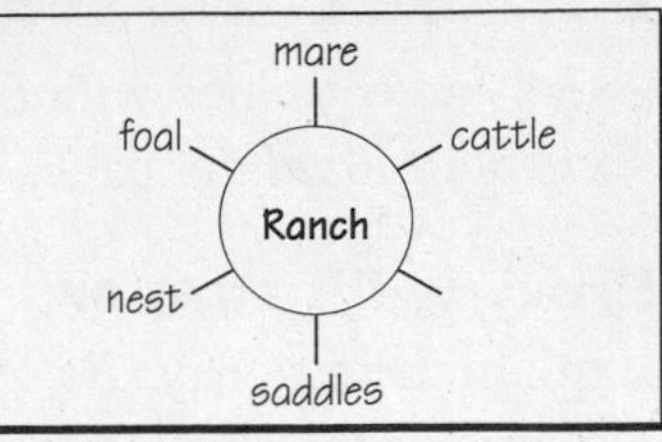

Transparency 4

Build Background

At the *estancia,* the daily schedule includes a large midday meal followed by a *siesta.* Explain to students that a nap after lunch is a common practice in Spain and some Latin American countries. The workday then continues into the evening. Have students write their daily schedule, beginning when they wake up.

RESOURCES

Use *Scott Foresman ESL,* Grade 3, for additional instruction and activities.

- Chapter 1, "The Farm and the City"
- Video, Unit 1, "The Farm and the City"

Vocabulary: Homophones

Use these activities with the Vocabulary lesson and paragraph "Adventure at the Ranch," Teacher's Edition, *Scott Foresman Reading,* page 306.

Write these sentences on the board and read them aloud:

- It gets cold here, but I hear it's colder in Alaska.
- Bus fare is now $1. That's too much. I don't think it's fair!

Point out the homophones. Discuss how context clues can help you choose the correct meaning. Write the selection vocabulary words on the board. Have students copy these words onto index cards: *bridle, herd, mane,* and *reins*. Let volunteers find a picture of each word on the Adding English Poster. Then help pairs of students look for homophones for the words on their cards and write them on the backs. They can use dictionaries for help. Students may want to include pictures on their cards.

ADD ENGLISH WORDS

Through listening and watching, assess students' knowledge of selection vocabulary.

corral	**manes**	**bridles**
reins	**herd**	**calves**
brand	**initials**	

Have a Dialogue

Have pairs create and perform dialogues that use at least two of the vocabulary words. The rest of the class can listen for the words and confirm their meaning by pointing to the poster.

Guide students as they read "Adventure at the Ranch," Scott Foresman Reading, *page 306. Ask students how they will determine the correct meaning for any homophones they find.*

Students can participate in the Write About It activity that follows. If possible, have English language learners work in groups with students whose home language is English to brainstorm a list of things they might see at a ranch.

Present the Reading Selection

Use these activities with *On the Pampas,* Teacher's Edition, *Scott Foresman Reading,* pages 306–321.

Preview Illustrations

Explain the strategy: *Before I begin to read, I can look at the pictures in the story to get an idea of what it is about.* Have students study the words and pictures on pages 308–309. Use these words as you continue to preview the pictures. Ask questions such as: *In what countries could you see the* pampas? *What are the* gauchos *doing on pages 312–313?*

Develop Concepts

For this selection, students may need support in understanding the Spanish words found in the text. Have students skim the story for Spanish words and use a T-chart to list the Spanish words and their English equivalents. Let Spanish speaking students use their own knowledge to help the rest of the class.

Spanish	English
pampas	grasslands
gaucho	cowboy
siesta	nap

Transparency 24

Set Purposes

Students can participate in Set Purposes, Teacher's Edition, *Scott Foresman Reading,* page 307.

Encourage students to start webs, Graphic Organizer Transparency 4, on a topic they expect to read about in the story. Have students fill in the circle with a topic such as *horses, cowboys,* or *Argentina.* As they read the story, students can record words related to their topic. Remind them that they are using a strategy called Using a Word Web.

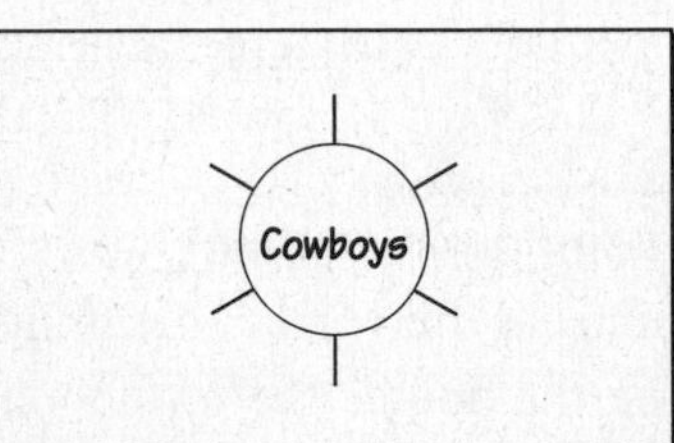

Transparency 4

Guide students as they read On the Pampas, Scott Foresman Reading, *pages 306–321. To support comprehension, use the suggestions in Meeting Individual Needs, ESL, in the Teacher's Edition.*

Selection Audio CD 5/Tape 15

Response Log

- Have students imagine that they are spending a week at an estancia. Ask them to write a list of things they would do to help the family.
- Have students draw and label a ranch scene similar to the ones in the story. They should include elements they see in the illustrations and on the Adding English Poster.

Practice Selection Concepts

To help students tell what they learned, choose from these activities.

- Have partners cover the center topic and then exchange the word webs they made while reading the story. Each student can read his or her partner's words and try to guess the topic. Then students can suggest additional words.
- Cut the ten important sentences into strips and display them for students to read. Have students arrange them in order and then use them as prompts to retell the story.

Ten Important Sentences
Page 25

Strategy: Self-Assess

Ask: *Did Using a Word Web help you see connections between words and understand the story better? How?*

Language Awareness

Provide supported practice by using the Adding English Grammar and Phonics Practice Masters, pages 119–120, with the suggestions below.

Grammar: Present, Past, and Future Verb Tenses

Write several verbs from the story on the board, such as *live, stay, ride.* Have a student make up a sentence using one of these verbs in the present tense. Then ask other students to make up sentences using the same verb in the past and future tenses. Point out that *-ed* must be added for the past tense and *will* for the future tense. List conjugations for common irregular verbs, such as *go, be,* and *have,* on the board.

Students can complete the Practice Master alone or with a partner.

Adding English
Grammar Practice Master
Page 119

Phonics: Inflected Forms with *-ed, -ing, -es*

Distribute the Practice Master. Have students listen, read, and repeat as you say the words in Exercise A. Make sure students understand that when endings are added to some base words, the spelling changes.

For Exercise B, have students read each sentence before writing their answers.

Adding English
Phonics Practice Master
Page 120

Base Words, Endings

PART 3

Connect Selection Concepts

Use these activities with Reader Response, Teacher's Edition, *Scott Foresman Reading,* page 321.

Literature Discussion Group

If possible, have English language learners work in groups with students whose home language is English to talk about the story, focusing on these questions:

- What did the author want to learn?
- Who helped her?
- How did the story end?
- What generalizations can you make about ranches and cowboys in the United States and in Argentina?

Learning How

Have students recall how the author learned to how to ride and handle horses during her summer at the estancia. Ask students to write sentences telling about something they would like to learn how to do well. Students can illustrate their sentences.

Reading Across Texts: "A Closer Look at Argentina," pages 322–323

To support students as they read a nonfiction article:

- Have students preview "A Closer Look at Argentina" by looking at the photographs and graph and reading a few words from each caption.
- Activate prior knowledge about the article by asking: What do you already know about Argentina? What did you learn about Argentina in the story, *On the Pampas*?
- Read the article with students.
- Compare "A Closer Look at Argentina" to *On the Pampas*. Ask: *What different kinds of information about Argentina do you learn in each selection?*

Assess

Refer to the list below to assess students' progress.

Reading

- ☐ Uses words related to fishing.
- ☐ Uses words related to ranching.
- ☐ Recognizes and makes valid generalizations.

Language Awareness

Grammar

- ☐ Recognizes and uses present, past, and future tense verbs.

Phonics

- ☐ Pronounces and decodes words with inflected endings *-ed, -ing,* and *-es.*

Learning Strategies

- ☐ Uses a word web to see relationships between words.
- ☐ Recognizes homophones and decides which meaning is being used.

Name ______________________________

Present, Past, and Future Verb Tenses

A. Underline the verb in each sentence.

1. I lived with my family in Buenos Aires.

2. Susanita lives at the estancia all year round.

3. Next summer I will live on the ranch again.

B. Circle the verb in parentheses that best completes each sentence.

4. Next summer I (visited, visit, will visit) La Carlota again.

5. Last year we (admired, admire, will admire) the belts at the general store.

6. I (wanted, want, will want) to visit the ranch every summer.

7. I hope that I (was, am, will be) a good gaucho someday!

C. Imagine that you will go to a ranch. Talk with a partner. Then write what you will do.

At a ranch, I will ______________________________

____

____

____

____

____

Name ___________________________________

Inflected Forms with *-ed, -ing, -es*

Phonics

A. Listen to the words. Read the words. Then say the words.

read	ride	fry	drag	cry
reading	riding	fried	dragged	cries

B. Write a word from the box to complete each sentence.

chased	tries	grazing	sipping

1. María _________ to lasso a calf.

2. The cattle spent time _________ on the pampas.

3. Susanita and María enjoyed _________ orange soda.

4. María _________ the horses into the corral.

C. Say the underlined words. Read the paragraph to a partner. Then listen as your partner reads it to you.

I wanted to live at the estancia all year. I liked to see the cattle grazing, and the gauchos riding and yelling. Susanita loved to gallop all day on her horse. At night, she spent her time reading and sipping tea. Sometimes she listened to the gauchos' stories.

The Storm

Pages 324–343

Crossing Cultures • In this lesson, students read about a boy who rides out a tornado in a barn with only horses for company. Have volunteers talk about the worst weather they ever experienced. Where were they? Was it a tornado, cyclone, drought, hurricane, or blizzard? How did they protect themselves?

PART 1

Preview the Skill Lesson

Use these activities with the Skill Lesson: "Summer Surfers," Teacher's Edition, *Scott Foresman Reading*, pages 324–325.

Activate Prior Knowledge

Show Adding English Poster 14 and have students identify what they see. Have students tell if they have ever been to the beach or seen people surfing. Encourage them to brainstorm words related to the beach. Use a web, Graphic Organizer Transparency 4, to record student responses.

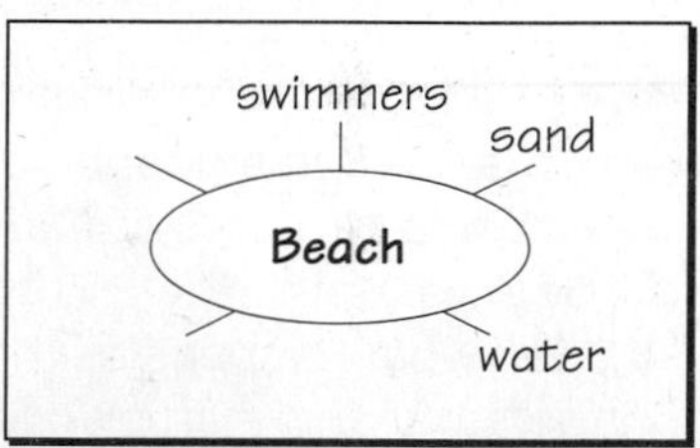

Transparency 4

Understand Words in Context

Introduce the Skill Lesson literature by previewing vocabulary at the right. List the vocabulary words on the board. Then read the following passage and pantomime the underlined words. Encourage students to imitate your gestures.

> As I stood on the <u>shore</u> of the sandy beach, I saw a huge <u>wave</u>! It looked like a wall of water. Suddenly, one <u>surfer</u> was standing on her <u>board</u>. She rode the <u>wave</u> alone, except for a large sea animal—a <u>seal</u>—that swam next to her. The wave <u>pushed</u> them both toward the <u>shore</u> with strength and speed.

Have students demonstrate comprehension of the words by pointing to the pictures on the poster. All students could benefit from reviewing this vocabulary before they begin reading the Skill Lesson selection.

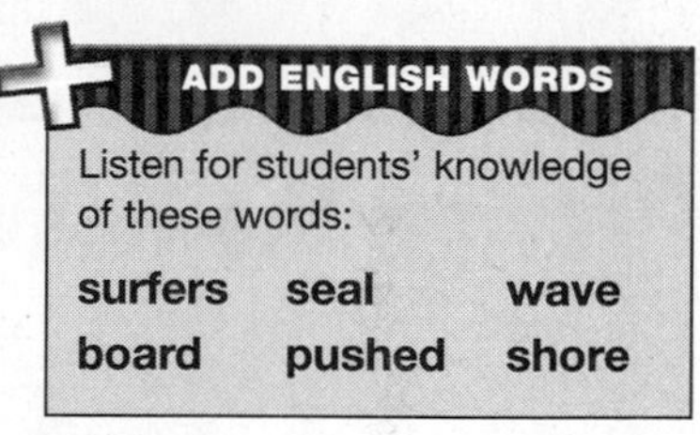
ADD ENGLISH WORDS

Listen for students' knowledge of these words:

surfers	seal	wave
board	pushed	shore

Present the Comprehension Strategy

Comprehension: Predicting

Use Comprehension Strategies, *Adding English Guide*, page 10, to introduce Predicting.

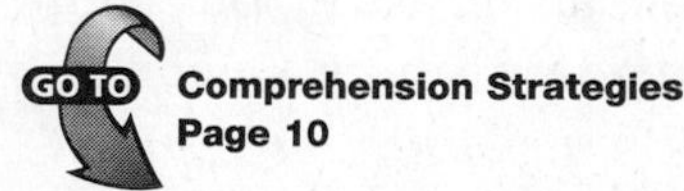

Relate to Personal Experience

Suggest familiar experiences, such as studying or not studying for a quiz, forgetting to set the alarm clock, practicing a sport, or seeing dark clouds in the sky. For each one, ask students to predict the result or what happens next.

Read

Guide students as they read "Summer Surfers," Scott Foresman Reading, *pages 324–325. Remind them to stop reading at the bottom of page 324 and try to predict what will happen to Ben in the rest of the story.*

Selection Audio CD 6/Tape 16

Practice

Have students tell the story to each other. Ask them to share the predictions they made about what would happen to Ben. Students can use the Adding English Poster for vocabulary support.

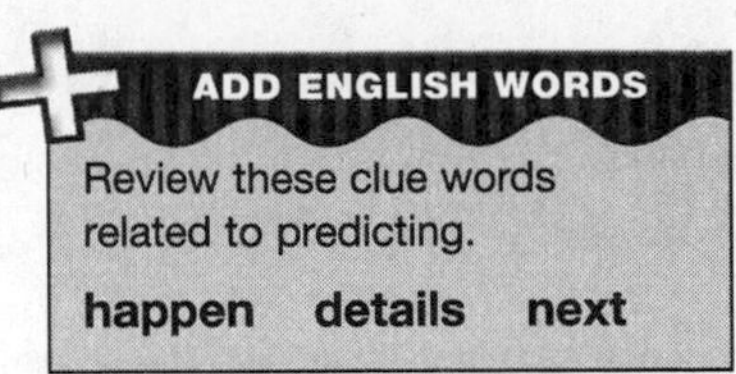

Assess

If... students were not able to make predictions about the story,

then... list a detail or picture description from the story on the board and have students recall what happened next in the story. Ask: *Could you predict that this would happen from this detail?* Repeat with other details and have students tell which helps them predict what happens next. Remind students to rely on past events in the story and their own knowledge when making predictions.

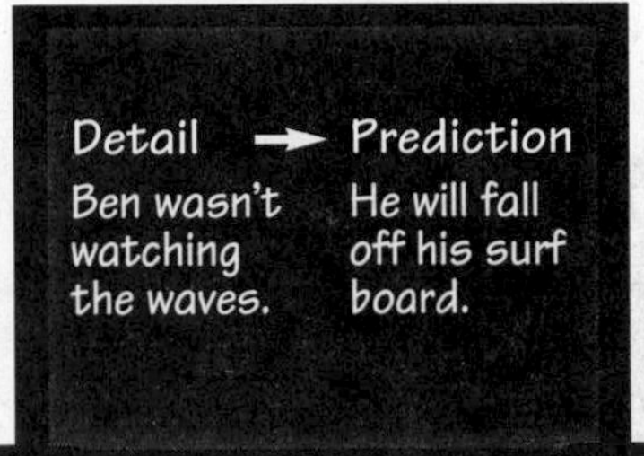

PART 2

Preview the Reading Selection

Use these activities before reading the selection *The Storm*, Teacher's Edition, *Scott Foresman Reading*, pages 326–340.

Activate Prior Knowledge

Point to the Adding English Poster and discuss the pictures depicting the words at the right. Encourage students to describe where the scenes take place. Have students share any knowledge of tornadoes or bad thunderstorms.

ADD ENGLISH WORDS

Listen for students' knowledge of words related to tornadoes.

thunderstorm **barn**
wind **funnel**
saved

Build Background

Display a weather map of the United States. Point to your state and mark it. Then point to Indiana and mark it. Talk about today's weather in your state and in Indiana. Ask: *Is it sunny, windy, warm, icy, rainy, or cold?* Write the weather words on the board.

Use Cause and Effect

Have students think about some of the effects caused by the weather. Record them on a cause and effect chart, Graphic Organizer Transparency 18. Students can use the Adding English Poster for ideas.

RESOURCES

Use *Scott Foresman ESL*, Grade 3, for additional instruction and activities.

- Chapter 8, "Weather and People"
- Video Unit 4, "Living Things Adapt"

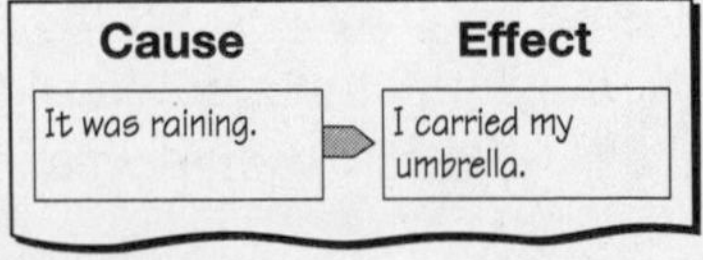

Transparency 18

Vocabulary: Antonyms

Use these activities with the Vocabulary Lesson and paragraph "In the Path of the Twister," Teacher's Edition, *Scott Foresman Reading*, page 326.

Write the vocabulary words for the selection on the board. Have students look for pictures of the words on the Adding English Poster. Explain that words that have opposite meanings are called antonyms. Give them some examples, such as: *up/down*, *right/left*. Challenge students to dramatize the opposite of the word *coaxed* (pushed away).

ADD ENGLISH WORDS

Through listening and watching, assess students' knowledge of selection vocabulary.

wail	**tornado**
accident	**coaxed**
soothing	**nuzzled**

Use Flash Cards

Ask students to make two-sided flash cards for the vocabulary words. On one side they can write the word, and on the other they can draw a picture depicting the word. Have volunteers hold up the picture side of a card. Encourage others in the class to say the word and then name an antonym if possible.

Read

Guide students as they read "In the Path of the Twister," Scott Foresman Reading*, page 326. Ask them how they can use antonyms to find the meaning of words they don't know.*

Students can participate in the Talk About It activity that follows. If possible, have English language learners work in groups with students whose home language is English to talk about Justin's feelings and actions during the storm.

Present the Reading Selection

Use these activities with *The Storm*, Teacher's Edition, *Scott Foresman Reading*, pages 326–340.

Preview Title and Illustrations

Explain the strategy: *When I begin to read, I look at the title and the pictures to get an idea of what the story will be about.* Encourage students to look at the title of the story and at the picture of Jonathan on page 327. Ask: *What does the picture tell you about Jonathan? What do you think will happen next?* Continue previewing the pictures. Then have students begin a story prediction from previewing chart, Graphic Organizer Transparency 1.

Title *The Storm*

Read the title and look at the pictures in the story. What do you think a problem in the story might be?

I think a problem might be *Jonathan gets caught in a tornado.*

Transparency 1

Strategy: Using a Story Prediction from Previewing Chart

Explain the strategy: *When I want to predict the problems in a story, I can use a chart. It is a strategy called Making Predictions from Previewing.* Be sure students understand that a problem is a question or issue that must be answered, and a solution is the answer. Model filling out the first part of the chart. Have students begin their own charts.

Develop Concepts

For this selection, students may need help in understanding that *The Storm* is realistic fiction. Help students understand that the story is based on a real weather event. As students read, pause to check whether they know which parts are factual.

Set Purposes

Students can participate in Set Purposes, Teacher's Edition, *Scott Foresman Reading*, page 327. Remind students that they are using a strategy called Making Predictions from Previewing.

Guide students as they read The Storm, Scott Foresman Reading, *pages 326–340. To support comprehension, use the suggestions in Meeting Individual Needs, ESL, in the Teacher's Edition.*

Response Log

- Have students draw Jonathan's farm as it looked before the storm and how it looked after the storm. Encourage students to refer to the Adding English Poster and the story illustrations for ideas and to write a descriptive sentence under each picture.
- Encourage students to imagine that they are one of Jonathan's horses. Have them write sentences describing how they feel when the storm hits.

Practice Selection Concepts

To help students tell what they learned, choose from these activities:

- Have students complete their story prediction from previewing charts by illustrating a problem from the story.
- Pair students and distribute the ten important sentences. Ask them to find sentences that help them predict problems in the story. Then have them look for sentences that tell about solutions to those problems.

ADD ENGLISH WORDS

Can students find titles of other stories like this one? Have them use this term as they search.

realistic fiction

Selection Audio CD 6/Tape 16

Title *The Storm*

Read the title and look at the pictures in the story. What do you think a problem in the story might be?

I think a problem might be *Jonathan gets caught in a tornado.*

After reading *The Storm*, draw a picture of one of the problems in the story.

Transparency 1

Ten Important Sentences Page 26

Strategy: Self-Assess

Ask: *Did Making Predictions from Previewing help you understand the story? How?*

Language Awareness

Provide supported practice by using the Adding English Grammar and Phonics Practice Masters, pages 127–128, with the suggestions below.

Grammar: Verb Tenses

Write the following sentences on the board:

The storm broke the trees at the farm.
Jonathan likes big storms.
Everyone will clean up tomorrow.

Talk about the meanings of past, present, and future. Point out that context clues help determine the correct verb tense in a sentence. Have students find the verb in each sentence and tell whether it is past, present, or future tense.

Students can complete the Practice Master individually or with a partner.

Adding English Grammar Practice Master Page 127

Phonics: Consonant Sounds /j/, /ks/, /kw/

Distribute the Practice Master. Have students listen, read, and repeat as you say the words in Exercise A. Then have students say the words aloud and use them in sentences. Write *large*, *coax*, and *square* on the board. Ask them to identify the sounds made by *g, x,* and *qu*. Divide the class into pairs. Encourage them to name other words with /j/, /ks/, and /kw/.

For Exercise B, have students read the riddles aloud before they choose an answer.

Adding English Phonics Practice Master Page 128

ADD ENGLISH WORDS

Students may have trouble pronouncing /j/, /ks/, and /kw/ in blends with other consonant sounds. Provide practice with these sounds in isolation using words such as the following:

jelly **fudge** **fix**
socks **quote** **quilt**

PART 3

Connect Selection Concepts

Use these activities with Reader Response, Teacher's Edition, *Scott Foresman Reading*, page 340.

Literature Discussion Group

If possible have English language learners work in groups with students whose home language is English to talk about *The Storm*, focusing on these questions:

- What did you like about the story?
- What did Jonathan do that you liked?
- What would you say if you met Jonathan?

Storm Stories

Ask students to think about another story they know about a storm, such as *The Wizard of Oz* or *Twister*. Have students tell the stories to each other. Then have groups compare and contrast one of the other stories with the main selection.

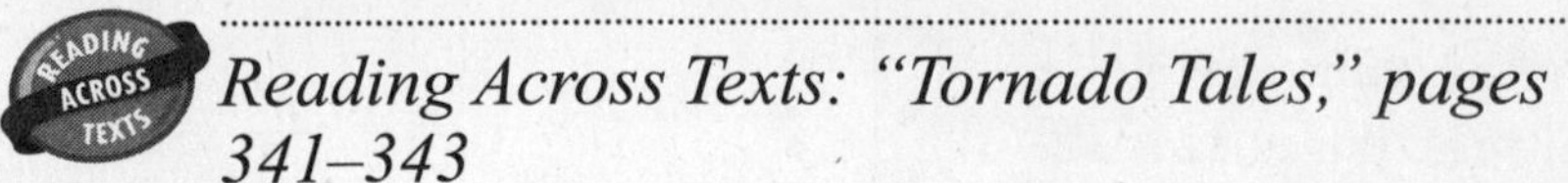

Reading Across Texts: "Tornado Tales," pages 341–343

To support students as they learn about and read an informational article:

- Activate prior knowledge by asking students to share their own "storm stories"—about storms they've experienced or heard about.
- Ask students to look at the title and illustrations and predict what the article will be about.
- Ask students to find the similarities and differences between *The Storm* and "Tornado Tales." Encourage them to use a Venn diagram, Graphic Organizer Transparency 21, to organize their findings.

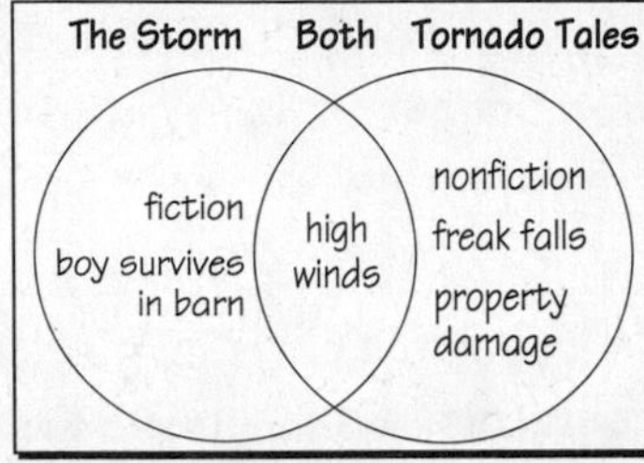

Transparency 21

Assess

Refer to the list below to assess students' progress.

Reading

- ☐ Uses words related to tornadoes and other storms.
- ☐ Makes predictions about events in a story.
- ☐ Distinguishes between realistic fiction and an informational article.

Language Awareness

Grammar

- ☐ Identifies and uses correct verb tenses.

Phonics

- ☐ Pronounces and decodes words with /j/, /ks/, and /kw/.

Learning Strategies

- ☐ Uses a story prediction from previewing chart.
- ☐ Uses antonyms to understand the meaning of unfamiliar words.

Name ______________________________

Grammar

Verb Tenses

A. Underline the verb in each sentence.

1. Jonathan rides the bus home every day.
2. Jonathan turned on the radio.
3. He heard a rumble of thunder.
4. The trees swayed in the wind.

B. Choose the word in parentheses that correctly completes each sentence.

5. Yesterday, Jonathan ________________ the snakelike tornado. (watched/watches)

6. He ________________ the animals. (save/saved)

7. The horses _________ the sugar cubes. (eat/eats)

8. After the storm, Jonathan ________________ proud. (feels/felt)

C. What was the weather like yesterday? Talk with a partner about it. Draw a picture of the weather. Then write a sentence to go with the picture.

Yesterday ______________________________

____

Name ______________________________

Phonics

Consonant Sounds /j/, /ks/, /kw/

A. Listen to the words. Read the words. Then say the words.

huge edge mix fox quick quiet

B. Choose a word to answer each riddle. Write it on the line.

queen	page	squirrel	box

1. You can put things inside me. What am I?

I am a ________________.

2. You will find me in every book. I usually have words and pictures. What am I?

I am a ________________.

3. I am small and have a fuzzy tail. I eat nuts. What am I?

I am a ________________.

4. My husband is the king. Who am I?

I am the ________________.

C. Complete the paragraph. Choose a word from the box that means the opposite of the word in parentheses. Read your paragraph to a partner.

fix	large	quiet	quickly

Many ____________ (small) clouds covered the sky. Thunder roared and lightning flashed. For one moment, all was ____________ (loud). When Jonathan saw the twister, he moved ____________ (slowly). After the storm, Jonathan's family would have to ____________ (break) all the damage.

Rikki-tikki-tavi

Pages 344–365

Crossing Cultures • In this lesson, students read a story about a mongoose who protects a British boy and his family from deadly snakes. Students from some cultural backgrounds may not be familiar with keeping animals as pets. Discuss how the treatment of Rikki-tikki compares to the treatment of animals in students' home cultures.

Preview the Skill Lesson

Use these activities with the Skill Lesson: "Another Death on the Ranch," Teacher's Edition, *Scott Foresman Reading,* pages 344–345.

Activate Prior Knowledge

Display Adding English Poster 15 and ask students to tell what they see. Ask: *What do you know about ranches and farms?* Encourage them to focus on the poster elements related to farms and animals. Use a three-column chart, Graphic Organizer Transparency 25, to describe farm animals.

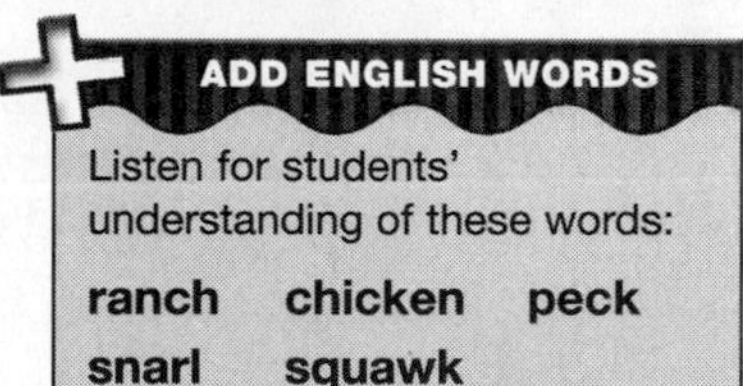

Animal	What sound they make	What they look like
chicken	squawk	covered with feathers

Transparency 25

Use Context Clues

Introduce the Skill Lesson literature by listing the words on the board. Explain the strategy: *When I read a word I don't know, I can look for other words before and after it to help me understand it.* Then read aloud the following paragraph.

> **Last night at the ranch I saw the shadow of a huge creature near the henhouse. I heard it snarl like a wild dog. Every chicken was too nervous to peck for food or make a sound. Not one squawk could be heard. I couldn't see the creature very clearly, and after I turned on the light, it ran into the woods.**

Have students show their comprehension of the underlined words by pointing to pictures on the Adding English Poster. Ask which context clues helped them understand the words. Then have students make a snarling noise. Ask them what kinds of animals snarl. Have students make a squawking noise. Ask them what animals squawk. All students could benefit from this vocabulary preview before they read the Skill Lesson selection.

ADD ENGLISH WORDS

Listen for students' understanding of these words:

ranch **chicken** **peck** **snarl** **squawk**

Present the Comprehension Strategy

Comprehension: Drawing Conclusions

Use Comprehension Strategies, *Adding English Guide,* page 10, to introduce Drawing Conclusions.

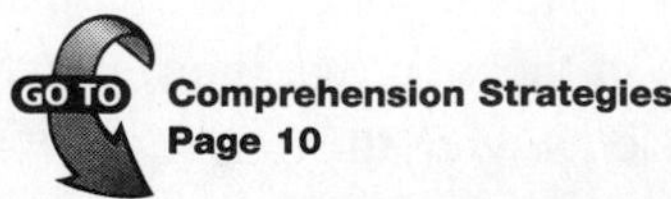

Relate to Personal Experience

Invite students to think about a time at home when something was missing or broken. Ask them to remember who they thought was responsible for the problem and why they thought so. Have students share these stories. Give an example: *I lost my pencil and thought my sister took it, but then I found it in my schoolbag.* Tell students they were drawing conclusions. Ask them to tell how they arrived at those conclusions. Were they right or wrong?

Guide students as they read "Another Death on the Ranch," Scott Foresman Reading, *pages 344–345. Remind them to look for details that can help them draw conclusions.*

Selection Audio CD 6/Tape 17

ADD ENGLISH WORDS

These idioms appear in "Another Day on the Ranch." Explain that these phrases have special meanings.

"He was too chicken" means "He was afraid."

"You put your life on the line" means "You are in danger."

Practice

Have the students draw conclusions about Hank the Cowdog. What is he like? What details in the story helped students decide? Students can use the Adding English Poster as a vocabulary aid.

Assess

If... students are not able to draw conclusions about Hank,

then... have them read the following statements. Help students look at the story to decide if each conclusion is valid.

- Hank is a hard-working dog with a sense of humor.
- The chickens appreciate Hank's detective work.
- The *Original Adventures of Hank the Cowdog* is a humorous book.

ADD ENGLISH WORDS

Review these clue words related to drawing conclusions.

details	**decisions**
characters	**events**

PART 2

Preview the Reading Selection

Use these activities before reading *Rikki-tikki-tavi,* Teacher's Edition, *Scott Foresman Reading,* pages 346–363.

Activate Prior Knowledge

Ask students to look at the parts of the Adding English Poster that depict the words at the right. Write the words on the board. Ask students what they might see in a garden. Record students' ideas on a web.

ADD ENGLISH WORDS

Listen for students' knowledge of the following words.

mongoose	**eggs**
saved	**hole**

Build Background

Display a world map and point to India, where the selection takes place. Encourage any students from India or neighboring countries to share information about climate and animal life. Show pictures of a mongoose and a cobra. Have students ever seen these animals? Ask what other animals a mongoose looks like. Then ask what other snakes students have seen or know about

Compare and Contrast

- Ask students to tell what pets they have. List the various pets on the board.
- Ask students to describe each pet's behavior. Write the responses on the board next to the name of the animal. Have students think about the behavior of snakes and their enemies. Have students use a Venn diagram, Graphic Organizer Transparency 21, to compare snakes with another animal they know well. Explain to students that they will read about a very loyal pet, a mongoose.

Vocabulary: Unfamiliar Words

Use these activities with the Vocabulary Lesson and paragraph "Brave Dog!," Teacher's Edition, *Scott Foresman Reading,* page 346.

Write sentences on the board using the vocabulary words. Underline the vocabulary words. Have students read the sentences aloud and then decide with a partner what they think each vocabulary word means. Have volunteers share their definitions with the class and point to other words in the sentence that helped them understand the vocabulary word. Students can refer to the Adding English Poster for support.

Use Pantomime

Let students take turns pantomiming the words for others to guess. Add props as needed, such as a rope to coil, or a trophy to hold up in triumph.

Guide students as they read "Brave Dog!," Scott Foresman Reading, *page 346. Ask them how they can use context clues to find the meaning of words they don't know.*

Students can participate in the Write About It activity that follows. If possible, have English language learners work with students whose home language is English to list important details about Topper's act of bravery.

RESOURCES

Use *Scott Foresman ESL,* Grade 3, for additional instruction and activities.

- Chapter 7, "Plants, Animals, and Climate"
- Video, Unit 4, "Living Things Adapt"

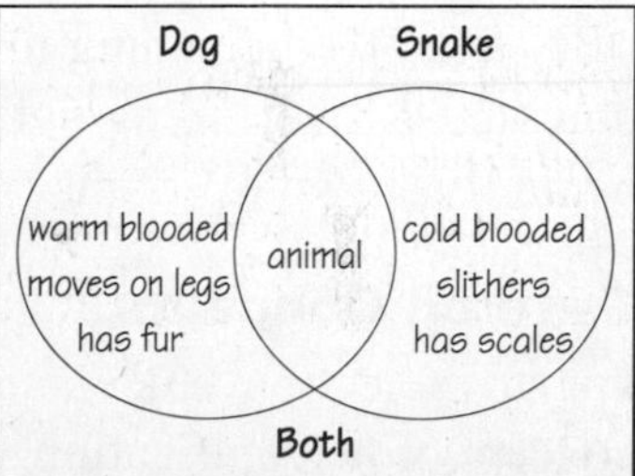

Transparency 21

ADD ENGLISH WORDS

Through listening and watching, assess students' knowledge of selection vocabulary.

cobra **coiled**
plunged **lame**
triumph

Present the Reading Selection

Use these activities with *Rikki-tikki-tavi,* Teacher's Edition, *Scott Foresman Reading,* pages 346–363.

Preview Illustrations

Explain the strategy: *Before I begin to read, I can look at the pictures in the story to get an idea of what the story will be about.* Invite students to look at the picture on pages 346–347. Ask: *What are the animals in the picture doing? What is in the background?* Continue previewing the pictures. Begin a plot structure diagram, Graphic Organizer Transparency 11, to organize information from previewing illustrations.

Strategy: Using a Plot Structure Diagram

Explain the strategy: *When I want to understand what happens in a story, I can use a strategy called Using a Plot Structure Diagram.* Be sure students understand that they will look at the story from the beginning to the turning point and then to the outcome. Model filling out the Title and Setting. Have students begin their own diagrams.

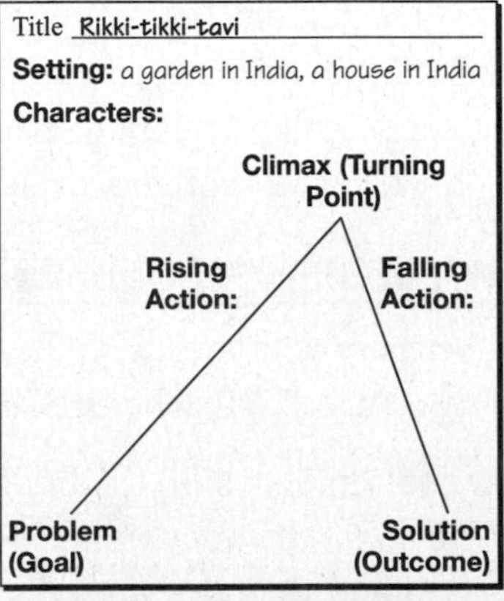

Transparency 11

Develop Concepts

For this selection, students may need help in understanding the concept of personification. Explain that writers sometimes give animals or things human qualities. Have students brainstorm some things people do, such as talk, think, and love. Review some of the humanlike things that Hank did in "Another Death at the Ranch." Reread the first paragraph. Ask students whether they think a dog can feel "a sense of responsibility."

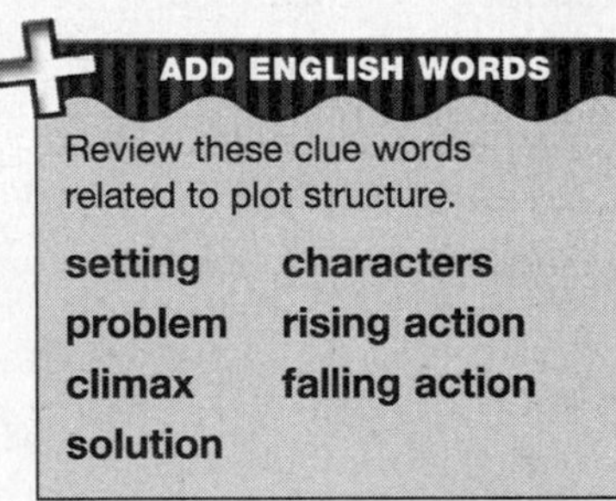

Set Purposes

Students can participate in Set Purposes, Teacher's Edition, Scott Foresman Reading, page 347. Encourage students to watch for the characters, rising action, problem, climax, falling action, and outcome as they read the story. Discuss the meaning of these terms from the plot structure diagram. Remind students that they are using a strategy called Using a Plot Structure Diagram.

Guide students as they read Rikki-tikki-tavi, Scott Foresman Reading, *pages 346–363. To support comprehension, use the suggestions in Meeting Individual Needs, ESL, in the Teacher's Edition.*

Selection Audio CD 6/Tape 17

Response Log

- Have students write sentences about their favorite animal from the story.
- Have students illustrate their favorite part of the story and write a caption to explain their picture.

Practice Selection Concepts

To help students tell what they learned, choose from these activities.

- Help students complete their plot structure diagrams. Let individuals share the Problem, Climax, and Solution with the class.
- Distribute the ten important sentences. Divide the class into two groups. Have Group A act out the first five sentences, with a narrator reading the sentences aloud. Group B can do the same with sentences 6–10.

Strategy: Self-Assess

Ask: *Did Using a Plot Structure Diagram help you understand the sequence of events in the story? What parts of the diagram were the most helpful? How?*

Language Awareness

Provide supported practice by using the Adding English Grammar and Phonics Practice Masters, pages 135–136, with the suggestions below.

Grammar: Review of Verbs

Write the following sentence on the board: *Rikki-tikki killed the snakes and saved the family.* Ask students to find verbs. Ask if they are in the past, present, or future. (past) Have students rewrite the sentence, changing the verbs to present and then future tense. Invite students to make up other sentences based on the story, using different verb tenses. Help students complete the Practice Master by reading sentences aloud slowly while they raise their hands when they hear a verb.

Phonics: Base Words

Write *quickly* on the board. Circle *quick* and say that it is the base word. Point out that new words can be made from base words using endings such as *-ed, -ing, -ly, -ness, -less,* and *-ful* or prefixes such as *un-* or *dis-*. Distribute the Practice Master. Have students listen, read, and repeat as you say the words in Exercise A. Ask students to use the words in sentences. For Exercise B, have students say the words aloud before answering.

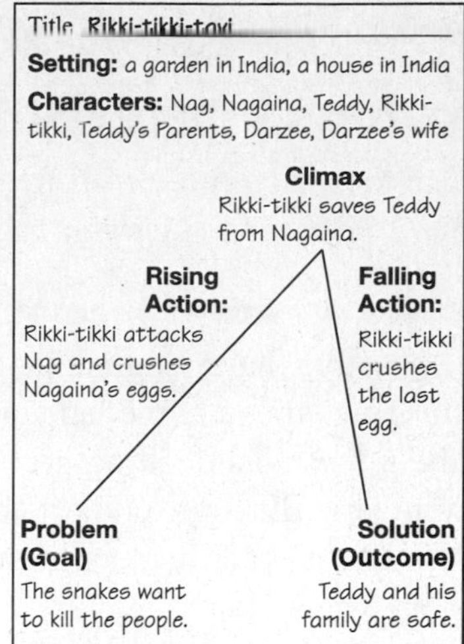

Transparency 11

Ten Important Sentences Page 27

Adding English Grammar Practice Master Page 135

Adding English Phonics Practice Master Page 136

Base Words, Endings

PART 3

Connect Selection Concepts

Use these activities with Reader Response, Teacher's Edition, *Scott Foresman Reading,* page 363.

Write an Advertisement for the Story

If possible, have English language learners work in groups with students whose home language is English. Ask them to think about the most exciting part of the story, the climax. Have them write and illustrate a short advertisement highlighting the climax, to interest other readers in the story. Encourage them to use story vocabulary.

Connect with the Story

Ask students to imagine they are Teddy. Would they like living in his house? How would they protect themselves from snakes and other creatures? Have them discuss their ideas in groups.

Reading Across Texts: "The Deadly Cobra," pages 364–365

To support students as they read a picture encyclopedia:

- Have students preview "The Deadly Cobra" by looking at the pictures and reading a few words from each caption. Explain that this selection can be read in any order. Read the introduction with students.
- Ask: *What kind of information about cobras does this article provide? How does this kind of article help you better understand the fear of cobras in* Rikki-tikki-tavi? Students can chart the information they learn about cobras in this article and compare it to information about cobras in *Rikki-tikki-tavi*.

Assess

Refer to the list below to assess students' progress.

Reading

- ☐ Uses words related to farm animals and wild animals.
- ☐ Draws conclusions about characters and events in a story.
- ☐ Understands the concept of personification.

Language Awareness

Grammar

- ☐ Identifies and uses present-, past-, and future-tense verbs.

Phonics

- ☐ Pronounces and decodes new words by looking at base words.

Learning Strategies

- ☐ Uses a plot structure diagram to understand the sequence of events in a story.
- ☐ Uses context clues to find the meaning of unfamiliar words.

Name ________________________________

Review of Verbs

A. Draw a box around the verb in each sentence.

1. The snake plunged into the river.

2. It rushed into the tall grass.

3. Snakes strike at their enemies.

4. The mongoose will smash the snake's eggs.

B. Choose a verb from the box to complete each sentence.

barked	slither	will break

5. I am a snake. I don't have legs to walk, so I

_______________ across the ground.

6. I am a mongoose. If I see a snake's eggs,

I _______________ them.

7. I am a dog. I saw a cat run by.

I _______________ at it.

C. Think about how Rikki-tikki saved the family. Talk with a partner. Then write from Rikki-tikki's point of view about how to protect people.

To protect people you need to ____________________

____

____

____

____

Name ______________________

Base Words

A. Listen to the words. Read the words. Then say the words.

winning   unzip   coiled   jumped   licking

B. Match the base word in the first column with the new word in the second column.

1. quick	**a.** unlock
2. play	**b.** quickly
3. lock	**c.** sensible
4. sense	**d.** playful
5. hide	**e.** frightened
6. forget	**f.** tingled
7. frighten	**g.** hiding
8. tingle	**h.** forgetful

C. Say the underlined words. Read the paragraph to a partner. Then listen as your partner reads it to you.

A rattlesnake was coiled on a rock, sunning itself in the afternoon. Suddenly an eagle flew above the rattler. It spied the snake slithering quickly into the tall grass. In an instant the bird swooped down, caught the snake, and carried it away.

Half-Chicken

Pages 376–393

Crossing Cultures • In this lesson, students read folktales that explain why some things are the way they are. Provide aid with dialect that is specific to certain cultures, such as *Bruh* (brother) and *Sis* (sister). Invite volunteers to tell folktales from their home cultures.

PART 1

Preview the Skill Lesson

Use these activities with the Skill Lesson: "Blue Jay Takes the Heat," Teacher's Edition, *Scott Foresman Reading,* pages 376–377.

GO TO Poster Tips Page 16

Activate Prior Knowledge

Invite students to tell what they know about birds. Then ask students to identify the birds they see in Adding English Poster 16 and describe what they are doing. Allow students to use their home language as necessary. Brainstorm a list of vocabulary related to birds: *beak, wings, feathers, nest, fly,* and so on. Have students draw pictures of birds, then label them and write captions using the vocabulary words.

Use Total Physical Response

Introduce the Skill Lesson literature by previewing the vocabulary at right. Write the vocabulary words on the board. Have students point to parts of the poster that relate to the vocabulary. As you read the passage that follows, have students follow the directions and act out each underlined word. Model by pantomiming how to cook a chicken over an open fire.

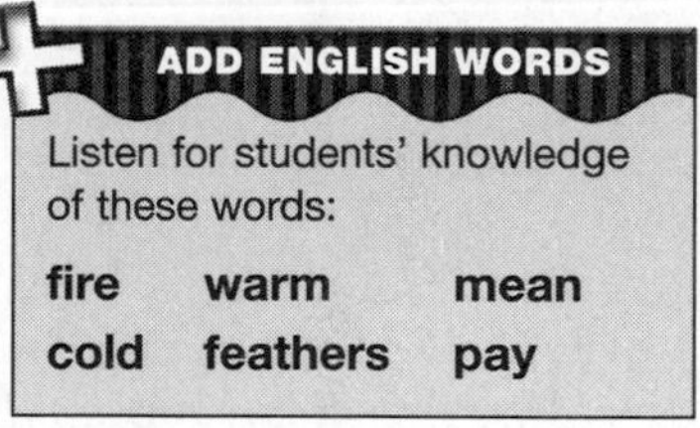

> First we have to buy a chicken. A farmer will sell us a chicken, so let's pay him some money. Then we have to take off all the feathers. Let's do that together. Don't be mean and make me do all the work! We'll cook the chicken outdoors over a fire. Don't step too close to the fire—it's hot! Are you cold or warm? Show me how we look when we're cold. Brrr! Show me how we look when we're warm. Put the chicken on the fire to cook. Soon we can eat!

Guide students to act out the meaning of each word. Allow students to use the Adding English Poster for support. Other students in the class may benefit from this strategy.

Present the Comprehension Strategy

Comprehension: Paraphrasing

Use Comprehension Strategies, *Adding English Guide,* page 10, to introduce Paraphrasing.

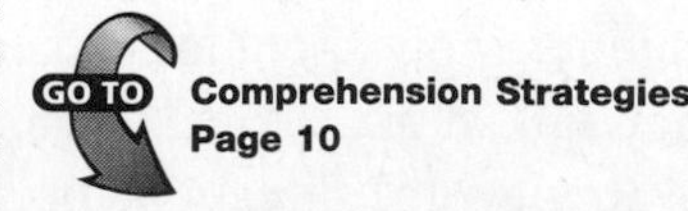
GO TO Comprehension Strategies Page 10

Relate to Personal Experience

Have students bring in a set of English directions for playing a board game, preparing a favorite food, or doing some other activity that they know how to do. In groups, students can explain the process in their own words. Ask students whether they generally prefer to read the directions for a new game or activity themselves or to listen to someone's paraphrase of the directions.

Guide students as they read "Blue Jay Takes the Heat," Scott Foresman Reading, *pages 376–377. Remind them to think about how they could retell the story in their own words.*

Selection Audio CD 7/Tape 19

Practice

Have students paraphrase passages in "Blue Jay Takes the Heat." Encourage them to use the Adding English Poster for support.

Assess

If... students are not able to paraphrase parts of the story,

then... have them decide which of the following best paraphrases the second paragraph.

- Alcee Lingo feels sorry for Bruh Blue Jay since he is very cold.
- Alcee Lingo is very cold because he does not have any feathers. Bruh Blue Jay feels sorry for Alcee Lingo.
- Sis Blue Jay gets some feathers for Bruh Blue Jay. That's because Bruh Blue Jay is very cold.

ADD ENGLISH WORDS

Review these clue words related to paraphrasing:

explain **meaning**
own words

PART 2

Preview the Reading Selection

Use these activities before reading the selection "Half-Chicken," Teacher's Edition, *Scott Foresman Reading,* pages 378–391.

Activate Prior Knowledge

Ask students to point to the parts of the Adding English Poster that picture the words at the right. Ask where hens, chicks, roosters, and weather vanes are usually found. Discuss what the students know about animals and activities on a ranch or farm. Then talk about weather vanes: what they look like and what they do. Review the directions north, south, east, and west.

ADD ENGLISH WORDS

Listen for students' knowledge of the following words related to farm or ranch life:

vane **rooster** **wind**
hen **chicks**

Build Background

Display various stuffed or toy animals, or cutouts of photographs including a hen, rooster, and chicks. Also display a weather vane or a picture of one. Have the class study the Adding English Poster and explain how they could use these items to model the actions it shows. Then have students act out the scenes they see on the poster, using some or all of the props. Encourage students to use the vocabulary words as they act out the scenes.

RESOURCES

Use *Scott Foresman ESL,* Grade 3, for additional instruction and activities.

- Chapter 1, "The Farm and the City"
- Video, Unit 1, "The Farm and the City"

Ask Questions

Have volunteers describe what they see in the Adding English Poster and name some of the items that relate to animals. Have students generate a list of questions about the poster. Guide students to ask questions about the animals and activities shown, using the vocabulary words. Write the questions on the board and let pairs choose questions to ask each other and try to answer.

Vocabulary: Synonyms

Use these activities with the Vocabulary Lesson and paragraph: "A Fresh Start," Teacher's Edition, *Scott Foresman Reading,* page 378.

Write the vocabulary words at right on the board. Distribute index cards with these synonyms written on them: *good-byes, knotted, special matching outfits, proud, advised, threw.* Have students match each word to its synonym. Have students look for illustrations of the words on the Adding English Poster.

ADD ENGLISH WORDS

Through listening and watching, assess students' knowledge of selection vocabulary.

farewells	**tangled**
uniforms	**vain**
suggested	**flung**

Use Personalization

Help students relate the vocabulary words to familiar situations. For example:

- Write *farewells* on the board and have students wave good-bye. Students can tell about a time they bid farewell to a friend or relative.
- Repeat with the other words by having students relate each one to their own experiences.

Guide students as they read "A Fresh Start," Scott Foresman Reading, *page 378. Ask how they can use synonyms to understand unfamiliar words.*

Students can participate in the Write About It activity that follows. If possible, have English language learners work in groups with students whose home language is English to discuss moving to a new neighborhood or school. Then have students draw some aspect of the move and label each part of the picture.

Present the Reading Selection

Use these activities with *Half-Chicken,* Teacher's Edition, *Scott Foresman Reading,* pages 378–391.

Preview Title and Illustrations

Explain the strategy: *Before I read, I look at the title and pictures to get an idea of what the story will be about.* Have students read the title and look at the picture on pages 378–379. Ask: *What do you see in the picture? What do you think the title means?* Continue previewing the pictures. Have students begin a story prediction from previewing chart, Graphic Organizer Transparency 1.

Title Half-Chicken

Read the title and look at the pictures in the story. What do you think a problem in the story might be?

I think a problem might be some-one tries to cook the half-chicken.

Transparency 1

Strategy: Making Predictions from Previewing

Explain the strategy: *When I want to predict the problems in a story, I can use a chart. It is a strategy called Making Predictions from Previewing.* Be sure that students understand that a *problem* is a question or issue that has to be answered, and a *solution* is the answer. Model filling out the first part of the chart. Then have students begin their own charts.

Develop Concepts

Students may need support in understanding that the story is a folktale passed down through the generations. It contains elements of both fact and fantasy. Have students read the title. Then ask: *Can a half-chicken be alive? What parts of the story might be real? What parts of the story might be make-believe?* Help students understand real and make believe by posing situations. Students can identify them as fact or fiction.

Chickens can hop. (real, fact)

Chickens can talk. (make believe, fiction)

Encourage students to share other stories they know that feature animals with human abilities, such as the Chinese "Lon Po Po" and the American "Three Little Pigs."

Help students with the following terms:

real	**make-believe**
fact	**fiction**

Set Purposes

Students can participate in Set Purposes, Teacher's Edition, *Scott Foresman Reading,* page 379. Let volunteers read aloud the problems they predicted on their story prediction from previewing charts. Remind students that they are using a strategy called Making Predictions from Previewing. Encourage students to watch for problems as they read the story.

Guide students as they read "Half-Chicken," Scott Foresman Reading, *pages 378–391. To support comprehension, use the suggestions in Meeting Individual Needs, ESL, in the Teacher's Edition.*

Selection Audio CD 7/Tape 19

Response Log

- Have students write a short thank-you letter from Half-Chicken to the water, fire, or wind. Students can refer to the Adding English Poster for support and draw pictures to help express their ideas.
- Ask students to list ways that Half-Chicken is different from other animals in real life and in the story. Have students draw Half-Chicken and label each part to show how he is special.

Practice Selection Concepts

To help students tell what they learned, choose from these activities.

- Have students illustrate a problem from the story to complete their story prediction from previewing charts.
- Have partners read the ten important sentences aloud and then take turns paraphrasing he last four sentences.

Strategy: Self-Assess

Ask: *Did Making Predictions from Previewing help you understand the story?* Let volunteers show the pictures they drew on their charts. Discuss the solutions to the problems in the story.

Graphic Organizer 10

Ten Important Sentences Page 30

Language Awareness

Provide supported practice by using the Adding English Grammar and Phonics Practice Masters, pages 143–144, with the suggestions below.

Grammar: Adjectives

Write the following sentences on the board: *The rooster crowed. The mean rooster crowed.* Read each sentence aloud. Ask: *How are these sentences the same? How are they different?* Guide students to see that the second sentence contains the adjective *mean*. Explain that an *adjective* is a word that describes a noun or a pronoun. Have students find the noun that *mean* describes. *(rooster)*. Write other sentences with adjectives on the board. Have volunteers identify the adjectives and find the nouns or pronouns they describe.

Students can complete the Practice Master alone or with a partner.

Adding English Grammar Practice Master Page 143

Base Words, Endings

Phonics: Inflected Forms with *-es*

Distribute the Practice Master. Have students listen, read, and repeat as you say the words in Exercise A. Then ask students to read the words aloud themselves. Ask questions such as *How do you spell one box? How do you spell more than one box? If two people reach up high, what does one person do?*

For Exercise B, have students read each sentence aloud before writing the answer.

Adding English Phonics Practice Master Page 144

PART 3

Connect Selection Concepts

Use these activities with Reader Response, Teacher's Edition, *Scott Foresman Reading,* page 391.

Literature Discussion Group

If possible, have English language learners to work in small groups with students whose home language is English. Together they should talk about *Half-Chicken,* focusing on the following:

- What does Half-Chicken look like?
- How does Half-Chicken react to all the attention he gets?
- What happens to Half-Chicken on his way to Mexico City?
- How does Half-Chicken get out of the soup pot?
- What happens to Half-Chicken at the end of the story?

You're So Vane!

Have students draw their own weather vanes, with any animal they select as the top. Encourage students to choose an animal known for a specific trait, such as a wise owl, a stubborn donkey, a slow turtle, a fast rabbit, a sly fox and so on. After students draw their weather vanes, have them write sentences explaining how this animal came to be a weather vane.

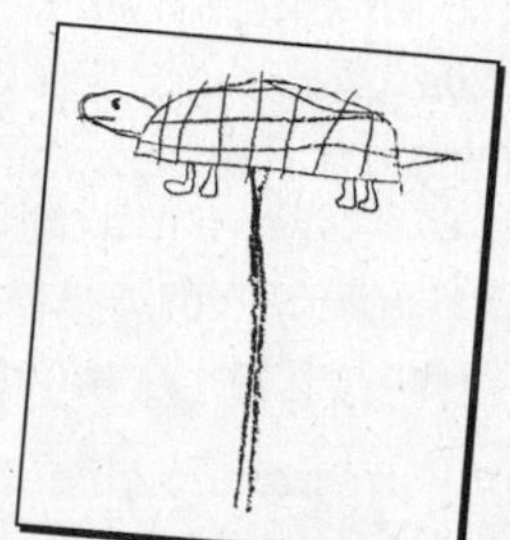

Reading Across Texts: "Chicken Farming," pages 392–393

To support students as they read a picture encyclopedia:

- Have students preview "Chicken Farming" by looking at the pictures and reading a few words from each caption.
- Explain that this selection can be read in any order. Read the introduction with students. Have students look at the pictures and read the captions. After reading, ask: *How is the information about chickens in this article different from a folktale about a chicken?*

Assess

Refer to the list below to assess students' progress.

Reading

- ☐ Uses words related to folk tales.
- ☐ Uses words related to birds.
- ☐ Paraphrases text.
- ☐ Previews title and illustrations to predict a story's events.

Language Awareness

Grammar

- ☐ Identifies and uses adjectives.

Phonics

- ☐ Pronounces and recognizes inflected forms with *-es.*
- ☐ Adds *-es* to words ending in *sh, ch, s, ss,* and *x.*

Learning Strategies

- ☐ Uses a Story Prediction from Previewing Chart.
- ☐ Uses synonyms to learn and remember unfamiliar vocabulary.

Name ____________________________________

Adjectives

A. Circle the adjective in each sentence.

1. The cold wind blew.

2. The mean bull charged.

B. Choose an adjective to complete each sentence. Write it on the line.

3. Look at the __________ string. (chicks/tangled)

4. The guards wear __________ uniforms. (red/rooster)

5. There are __________ chicks. (wind/five)

6. The __________ hen is here. (mean/flung)

7. The __________ fire feels good. (feathers/warm)

8. The __________ rooster crowed. (farewells/vain)

C. Imagine that you are a farm animal. Where would you go if you left the farm? Talk with a partner. Then write two sentences that tell where you would go and what would happen.

If I left the farm, I'd go to ____________________

____

____

____

____

____

____

Name ______________________________

Phonics

Inflected Forms with -es

A. Listen to the words. Read each word. Then say each word.

dishes reaches buses passes boxes

B. Add *-es* to the word in parentheses. Write the new word to complete each sentence.

1. The stream was blocked by __________ (branch).
2. The viceroy blew __________ (kiss) to his subjects.
3. We washed the __________ (dish) after dinner.
4. Did Half-Chicken meet any __________ (fox)?
5. Five __________ (bus) took the children to the palace.

C. Say the underlined words. Read the poem to a partner. Then listen as your partner reads it to you.

When we wash the dishes,
We think about wishes.
We wonder just what can come true.
We wish for big boxes,
All filled with toy foxes.
I would like to see that. Wouldn't you?

Blame It on the Wolf

Pages 394–419

Crossing Cultures • In this lesson, students read a play that contains characters and plots from traditional European fairy tales, centering on the wolf's reputation as a villain. Since students may not know these fairy tales, you may want to sketch the plots of "The Three Little Pigs" and "Little Red Riding Hood." Invite volunteers to tell fairy tales from their home cultures.

PART 1

Preview the Skill Lesson

Use these activities with the Skill Lesson: "Wolves," Teacher's Edition, *Scott Foresman Reading,* pages 394–395.

Activate Prior Knowledge

Invite volunteers to share what they know about Adding English Poster 17. Talk about the wolves shown. Have students brainstorm a list of words that describe wolves. Use a web, Graphic Organizer Transparency 5, to record students' responses.

Poster Tips Page 16

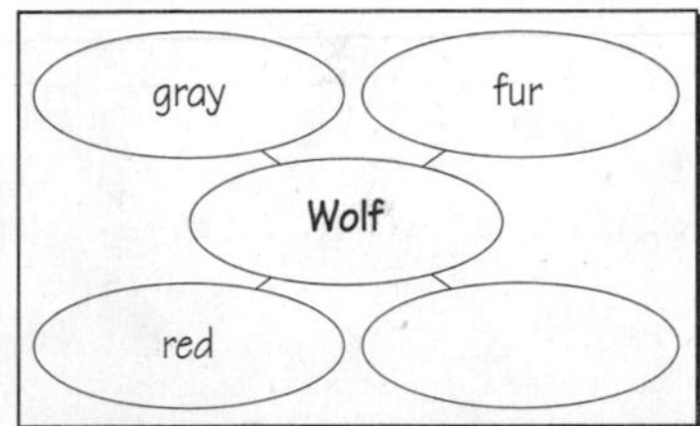

Transparency 5

Use Context Clues

Introduce the Skill Lesson literature by previewing the vocabulary at right. Write the vocabulary words on the board. Have students point out pictures of the vocabulary words on the Adding English Poster. As you read the following paragraph, have students listen for the vocabulary words. Explain the strategy: *When I hear a word I don't know, I listen for other words I know to help me figure out the meaning.*

> **In the mountains, we see a wolf. "The wolf looks like a dog!" Luis says, "but I know it is a wild animal." A group of wolves, at least ten of them, run across the snow. They have thick, soft hair called fur. Some of the wolves are red like fire, and others are gray like storm clouds. The wolves are so slender that they can fit in small places. If they eat more food, they will not be as skinny.**

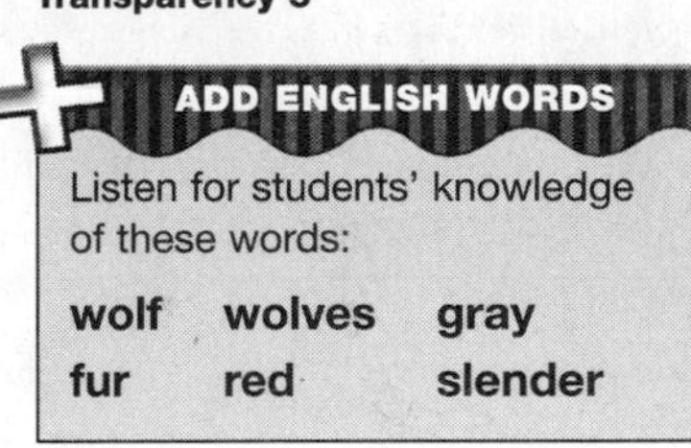

ADD ENGLISH WORDS

Listen for students' knowledge of these words:

wolf	**wolves**	**gray**
fur	**red**	**slender**

Write the context clues from the paragraph on the board and have students match them with the vocabulary words. Other students in the class may also benefit from reviewing this vocabulary before reading "Wolves."

Present the Comprehension Strategy

Comprehension: Compare and Contrast

Use Comprehension Strategies, *Adding English Guide,* page 10, to introduce Compare and Contrast.

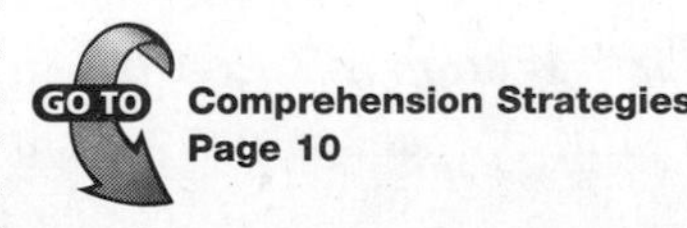

Comprehension Strategies Page 10

Relate to Personal Experience

Have students think about how school is the same as home and how it is different. In groups, students can list some of the differences and similarities in their own words. Then have students fold a piece of paper in half. On the left, they can draw a picture of eating lunch at home. On the right, they can draw a picture of eating lunch at school. Have students explain how the two meals are similar and different because of their setting.

Guide students as they read "Wolves," Scott Foresman Reading, *pages 394–395. Remind them to think about how gray wolves and red wolves are the same as and different from each other.*

Selection Audio CD 7/Tape 19

ADD ENGLISH WORDS

Review these clue words related to comparing and contrasting:

similarities **differences**
alike **different**

Practice

Have students compare and contrast gray wolves and red wolves. Encourage students to use the Adding English Poster for help in showing the similarities and differences between these two types of wolves.

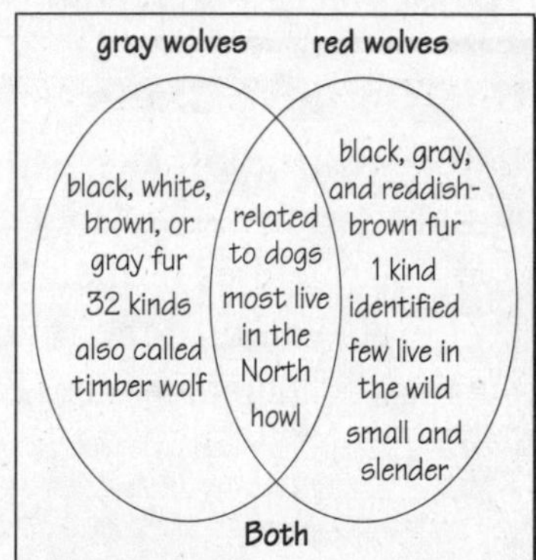

Transparency 21

Assess

If... students are not able to compare and contrast gray wolves and red wolves,

then... help them show the similarities and differences on a Venn diagram, Graphic Organizer Transparency 21.

PART 2

Preview the Reading Selection

Use these activities before reading the selection *Blame It on the Wolf,* Teacher's Edition, *Scott Foresman Reading,* pages 396–417.

Activate Prior Knowledge

Ask students to point to the parts of the Adding English Poster that picture the words at the right. Direct their attention to the courtroom setting, including the stage and judge. Ask students what they think a court is like, based on what they see in the poster and on what they already know. Ask: *What happens in a court? Who is in a courtroom?* Begin a K-W-L chart, Graphic Organizer Transparency 7, about courts and trials.

ADD ENGLISH WORDS

Listen for students' understanding of the following words related to a courtroom trial:

judge **jury** **stage**
verdict **trial** **twin**

Strategy: Using a K-W-L Chart

Explain the strategy: *When I want to learn new facts, I can use a chart. It is a strategy called Using a K-W-L* Chart. Point out what each letter means and model filling out the K column. Have students begin their own charts.

K What I Know	W What I Want to Know	L What I Learned
A judge is in charge of the courtroom.		

Transparency 7

RESOURCES

Use *Scott Foresman ESL*, Grade 5, for additional instruction and activities.

- Chapter 10, "What Makes a Good Story?"
- Video, Unit 5, "Reading Fun"

Build Background

Display photographs of scenes from plays. Explain how a play is different from a movie. The actors and actresses perform on a stage in front of an audience. They wear costumes and there is scenery, but it all takes place in this small area. The audience uses imagination to picture in their minds things that aren't shown.

Practice New Words

Ask students to brainstorm ways they can learn new words, such as listening to the word, drawing pictures of the word, looking at the word, saying the word silently, saying it out loud, and writing it. Partners can use these methods to practice the vocabulary words. Encourage students to point at the appropriate images on the Adding English Poster as they say and write the words.

Vocabulary: Context Clues

Use these activities with the Vocabulary Lesson and paragraph: "Live News Report," Teacher's Edition, *Scott Foresman Reading,* page 396.

Create a question-and-answer dialogue that uses each vocabulary word in context. For example: *If the defendant is found* guilty *in court, will he have to go to jail? What does* guilty *mean? We sat in the* courtroom. *The judge sat in front, facing us. What does* courtroom *mean?* Students can point to an illustration of each word on the Adding English Poster as they answer the questions.

ADD ENGLISH WORDS

Observe students and listen to their responses to assess their comprehension of selection vocabulary.

character **courtroom**
guilty **evidence**
rescued

Use Synonyms

Write the word *rescued* on one side of an index card. On the other side, write the synonym *saved*. Explain that we can often figure out what a word means by knowing other words with the same meaning—synonyms. Continue with the following words and their synonyms: *character (person), evidence (proof),* and *guilty (wrong).*

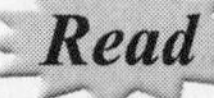

Guide students as they read "Live News Report," Scott Foresman Reading, *page 396. Ask how they can use synonyms to find the meanings of new words.*

Students can participate in the Talk About It activity that follows. First have English language learners work in groups with students whose home language is English to retell the story of Goldilocks.

Present the Reading Selection

Use these activities with *Blame It on the Wolf,* Teacher's Edition, *Scott Foresman Reading,* pages 396–417.

Preview Illustrations

Explain the strategy: *When I start to read, I first look at the pictures to get an idea of what the story will be about.* Have students look at the pictures on pages 396–397 and 399. Ask: *Where do you think the story takes place? What is the wolf doing?* Continue previewing the pictures.

Develop Concepts

Support students' understanding of the selection by reminding them that the wolf is often the villain or "bad guy" in Western fairy tales and folktales. Talk about reasons why some people fear wolves, such as the creature's fierce appearance and scary howl.

Students also may need help following the format of a play. Go over the cast and setting on page 398 together. Point out the scene numbers, stage directions, and characters' names in the body of the play. Make sure students understand that the characters' names tell who is talking.

Set Purposes

Students can participate in Set Purposes, Teacher's Edition, *Scott Foresman Reading,* page 397. Help students fill in the W column on their K-W-L charts about courts and trials. Remind students that they are using a strategy called Using a K-W-L Chart.

Guide students as they read "Blame It on the Wolf," Scott Foresman Reading, *pages 396–417. To support comprehension, use the suggestions in Meeting Individual Needs, ESL, in the Teacher's Edition.*

Response Log

- Have students write their opinion of the ending of the play. Did it change their opinion about the wolf? If so, how? Students can use the poster to recall courtroom-related vocabulary.
- Ask students to list other animals that have a reputation for causing trouble, such as cats that scratch furniture and snakes that frighten people. Students can draw captioned cartoons to portray mischievous or destructive animals.

ADD ENGLISH WORDS

Help students with the following terms:

hero **villain**
play **cast**
setting **scene**
stage directions

K What I Know	W What I Want to Know	L What I Learned
A judge is in charge of the courtroom.	What does a jury do?	

Transparency 7

Selection Audio CD 7/Tape 20

Practice Selection Concepts

To help students tell what they learned, choose from these activities.

- Help students complete the L column in their K-W-L charts about courts and trials.
- Students can use the ten important sentences as the basis for a skit about the wolf's trial. They can select parts, including the Wolf, Judge, Hansel, Little Red, Old Red, and Auntie Pot Pie. The group can present its skit to the class.

Strategy: Self-Assess

Ask: *Did Using a K-W-L Chart help you learn more about courts and trials?* Have students explain what they liked about the strategy.

K What I Know	W What I Want to Know	L What I Learned
A judge is in charge of the courtroom.	What does a jury do?	A jury decides if the defendant is guilty or not.

Transparency 7

Ten Important Sentences
Page 31

Language Awareness

Provide supported practice by using the Adding English Grammar and Phonics Practice Masters, pages 151–152, with the suggestions below.

Grammar: Using Adjectives to Improve Sentences

Write the following pair of sentences on the board: *The wolf howled. The slender, red wolf howled.* Read each sentence aloud. Ask: *How are these sentences the same? How are they different?* Guide students to see that both sentences are about a wolf, but the second sentence contains the adjectives *slender* and *red*. Explain that an adjective is a word that describes a noun or a pronoun. Discuss how writers improve their sentences by adding adjectives that tell more about the nouns and pronouns. Talk about how the second sentence is more interesting than the first one because the adjectives help readers get a better picture of the wolf.

Write other sentences on the board. Have volunteers add adjectives to each sentence.

Students can complete the Practice Master alone or with a partner.

Adding English
Grammar Practice Master
Page 151

Phonics: Contractions

Distribute the Practice Master. Have students listen, read, and repeat as you say the words in Exercise A. Then ask students to read the words aloud themselves. Explain that a contraction is a word created by combining two words and removing one or more letters. The removed letters are replaced by an apostrophe. Write an example on the board: *they are = they're.*

For Exercise B, have students read the sentences aloud before they write the contraction.

Adding English
Phonics Practice Master
Page 152

PART 3

Connect Selection Concepts

Use these activities with Reader Response, Teacher's Edition, *Scott Foresman Reading,* page 417.

Write a News Broadcast

If possible, have English language learners to work in small groups with students whose home language is English. Have each group write and deliver a television news broadcast about *Blame It on the Wolf.* Use these prompts to get students started:

- What evidence did the Three Little Pigs provide?
- What did Hansel and Gretel report to the court?
- What was Chicken Little's story?
- How did the jury find out that the wolf didn't eat Old Red?

Spin City

Blame it On the Wolf draws on the wolf's traditional identification with evil. Invite students to list animals that appear in other stories, such as the mongoose, snake, and panda. Have students sort the animals according to their reputations as good or bad creatures. Then ask each student to select one creature and explain how it is regarded and why. Students can draw a picture of the animal to use as a visual as they deliver their explanation.

Reading Across Texts: "What Is the Supreme Court?" pages 418–419

To support students as they read an informational article:

- Have students preview the article. What do students already know about the Supreme Court? What kind of information do they think this article will provide?
- Have students take notes as directed on page 418. Help students generate the questions they want to have answered before they take their notes.
- Compare "What Is the Supreme Court?" to *Blame It on the Wolf.* How are these two selections related?

Assess

Refer to the list below to assess students' progress.

Reading

- ☐ Uses words related to wolves.
- ☐ Uses words related to courts and trials.
- ☐ Uses words related to plays.
- ☐ Compares and contrasts two people, settings, or ideas.

Language Awareness

Grammar

- ☐ Uses adjectives to improve sentences.

Phonics

- ☐ Pronounces contractions and identifies the words from which they are formed.

Learning Strategies

- ☐ Uses a K-W-L Chart.
- ☐ Uses context clues to learn unfamiliar vocabulary.

Name ______________________________

Using Adjectives to Improve Sentences

A. Underline the adjective in each sentence.

1. The wolves walked on the snowy trail.

2. The gray wolves played in the snow.

B. Choose an adjective to complete each sentence.

3. The __________ wolf was the color of storm clouds. (gray/brick)

4. The __________ sky looked like fire. (slender/red)

5. The __________ snow covered the house. (green/thick)

6. The pigs lived in a __________ house. (brick/bread)

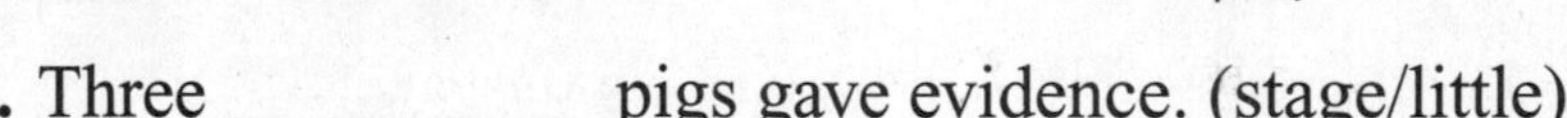

7. Three __________ pigs gave evidence. (stage/little)

C. Choose an adjective from the box to describe each character or pair of characters.

afraid	evil	hungry	innocent

Hansel and Gretel: ____________________

Chicken Little: ____________________

Auntie Pot Pie: ____________________

Wolf: ____________________

Name ______________________________

Contractions

A. Listen to the words. Read each word. Then say each word.

I'm

don't

she's

he's

they're

B. Read each sentence. Then make a new sentence. Use a contraction from the box for the underlined words.

isn't	can't	didn't	don't

1. Do not touch the wolf! ________ touch the wolf!

2. You cannot play with it. You ________ play with it.

3. The wolf is not a pet. The wolf ________ a pet.

4. I did not play with the wolf. I ________ play with the wolf.

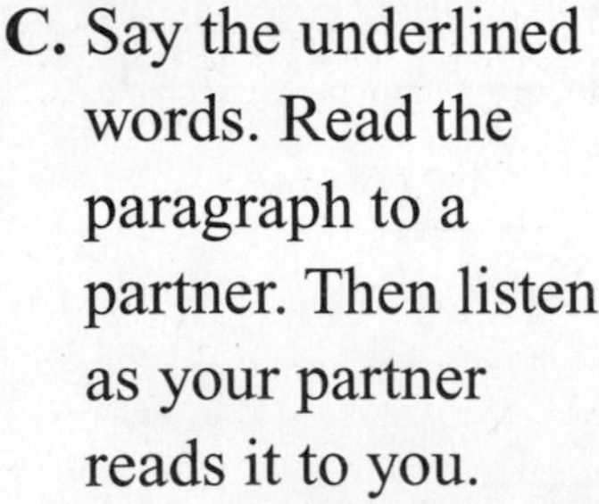

C. Say the underlined words. Read the paragraph to a partner. Then listen as your partner reads it to you.

I'm reporting to you from the courtroom. The wolf is on trial, but he didn't do it! He's innocent! You don't have to trust me—just ask Hansel and Gretel. They're honest. It isn't fair that the wolf is getting the blame. We're out of time, so I can't talk anymore.

Lou Gehrig: The Luckiest Man

Pages 420–441

Crossing Cultures • In this lesson, students read about two famous baseball players. Share information about baseball and its important place in American culture. Encourage students to tell about favorite sports in their home cultures.

PART 1

Preview the Skill Lesson

Use these activities with the Skill Lesson: "Cal Ripken, Jr.," Teacher's Edition, *Scott Foresman Reading,* pages 420–421.

Activate Prior Knowledge

Ask students what images of baseball they see in Adding English Poster 18. Allow students to use their home language as necessary. Draw a simple baseball diamond on the board and have students fill it with words that describe the game.

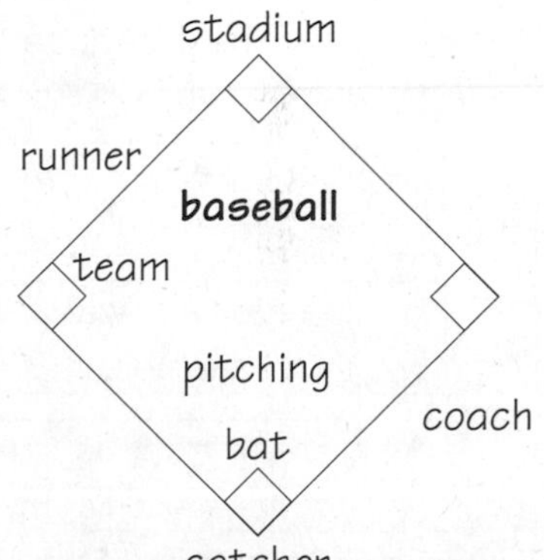

Use Total Physical Response

Introduce the Skill Lesson literature by previewing the vocabulary at right. Write the words on the board. Have students point to parts of the Adding English Poster that relate to the vocabulary. As you read the passage that follows, have students follow the directions and act out each underlined word.

> Here we are in the baseball stadium. Look at all the the people! There's a coach helping a player. Show me how you would give advice to a baseball player. Stop! The baseball is coming our way! Reach up and catch it! Now, throw it back. The catcher got it! Act out how a catcher catches a baseball. Here is the pitch. Pretend that you're pitching the ball too. Isn't it great to be part of a baseball team?

Have students talk about the poster, using as support the words on the list and words from the baseball diamond.

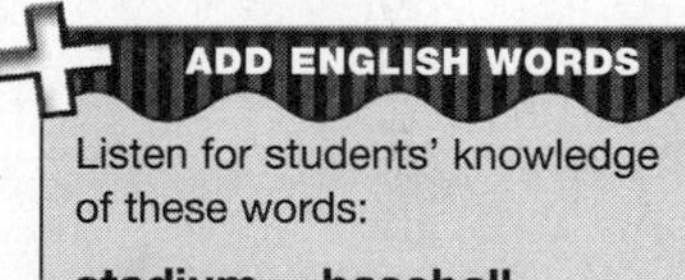

ADD ENGLISH WORDS

Listen for students' knowledge of these words:

stadium	**baseball**
catcher	**team**
coach	**pitching**

Present the Comprehension Strategy

Comprehension: Text Structure

Use Comprehension Strategies, *Adding English Guide,* page 10, to introduce Text Structure.

Relate to Personal Experience

Have students think about how they organize their possessions, such as collections and photographs. For example, students may arrange their photographs in chronological order. Ask students to draw "snapshots" of three important events in their lives and arrange them in time order.

Guide students as they read "Cal Ripken, Jr.," Scott Foresman Reading, *pages 420–421. Remind them to think about how the writer organizes the text.*

Selection Audio CD 7/Tape 21

Practice

Have students retell the events in Cal Ripken, Jr.'s life in order. Encourage them to use clue words that link events in time order.

Assess

If... students are not able to retell key events in the life of Cal Ripken, Jr., in chronological order,

then... have them arrange these sentence strips in chronological order, using the clue words as hints.

- As young as age four, Cal took advantage of his father's job.
- At age nine he was allowed to chase fly balls during batting practice.
- As a freshman, he was determined to be on his high school baseball team.
- Once he was on a team, he continued to work hard.

ADD ENGLISH WORDS

Review these words related to text structure.

organized **dates**
ages **clue words**
chronological order

PART 2

Preview the Reading Selection

Use these activities before reading the selection *Lou Gehrig: The Luckiest Man,* Teacher's Edition, *Scott Foresman Reading,* pages 422–438.

ADD ENGLISH WORDS

Listen for students' understanding of the following words related to baseball:

home run **bat** **fans**
teammate **umpire** **lucky**

Activate Prior Knowledge

Ask students to find the parts of the Adding English Poster that picture the words at the right. Encourage students to talk about the fun of playing and watching a baseball game.

Strategy: Making Predictions from Vocabulary

Explain the strategy: *When I want to use vocabulary words to predict what a selection will be about, I can use a chart.* Say the words and phrases and invite students to repeat them. Model how to fill out the "Words and Phrases" box on the story prediction from vocabulary chart, Graphic Organizer Transparency 3. Have students begin their own charts.

Build Background

Display a baseball, bat, and other baseball paraphernalia. Have students act out the scenes they see on the Adding English Poster, using some or all of the props. Encourage students to use the vocabulary words to explain what they are doing as they act out the scenes.

Vocabulary: Context Clues

Use these activities with the Vocabulary Lesson and paragraph "Book Report: Lou Gehrig," Teacher's Edition, *Scott Foresman Reading,* page 422.

Create a question-and-answer dialogue that uses each word at right in context. For example: *Will the pitcher start slowly and then* gradually *throw balls faster and faster? What does* gradually *mean? There were many* immigrants *at the game. They had just moved to America from other countries. What does* immigrants *mean?*

Remind students that pictures as well as words can help them understand words they don't know. Encourage them to look at the Adding English Poster for help in defining the vocabulary words.

Use Antonyms

Write *courageous* on the board. Next to it, write its antonym, *afraid.* Explain that we can sometimes figure out what a word means by knowing its opposite. Then write *convinced* and *gradually* and *quickly* and *discouraged*. Have students match the antonym pairs.

Guide students as they read "Book Report: Lou Gehrig," Scott Foresman Reading, *page 422. Ask them how they can use antonyms as they read.*

Students can participate in the Write About It activity that follows. Have English language learners work in groups with students whose home language is English to brainstorm the names of well known athletes. Then have students select the athlete they admire most and tell why.

Title Lou Gehrig: The Luckiest Man

Look at the selection title above and the list of words and phrases below. Write sentences that predict who and what this story might be about.

Words and Phrases

home run, bat, teammate, umpire, fans, lucky

Transparency 3

RESOURCES

Use *Scott Foresman ESL,* Grade 6, for additional instruction and activities.

- Chapter 3, "Types of Fitness"
- Video, Unit 2, "Good Sports"

ADD ENGLISH WORDS

Through listening and watching, assess students' knowledge of selection vocabulary.

courageous **immigrants**
engineer **convinced**
gradually

Present the Reading Selection

Use these activities with *Lou Gehrig: The Luckiest Man,* Teacher's Edition, *Scott Foresman Reading,* pages 422–438.

Preview Title and Illustrations

Explain the strategy: *Before I start to read, I look at the title and pictures to get an idea of what the story will be about.* Have students read the title and copy it onto the top line of their story prediction from vocabulary charts. Remind students that they are using the strategy called Making Predictions from Vocabulary. Next, have students look at the picture and caption on page 422. Ask: *When was Lou Gehrig born? When did he die? How old was he when he died?* Continue previewing the pictures.

Develop Concepts

For this selection, students may need support in understanding the tragedy of Lou Gehrig's illness and early death. Discuss how some exceptional athletes are heroes to many people. Talk about reasons why people admire certain athletes, such as for their skills, their dedication to the sport, or their kindness to fans. Have students think about the title. Then ask: *Why do you think Lou Gehrig could be considered the "luckiest man"?* Help students understand that Lou Gehrig appreciated his talent and luck in getting to play a game he loved, even though his time was short.

Set Purposes

Students can participate in Set Purposes, Teacher's Edition, *Scott Foresman Reading,* page 423. Let volunteers share their predictions from their story prediction from vocabulary charts.

Guide students as they read "Lou Gehrig: The Luckiest Man," Scott Foresman Reading, *pages 422–423. To support comprehension, use the suggestions in Meeting Individual Needs, ESL, in the Teacher's Edition.*

Response Log

- Have students list what would make them feel lucky, such as having a family, safety, or their health. Students can refer to the Adding English Poster and draw pictures to help express their ideas.
- Ask students to make a poster advertising an athletic game they would like to see. The game can be a match between real athletes or teams or an imaginary pairing. Students should use both words and pictures to announce the event and generate interest for it.

ADD ENGLISH WORDS

Help students with the following terms:

heroic **exceptional** **tragedy**

Title Lou Gehrig: The Luckiest Man

Look at the selection title above and the list of words and phrases below. Write sentences that predict who and what this story might be about.

Words and Phrases

home run, bat, teammate, umpire, fans, lucky

Characters: Lou Gehrig, teammates, coach, fans

Transparency 3

Selection Audio CD 7/Tape 21

Title Lou Gehrig: The Luckiest Man

Look at the selection title above and the list of words and phrases below. Write sentences that predict who and what this story might be about.

Words and Phrases

home run, bat, teammate, umpire, fans, lucky

Characters: Lou Gehrig, teammates, coach, fans

Problem: A baseball player wants to hit a home run.

Events: The player will practice with his teammates.

Outcome: Lou Gehrig got sick and had to stop playing baseball. He died soon after.

Transparency 3

Practice Selection Concepts

To help students tell what they learned, choose from these activities.

- Help students complete the "outcome" section of their story prediction from vocabulary charts.
- Cut the ten important sentences into strips and have students work in groups to arrange them in order. Remind students to look for clue words to help them find the chronological order.

Ten Important Sentences
Page 32

Strategy: Self-Assess

Ask: *Did Making Predictions from Vocabulary help you understand the selection?* Have students tell how closely their predictions matched the outcome of the story.

Language Awareness

Provide supported practice by using the Adding English Grammar and Phonics Practice Masters, pages 159–160, with the suggestions below.

Grammar: Comparative and Superlative Adjectives

Display a golf ball and a baseball. Write the following sentence on the board: *The baseball is bigger than the golf ball.* Then set a basketball near the others balls. Write: *The basketball is the biggest ball.* Read each sentence aloud. Ask: *How many balls are being compared in the first sentence?* (two) *How many balls are being compared in the second sentence?* (three). Explain that adjectives change form to show two or more things are being compared. The *-er,* or *more,* form shows two things are being compared, while the *-est,* or *most,* form shows that three or more things are being compared. Write other adjectives on the board and have students identify them as comparative or superlative.

Students can complete the Practice Master alone or with a partner.

Adding English
Grammar Practice Master
Page 159

Phonics: Possessives

Distribute the Practice Master. Have students listen, read, and repeat as you say the word groups in Exercise A. Use realia to guide students in practicing possessive nouns.

For Exercise B, have students read each sentence pair aloud before writing an answer.

Adding English
Phonics Practice Master
Page 160

PART 3

Connect Selection Concepts

Use these activities with Reader Response, Teacher's Edition, *Scott Foresman Reading,* page 438.

Literature Discussion Group

Invite English language learners to work in groups with students whose home language is English to talk about *Lou Gehrig: The Luckiest Man,* centering on the following questions:

- Who was Lou Gehrig? Why is he famous?
- What happened to him?
- Why did Lou Gehrig think he was the luckiest man?
- What words do you think best describe Lou Gehrig?

My Hero

Have students create a plaque or trophy honoring Lou Gehrig. Students can start by designing the award, then write a citation that explains why Gehrig deserves the award. Encourage students to use the words they generated in their literature discussion group.

Reading Across Texts: "The Baseball Hall of Fame," pages 439–441

To support students read an informational article:

- Have students study the pictures on pages 439–441. Ask which objects and images look familiar. Have volunteers read the captions aloud. Then check comprehension by asking students to point out certain parts of the pictures.
- Use the Adding English Poster to build background about the popularity of baseball and baseball souvenirs. Have students find pictures of the vocabulary words on the poster.
- Ask students: *How is "The Baseball Hall of Fame" like "Lou Gehrig: The Luckiest Man"?* Record their responses on a main idea chart, Graphic Organizer Transparency 15. Have students refer to the Adding English Poster and the reading selections.

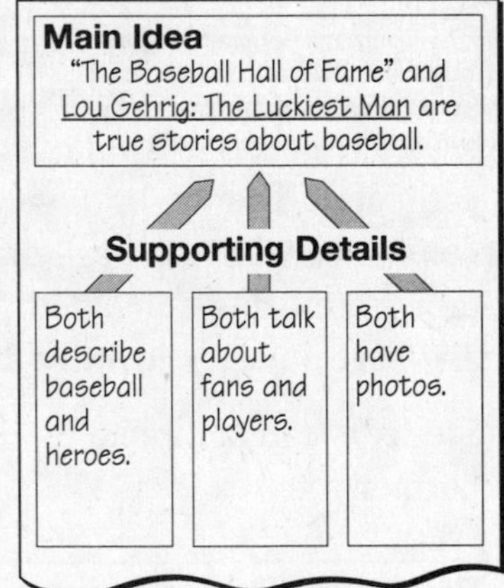

Transparency 15

Assess

Refer to the list below to assess students' progress.

Reading

- ☐ Uses words related to baseball.
- ☐ Identifies chronological text structure.
- ☐ Previews titles and illustrations to predict a story's events.

Language Awareness

Grammar

- ☐ Identifies and uses comparative and superlative adjectives.

Phonics

- ☐ Pronounces and creates possessive nouns.

Learning Strategies

- ☐ Uses a story prediction from vocabulary chart.
- ☐ Uses context clues to learn unfamiliar vocabulary.

Name ______________________________

Comparative and Superlative Adjectives

A. Underline the comparative adjective. Circle the superlative adjective.

1. Babe Ruth was luckier than Ty Cobb.

2. Lou Gehrig was the luckiest man of all.

B. Choose the comparative or superlative adjective to complete each sentence.

3. Amy is __________ than Max. (taller/tallest)

4. Miguel is the __________ player of all. (taller/tallest)

5. My hair is __________ than yours. (longest/longer)

6. T'Aysha's hair is the __________ on the team. (longest/longer)

7. Yohei is a __________ player than John. (stronger/strongest)

8. Lisa is the __________ player on the team. (stronger/strongest)

C. Choose one sport you like. Talk with a partner about it. Then write sentences telling how to play it well.

My favorite sport is ______________________________

____

____

____

____

Name ____________________________________

Possessives

Phonics

A. Listen to the words. Read the words. Then say the words.

Lou's uniform	school's team	league's most valuable player	city's stadium

B. Write a possessive noun to complete each sentence.

1. The baseball belongs to Tran.
It is __________ baseball. (Tran/Tran's)

2. The bat belongs to Nick. It is
__________ bat. (Nick/Nick's)

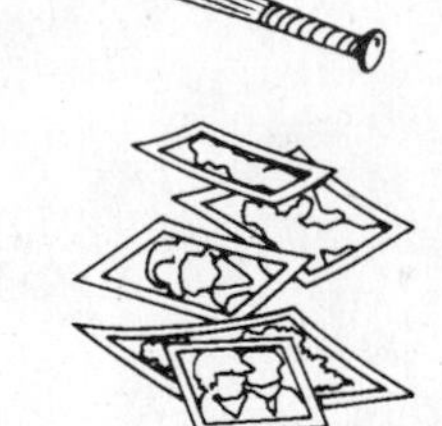

3. The photos belong to Lisa. They are
__________ photos. (Lisa's/Lisa)

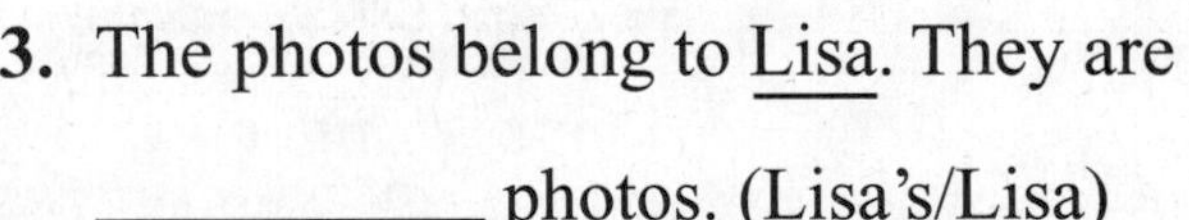

4. The cards belong to Ashley. They are
__________ cards. (Ashley/Ashley's)

C. Say the underlined words. Read the paragraph to a partner. Then listen as your partner reads it to you.

Maria's bat is at home. Janal's baseball is in his locker. Lashauna's glove is in the car. Matt's uniform is at school. Kyoko's sneakers are lost. The school's bases are broken. The city's baseball field is muddy. How can they play baseball now?

The Disguise

Pages 442–467

Crossing Cultures • In this lesson, students read about a girl who pretends to be a boy so that she can go to school. Ask students if there are things only girls or only boys can do in their home cultures. Do they think that is fair?

PART 1

Preview the Skill Lesson

Use these activities with the Skill Lesson: "Korean Foods," Teacher's Edition, *Scott Foresman Reading,* pages 442–443.

Poster Tips
Page 16

Activate Prior Knowledge

Invite students to share information about special foods and typical meals in their home. Have students work in groups to create menus for a day's meals in their home, then draw pictures of the meals and label each food. Ask students what foods they see on Adding English Poster 19. Let students raise their hands to show which foods they like to eat.

Use Context Clues

Introduce the Skill Lesson literature by previewing the vocabulary at the right. Write the vocabulary words on the board. Have students point to parts of the Adding English Poster that relate to vocabulary. As you read the paragraph below, have students listen for the vocabulary words. Encourage them to listen for context clues—words they know that will help them figure out the meaning of each vocabulary word.

Listen for students' knowledge of these words:

vegetables	**spices**
rice	**grains**
fruits	**eggs**

> At the grocery store, we saw many vegetables—carrots, peas, cabbage, and corn. We got some fruits—apples, pears, and bananas. Mother also bought spices, like salt, pepper, and cinnamon. There were many grains for sale, including rice, wheat, oats, and barley. The rice looked like little white seeds. Last, I got a box of smooth, white eggs.

Write the context clues from the paragraph on the board and have students match them with the vocabulary words. Other students in the class may also benefit from reviewing this vocabulary before reading "Korean Foods."

Present the Comprehension Strategy

Comprehension: Summarizing

Use Comprehension Strategies, *Adding English Guide,* page 10, to introduce Summarizing.

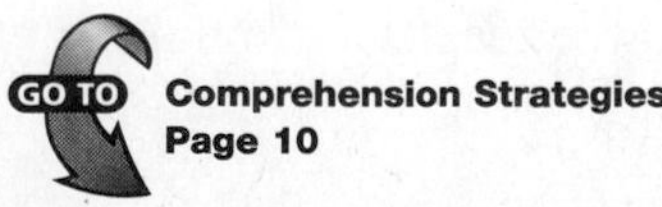

Comprehension Strategies
Page 10

Relate to Personal Experience

Have students think about a television show they recently watched. Ask them to create a three-panel cartoon that summarizes the key events in the show. Students who have watched the same show may enjoy working in pairs.

Guide students as they read "Korean Foods," Scott Foresman Reading, *pages 442–443. Remind them to think about the main idea of the selection so they can summarize it in their own words.*

Selection Audio CD 1/Tape 19

ADD ENGLISH WORDS

Review these key words related to summarizing:

statement **main**
idea **short**
unnecessary

Practice

Have students summarize "Korean Foods" in their own words. Remind them that their summaries should be brief but must tell the main idea of the article. Encourage students to use the Adding English Poster for help in identifying the foods.

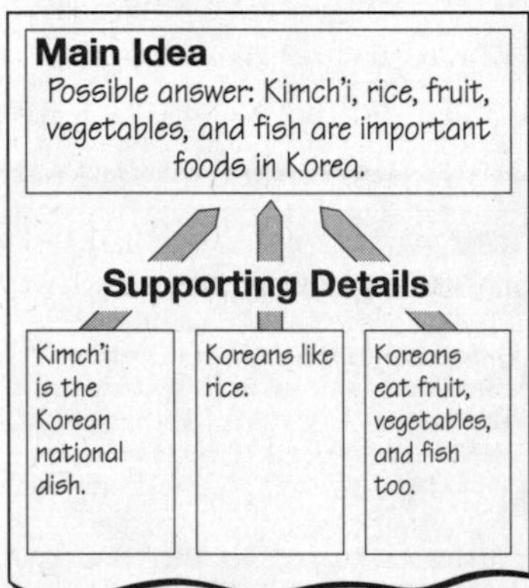

Transparency 15

Assess

If... students are not able to summarize "Korean Foods,"

then... help them use a main idea chart, Graphic Organizer Transparency 15, to list the main idea and supporting details.

PART 2

Preview the Reading Selection

Use these activities before reading the selection *The Disguise*, Teacher's Edition, *Scott Foresman Reading,* pages 444–465.

Activate Prior Knowledge

Ask students to point out the parts of the Adding English Poster that show the words at the right. Direct their attention to the alphabet and other pictures related to education. Ask students what they know about schools in the United States and other countries. Ask: *What do you think boys and girls learn in school in Korea? How do you think school might be different in Korea than it is in America?* Encourage any Korean students to share their knowledge. Begin a K-W-L chart, Graphic Organizer 7, about education around the world.

ADD ENGLISH WORDS

Listen for students' knowledge of the following words:

alphabet **soldier**
jacket **son**
secret **swim**

Strategy: Using a K-W-L Chart

Explain the strategy: *When I want to learn new facts, I can use a chart. It is a strategy called Using a K-W-L Chart.* Point out what each letter means and model filling out the K column. Have students begin their own charts with things they know about education in the United States and other countries.

K What I Know	W What I Want to Know	L What I Learned
School is very important for children in all countries.		

Transparency 7

Build Background

Arrange students in small groups. Have each group play charades, pantomiming the vocabulary words for each other to guess. For example, a student could mime a breast stroke or a crawl for *swim*. Students can switch roles and continue the activity until everyone has had a chance to act out a word.

Words I Recognize

Write *alphabet, soldier, jacket, son, secret,* and *swim* on the board. Explain that we can often recognize new words because they look like words we already know. (For example, the Spanish word *chaqueta* looks and sounds similar to its English equivalent, *jacket*.) Sometimes the words are identical or almost so. Other times, they share word parts, such as prefixes, suffixes, or roots. Invite students to study the vocabulary words and see if they are similar to any words they know from their home language or English. Have volunteers identify the similar words and describe the connection between them.

ADD ENGLISH WORDS

Ask students whose home language is Spanish to teach the class these Spanish words.

chaqueta (jacket)
secreto (secret)
alfabeto (alphabet)

Vocabulary: Antonyms

Use these activities with the Vocabulary Lesson and paragraph "Letter to Mother from School," Teacher's Edition, *Scott Foresman Reading,* page 444.

Write the following sentences on the board and have students act them out: *We squatted down to hide behind the desks. If we stood, everyone would see us.* Explain that we can sometimes figure out what a word means by knowing its opposite, as with *squatted* and its antonym *stood*. Then write the other vocabulary words on the chalkboard. Next to them, write *safe* and *uncover*. Explain that these are antonyms for two of the vocabulary words. Have students match the antonym pairs.

RESOURCES

Use *Scott Foresman ESL,* Grade 3, for additional instruction and activities.

- Chapter 2, "Life in the City"
- Video, Unit 1, "The Farm and the City"

ADD ENGLISH WORDS

Through listening and watching, assess students' knowledge of selection vocabulary.

cautious	**disguise**
dangerous	**chanting**
principal	**suspected**
recite	**squatted**

Picture-Word Cards

Students can make cards to help them remember difficult words. Have them write the word in English and their home language, then add synonyms or antonyms, if possible, and a picture to illustrate the word. The card for *dangerous* might include the antonym *safe*, the Spanish word *peligroso*, and a drawing of a lion.

Guide students as they read "Letter to Mother from School," Scott Foresman Reading, *page 444. Ask how they can use antonyms to learn new words.*

Students can participate in the Talk About It activity that follows. Have English language learners work in groups with students whose home language is English to talk about whether going to school is important.

Present the Reading Selection

Use these activities with *The Disguise,* Teacher's Edition, *Scott Foresman Reading,* pages 444–465.

Preview Illustrations

Explain the strategy: *Before I read, I look at the pictures to get an idea of what the story will be about.* Have students look at the picture on pages 444–445. Ask: *Who do you think these people are? Where are they? What do you think they are doing?* Continue previewing the pictures, paying special attention to the main characters and the setting of the story.

Develop Concepts

For this selection, students may need support in understanding many aspects of Korean culture mentioned in the story. Make sure students understand that the story took place more than one hundred years ago, and point out that life in Korea has changed since then. Let any Korean students share their expertise on modern Korean culture. Then discuss cultural issues from the story that may surprise students, such as the nature of the Chinese and Korean alphabets, the role of women, and the value placed on reciting loudly in school. Invite students who are familiar with Chinese or Korean characters to write some sample letters to show the class.

Set Purposes

Students can participate in Set Purposes, Teacher's Edition, *Scott Foresman Reading,* page 445. Help students fill in the W column on their K-W-L charts about education around the world. Remind students that they are using a strategy called Using a K-W-L Chart.

Guide students as they read The Disguise, Scott Foresman Reading, *pages 444–465. To support comprehension, use the suggestions in Meeting Individual Needs, ESL, in the Teacher's Edition.*

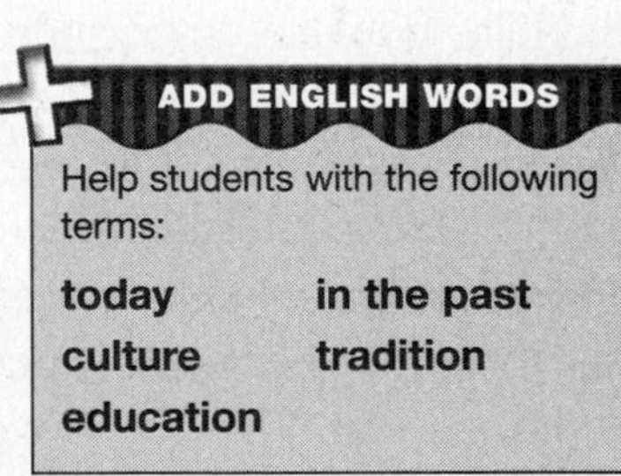

K What I Know	W What I Want to Know	L What I Learned
School is very important for children in all countries.	What was education like for girls 100 years ago in Korea?	

Transparency 7

Selection Audio CD 8/Tape 22

Response Log

- Have students list which school subject they like the best and why. For example, students might like math because they enjoy solving problems or science because they learn about animals.
- Ask students to draw a picture of your classroom and label each person and object they include. Guide students to refer to the Adding English Poster for support.

K What I Know	W What I Want to Know	L What I Learned
School is very important for children in all countries.	What was education like for girls 100 years ago in Korea?	Girls were not allowed to go to school in Korea 100 years ago.

Transparency 7

Ten Important Sentences
Page 33

Practice Selection Concepts

To help students tell what they learned, choose from these activities.

- Help students complete the L column of their K-W-L charts about education around the world.
- Group students; one student writes the letters of the alphabet vertically on a sheet of paper. Give groups the ten important sentences. Have each student match an alphabet letter to the first letter in the sentence.

Strategy: Self-Assess

Ask: *Did Using a K-W-L Chart help you learn more about education around the world?* Have students explain how.

Language Awareness

Provide supported practice by using the Adding English Grammar and Phonics Practice Masters, pages 167–168, with the suggestions below.

Grammar: Adverbs

Write the following sentences on the board: We swim. We swim slowly. Read each sentence aloud. Ask: *How are these sentences the same? How are they different?* Guide students to see that both sentences are about swimming, but the second sentence uses a word that tells *how* we swim—*slowly*. Explain that most adverbs describe verbs.

Write other sentences with adverbs on the board. Have volunteers identify the adverbs and the words they describe.

Students can complete the Practice Master alone or with a partner.

Adding English
Grammar Practice Master
Page 167

Phonics: Suffixes

Distribute the Practice Master. Have students listen, read, and repeat as you say the words in Exercise A. Then discuss the base words. Pair students to identify the suffix in each word. Invite students to use the words in sentences.

Have students say aloud the words in Exercise B before matching them.

Adding English
Phonics Practice Master
Page 168

PART 3

Connect Selection Concepts

Use these activities with Reader Response, Teacher's Edition, *Scott Foresman Reading,* page 465.

Dramatizing

Have English language learners work in small groups with students whose home language is English to act out *The Disguise,* focusing on these scenes:

- Induk working at home with her tutor
- Mother telling Induk the tale of the Chinese girl who wanted to be a soldier
- Induk's first day in school
- Induk winning a prize for reciting

Citizen of the World

Invite students to teach the class a brief lesson about their home culture, focusing on one element such as food, music, art, clothing, sports, or family traditions. Students can work on their own or with a partner who shares the same cultural background. Encourage students to bring in objects such as photographs, samples of food, or souvenirs from festivals or holidays.

ADD ENGLISH WORDS

Use the Adding English Poster to help students with the following words:

locker	**visitors**
souvenirs	**photo**
bases	**uniforms**

Reading Across Texts: "Chinese Calligraphy," pages 466–467

To support students as they read a Web site article:

- Have students preview the article. Have students notice the parts of the article that they might see if they were looking at it on the World Wide Web.
- Activate prior knowledge by talking about symbols students know that stand for words or letters. Do students know languages that use special symbols? Can they identify symbols that resemble what they stand for?
- Read the text together. Students can participate in the discussion questions shown on page 466.

Assess

Refer to the list below to assess students' progress.

Reading

- ☐ Uses words related to foods.
- ☐ Uses words related to schools and education.
- ☐ Summarizes a selection.

Language Awareness

Grammar

- ☐ Identifies adverbs and uses them in sentences.

Phonics

- ☐ Correctly pronounces and decodes words with suffixes.

Learning Strategies

- ☐ Uses a K-W-L chart.
- ☐ Uses antonyms to learn unfamiliar vocabulary.

Name ______________________________

Grammar

Adverbs

A. Circle the adverb in each sentence.

1. We ran quickly.

2. The bus moved slowly.

B. Choose an adverb from the box to describe the underlined word in each sentence. Write it on the line.

easily	loudly	proudly	tightly

3. Induk's hair was <u>braided</u> ____________.

4. She ____________ <u>learned</u> the alphabet.

5. She <u>recited</u> the lessons ____________.

6. She ____________ <u>accepted</u> the award.

C. What advice would you give a new student about how to do well in school? Talk with a partner. Then write sentences about what you would say.

To do well in school, you should ________________

Name ______________________________

Suffixes

A. Listen to the words. Read each word. Then say each word.

B. Draw a line to match each word with its meaning.

1. hopeful — **a.** causing danger

2. slowly — **b.** full of hope

3. dangerous — **c.** without a home

4. homeless — **d.** in a slow manner

C. Say the underlined words. Read the paragraph to a partner. Then listen to your partner read it.

Education is important. At school we learn about beautiful animals. We even read about some poisonous ones! Our teacher treats us kindly, so I like going to school. The time passes quickly.

We had some excitement yesterday. Our snake got out of its cage! We backed away uneasily, but the teacher told us not to worry. She's fearless! She picked up the snake and put it back in the cage.

Keepers

Pages 468–484

Crossing Cultures • In this lesson, a grandmother is the keeper of her family's history, the person who passes down stories from generation to generation. Ask students who are the important family members in their home cultures.

Preview the Skill Lesson

Use these activities with the Skill Lesson: "One Particular Small, Smart Boy," Teacher's Edition, *Scott Foresman Reading,* pages 468–469.

Activate Prior Knowledge

Ask students to identify familiar objects and activities from Adding English Poster 20. Remind students that what they already know can help them learn new things. Then ask students which pictured item could be a special gift for a family member. Have students walk to the poster, point to and name an item, and tell to whom they would give it and why. Allow students to use their home language as necessary. Use a T-chart, Graphic Organizer Transparency 24, to list items from the poster and the reasons why students might want them.

Item	Reason
egg	to eat
salt	to eat
chocolate	for gift

Transparency 24

Use Context Clues

Introduce the Skill Lesson literature by previewing the vocabulary at the right. Write the vocabulary words on the board. Have students listen for words as you read the following paragraph. Direct them to listen for context clues, such as *crush, the shell will break, dirt,* and *very big person.*

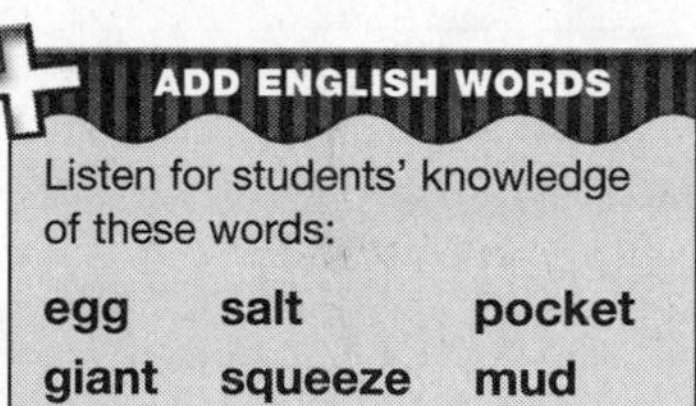

> "Don't squeeze the egg! If you crush it, the shell will break and it won't be good to eat," Mom said. "And don't get mud all over your pants. The dirt never comes out." Then Mom gave me a kiss. I put the hard-boiled egg and a packet of salt to sprinkle on it in my jacket pocket. I felt like a giant—a very big person—because today was a special day. It was my birthday! I couldn't wait to see my cake and presents.

Write the context clues from the paragraph on the chalkboard. Guide students to match each clue to its corresponding vocabulary word. Other students may benefit from reviewing this vocabulary.

Present the Comprehension Strategy

Comprehension: Plot

Use Comprehension Strategies, *Adding English Guide,* page 10, to introduce Plot.

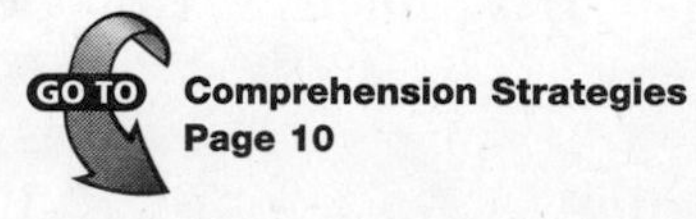

Relate to Personal Experience

Ask students to think about a television show they recently watched. Pair students who watched the same show to talk about the plot, the events that happened in the show. Guide them to identify the problem or conflict in the show, as well as the climax and the resolution.

Guide students as they read "One Particular Small, Smart Boy," Scott Foresman Reading, *pages 468–469. Remind them to think about the plot as they read.*

Practice

Have students describe the plot of "One Particular Small, Smart Boy" in their own words. Remind them to identify the conflict, climax, and resolution. Students can work in pairs or small groups.

Assess

If... students are not able to identify the plot elements in "One Particular Small, Smart Boy,"

then... help them complete a plot diagram using Graphic Organizer Transparency 11.

Selection Audio CD 8/Tape 23

Title One Particular Small, Smart Boy
Setting: a country road, once upon a time
Characters: a little boy, a giant

Rising Action A boy meets a giant. The boy pretends to squeeze rocks into water and salt.

Climax (Turning Point) The boy says he will squeeze the giant's hand into mud.

Falling Action The giant runs away.

Problem (Goal) The giant wants to eat the boy.

Solution (Outcome) The boy is safe because he tricked the giant.

Transparency 11

ADD ENGLISH WORDS

Review these key words related to plot.

plot **conflict**
climax **resolution**

PART 2

Preview the Reading Selection

Use these activities before reading the selection *Keepers,* Teacher's Edition, *Scott Foresman Reading,* pages 470–484.

Activate Prior Knowledge

Ask students to point out parts of the Adding English Poster that picture the words at the right. Encourage students to talk about the kinds of things people need and want, things they buy for themselves and receive as gifts. Discuss what makes a gift special.

Strategy: Making Predictions from Vocabulary

Explain the strategy: *I can predict what a story will be about by looking at the vocabulary words. It is a strategy called Making Predictions from Vocabulary.* Write the vocabulary on the board and model how to fill out the "Words and Phrases" box on the chart. Have students begin their own charts.

ADD ENGLISH WORDS

Assess students' understanding of the following words related to birthdays:

glove **present**
birthday **storyteller**
antique **chocolates**

Title Keepers

Look at the selection title above and the list of words and phrases below. Write sentences that predict who and what this story might be about.

Words and Phrases:
glove, present, birthday, storyteller, antique, chocolates

Transparency 3

Build Background

Hold up a baseball glove, birthday card, box of chocolates, and wrapped present. If possible, also display an antique. Then have students act out the scenes on the poster, using some or all of the props. Encourage students to use the vocabulary words as they act out the scenes.

In My Own Words

Invite students to use a combination of words and actions to paraphrase the vocabulary words. Model by saying: *a glove is the mitt you wear to protect your hand when you play baseball.* Pantomime catching a baseball in a glove. For *birthday*, a student could say: "the day you were born" and mime blowing out the candles on a birthday cake. Encourage students to be creative as they paraphrase each word. Allow students to use their home languages, if necessary.

Vocabulary: Homonyms

Use these activities with the Vocabulary Lesson and paragraph "Family Stories," Teacher's Edition, *Scott Foresman Reading,* page 470.

Write the following sentence on the board: *We played baseball on the diamond in the park.* Ask what *diamond* means. Have students think of another meaning for *diamond.* (a gemstone) Use that meaning of in a sentence such as: *I have a diamond ring.* Explain that some English words are spelled the same but have different meanings. Point out that the best way to tell what these words mean is to see how they are used in a sentence. Encourage students to think of other homonym pairs, referring to the Adding English Poster for ideas.

Use Synonyms

Write these words on the board: *thinking, surely, teased.* Have students match each word to its synonym: *considering, definitely, taunted.* Students may want to use their dictionaries for help. Suggest that they also use the Adding English Poster for support.

Guide students as they read "Family Stories," Scott Foresman Reading, *page 470. Ask them how they can decide on the correct meaning as homonyms.*

Students can participate in the Write About It activity that follows. Invite English language learners to share special family stories in groups with students whose home language is English. Guide students to think about use the elements of plot—conflict, climax, and resolution—in their stories.

RESOURCES

Use *Scott Foresman ESL,* Grade 5, for additional instruction and activities.

- Chapter 10, "What Makes a Good Story?"
- Video, Unit 5, "Reading Fun"

ADD ENGLISH WORDS

Observe students and listen to their responses to assess their comprehension of selection vocabulary:

stroke	**reminder**
considering	**taunted**
diamond	**grounders**
definitely	

Present the Reading Selection

Use these activities with *Keepers,* Teacher's Edition, *Scott Foresman Reading,* pages 470–484.

Preview Illustrations

Explain the strategy: *Before I read, I look at the pictures to get an idea of what the story will be about.* Have students look at the picture on pages 470–471. Ask: *Who do you think this person is? What do you think he is doing?* Continue previewing the pictures.

Develop Concepts

Students may need support in understanding Little Dolly's dialect, or the way English is spoken by some people or in a certain places. Also discuss how traditions are important in families and communities. Have students read the story title. Then ask: *What do you think a "keeper" might be?* Have students fill in their charts. Remind them that they are using the strategy called Making Predictions from Vocabulary. Guide students to see that things worth keeping may not always be real items; they can be stories and memories.

Set Purposes

Students can participate in Set Purposes, Teacher's Edition, *Scott Foresman Reading,* page 471. Let volunteers read aloud their predictions from their charts.

Guide students as they read Keepers, Scott Foresman Reading, *pages 470–484. To support comprehension, use the suggestions in Meeting Individual Needs, ESL, in the Teacher's Edition.*

Response Log

- Have students draw a picture of the gift they would buy or make to mark a family member's special event, such as a birthday or accomplishment. Then have students write a sentence telling why they would select this particular present. Students can refer to the Adding English Poster for support.
- Invite groups of students to brainstorm a list of gifts they could make. Students can draw a picture of one of the gifts and write how it is made. For example, the ingredients for cookies or the steps in making a papier-mâché piñata.

Title Keepers

Look at the selection title above and the list of words and phrases below. Write sentences that predict who and what this story might be about.

Words and Phrases:
glove, present, birthday, storyteller, antique, chocolates

Characters: a boy and his grandmother

Problem: Someone wants a special birthday present.

Events: The person can't decide among gloves, chocolates, or antiques. The person will listen to a storyteller.

Outcome:

Transparency 3

ADD ENGLISH WORDS

Help students understand the following terms:

heritage **history**
ancestors **memories**
tradition

Selection Audio CD 8/Tape 23

Practice Selection Concepts

To help students tell what they learned, choose from these activities.

- Help students complete the "outcome" section of their story prediction from vocabulary charts.
- Cut the ten important sentences into strips and have students work in groups to arrange them in order. Then work with the class to divide the sentences into groups of plot elements: problem, climax, and resolution.

Strategy: Self-Assess

Ask: *Did Making Predictions from Vocabulary help you understand the story?* Have students tell how closely their predictions matched the story's outcome.

Title Keepers

Look at the selection title above and the list of words and phrases below. Write sentences that predict who and what this story might be about.

Words and Phrases:

glove, present, birthday, storyteller, antique, chocolates

Characters: a boy and his grandmother

Problem: Someone wants a special birthday present.

Events: The person can't decide among gloves, chocolates, or antiques. The person will listen to a storyteller.

Outcome: Kenyon makes Little Dolly a book of her stories. Kenyon will become the family's "keeper."

Transparency 3

Ten Important Sentences Page 34

Language Awareness

Provide supported practice by using the Adding English Grammar and Phonics Practice Masters, pages 175–176, with the suggestions below.

Grammar: Using Adverbs to Improve Sentences

Adding English Grammar Practice Master Page 175

Write the following sentences on the board: *I walk home. I walk home quickly.* Guide students to see that the second sentence uses a word that tells how we walk—*quickly.* Remind students that adverbs are words that describe verbs, adjectives, or other adverbs. Discuss how adding the adverb improves the sentence by making it more precise and descriptive. Demonstrating three ways of walking home: slowly, at a normal pace, and quickly. Then have students vote on which sentence (or both) described the walk. They should see that all three walks are described by the first sentence, but the second sentence describes only the fast-paced walk. Write other sentences without adverbs. Have volunteers add adverbs. Discuss how the adverbs improve the sentences.

Students can complete the Practice Master alone or with a partner.

Phonics: Syllabication

Adding English Phonics Practice Master Page 176

Distribute the Practice Master. Have students listen, read, and repeat as you say the words in Exercise A. Then ask students to read the words aloud themselves. Teach students how to tap out the number of syllables in a word. Write the words on the board and demonstrate how to draw vertical lines to divide them into syllables.

For Exercise B, have students read the sentences aloud before writing their answers.

PART 3

Connect Selection Concepts

Use these activities with Reader Response, Teacher's Edition, *Scott Foresman Reading,* page 484.

Dramatize

If possible, place English language learners in small groups with students whose home language is English. Invite groups to act out one of the following scenes from *Keepers:*

- Kenyon shopping for a gift for Little Dolly
- Kenyon deciding to buy himself the baseball glove
- Little Dolly's birthday party
- Little Dolly opening Kenyon's gift

Party Time

Students can describe parties for special times, such as birthdays, anniversaries, and holidays. Encourage students to describe the foods they eat, the songs they sing, and the customs they follow. Students can draw pictures of a family party and label each part.

Reading Across Texts: "Have-a-Ball! Cake," pages 485

To support students as they read a recipe:

- Activate prior knowledge by talking about different recipe formats, abbreviations in recipes, and experiences students have had with following recipes.
- After students have read the recipe, have them identify words that tell the order for making the cake. Talk about what students would do to make the cake look like another kind of ball.

Assess

Refer to the list below to assess students' progress.

Reading

- ☐ Uses words related to birthdays, shopping and gift-giving.
- ☐ Identifies the plot of a story, including conflict, climax, and resolution.

Language Awareness

Grammar

- ☐ Uses adverbs to improve sentences.

Phonics

- ☐ Pronounces and decodes multisyllabic words.

Learning Strategies

- ☐ Uses a story prediction from vocabulary chart.
- ☐ Uses context clues to find the meanings of homonyms.

Name ______________________________

Using Adverbs to Improve Sentences

A. Circle the adverb in each sentence.

1. Little Dolly carefully lifted the gift from the box.

2. She delicately touched the handmade book.

B. Choose an adverb from the box to improve each sentence.

carefully	nearly	loudly	very	easily

3. Grandmother snored ___________.

4. She got tired ___________ since her stroke.

5. Kenyon studied ___________ hard.

6. He did his homework ___________.

7. Kenyon was ___________ done when the phone rang.

C. Imagine that you are planning a birthday party for a family member. Talk about it with a partner. Write sentences telling what you would do and eat.

At the party is ______________________________

____

____

____

____

____

Name ________________________________

Phonics

Syllabication

A. Listen to the words. Read each word. Then say each word.

letters

dollar

grandmother

neighborhood

storyteller

B. Write a word from the box to complete each sentence.

baseball	supermarket	dollar	holiday

1. The muffin cost one ________________.
2. Valentine's Day is my favorite ________________.
3. Lou Gehrig was a great ________________ player.
4. We buy food in a ________________.

C. Say the underlined words. Then read the paragraph to a partner. Listen as your partner reads it to you.

Yesterday I went shopping in the supermarket. I needed food for the holidays. I decided to make strawberry shortcakes for my grandmother. They are her favorite. My grandmother is a storyteller. Once she told me a story about a pretty box, but my dog interrupted her. I never heard the end of the story!

Amazing Alice!

Pages 496–517

Crossing Cultures • Throughout this lesson about traveling in the United States long ago, encourage students to ask questions about pictures and texts. To convey high expectations of English language learners, wait for them as they formulate questions, showing confidence that they can express themselves.

PART 1

Preview the Skill Lesson

Use these activities with the Skill Lesson: "Stagecoaches, Then … and Now," Teacher's Edition, *Scott Foresman Reading,* pages 496–497.

Poster Tips
Page 16

Activate Prior Knowledge

Ask students to tell what they see in Adding English Poster 21. Have students discuss stagecoaches they have seen on television or in a movie. Ask: *How are stagecoaches and present-day cars similar? How are they different?* Use a Venn diagram, Graphic Organizer Transparency 21, to record students' responses.

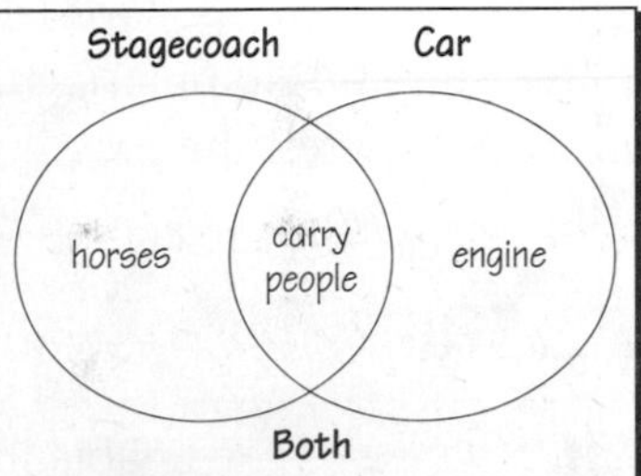

Transparency 21

Recognize Vocabulary Words

Introduce the Skill Lesson literature by previewing the vocabulary at the right. List the vocabulary words on the board. Have students listen for them as you read the passage that follows.

> I was traveling by <u>stagecoach</u>. There were no other <u>passengers</u>. I was alone, except for the horses pulling the large wooden coach along the muddy, bumpy <u>roads</u>. Bags of <u>mail</u> bumped against me on the hard wooden seat. I wondered for whom the letters were. As the sky grew dark, I was afraid robbers would try to stop the stagecoach. Then I woke up. I had dreamed I was in a <u>Western</u>.

As you reread the passage, have students point to parts of the Adding English Poster that relate to the vocabulary words. Ask: *What is the passage about?* (a stagecoach ride) *What is the main idea of the passage?* (The narrator is nervous about traveling alone.) Have students look for details that support the main idea.

ADD ENGLISH WORDS

Have students use these selection vocabulary words in sentences. Encourage them to use as many as possible to tell about the poster.

Westerns **roads**
passengers **mail**
stagecoach

Present the Comprehension Strategy

Comprehension: Summarizing

Use Comprehension Strategies, *Adding English Guide,* page 10, to introduce Summarizing.

Comprehension Strategies
Page 10

Relate to Personal Experience

Have students think of a time they took a ride—in a car, on a bus, on an airplane, on a bicycle, or by some other mode of transportation—and something happened that made the trip memorable. In groups, have students tell about their trip, summarizing in one or two sentences what happened. Remind students to tell only their most important ideas.

Guide students as they read "Stagecoaches, Then . . . and Now," Scott Foresman Reading, *pages 496–497. Remind them to think about the most important ideas in the article.*

Selection Audio CD 9/Tape 25

Practice

Have students summarize the selection. Remind them that they should only tell the most important ideas.

Assess

If... students are unable to summarize the article,

then... ask them to reread the article slowly. Say: *As you read each sentence, ask yourself, "Is this an important idea?"* Write the following sentences on the board. Have students choose the one that best summarizes the article. (sentence 3)

1. Teams of galloping horses pulled the stagecoaches.
2. Robbers who attacked stagecoaches were referred to as road agents.
3. Stagecoaches provided a way for passengers and mail to travel swiftly between places in the newly settled West.

ADD ENGLISH WORDS

Review these words related to summarizing.

summary **main idea** **details**

PART 2

Preview the Reading Selection

Use these activities before reading "Amazing Alice!," Teacher's Edition, *Scott Foresman Reading,* pages 498–515.

Activate Prior Knowledge

Involve students in talking about parts of the Adding English Poster that picture the words at the right. Direct their attention to the motorcar and invite them to tell what they know about early automobiles. Ask students to tell how cars today are similar to and different from earlier models.

ADD ENGLISH WORDS

Listen for students' knowledge of words related to automobiles.

motorcar **driver** **seat**
road map **axle** **steers**

Build Background

Show students a map of the route Hermine and Alice took from New York to California. Tell students that roads today are much more smooth and dry than they were ninety years ago. Also, early cars did not move as quickly as modern cars. Have students talk about what such a journey might have been like a long time ago.

Word Riddles

Have partners write a riddle for each vocabulary word, using the Adding English Poster for ideas. For example: *I steer the car. Who am I?* (the driver) *You sit on me. What am I?* (a seat) Have students take turns reading their riddles for classmates. The student who guesses correctly then points out the answer on the Adding English Poster.

Vocabulary: Synonyms

Use these activities with the Vocabulary Lesson and paragraph "Postcard from a Cross-country Trip," Teacher's Edition, *Scott Foresman Reading,* page 498.

Write the selection vocabulary words on the board. Then write these sentences: *Pamela drove carefully because there were ravines on both sides of the road. She didn't want the car to slide into one of those steep valleys.* Ask students to read the sentences and find a vocabulary word. (*ravines*) Can they find a synonym for *ravines*? (*valleys*) Have students identify other vocabulary words pictured on the Adding English Poster and use dictionaries to look up synonyms for *crank* and *dependable.*

Make Crossword Puzzles

Write the vocabulary words on the board. Discuss the meaning of each word, referring to the poster for support. Then show students how to make a crossword puzzle by interlacing the words, numbering them, and writing definitions. Pass out graph paper and have pairs create puzzles. For clues, they can draw pictures and/or write simple definitions of the words.

Guide students as they read "Postcard from a Cross-country Trip," Scott Foresman Reading, *page 498. Ask them how thinking of synonyms might help them understand an unfamiliar word.*

Students can participate in the Write About It activity that follows. If possible, have English language learners work with partners whose home language is English. Before they begin writing, pairs can list things they know about the place they would like to visit.

RESOURCES

Use *Scott Foresman ESL,* Grade 4, for additional instruction and activities.

- Chapter 11, "Regions of Our Country"
- Video, Unit 6, "Regions and States"

ADD ENGLISH WORDS

Through listening and watching, assess students' knowledge of selection vocabulary.

forge	**blacksmith**
crank	**dependable**
ravines	**telegraph**

Present the Reading Selection

Use these activities with "Amazing Alice!," Teacher's Edition, *Scott Foresman Reading,* pages 498–515.

Preview Headings and Illustrations

Explain the strategy: *Before I begin to read a story, I read the headings and look at the pictures to see what the story is about.* Discuss the illustration on pages 498–499. Then call attention to the dates and headings throughout the selection and to the map at the top of each spread. Ask: *When does the story take place? What is it about?* Make sure students notice the progress of the car from map to map. Begin a time line about the story using Graphic Organizer Transparency 16.

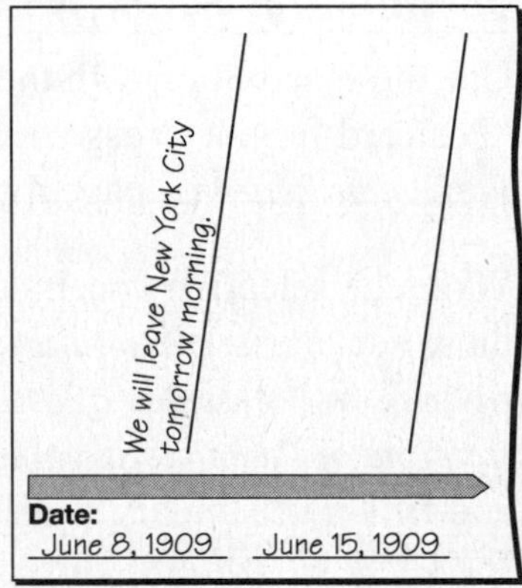

Transparency 16

Strategy: Using a Time Line

Explain the strategy: *When I want to understand when and in what order things happen, I can use a diagram. It is a strategy called Using a Time Line.* Call attention to the arrow and the lines for writing dates and events. Model filling in the first date. Write *June 8, 1909.* Have students begin their own time lines by filling in 5 dates from the story headings.

Develop Concepts

Students may need support understanding which parts of this story are historical and which are made-up. The selection is a series of journal entries based on a cross-country car trip. The characters and events are real, but the journal entries and the character's words and thoughts are made up by the author. Have the students ever kept a journal or diary? What kinds of things did they write about?

Set Purposes

Students can participate in Set Purposes, Teacher's Edition, *Scott Foresman Reading,* page 499. Encourage them to watch for what happened on the dates they wrote on their time lines. Remind students that they are using a strategy called Using a Time Line.

Guide students as they read "Amazing Alice!," Scott Foresman Reading, *pages 498–515. To support comprehension, use the suggestions in Meeting Individual Needs, ESL, in the Teacher's Edition.*

Selection Audio CD 9/Tape 25 Side 1

Response Log

- Have students imagine what happened on the trip back to New York and write a journal entry to describe it. They can use the Adding English Poster for ideas.
- Have students write a headline for a newspaper article that might have been written about the women's cross-country trip. They can draw a picture to accompany their headline.

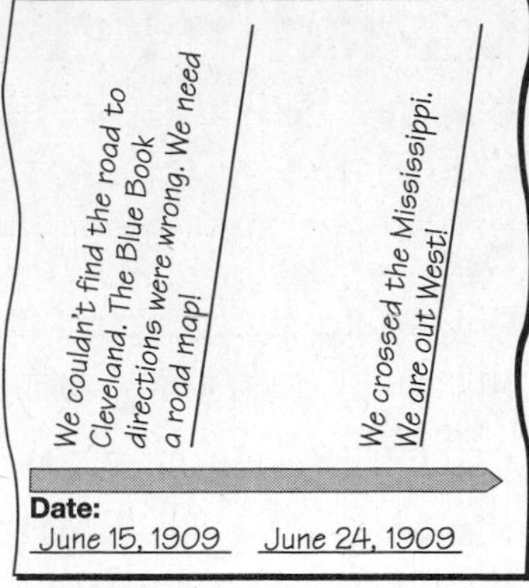

Transparency 16

Practice Selection Concepts

To help students tell what they learned, choose from these activities.

- Help students complete their time lines for the story. Have students summarize what happened on each date they selected.
- Distribute copies of the ten important sentences. Have students underline details that show why Alice was so amazing.

Ten Important Sentences Page 33

Strategy: Self-Assess

Ask: *Did Using a Time Line help you understand when and in what order things happened in the story?*

Language Awareness

Provide supported practice by using the Adding English Grammar and Phonics Practice Masters, pages 183–184, with the suggestions below.

Grammar: Pronouns

Write the following on the board: *When Jenny gets here, she will feed the dogs. They will be glad to see her.* Read the sentences aloud. Then point to *she* and say: She *is a pronoun. A pronoun takes the place of a noun. The word* she *stands for* Jenny. Circle *she.* Point to *They* and say: *The word* they *is a pronoun.* They *stands for* dogs. Circle *They.* Point to *her* and say: Her *is a pronoun.* Her *stands for* Jenny. Circle *her.*

Students can complete the Practice Master alone or with a partner.

Adding English Grammar Practice Master Page 183

Phonics: Prefixes

Distribute the Practice Master. Have students listen to and read the words in Exercise A. Then students should say the words aloud. Discuss the meanings of the base words and how the prefixes change their meanings.

For Exercise B, have students read the sentences aloud before they choose their answers.

Adding English Phonics Practice Master Page 184

PART 3

Connect Selection Concepts

Use these activities with Reader Response, Teacher's Edition, *Scott Foresman Reading,* page 515.

Dramatize

If possible, have English language learners work in groups with students whose home language is English to act out scenes from "Amazing Alice!" for the class.

Modern-Day Road Trip

Provide groups of students with a road atlas of the United States. Ask them to look for routes that go from New York City to San Francisco. Write the interstate numbers on the board. Students may also plan other road trips.

Reading Across Texts: "Keeping a Road Journal," pages 516–517

To support students as they read a how-to article:

- Have students preview the article. How is the article organized? What will students learn how to do?
- Activate prior knowledge by talking about journals. Who might use a journal and for what purpose(s)? Have students ever kept a journal?
- Before reading, have students look at the headings on the journal pictured. Together, fill in the journal for one or two days. Then read the article.
- Compare "Keeping a Road Journal" to *"Amazing Alice!"* How are the journals alike? How are they different? Use a Venn diagram to chart student responses.

Assess

Refer to the list below to assess students' progress.

Reading

- ☐ Uses words related to traveling by stagecoach and by car.
- ☐ Summarizes a selection.

Language Awareness

Grammar

- ☐ Identifies and uses pronouns correctly.

Phonics

- ☐ Recognizes and decodes words with prefixes.

Learning Strategies

- ☐ Uses a time line.
- ☐ Uses synonyms to find the meanings of unfamiliar words.

Name ______________________________

Pronouns

A. Read the sentences. Circle the pronouns.

1. Hermine was young when she went on the trip.
2. Hermine said, "Alice, I want to go on the trip with you."
3. "We will go in the motorcar to California if it will take us that far," Alice said.
4. Alice said, "Minna, I want you to ride with me."

B. Read the sentences. Circle the correct pronouns to complete the sentences.

5. Mr. Kelsey told Alice that (him/she) was a good driver.
6. Alice told Hermine, "(We/I) am glad (you/her) are going."
7. The motorcar was stuck, and (it/them) would not move.
8. People cheered when (me/they) saw Alice.

C. Think about traffic signs and what they mean. Talk with a partner. Draw a picture of the traffic sign and write about it.

One traffic sign is ______________________

____

It means ______________________

____

____

Name ______________________________

Prefixes

Phonics

A. Listen to the words. Read the words. Then say the words.

unlucky	miscount	reread
incorrect	disappear	submarine

B. Read the sentences. Choose the word that completes each sentence. Write it on the line.

1. Four women rode ____________ the motorcar. (impossible/inside)
2. Were ____________ dangers ahead? (unseen/unhooked)
3. They hoped they wouldn't ____________ any supplies. (mister/misplace)
4. Today, nothing could make Alice ____________! (unhappy/unopened)

C. Say the underlined words. Read the paragraph to a partner. Then listen as your partner reads it to you.

The stagecoach was ready to go. The passengers were impatient to be on their way. But it would be unwise to start out in the snow. The unhappy passengers went inside the inn. They reread old magazines. By the next day, the snow had disappeared.

A Peddler's Dream

Pages 518–535

Crossing Cultures • As students read this story about an immigrant, point out the German words on page 524. Have them imagine Solomon when he first arrived in the United States where most people spoke English. Which language did he probably speak most often? In which language did he probably write the letters home? What language did he use when he waited on customers? Remind students that knowing two languages is a valuable skill.

PART 1

Preview the Skill Lesson

Use these activities with the Skill Lesson: "Atalanta's Race," Teacher's Edition, *Scott Foresman Reading,* pages 518–519.

Poster Tips
Page 16

Activate Prior Knowledge

Ask students to tell what kind of race they see in Adding English Poster 22. What kinds of races have students participated in or watched? Are those races different from the race shown on the poster? How?

Recognize Vocabulary Words

Introduce the Skill Lesson literature by previewing the vocabulary at the right. List the vocabulary words on the board. Have students point to pictures in the Adding English Poster that relate to the vocabulary. Prompt them to listen for the vocabulary words as you read the passage that follows.

> Hannah goes to the library each Saturday to check out books. Sometimes it is a challenge for her to find books she likes. Last week she got a book about a princess who decided to marry a gardener. She chose him because he had an apple orchard and she liked apples—not red ones, but yellow or golden colored apples. Hannah thought the story was silly. Another book was about a dog sled race. Hannah didn't find out until the last page which team won and which teams lost the race.

Have students make word cards for the vocabulary words. As you reread the passage, students can hold up the correct card whenever they hear a vocabulary word. All students in the class would benefit from reviewing this vocabulary.

ADD ENGLISH WORDS

Listen for students' knowledge of these words:

race	**marry**
challenge	**golden**
apple	**won**
lost	

Present the Comprehension Strategy

Comprehension: Plot

Use Comprehension Strategies, *Adding English Guide,* page 10, to introduce Plot.

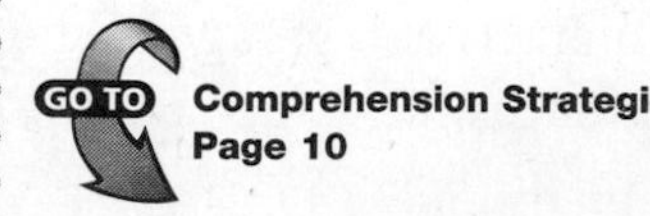

Comprehension Strategies
Page 10

Relate to Personal Experience

In groups, have students think of a story that they have read in class. Have the group members discuss what happened in the story. Ask them to recall the main problem, how the characters tried to solve the problem, and how the problem was solved. Have a volunteer from each group report to the class the plot elements of their story.

Guide students as they read "Atalanta's Race," Scott Foresman Reading, *pages 518–519. Remind them to look for a problem and the events that lead to its resolution.*

Selection Audio CD 9/Tape 26

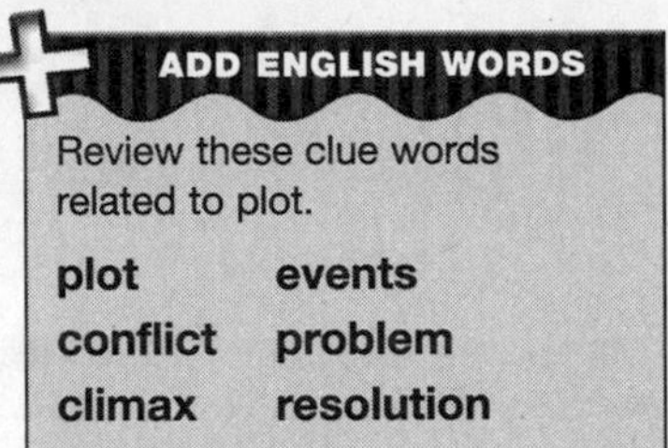

ADD ENGLISH WORDS

Review these clue words related to plot.

plot	**events**
conflict	**problem**
climax	**resolution**

Practice

Have students describe the plot of the story, listing the events and identifying the problem or conflict, the climax, and the resolution.

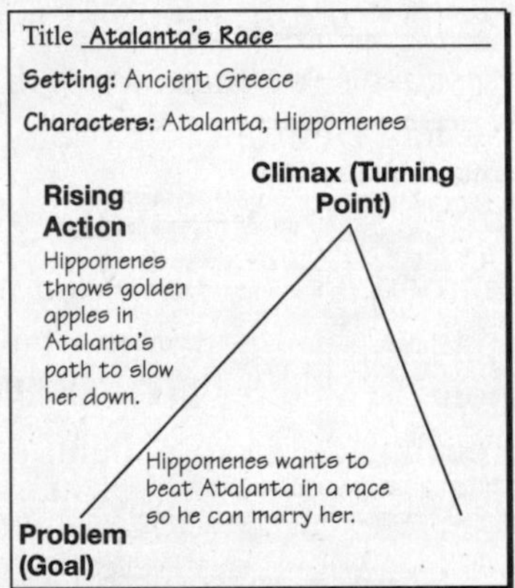

Transparency 11

Assess

If... students cannot identify the plot elements of the story,

then... help them to complete a plot structure diagram, Graphic Organizer Transparency 11, about the story. Ask questions such as: *Whom did Atalanta say she would marry? What did Hippomenes challenge himself to do? What was his goal? What events happened that helped him accomplish his goal?* Record students' responses in the appropriate places on the diagram.

PART 2

Preview the Reading Selection

Use these activities before reading *A Peddler's Dream,* Teacher's Edition, *Scott Foresman Reading,* pages 520–534.

ADD ENGLISH WORDS

Listen for students' knowledge of words related to a store.

dream	**store**
clerk	**stories**
customers	**peddler**

Activate Prior Knowledge

Involve students in talking about parts of the Adding English Poster that picture the words at the right. Invite students to tell what they know about shopping. Who shops in a store? Who buys from a peddler? Is shopping the same in all countries and cultures? Encourage students to describe shopping experiences of various kinds—in stores and open-air markets; by mail, phone, or the Internet; at a garage sale or flea market. How are these experiences the same and how are they different?

Build Background

Explain that today people shop in big department stores and ask students to give examples of these stores. Then explain that years ago, people shopped in small stores or bought things from peddlers who pushed or rode a cart from place to place. Display objects that peddlers would sell, such as kitchen gadgets, ribbons, and medicines. Ask students what peddlers sell today. (Possible responses: hot dogs, fruit, books)

Vocabulary: Antonyms

Use these activities with the Vocabulary Lesson and paragraph "My Dreams May Come True," Teacher's Edition, *Scott Foresman Reading,* page 520.

Review with students that words with opposite meanings are called antonyms and that students can use an antonym to help figure out the meaning of an unfamiliar word. Write this sentence on the board: *Some of the peddler's boxes were bound together with ribbon, but others were left untied.* Pantomime tying and untying, if necessary. Ask: *Which word in the sentence means the opposite of* bound*?* Have a volunteer circle *untied.* Continue with the following sentences: *The peddler sold many beautiful buttons to customers who eagerly purchased them. A lamb playfully skipped over to the fence and watched the tired peddler as he trudged along the road. After peddling most of his goods, the peddler spent a day in the town purchasing new supplies.*

Guide students as they read "My Dreams May Come True," Scott Foresman Reading, *page 520. Ask them how thinking of antonyms might help them understand an unfamiliar word.*

Students can participate in the Talk About It activity that follows. When possible, have English language learners work with partners whose home language is English. Students should list things they brought with them to the new place and things they know about the new place.

RESOURCES

Use *Scott Foresman ESL,* Grade 5, for additional instruction and activities.

- Chapter 7, "Coming to America"
- Video, Unit 4, "Settling America"

ADD ENGLISH WORDS

To check understanding of word meanings, have students pantomime an action involving these selection vocabulary words.

bound	**fortune**
trudged	**quarters**
mission	**peddling**
purchased	

Present the Reading Selection

Use these activities with *A Peddler's Dream,* Teacher's Edition, *Scott Foresman Reading,* pages 520–534.

Preview Title and Illustrations

Explain the strategy: *Before I begin to read a story, I read the title and look at the pictures to see what the story is about.* Point out the illustration on pages 520–521 and have students discuss what the time and place of the scene might be. Encourage comments and speculations about the setting of the story as students continue previewing the pictures. Begin a story sequence chart, Graphic Organizer Transparency 12.

Strategy: Using a Story Sequence Chart

Explain the strategy: *When I want to understand the events in a story, I can use a chart. It is a strategy called Using a Story Sequence Chart.* Remind students that sequencing is putting events in order. Call attention to the labeled boxes on the chart and the arrows connecting the *Problem* and *Solution* boxes. Model filling in the story title and a character based on the title and illustrations. Then have students begin their own charts by writing the story title and possible characters in the appropriate boxes.

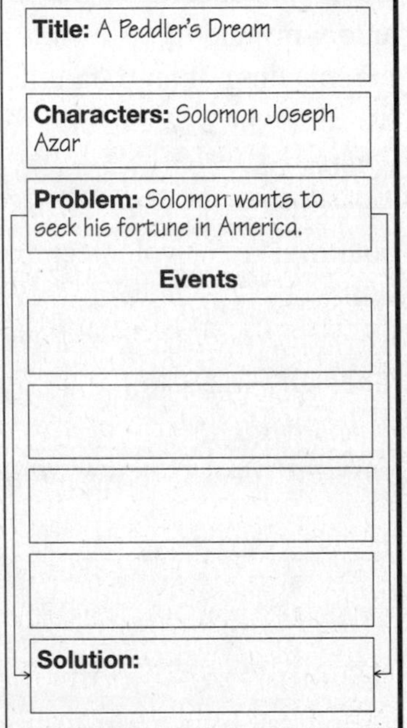

Transparency 12

Develop Concepts

Students may need support in understanding the persistence of Solomon in achieving his goal. Have them think about other people who did not give up in trying to achieve their goals. Encourage students to share stories about members of their own families who were persistent in following their goals. Ask questions such as: *What problems did the person face? What did the person do to overcome the problems? Would it have been easy just to give up and forget about the goals?*

Set Purposes

Students can participate in Set Purposes, Teacher's Edition, *Scott Foresman Reading,* page 521. Encourage students to look for a problem or goal and to notice the order of events in the story as they read. Remind them that they are using a strategy called using a story sequence chart. They may want to fill in their charts as they read.

Guide students as they read A Peddler's Dream, Scott Foresman Reading, *pages 520–534. To support comprehension, use the suggestions in Meeting Individual Needs, ESL, in the Teacher's Edition.*

Selection Audio CD 9/Tape 26

Response Log

- Have students draw a picture of one of the characters in the story and write a sentence or two describing the character.
- Have students reread Solomon's letter. Then have students write about people they would miss if they moved away.

Practice Selection Concepts

To help students tell what they learned, choose from these activities.

- Help students complete their story sequence charts. Partners can discuss their answers.
- Distribute copies of the ten important sentences. Have students work in groups to discuss the sentences and decide which ones tell about events that helped to make Solomon's dream come true. Students can draw pictures to illustrate one of those events.

Strategy: Self-Assess

Ask: *Did Using a Story Sequence Chart help you understand the problem and the events that led to its solution? How?*

Title: A Peddler's Dream

Characters: Solomon Joseph Azar, Mr. Lindheimer, Mr. Hart, Marie

Problem: Solomon wants to seek his fortune in America.

Events

Solomon becomes a peddler.

Solomon is robbed.

Solomon goes to work for Mr. Hart.

The store burns down.

Solution: Solomon builds the store of his dreams.

Transparency 12

Ten Important Sentences Page 34

Language Awareness

Provide supported practice by using the Adding English Grammar and Phonics Practice Masters, pages 191–192, with the suggestions below.

Grammar: Subject and Object Pronouns

Offer a pencil to a student. Write on the board: *She took it.* Explain to students that *she* takes the place of the student's name and that *it* takes the place of *pencil.* Perform other simple actions and invite students to dictate sentences with subject and object pronouns.

Students can complete the Practice Master alone or with a partner.

Adding English Grammar Practice Master Page 191

Phonics: Words with Silent Consonants *kn, gn, wr, mb*

Distribute the Practice Master. Have students listen and read as you say the words in Exercise A. Then students should say the words aloud. Have students figure out which letter is silent in each word.

For Exercise B, have students read the sentences aloud before they choose their answers.

Adding English Phonics Practice Master Page 192

PART 3

Connect Selection Concepts

Use these activities with Reader Response, Teacher's Edition, *Scott Foresman Reading,* page 534.

Literature Discussion Group

When possible, have English language learners work in groups with students whose home language is English. Together they should discuss the story, focusing on these questions:

- Would becoming a peddler help Solomon reach his goal in the United States today? Explain your answer.
- Is the store shown on pages 484 and 485 different from the stores in which your family shops? If so, in what ways?

Make a Picture Book

Ask groups of students to create a simple picture book that tells the story of Solomon's dream. They can use their story sequence chart for ideas. Each page should have a picture and one or two sentences of text.

ADD ENGLISH WORDS

Use the Adding English Poster to help students with the following words:

welcome	**years**
immigrants	**Ellis Island**
arrived	**ports of entry**

Reading Across Texts: "Welcome to the United States," page 535

To support students as they learn about and read an informational article:

- Remind students to read the title, the key, and the labels of the graph first. Ask what this graph is about.
- Ask: *Did someone in your family come to the United States from another country? Do you know what city your relatives arrived in and when? What country did they come from? Where did they settle?*
- Have students compare "Welcome to the United States" with *A Peddler's Dream.* Divide the class into two groups. One group should list how the two selections are alike. The other group should list how they are different.

Assess

Refer to the list below to assess students' progress.

Reading

- ☐ Uses words related to shopping, stores, and peddlers.
- ☐ Understands and identifies plot elements in a story.

Language Awareness

Grammar

- ☐ Identifies and uses subject and object pronouns.

Phonics

- ☐ Decodes words with silent consonants.

Learning Strategies

- ☐ Uses a story sequence chart.
- ☐ Uses antonyms to find the meanings of unfamiliar words.

Name ______________________________

Subject and Object Pronouns

A. Read the sentences. Circle the pronouns in each sentence.

1. Solomon dreamed about the store he would have.

2. The shop owner told him, "You should try peddling."

3. The Lindheimers asked Solomon if he would stay and work for them.

4. "Mr. Hart, I think Solomon can help you," said Mr. Lindheimer.

B. Read the sentences. Circle the correct pronouns to complete the sentences.

5. Customers liked Solomon because (he/him) greeted (they/them) with a smile.

6. Solomon wrote to Marie, "(Me/I) will soon return, and (we/us) will be married."

7. "The store! (It/Them) is on fire!" cried Solomon as (him/he) woke Marie.

8. Solomon thought about the dream and how (her/it) had finally come true.

C. Talk with a partner about something you like to buy in a store. Write about it and why you like it.

I like to buy ______________________________

____

____

____

____

Name ___________________________________

Words with Silent Consonants *kn, gn, wr, mb*

A. Listen to the words.
Read the words.
Then say the words.

knot gnome wren lamb

B. Read the sentences. Write the word that completes each sentence.

1. The peddler ____________ on the door of the farmhouse. (kitchen/knocked)

2. He displayed the ____________, mirrors, and other goods in his pack. (combs/cheats)

3. He had netting to protect a horse from buzzing ____________.(grabs/gnats)

4. A ____________ pen had a gold point and a carved pearl handle. (walking/writing)

5. The peddler painted a ____________ on his cart. (sign/song)

C. Say the underlined words. Read the paragraph to a partner. Then listen as your partner reads it to you.

The peddler took the <u>wrong</u> road and lost his way. Then he saw a <u>sign</u> that pointed to the town where he was going. He <u>climbed</u> a steep hill and thought about stopping to rest. But he <u>knew</u> he had to keep on going, so that he would reach the town before night.

The Race for the North Pole

Pages 536–555

Crossing Cultures • In this lesson, students read about polar regions and famous people who explored them. The explorers in one selection are considered famous. Ask students if they know of someone from their home culture who is famous for exploring or discovering a new place. What did he or she discover? If time allows, help students use the Internet or library to research explorers from their home cultures.

PART 1

Preview the Skill Lesson

Use these activities with the Skill Lesson: "Polar Lands," Teacher's Edition, *Scott Foresman Reading,* pages 536–537.

Activate Prior Knowledge

Ask students to tell what they see in Adding English Poster 23. What part of the world is shown? What words can students think of to describe the climate and land in the poster? Encourage students to compare and contrast the pictures they see with places they have lived or visited. Begin a Venn diagram, Graphic Organizer Transparency 21, to record students' responses.

Poster Tips Page 16

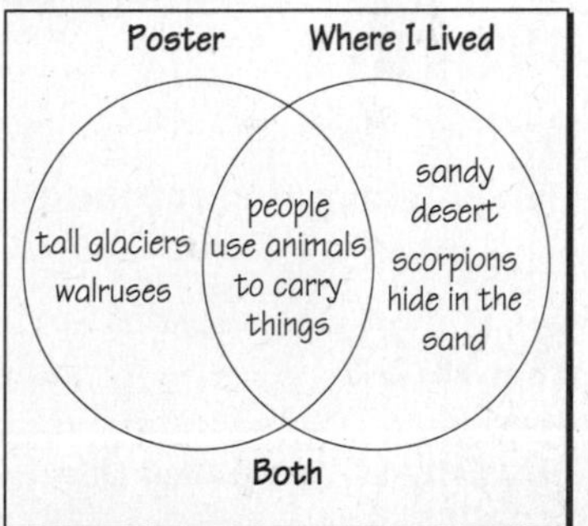

Transparency 21

Recognize and Use Vocabulary Words

Introduce the Skill Lesson literature by previewing the vocabulary at the right. List the vocabulary words on the board. Have students point to elements of the Adding English Poster that relate to the vocabulary. Then have students listen for the vocabulary words as you read the passage that follows.

> **Earth turns on an imaginary line, or axis. Each end of the line is called a pole. The pole at the top is called the North Pole. The bottom pole is called the South Pole. Both poles are very cold and have large, ice-covered areas. These icy spots are frozen all year round. Mounds of ice and snow surround the poles on all sides.**

Have students draw pictures of themselves on an imaginary visit to the North or South Pole. Tell them to write sentences about their pictures, using vocabulary words. Students can refer to the Adding English Poster for ideas. All students in the class may benefit from reviewing this vocabulary before reading the skill lesson selection.

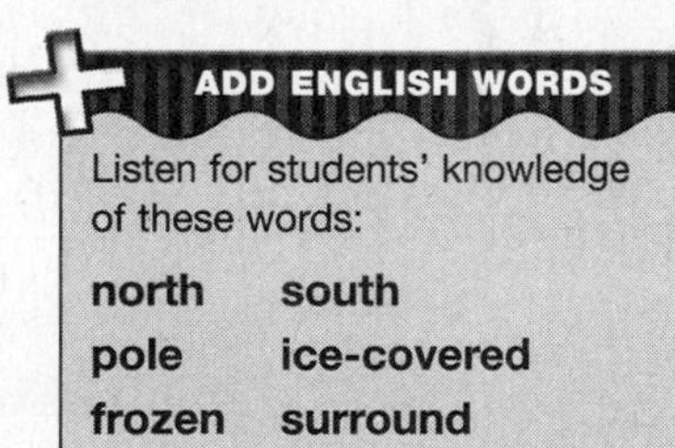

ADD ENGLISH WORDS

Listen for students' knowledge of these words:

north	**south**
pole	**ice-covered**
frozen	**surround**

Present the Comprehension Strategy

Comprehension: Graphic Sources

Use Comprehension Strategies, *Adding English Guide,* page 10, to introduce Graphic Sources.

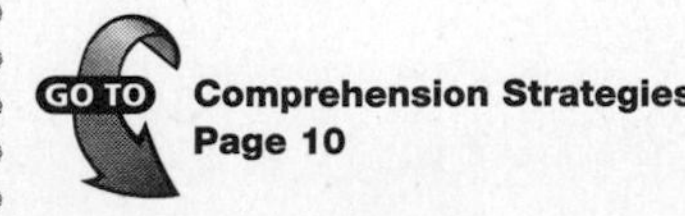

Comprehension Strategies Page 10

Relate to Personal Experience

Show a map of your area. Have a volunteer point out where your school is located. Have students tell how a street map is helpful and when they have used such a map. Remind students that maps are geographic sources that can help readers understand the places they read about. Have partners talk about how to get from their homes to the school and then draw a simple map to show the routes. Students' maps can be general, showing only landmarks and directions.

Guide students as they read "Polar Lands," Scott Foresman Reading, *pages 536–537. Remind them to refer to the map to find the places mentioned in the article.*

Selection Audio CD 9/Tape 27

Practice

Have students name the places that are mentioned in "Polar Lands" and point out those that are shown on the map.

Assess

If... students cannot point out places mentioned in the article,

then... ask them to reread the article in pairs. One student can read the text aloud while the other studies the map. The reader should pause after saying each place name until the map reader points out the place on the map or determines that it is not shown. Partners can switch parts halfway through the article.

ADD ENGLISH WORDS

Review these clue words related to graphic sources.

illustration	**chart**
graph	**map**
diagram	**table**
list	**map key**
time line	**scale drawing**

PART 2

Preview the Reading Selection

Use these activities before reading "The Race for the North Pole," Teacher's Edition, *Scott Foresman Reading,* pages 538–553.

Activate Prior Knowledge

Ask students if they have experienced a major winter snowstorm. What were the conditions outside? What clothing did they wear? Encourage students to use the Adding English Poster for support. Have students talk about how they might prepare for a long journey to a place that is covered with ice, snow, and extremely cold water.

ADD ENGLISH WORDS

Listen for students' knowledge of words related to Arctic expeditions.

expedition	**Inuit**
sledge	**survive**
supplies	**explorer**

Build Background

Show students pictures of explorers and their dog sleds arriving at the North Pole. Explain that the dogs pulled sleds that carried supplies for the explorers. Tell students that the explorers in the main selection had very little food other than walrus meat. In addition, they had to bring all of their supplies on their sleds.

Use Brainstorming

Have students brainstorm a list of the most important items needed by Arctic explorers. Students should choose two items from the list and talk with a partner about why the items are important. Students should use selection vocabulary words when possible.

Vocabulary: Multiple-Meaning Words

Use these activities with the Vocabulary Lesson and paragraph "Arctic Mission!," Teacher's Edition, *Scott Foresman Reading,* page 538.

Write the following sentences on the board and read them aloud: *I am navigating an airplane. I am navigating a boat. I am navigating over this land that is full of mountains.* Have students act out each sentence as they say it aloud. For example, students can sit in a chair and pretend to steer an airplane or row a boat, or they can to pretend to hike through mountains (a group of desks).

Use Word Riddles

Write word riddles on the board and have students choose vocabulary words to answer them. For example: *We are large animals with tusks, and we live where it is cold. What are we?* (*walruses*) *I am a section of Earth. What am I?* (*region*) *We are huge chunks of ice. What are we?* (*glaciers*) Point to the Adding English Poster, maps, posters, or other objects to guide students.

Guide students as they read "Arctic Mission!," Scott Foresman Reading, *page 538. Ask them how context clues can help them choose the correct meaning of a multiple-meaning word.*

Students can participate in the Write About It activity that follows. Before they begin writing, have English language learners work with partners whose home language is English to discuss and list things they know about the Arctic.

RESOURCES

Use *Scott Foresman ESL,* Grade 5, for additional instruction and activities.

- Chapter 3, "The Earth Is Not Flat!"
- Video, Unit 2, "Explorers"

ADD ENGLISH WORDS

Through listening and watching, assess students' knowledge of selection vocabulary.

region **navigate**
glaciers **walruses**
adventure

Present the Reading Selection

Use these activities with "The Race for the North Pole," Teacher's Edition, *Scott Foresman Reading,* pages 538–553.

Preview Headings and Illustrations

Explain the strategy: *Before I begin to read a selection, I read the heading and look at the pictures and other graphic sources to see what the selection will be about.* Point out the photographs on page 539. Ask: *What do you think these men are wearing? Why?* Continue previewing the illustrations. Call attention to the table on page 548 and the map on page 550. Have students read and discuss the headings.

Develop Concepts

Students may need support in understanding that Matthew Henson was an experienced traveler before he went with Robert Peary on the Nicaragua expedition. Use a world map to point out Maryland, where Matthew grew up; China, Japan, the Philippines, France, Africa, and Russia, where he traveled with Captain Childs; and Nicaragua and Greenland, where he went with Robert Peary. Ask: *What skills do you think Matthew Henson might have learned from so much sailing experience?*

Set Purposes

Students can participate in Set Purposes, Teacher's Edition, *Scott Foresman Reading,* page 539.

Strategy: Using a Character Traits Web

Explain the strategy: *When I want to understand what a person is like, I can use a chart. It is a strategy called Using a Character Traits Web.* Model writing *Matthew Henson* in the center oval. Say: *The photograph on page 551 shows Matthew Henson at the North Pole. I think that anyone who makes the journey to the North Pole must be very brave. I am going to write brave as a character trait.* Model writing *brave* in one of the ovals. Have students begin separate character traits webs for Matthew Henson and Robert Peary, based on information in the selection titles, photographs, and other graphic sources. Remind them that the explorers' thoughts and actions reveal their character traits.

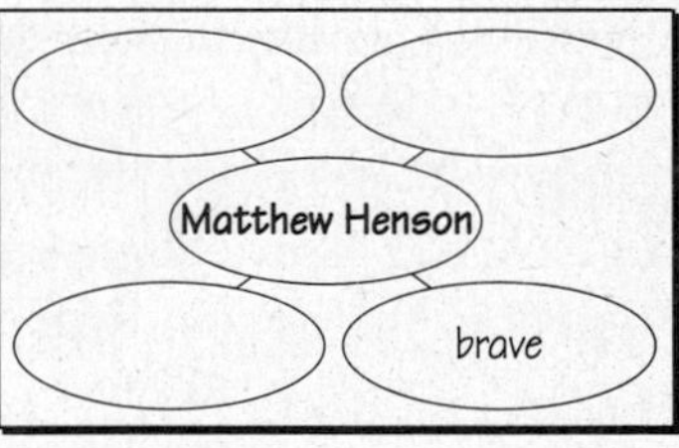

Transparency 5

Guide students as they read "The Race for the North Pole," Scott Foresman Reading, *pages 538–553. To support comprehension, use the suggestions in Meeting Individual Needs, ESL, in the Teacher's Edition.*

Selection Audio CD 9/Tape 27

Response Log

- Have students write about a place they'd like to explore and list supplies they would need for the expedition.
- Have students draw a picture to show how they would dress for an expedition to the North Pole. Tell them to write captions for their drawings. Students can use the selection illustrations and the Adding English Poster as references.

Practice Selection Concepts

To help students tell what they learned, choose from these activities.

- Help students complete their webs for Matthew Henson and Robert Peary. Encourage them to draw more ovals on the webs, if needed. Have them share their webs in small groups.
- Distribute the ten important sentences. Have partners take turns reading the sentences aloud. Then have students choose the sentence that tells about the part of the biography they like best. Students can draw pictures to illustrate their sentences and then share them with the class.

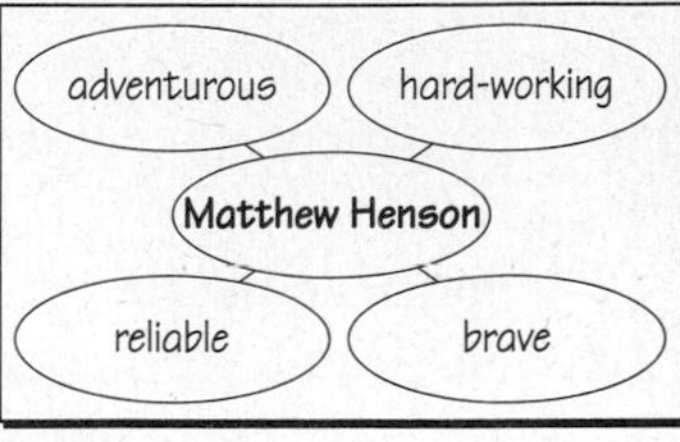

Transparency 5

Ten Important Sentences Page 35

Strategy: Self-Assess

Ask: *Did Using a Character Traits Web help you understand what Matthew Henson and Robert Peary were like? How?*

Language Awareness

Provide supported practice by using the Adding English Grammar and Phonics Practice Masters, pages 199–200, with the suggestions below.

Grammar: Pronouns and Their Referents

Write the following on the board: *Julie will play with the kitten. It will be glad to see her.* Read the sentences aloud. Then invite a volunteer to circle the pronouns. (*it, her*) Ask other volunteers to indicate which noun each pronoun refers to, or stands for. (*kitten, Julie*) Point out that pronouns need a clear referent, or noun to refer to.

Students can complete the Practice Master alone or with a partner.

Adding English Grammar Practice Master Page 199

Phonics: Plural Possessives

Distribute the Practice Master. Have students listen, read, and repeat as you say the words in Exercise A. Prompt students to use the words in sentences.

For Exercise B, have students read each sentence aloud before they write an answer.

Adding English Phonics Practice Master Page 200

PART 3

Connect Selection Concepts

Use these activities with Reader Response, Teacher's Edition, *Scott Foresman Reading,* page 553.

Literature Discussion Group

When possible, have English language learners work in groups with students whose home language is English. Together they should talk about "The Race for the North Pole," focusing on these questions:

- What happened in the story?
- How did Matthew Henson and Robert Peary meet?
- How do you think Matthew Henson felt when Robert Peary chose others to go with him to the North Pole? Why?

Personal Treks

Ask students to write about an imaginary trek. Have them describe where they went, what happened, and how they finally reached their destination. Encourage them to illustrate their descriptions.

Reading Across Texts: "The North Pole," pages 554–555

To support students as they read a picture encyclopedia:

- Have students preview "The North Pole" by looking at the pictures and reading a few words from each caption. Explain that this selection can be read in any order. Read the introduction with students.
- Ask: *What kind of information about going to the North Pole does this article provide? How does this kind of article help you better understand "The Race for the North Pole?"*

Assess

Refer to the list below to assess students' progress.

Reading

- ☐ Uses words related to polar regions and Arctic exploration.
- ☐ Uses graphic sources of information.

Language Awareness

Grammar

- ☐ Uses pronouns and identifies their referents.

Phonics

- ☐ Identifies and decodes plural possessive nouns.

Learning Strategies

- ☐ Uses a character traits web.
- ☐ Uses context clues to choose the correct meaning of multiple-meaning words.

Name ____________________________

Grammar

Pronouns and Their Referents

A. Read each sentence. Circle the pronoun. Draw a line under the noun it refers to.

1. The explorers were gone for a year, so they needed lots of supplies.
2. Mrs. Peary was happy that she could go on the trip.
3. The ice was so thick it stopped the ship.
4. Now Matthew would build the house he needed.

B. Read the sentences. Choose a word from the box to complete each sentence.

them	him	it	they

5. The Inuit liked Matthew Henson and taught _________ many of their ways.
6. Matthew cracked the whip in the air over the dogs to make _________ start.
7. When the dogs were tied to the sledge, _________ spread out.
8. A walrus roared as _________ ran to the sledge.

C. Talk with a partner about an arctic animal: polar bear, seal, walrus, reindeer, or caribou. Then write about the animal.

One arctic animal is the ____________________________

It ____________________________

____

____

____

____

Name ________________________________

Plural Possessives

Phonics

A. Listen to the words. Read the words. Then say the words.

birds' nest seals' fur owls' chicks

B. Read the sentences. Choose a word from the box to complete each sentence.

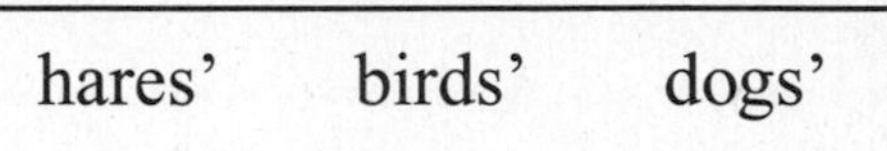
hares' birds' dogs'

1. The sledge ____________ hair has fur underneath to keep the dogs warm.

2. The arctic ____________ coats grew white as fall ended.

3. Ground squirrels were looking for nests of ____________ eggs to eat.

C. Say the underlined words. Read the paragraph to a partner. Then listen as your partner reads it to you.

My grandfather and I sat on my grandparents' porch, and he told me stories of great explorers traveling to the North Pole. He said the explorers' sled had long oak runners and was stacked high with supplies. He also told me the sled dogs' harnesses had to be tied tightly to the sled so dogs weren't left behind. Once, my grandfather showed me his old sleds. The sleds' runners were worn, but they still worked!

Into the Sea

Pages 556–575

Crossing Cultures • In this lesson, students read about the importance of wetlands, the experiences of a sea turtle, and the work of an underwater photographer. Ask students about how their home cultures value or use similar bodies of water.

PART 1

Preview the Skill Lesson

Use these activities with the Skill Lesson: "Saving Our Wetlands," Teacher's Edition, *Scott Foresman Reading,* pages 556–557.

Poster Tips
Page 16

Activate Prior Knowledge

Ask students to tell what they see in Adding English Poster 24. What do students already know about such places? Ask them to point to the turtle, sharks, and dolphins and compare and contrast what they know about these animals.

ADD ENGLISH WORDS

Use these words in questions. Have students use the words to answer your questions.

saving	**wetlands**
swamps	**marshes**
nursery	**migrating**

Recognize and Use Vocabulary Words

Introduce the Skill Lesson literature by previewing vocabulary at the right. List the vocabulary words on the board. Have students point to elements in the Adding English Poster that relate to the vocabulary. Then have students listen for the vocabulary words as you read the passage that follows.

> Many farmers are helping restore Earth to its natural state. They plant grass and trees near streams to keep the soil from being washed away and to provide homes for animals. They plant trees near swamps and marshes to provide protection and resting places for migrating birds. These wetlands are also a nursery for baby fish and turtles. Saving Earth and its creatures is important to farmers.

Have students work in groups to create phrases using the vocabulary words. Students can refer to the paragraph and the Adding English Poster for ideas. Have students illustrate their phrases. All students could benefit from reviewing this vocabulary before reading the Skill Lesson selection.

Present the Comprehension Strategy

Comprehension: Author's Purpose

Use Comprehension Strategies, *Adding English Guide,* page 10, to introduce Author's Purpose.

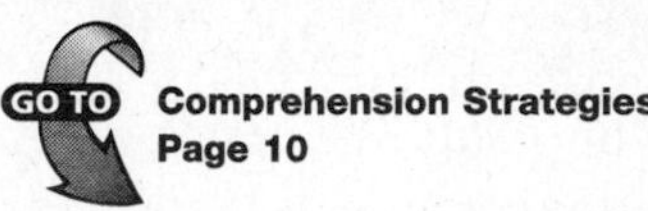

Comprehension Strategies
Page 10

Relate to Personal Experience

Remind students that an author's purpose is his or her reason for writing something and that some purposes for writing are to entertain, to inform, to express, and to persuade. Display a comic strip that students are familiar with and ask: *What purpose or purposes do you think the cartoonist had for writing this comic strip?* (to entertain or amuse) Have students turn to the selection "Polar Lands" on pages 536–537 of their books. Ask: *What purpose or purposes do you think the author had for writing "Polar Lands"?* (to inform) Tell students that predicting an author's purpose can help them decide what to look for when they read.

Guide students as they read "Saving Our Wetlands," Scott Foresman Reading, *pages 556–557. Remind them to think about why the author wrote it.*

Selection Audio CD 10/Tape 28

Practice

Have students recall details from "Saving Our Wetlands" and discuss the author's purpose in writing it.

Assess

If... students cannot recall details from the selection and identify the author's purpose,

then... ask: *Do you think this selection is fiction or nonfiction? How can you tell?* When students have identified the piece as nonfiction, ask questions to help them recognize the author's purpose: *Does the article give facts or information? Does it make you laugh or smile? Does the author tell what he thinks? Does he tell readers to do something?*

ADD ENGLISH WORDS

Review these clue words related to author's purpose.

purpose **entertain**
inform **express**
persuade

PART 2

Preview the Reading Selection

Use these activities before reading *Into the Sea,* Teacher's Edition, *Scott Foresman Reading,* pages 558–571.

Activate Prior Knowledge

Involve students in talking about parts of the Adding English Poster that picture the words at the right. Ask students what they know about sea turtles and other animals shown. Use a T-chart, Graphic Organizer Transparency 24, to record students' responses.

ADD ENGLISH WORDS

Listen for students' knowledge of words related to sea turtles.

sea turtle **paddle**
dive **floats**
underwater **nest**
hatch

Build Background

Show students pictures of turtles, crabs, jellyfish, sea stars, water striders, barnacles, sharks, and other creatures from *Into the Sea.* Together, create a bulletin board display of pictures and captions. Students can refer to the display as they read the selection.

Animals I See	What the Animals Are Doing
turtle	diving underwater

Transparency 24

Word Card Game

First, each student should make a set of cards for the vocabulary and write a sentence using each word. To play the game, one student reads a sentence, leaving out the vocabulary word. The partner supplies the missing word by holding up the word card that fits the sentence. Students can refer to the Adding English Poster for ideas in creating their sentences.

RESOURCES

Use *Scott Foresman ESL,* Grade 5, for additional instruction and activities.

- Chapter 5, "Precious Water"
- Video, Unit 3, "Water, Water Everywhere"

Vocabulary: Multiple-Meaning Words

Use these activities with the Vocabulary Lesson and paragraph "Out of the Nest," Teacher's Edition, *Scott Foresman Reading,* page 558.

Write these vocabulary words on the board: *coral, awkward,* and *current.* Then write this sentence: *The fish was coral with dark blue stripes.* Ask: *Does* coral *mean "a stony or skeletal creature in the sea" or "deep pink or red"?* Point out that context clues can help students choose the correct meaning. Continue with these sentences and word meanings: *The crab was awkward and slow as it moved along the reef.* (*awkward:* "difficult" or "embarrassing, clumsy") *The wind blowing on the ocean's surface caused the current.* (*current:* "flow of water" or "flow of electricity")

ADD ENGLISH WORDS

Through listening and watching, assess students' knowledge of selection vocabulary.

protection	**awkward**
flippers	**muscles**
current	**ridges**
coral	**underside**

Use Word Riddles

Write the vocabulary words on the board. Have partners write a riddle for each one. For example: *I am a long, narrow chain of hills, sometimes on the ocean bottom. What am I?* Have students take turns reading their riddles and providing two answer choices while the rest of the class tries to guess the vocabulary word that is the answer. Students can use the Adding English Poster for ideas in creating their riddles.

Guide students as they read "Out of the Nest," Scott Foresman Reading, *page 558. Ask them how context clues can help them choose the correct meaning of a multiple-meaning word.*

Students can participate in the Talk About It activity that follows. When possible, have English language learners work with partners whose home language is English to make a list of things they know about sea turtles.

Present the Reading Selection

Use these activities with *Into the Sea,* Teacher's Edition, *Scott Foresman Reading,* pages 558–571.

Preview Illustrations

Explain the strategy: *Before I begin to read, I look at the pictures and captions to see what the selection is about.* Call attention to the illustrations, especially on pages 558–559 and page 562. Ask: *Why are some of these fish brightly colored and not others?* Point out the different kinds of turtles shown on page 569. Continue discussing other illustrations.

Strategy: Using a Sequence Chart

Explain the strategy: *When I want to understand the things that happen in a selection and the order in which they happen, I can use a chart. It is a strategy called Using a Sequence Chart.* Use Graphic Organizer Transparency 22, to make a sequence chart, deleting "How to" at the top and "Steps in a Process" at the bottom. Call attention to the numbered boxes and the arrows. Say: *The illustration on page 560 shows a baby sea turtle breaking out of its egg, so I am going to write that in the first box on my chart.* Have students begin their own sequence charts, writing the selection title at the top and filling in the first box.

Transparency 22

Develop Concepts

Students may need support in understanding the variety of living things that live in the ocean. Explain that sea creatures range in size from microscopic to the 100-foot-long blue whales. Also say that most sea animals stay in the water, except for the female sea turtle, featured in *Into the Sea,* that returns to lay her eggs on the beach. Explain that although the story did not actually happen to a specific sea turtle, it tells about experiences sea turtles typically have.

Set Purposes

Students can participate in Set Purposes, Teacher's Edition, *Scott Foresman Reading,* page 559. Encourage them to notice when important things happen to the sea turtle and to write them on their charts as they read. They can continue their charts on a second page, changing the numbers 1–5 to 6–10. Remind students that they are using a strategy called using a sequence chart.

Guide students as they read Into the Sea, Scott Foresman Reading, *pages 558–571. To support comprehension, use the suggestions in Meeting Individual Needs, ESL, in the Teacher's Edition.*

Selection Audio CD 10/Tape 28

Response Log

- Have students list some of the ways people can harm sea turtles. Then have them write about how people can help protect turtles. Encourage students to brainstorm and discuss their ideas before they write.
- Have students draw a picture and caption of one event in the life of the sea turtle.

Practice Selection Concepts

To help students tell what they learned, choose from these activities.

- Help students complete their sequence charts.
- Distribute the ten important sentences. Have students check the selection to see if a sentence is illustrated and record the page number. Students can draw pictures of other sentences.

Strategy: Self-Assess

Ask: *Did Using a Sequence Chart help you understand the selection? How?*

Into the Sea

1. A baby sea turtle hatches on the beach.
2. The baby turtle pulls herself across the beach and into the ocean.
3. The turtle floats and eats plankton.

Transparency 22

Ten Important Sentences Page 36

Language Awareness

Provide supported practice by using the Adding English Grammar and Phonics Practice Masters, pages 207–208, with the suggestions below.

Grammar: Prepositions and Prepositional Phrases

Write the following sentence on the board: *A gentle wave carried the turtle into the sea.* Read the sentence aloud. Then point to *into* and say: Into *is a preposition. A preposition shows the relationship between a noun or pronoun and another word in a sentence.* List other prepositions on the board: *in, by, from, to, on, off, across, between, over,* and *through.* Say: *A prepositional phrase is a group of words that begins with a preposition and ends with a noun or a pronoun.* Point to *into the sea* and say: Into the sea *is a prepositional phrase.*

Students can complete the Practice Master alone or with a partner.

Adding English Grammar Practice Master Page 207

Base Words, Endings

Phonics: Schwa Sound

Distribute the Practice Master. Have students listen to and read as you say the words in Exercise A. Then students should repeat the words. Point out that a different letter makes the schwa sound in each word.

For Exercise B, have students read the sentences aloud before they choose their answers.

Adding English Phonics Practice Master Page 208

PART 3

Connect Selection Concepts

Use these activities with Reader Response, Teacher's Edition, *Scott Foresman Reading,* page 571.

Puppet Performance

Students can present a class puppet performance of *Into the Sea.* They can make puppets out of lightweight cardboard, with a ruler taped on the back for manipulating them, and the "character" (painted or made of construction paper) on the front. As a class, create a stage with a change of backdrops (beach, ocean, nighttime, daylight). Characters may include the sea turtle at different stages of her life, a crab, a sea star, a barracuda, sea horses, mussels, butterfly fish, and sharks. Narrators can take turns reading from the story while other students move the puppets.

Sea Creature Reports

Students can work in groups to share information about creatures that live in water, based on research in encyclopedias or on the Internet. Students can accompany their presentations with photographs and other illustrations.

Reading Across Texts: "I Work in the Ocean," pages 572–575

To support students as they read an informational article:

- Remind students to look at the pictures and read the captions before reading an informational article. Help them match the numbered captions with the photographs.
- Ask: *Who is this article about? Would you like to do the things that he does? Explain your answer.*
- Discuss how Norbert Wu might have used photographs to illustrate *Into the Sea.* What would the photographs look like? How would Wu take them?

ADD ENGLISH WORDS

Use the Adding English Poster to help students with the following words:

photograph	**sharks**
environment	**dolphins**
scuba diving	**pollution**

Assess

Refer to the list below to assess students' progress.

Reading

- ☐ Uses words related to wetlands, sea turtles, and other ocean life.
- ☐ Recognizes the author's purpose for writing a selection.

Language Awareness

Grammar

- ☐ Uses prepositions and prepositional phrases.

Phonics

- ☐ Pronounces words with the schwa sound.

Learning Strategies

- ☐ Uses a sequence chart.
- ☐ Uses context clues to choose the correct meaning of multiple-meaning words.

Name ______________________________

Prepositions and Prepositional Phrases

A. Read the sentences. Circle the preposition. Draw a line under the prepositional phrase.

1. A sea turtle must drag its body across the beach.

2. Even the largest land turtle can lift its body off the ground.

3. Some freshwater turtles have webbing between their fingers and toes.

4. Sea turtles swim through the water.

B. Read the sentences. Write a preposition from the box to complete each sentence.

from	in	across	under	with	for

5. Turtles swim __________ a ledge to hide.

6. A baby turtle breaks away __________ the rest.

7. Turtles paddle __________ their flippers.

8. Wind makes waves __________ the ocean's surface.

9. Tiny fish hide __________ the seaweed.

10. Turtles dig holes in the sand __________ their eggs.

C. Talk with a partner about living things in the ocean. Then write about one animal that lives in the ocean.

____

____

____

____

____

Name ______________________________

Schwa Sound

A. Listen to the words. Read the words. Then say the words.

zebr_a_ chick_e_n penc_i_l pil_o_t circ_u_s

B. Read the sentences. Write the word from the parentheses that completes each sentence.

1. A hard shell is protection ____________ enemies. (alive/against)
2. Some fish live at the ____________ of the ocean. (bottom/button)
3. Turtles follow a ____________ in the sea. (connect/current)
4. Birds and amphibians need wetlands to ____________. (survive/suggest)
5. Turtle eggs are ____________. (feathery/leathery)

C. Say the underlined words. Read the paragraph to a partner. Then listen as your partner reads it to you.

Wetlands make excellent homes for turtles, salamanders, frogs, and snakes. There are ways to attract these and other animals to a restored wetland. Drag an old log to the north side of the wetland pool. In this location, shoreline grass and other vegetation will not shade the log. Painted turtles will appreciate this great place to lie in the sun!

Space Probes to the Planets

Pages 576–595

Crossing Cultures • In this lesson, students read about meteorites and about information collected by space probes to the planets. Have students help you make a list of names of the sun, Earth, and the moon in English and in their home languages. Invite students to teach the class, and you, how to say the names.

PART 1

Preview the Skill Lesson

Use these activities with the Skill Lesson: "Out-of-This-World Rocks," Teacher's Edition, *Scott Foresman Reading,* pages 576–577.

Activate Prior Knowledge

Ask students to tell what they see in Adding English Poster 25. What is the setting? What things do they see in the picture? Ask: *Where have you seen objects like these before?* Allow students to use their home language when needed. Use a T-chart, Graphic Organizer Transparency 24, to record students' responses.

GO TO Poster Tips Page 16

Things I See	Where I Have Seen Them Before
moons	outdoors
planets	on TV
spacesuit	museum

Transparency 24

Recognize and Use Vocabulary Words

Introduce the Skill Lesson literature by previewing vocabulary at the right. List the vocabulary words on the board. Have students point to elements in the Adding English Poster that relate to the vocabulary. Then have students listen for the vocabulary words as you read the passage that follows.

> **Most <u>meteorites</u> are found on the ground. Someone finds these <u>space rocks</u> on Earth, but usually no one sees them fall. Some meteorites look like rocks formed by volcanoes, because they have a <u>glassy</u> surface. Meteorites might be called part of the stardust from which the <u>solar system</u> was formed. They are pieces of the <u>planets</u>, the sun, moons, and <u>comets</u>.**

Have students make word cards for the vocabulary words and illustrate the words on the back of the cards. Read the passage again and have students hold up their word cards when they hear a vocabulary word.

ADD ENGLISH WORDS

Present these words in a web to help students understand their meanings and their relationships to one another.

comets **meteorites**
planets **space rocks**
glassy **solar system**

Present the Comprehension Strategy

Comprehension: Text Structure

Use Comprehension Strategies, *Adding English Guide,* page 10, to introduce Text Structure.

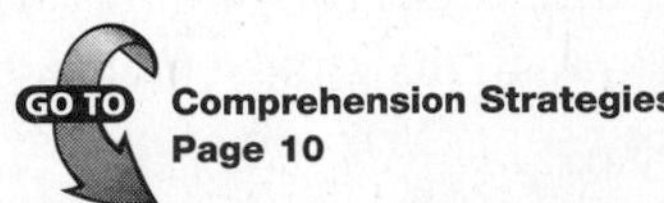
GO TO Comprehension Strategies Page 10

Relate to Personal Experience

Ask students to think about two similar but different things that they have or know about, such as two coins in a coin collection or two kinds of dogs. Have them write two sentences that tell how the things are alike and two sentences that tell how they are different. Students can share their comparison and contrast statements with a partner. Remind students that a writer can explain ideas by comparing and contrasting.

Guide students as they read "Out-of-This-World Rocks," Scott Foresman Reading, *pages 576–577. Remind students to think about whether the selection is fiction or nonfiction and how it is organized.*

Selection Audio CD 10/Tape 29

Practice

Have students tell whether "Out-of-This-World Rocks" is fiction or nonfiction and how the text is organized.

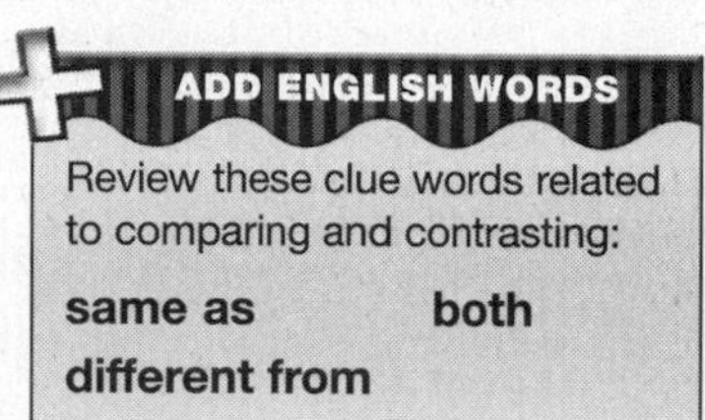

Assess

If... students cannot tell what kind of selection they have read and how it is organized,

then... ask them to reread the title and the first page of the article. Ask: *Do you think this selection is fiction or nonfiction? How can you tell?* Then have students compare a space rock and an Earth rock by rereading the first paragraph on page 577. Have them write their answers in a Venn diagram, Graphic Organizer Transparency 21. Point out that they have shown that the writer organized his ideas into compare-and-contrast statements.

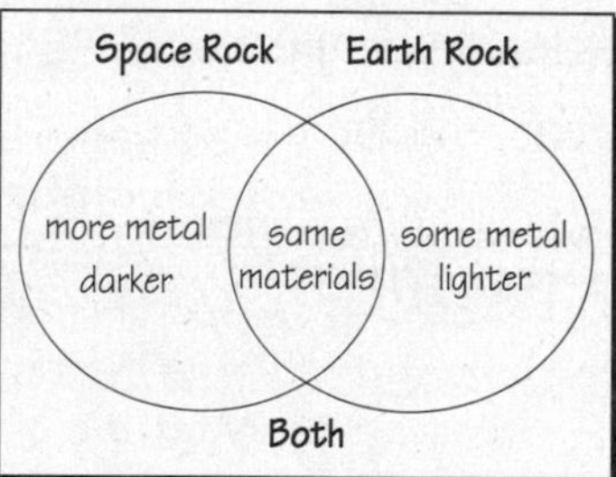

Transparency 21

PART 2

Preview the Reading Selection

Use these activities before reading *Space Probes to the Planets,* Teacher's Edition, *Scott Foresman Reading,* pages 578–593.

Activate Prior Knowledge

Have students look at the picture on pages 578–579. Then have them read the first sentence on page 580 and answer it. Why do they feel as they do? Do they think that they will visit another planet when they are older? Use the Adding English Poster to stimulate ideas.

ADD ENGLISH WORDS

Listen for students' knowledge of words related to space.

circle	**moons**
clouds	**spacesuits**
spin	**orbit**

Strategy: Using a K-W-L Chart

Tell students that they will read about our solar system, which has the sun at its center. Begin a K-W-L chart, Graphic Organizer Transparency 7, about the solar system. Explain the strategy: *When I want to learn new things that are facts, I can use a chart. It is a strategy called Using a K-W-L Chart.* Point out what each letter means, and model filling out the K column based on your discussion. Have students begin their own charts.

K What I Know	W What I Want to Know	L What I Learned
The sun is in the center. Mars is next to Earth. Saturn has rings.		

Transparency 7

Build Background

Ask students whether they think it is easy or difficult to get factual information about other planets. Then show students pictures of Mars taken by *Pathfinder* in 1997 (available from NASA on the Internet). Explain how these pictures were taken: A vehicle was sent to Mars. It had cameras and a computer on board. As it moved over the surface of Mars, it sent back pictures to scientists on Earth. It also brought back pieces of Mars for scientists to study.

RESOURCES

Use *Scott Foresman ESL*, Grade 2, for additional instruction and activities.

- Chapter 9, "Day and Night"
- Video, Unit 5, "How Time Changes"

Vocabulary: Context Clues

Use these activities with the Vocabulary Lesson and paragraph "Exploring a Planet," Teacher's Edition, *Scott Foresman Reading,* page 578.

Review with students that when they see an unfamiliar word as they read, they should look for words around it that give a definition or explanation of the word. Write these sentences on the board: *The colors of the planet in the photograph were* *__incredible__*. *It was unbelievable that anything so far away could be so beautiful.* Have students read the sentences and tell what the underlined word means. What context clue helped them know the meaning? Continue with sentences that use the other vocabulary words and that contain context clues for the meanings. Have students point out pictures on the Adding English Poster to show their understanding of the words.

ADD ENGLISH WORDS

Present these words in the context of your discussion about space.

incredible **atmosphere**
probes **spacecraft**
craters

Illustrated Sentences

Write the vocabulary words on the board. Have students work with a partner to write sentences using one or two of the words and then draw pictures to illustrate the sentences. An example sentence: *The spacecraft landed on the moon. It was incredible.* Students can use the Adding English Poster for ideas in creating their sentences and drawing their pictures.

Guide students as they read "Exploring a Planet," Scott Foresman Reading, *page 578. Ask them how using context clues can help them figure out the meaning of an unfamiliar word.*

Students can participate in the Write About It activity that follows. If possible, have English language learners work in pairs with students whose home language is English to talk about the characteristics of their real or imaginary planets.

Present the Reading Selection

Use these activities with *Space Probes to the Planets,* Teacher's Edition, *Scott Foresman Reading,* pages 578–593.

Preview Illustrations

Explain the strategy: *Before I begin to read a selection, I look at the pictures and read the captions to see what the selection is about.* Call attention to the spacecraft, or space probes, on pages 580 and 581, the row of labeled planets at the top of pages 582–590, and the chart on page 587. Make sure students notice the different colors and textures of the planets in the illustrations.

Develop Concepts

Students may need support in understanding the distances involved in space travel. For comparison, tell them that Earth's circumference—the distance from your town all the way around—is 25,000 miles. The distance from Earth to the moon is 250,000 miles; from Earth to Venus is 26 million miles; from Earth to Mars is 63 million miles.

Set Purposes

Students can participate in Set Purposes, Teacher's Edition, *Scott Foresman Reading,* page 579. Then have students continue their K-W-L charts by writing what they want to find out about the solar system in the W column. Remind students that they are using a strategy called Using a K-W-L Chart.

K What I Know	W What I Want to Know	L What I Learned
The sun is in the center.	Which planets have space probes landed on?	
Mars is next to Earth.		
Saturn has rings.	What are Saturn's rings made of?	
Pluto is the farthest planet.		

Transparency 7

Selection Audio CD 10/Tape 29

Guide students as they read Space Probes to the Planets, Scott Foresman Reading, *pages 578–593. To support comprehension, use the suggestions in Meeting Individual Needs, ESL, in the Teacher's Edition.*

Response Log

- Have students write a description of one of the planets and tell whether or not they would like to visit that planet.
- Have students draw a picture of themselves on another planet. Remind them to show the special equipment they will need to use. Have them use the book illustrations and the Adding English Poster for reference. They can write a caption to explain their picture.

Practice Selection Concepts

To help students tell what they learned, choose from these activities.

- Help students fill in the L column of their K-W-L charts.
- Distribute the ten important sentences. Write the following questions on the board. Have partners find the sentences that answer each question. *What are space probes and what do they carry?* (sentences 1, 10) *What information did the space probes collect?* (2) *What specific information did space probes find out about for six of the planets?* (3, 4, 5, 6, 7, 8) *What planet has not yet been explored by a space probe?* (9)

Strategy: Self-Assess

Ask: *Did Using a K-W-L Chart help you learn new information?*

K What I Know	W What I Want to Know	L What I Learned
The sun is in the center. Mars is next to Earth. Saturn has rings. Pluto is the farthest planet.	Which planets have space probes landed on? What are Saturn's rings made of?	Probes have landed on Venus and Mars. Saturn's rings are made of ice and icy rock. Uranus is tipped on its side.

Transparency 7

Ten Important Sentences
Page 37

Language Awareness

Provide supported practice by using the Adding English Grammar and Phonics Practice Masters, pages 215–216, with the suggestions below.

Grammar: Conjunctions

Write the following on the board: *Space probes have flown close to most of the planets, and probes have landed on Venus and Mars.* Read the sentence aloud. Then point to the word *and* and say: And *is a conjunction. A conjunction joins two sentences, phrases, or words.* Invite a volunteer to circle *and.* List other conjunctions on the board: *but, or, nor, for, yet.*

Students can complete the Practice Master alone or with a partner.

Adding English
Grammar Practice Master
Page 215

Phonics: Syllabication

Distribute the Practice Master. Have students listen as you slowly say the words in Exercise A. Then students should repeat, saying each syllable. After students repeat a word, ask how many syllables the word has.

For Exercise B, have students read each sentence aloud and repeat the underlined word before counting the syllables.

ADD ENGLISH WORDS

Some students may have difficulty pronouncing multi-syllabic words. Provide practice in saying just the base word, then add prefixes and suffixes. Discuss changes in word stress due to affixes.

write	**rewrite**
spell	**misspell**
beauty	**beautiful**

Adding English
Phonics Practice Master
Page 216

PART 3

Connect Selection Concepts

Use these activities with Reader Response, Teacher's Edition, *Scott Foresman Reading,* page 593.

Discussion Groups: Space Probes

If possible, have English language learners work in groups with students whose home language is English. Each group should focus on a question, such as the following, related to space probes:

- Imagine that you could have one picture from the selection to frame and hang up at home. Which would you choose? Why?
- What do people on Earth know about the surface of the planets from pictures taken by space probes?
- What have scientists discovered about Mars?

Changing Interests

Have students reread About the Author on page 592. Why does the author write for children? (She remembers what she liked to do and what she liked to learn about in her childhood.) Students can talk in groups about how their interests are the same as or different from when they were younger, in first or second grade.

Space exploration is exciting! I'd like to go to the moon someday.

Reading Across Texts: "Meet the Universe's Main Attraction. . .Gravity," pages 594–595

To support students as they read an informational article:

- Have students preview the article. Activate prior knowledge by asking what students already know about gravity. Begin a K-W-L chart and list facts students know about gravity under What I Know.
- Before students read, clarify the use of the word *attraction* in the title.
- Students can complete the K-W-L chart as they learn more about gravity from the article.

Assess

Refer to the list below to assess students' progress.

Reading

- ☐ Uses words related to space probes, planets, and the solar system.
- ☐ Recognizes different types of text structure.

Language Awareness

Grammar

- ☐ Identifies and uses conjunctions.

Phonics

- ☐ Uses syllabication to help pronounce and decode words with affixes.

Learning Strategies

- ☐ Uses a K-W-L chart.
- ☐ Uses context clues to identify the meanings of unfamiliar words.

Name ____________________________________

Conjunctions

A. Read the sentences. Circle the conjunction in each sentence.

1. Mercury is the closest planet to the sun, and it is covered with craters.

2. Venus is the hottest planet, but it is not the closest planet to the sun.

3. People can live on Earth, but they cannot live on the sun.

4. There may have been life on Mars once, but scientists are not sure.

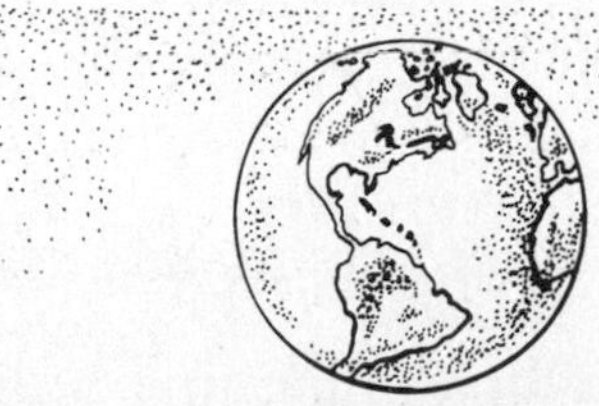

B. Read the sentences. Circle the conjunction that completes each sentence.

5. Jupiter is the fifth planet from the sun, (and/because) it is also the largest planet.

6. All the planets spin, (so/but) Jupiter spins faster than the others.

7. Three other planets have rings, (because/yet) no planet has as many as Saturn.

8. You could read more about one planet, (or/for) you could find out more about the entire solar system.

C. Talk with a partner about which planet you would most like to learn more about. Write some questions about this planet.

I would like to learn more about ______________.

Questions: ____________________________________

____

____

____

Name ______________________________

Syllabication

Phonics

A. Listen to the words. Then say the words. Count the number of syllables that you hear.

unexplored wonderful disappear useless

B. Read the sentences. Say the underlined words. Count the syllables. Write the number on the line.

1. Space probes have sent back beautiful pictures of Mars. ___
2. Is it impossible for life to exist on any planet but Earth? ___
3. Scientists make sure there are no unsafe conditions when launching probes. ___
4. There is no plan to discontinue launching space probes. ___

C. Work with a partner. Make new words by adding a syllable from the box. Use one new word in a sentence and write it below.

im	ful	un

wonder ______________________

possible ______________________

care ______________________

safe ______________________

broken ______________________

____

____

Koya's Cousin Del

Pages 606–629

Crossing Cultures • In this lesson, students read a story about a family's reunion with a famous relative. Encourage students to share memorable family reunions they have experienced. Where did the family gathering occur? Where did people travel from? What languages were spoken at the reunion?

Preview the Skill Lesson

Use these activities with the Skill Lesson: "Seeds," Teacher's Edition, *Scott Foresman Reading,* pages 606–607.

Activate Prior Knowledge

Point out the watermelon on Adding English Poster 26. Ask students if they have ever eaten watermelon. Can volunteers show the class how they would eat a watermelon slice, pantomiming each step in the process? Have them show how they would sit, how they would hold their arms and hands, and what they would do with the seeds. Record the steps on a steps in a process chart, Graphic Organizer Transparency 22.

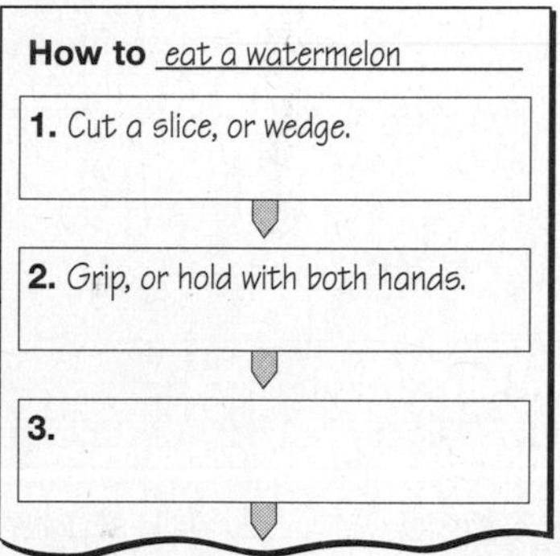

Transparency 22

Use Synonyms

Use the vocabulary words at right to preview the Skill Lesson literature. List them on the board. Explain the strategy: *Some words mean the same or nearly the same as other words. When I read a word I don't know, I look for other words around it that might mean the same thing.* Then write the following paragraph on the board and read it aloud.

> Today is very hot. My sister and I eat slices of watermelon to cool off. Each wedge is shaped like a crescent moon. We eat the juicy, red fruit sitting outside on a ledge near the street, gripping the wedges with both hands as the juice runs down our arms. We watch as the juice dribbles down on the curb. Eating watermelon makes us feel much cooler!

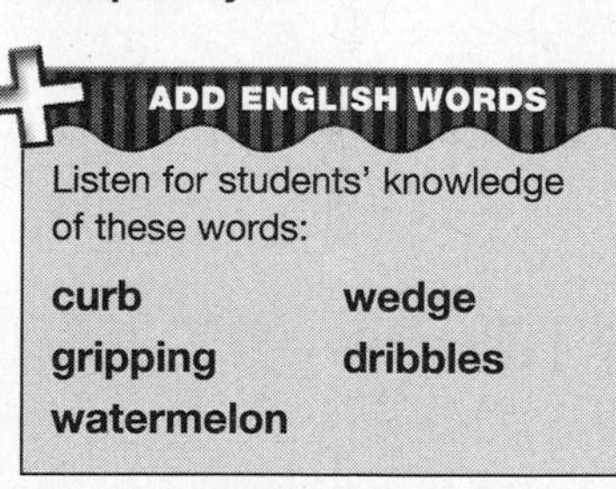

Have students tell what they think the underlined words mean. Let them find a picture on the Adding English Poster that relates to or illustrates each word. Then have them listen for another word or phrase with the same or nearly the same meaning as each vocabulary word in the paragraph.

Present the Comprehension Strategy

Comprehension: Visualizing

Use Comprehension Strategies, *Adding English Guide,* page 10, to introduce Visualizing.

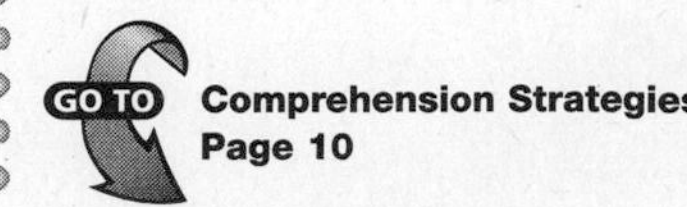

Relate to Personal Experience

Have students think of their favorite food. Talk about the five senses: sight, smell, sound, touch, taste. In groups, have students take turns describing their favorite foods, talking about each of the five senses. Students can try to visualize each other's favorite foods.

Guide students as they read "Seeds," Scott Foresman Reading, *pages 606–607. Remind them to look for details that tell how things look, sound, smell, taste, and feel.*

Selection Audio CD 11/Tape 31

Practice

Give students an opportunity to review the selection and describe what they visualized. Discuss what words created pictures in their minds. They can use the Adding English Poster as a vocabulary aid.

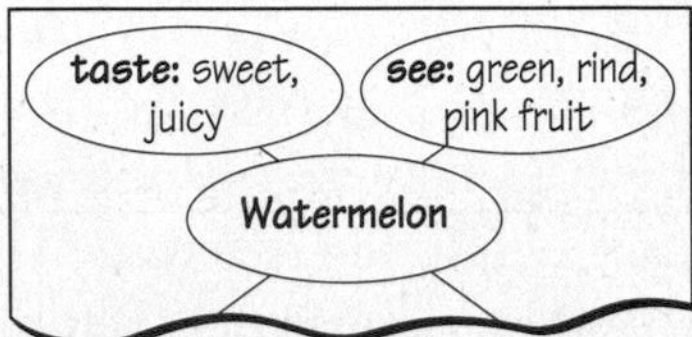

Transparency 5

Assess

If... students are not able to visualize what they read in "Seeds,"

then... have them make a sensory web using Graphic Organizer Transparency 5. Ask students to write the word *Watermelon* in the middle circle and fill in words from "Seeds" that describe watermelon.

ADD ENGLISH WORDS

Review these clue words related to visualizing:

visualize **details** **see**
hear **smell** **taste**
feel

PART 2

Preview the Reading Selection

Use these activities before reading "Koya's Cousin Del," Teacher's Edition, *Scott Foresman Reading,* pages 608–627.

Activate Prior Knowledge

Show the Adding English Poster to students and discuss the pictures referring to the words at the right. Ask students to talk about a time they went to concert or a public performance. Was there a big crowd? Did a famous person perform? Did they go with their families? How was their experience like what they see on the poster? How was it different?

ADD ENGLISH WORDS

Listen for students' knowledge of words related to a performance and families.

cousin **famous** **album**
parents **crowd**

Build Background

Draw a simple family tree on the chalkboard, including the family relations of brother, sister, mother, father, aunt, uncle, and cousin. Explain the family tree and label each family relationship. Invite students to make their own family trees, filling in the names of their relatives.

Use Brainstorming

To help students understand what the life of a famous person is like, have them think of a movie star or a famous rock star. Let students browse through newspaper or magazine articles about famous people. Discuss with students what they think it would be like to be famous. Guide students to think about both positive or fun, and negative or unpleasant things. Record students' responses on a T-chart, Graphic Organizer Transparency 24.

Strategy: Using a T-Chart

Explain the strategy: *When I want to list what is positive and what is negative about something, I can make a chart. It is a strategy called Using a T-Chart.* Model beginning a chart. Have students begin their own charts in small groups.

Vocabulary: Unfamiliar Words

Use these activities with the Vocabulary Lesson and paragraph "A Night to Remember," Teacher's Edition, *Scott Foresman Reading,* page 608.

Write the following paragraph on the board and read it aloud.

> The performers walked onto the stage of the packed auditorium and stepped up to the microphones. The applause of the impatient crowd grew louder. At last, the band began to play.

Have students identify the scene being described. Ask: *Do you know the meaning of all the underlined words?* Point out that even if you are unsure of a certain word, looking at the other words and deciding what would make sense can help you understand it. Help students locate pictures of the underlined words on the Adding English Poster.

Play Charades

Ask for seven volunteers to come to the front of the class. Write the vocabulary words on the board. Give each volunteer an index card containing one word and its definition. One at a time, have the volunteers pantomime clues to help the class guess the word. Start with easier words such as *microphones* and *autographs*. As class members guess the words, erase them from the board.

RESOURCES

Use *Scott Foresman ESL,* Grade 5, for additional instruction and activities.

- Chapter 2, "Uses of Sounds"
- Video, Unit 1, "Music to Your Ears"

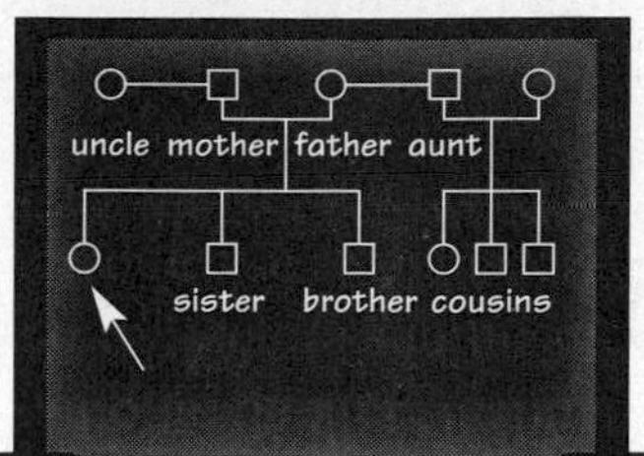

Good	Bad
Fans say that you are great.	Fans always want your time.

Transparency 24

ADD ENGLISH WORDS

Through listening and watching, assess students' knowledge of selection vocabulary.

performers	**imitation**
auditorium	**impatient**
microphones	**applause**
autographs	

Guide students as they read "A Night to Remember," Scott Foresman Reading, *page 608. Ask them how they will figure out the meanings of unfamiliar words.*

Students can participate in the Write About It activity that follows. When possible, have English language learners work in groups with students whose home language is English to list details about the performers and the concert.

Present the Reading Selection

Use these activities with "Koya's Cousin Del," Teacher's Edition, *Scott Foresman Reading,* pages 608–627.

Preview Illustrations

Explain the strategy: *Before I begin to read, I look at the pictures in the story to get an idea of what it will be about.* Invite students to look at the picture on page 612. Ask: *What is the man doing? What kind of person signs autographs? What do you think this story will be about?* Continue previewing the pictures.

Develop Concepts

For this selection, students may need help in understanding the literary technique of flashback. Explain that writers use flashback in stories to give information to the reader about something that happened in a character's past. Have students tell about another story or movie where the author used flashback.

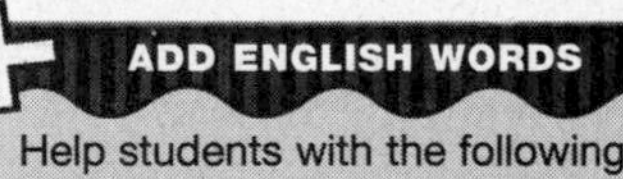

Help students with the following term:

flashback

Set Purposes

Students can participate in Set Purposes, Teacher's Edition, *Scott Foresman Reading,* page 609. Have students tell what *famous* means. They can use their T-charts about being famous as support.

Guide students as they read "Koya's Cousin Del," Scott Foresman Reading, *pages 608–627. To support comprehension, use the suggestions in Meeting Individual Needs, ESL, in the Teacher's Edition.*

Selection Audio CD 11/Tape 31

Response Log

- Have students write about Del. What kind of person is he? Would they like to meet him? Why or why not?
- Have students draw a picture of how music makes them feel. Ask them to write a word or two describing their picture.

Practice Selection Concepts

To help students tell what they learned, choose from these activities.

- Now that students have read about a rock star, have them work with a partner to add details to their T-charts about being famous. As a class, discuss whether the good outweighs the bad. Then have students vote on whether they would like to be famous.
- Distribute the ten important sentences and have students read and discuss them with a partner. Ask each student to choose one sentence and to visualize and draw the scene it describes.

Good	Bad
Fans say that you are great.	Fans always want your time.
You make a lot of money.	You don't have any privacy.

Transparency 24

Ten Important Sentences Page 38

Strategy: Self-Assess

Ask: *Did the strategy Using a T-Chart help you identify the positives and negatives of being famous? Why or why not?*

Language Awareness

Provide supported practice by using the Adding English Grammar and Phonics Practice Masters, pages 223–224, with the suggestions below.

Grammar: Review of Sentences and Sentence Punctuation

Adding English Grammar Practice Master Page 223

Write the following on the board: *Del plays the piano.* Ask students if it is a complete sentence and why they think so. Review that sentences need both a subject (a naming part) and a predicate (a doing part). Have students point out the subject and predicate in the sentence above. Ask volunteers to write complete sentences and share them with the class. Remind students that sentences must start with a capital letter and can be punctuated by periods, questions marks, and exclamation points. Students can complete the Practice Master individually or with a partner.

Phonics: Complex Spelling Patterns

Adding English Phonics Practice Master Page 224

Distribute the Practice Master. Have students listen, read, and repeat as you say the words in Exercise A. Prompt students to use the words in sentences. Write *light* on the board. Erase the *l* and demonstrate how to put other letters at the beginning of *-ight* to make rhyming words such as *sight* and *might.* Tell students that when they read words with complex spellings they should try to think of words that sound the same.

For Exercise B, have students read each word aloud before writing it in the blank.

Connect Selection Concepts

Use these activities with Reader Response, Teacher's Edition, *Scott Foresman Reading,* page 627.

Character Analysis

When possible, have English language learners work in groups with students whose home language is English. Together they should talk about the characters in "Koya's Cousin Del." Have each group make word webs describing three of the characters, using Graphic Organizer Transparency 5. Let each student tell which character he or she would most like to be and explain why.

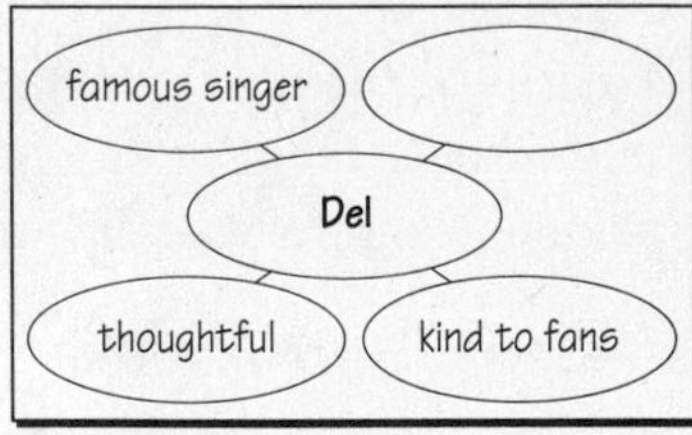

Transparency 5

We Are Famous

Have students pretend that they are famous people such as writers, singers, artists, actors, athletes, or scientists. Each student should choose one person and think about whether he or she would act differently toward other people if he or she were that famous person. Let students discuss their feelings with a partner.

Reading Across Texts: "On the Beat," pages 628–629

To support students as they read a picture encyclopedia:

- Have students preview "On the Beat" by looking at the pictures and reading a few words from each caption. Explain that this selection can be read in any order. Read the introduction with students.
- Activate prior knowledge about the topic of drums. What experiences have students had with drums? What kinds of drums have they played or heard others play?
- After students have read the page, talk about how this information is related to the story "Koya's Cousin Del."

Assess

Refer to the list below to assess students' progress.

Reading

- ☐ Uses words related to concerts and performances.
- ☐ Visualizes characters and events in a story.
- ☐ Understands the use of flashbacks in a story.

Language Awareness

Grammar

- ☐ Writes complete sentences with correct punctuation.

Phonics

- ☐ Pronounces and spells words with complex spelling patterns.

Learning Strategies

- ☐ Uses a T-chart to identify positives and negatives of an issue.
- ☐ Uses context clues to learn the meanings of unfamiliar words.

Name ____________________

Review of Sentences and Sentence Punctuation

A. Read the sentences. Write a period (.), a question mark (?), or an exclamation point (!) to end each sentence.

1. Koya and her family were at the airport___
2. Isn't that somebody famous___
3. You forgot to say good evening___
4. Your album is great, Del___

B. Draw a line to make a sentence.

Subject	Predicate
5. Koya and Loritha	**a.** missed his family.
6. Del	**b.** ran over to hug Delbert.
7. A teenage boy	**c.** were proud of their cousin.
8. Koya	**d.** wanted his mother to take a picture.

C. Talk with a partner about a special concert you would like to see. Write about it.

I would like to see ____________________

____

____

____

Name ______________________________

Complex Spelling Patterns

A. Listen to the words. Read the words. Then say the words.

light

caught

thought

B. Say the underlined words. Then make new words. Follow the spelling patterns.

<u>night</u>	<u>bought</u>	<u>caught</u>
1. f______	**4.** f________	**7.** t________
2. t______	**5.** br________	**8.** n________y
3. s______	**6.** th________	**9.** d________er

C. Write a rhyming word to complete each pair of lines. Read the sentences to your partner.

10. At 7:21, one exciting night,

Koya went to meet Del's fl________.

11. The gift that Cousin Del brought

was wonderful, Koya th________.

12. Seeing his hometown felt just right.

To Del it was a happy s________.

Children of Clay

Pages 630–647

Crossing Cultures • In this lesson, students read about a Pueblo family whose members work together to make beautiful pottery. Ask students if they have ever made pottery or sculpted with clay. Encourage them to describe their experiences and the objects they made. What other handicrafts do students know about? Let them share information—and samples of the crafts, if possible—with the class.

PART 1

Preview the Skill Lesson

Use these activities with the Skill Lesson: "From Drawing to Carousel Critter," Teacher's Edition, *Scott Foresman Reading,* pages 630–631.

GO TO Poster Tips Page 16

Activate Prior Knowledge

Point to the picture of the carousel on Adding English Poster 27 and ask students to describe what they see. Ask students if they've ever seen or ridden a carousel. Have them share what they know about carousels. Record students' responses on a web, Graphic Organizer Transparency 4.

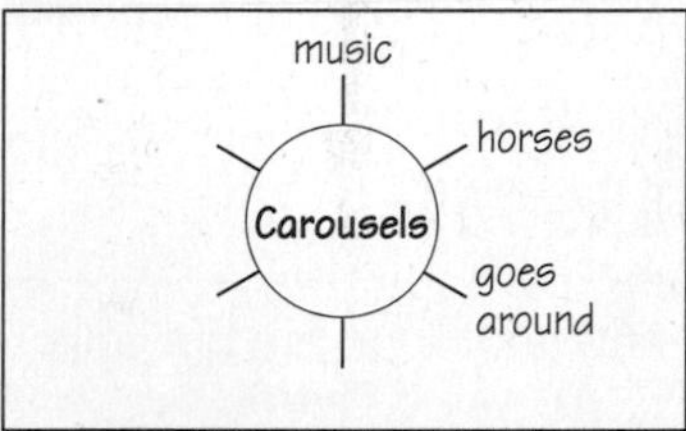

Transparency 4

Use Pictures

Use the vocabulary words at right to introduce the Skill Lesson literature. Write the words on the board. Explain the strategy: *I can use pictures to help me understand new words.*

Have students point to parts of the Adding English Poster that relate to the vocabulary. Model the strategy by pointing out images as you read the following passage.

> Last weekend I went to the fair. My favorite ride was the carousel. People sit on colorful painted critters as the ride goes round and round in circles. I rode on the deer painted brown with white spots. The person who designed this carousel must have been a real wizard. It was so beautiful that I went home and made a drawing of it on a piece of foam so I would not forget what it looked like.

Invite volunteers to point out the vocabulary words on the poster and to say a sentence about each word. Ensure that all students understand the less-familiar vocabulary in the passage.

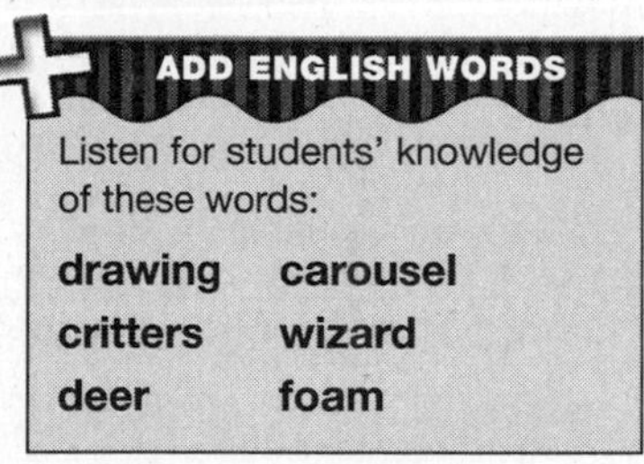

ADD ENGLISH WORDS

Listen for students' knowledge of these words:

drawing	**carousel**
critters	**wizard**
deer	**foam**

Present the Comprehension Strategy

Comprehension: Steps in a Process

Use Comprehension Strategies, *Adding English Guide,* page 10, to introduce Steps in a Process.

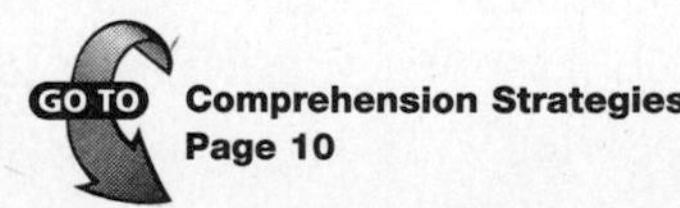
GO TO Comprehension Strategies Page 10

Relate to Personal Experience

Ask students to think about a simple task they do every day, such as brushing their teeth. Have them think about the steps they follow to complete the task. What do they do first? Next? Last? Have students list the steps. Record students' responses on the board.

1. First, run water on the toothbrush.
2. Next, put toothpaste on the toothbrush.
3. Then, brush your teeth in a circular motion.
4. Last, rinse your mouth.

Guide students as they read "From Drawing to Carousel Critter," Scott Foresman Reading, *pages 630–631. Encourage students to look for the steps the artist uses in creating carousel critters.*

Selection Audio CD 11/Tape 32

Practice

Give students an opportunity to tell each other the steps necessary to make a carousel critter. Encourage them to use the Adding English Poster for vocabulary support.

Assess

If... students are not able to tell the steps in making a carousel critter,

then... write the following sentences on strips of paper. Help students put them in order to show the steps in a process.

- Then, Milo traces the animal onto two pieces of foam.
- First, a child draws an animal.
- Last, he paints the animal.
- Next, he glues a pole between the two pieces.

ADD ENGLISH WORDS

Review these words related to steps in a process:

first **next** **last** **steps**

PART 2

Preview the Reading Selection

Use these activities before reading *Children of Clay,* Teacher's Edition, *Scott Foresman Reading,* pages 632–644.

Activate Prior Knowledge

Display the Adding English Poster and talk about the pictures that illustrate or relate to the words at the right. Have students talk about an art project they completed. How did they get the idea? What materials did they use? In pairs, have students use the vocabulary words to write sentences about art projects they've completed. Ask volunteers to share their sentences with the class.

ADD ENGLISH WORDS

Listen for students' knowledge of words related to artwork:

artists **clay**
create **designs**
shiny **piece**

Build Background

Display a map of the United States and point to New Mexico. Explain to students that a group of Native Americans, called Pueblos, lives there. Tell students that the Pueblos make works of art out of a clay that they dig from the land and mountains of New Mexico.

Ask Questions

Encourage students to think about what is involved in producing a work of art. Have them focus on a clay pot or figure and formulate several questions about its production. Begin a T-chart, Graphic Organizer Transparency 24, about how a work of clay is made. Students can use the Adding English Poster for aid.

Strategy: Asking Questions

Explain the strategy: *When I want to learn about something, I can ask questions about it. It is a strategy called Asking Questions.* Be sure students understand that when they ask questions, they must first think of what to ask and then find the answer. Model filling in the T-chart with questions based on your class discussion. Save the T-chart in order to fill in the answers after reading the selection.

Vocabulary: Multiple-Meaning Words

Use these activities with the Vocabulary Lesson and paragraph "Crafty Clay," Teacher's Edition, *Scott Foresman Reading,* page 632.

Display the Adding English Poster. Write the selection vocabulary words on the board. Ask volunteers to find the corresponding pictures on the poster. Tell students that some words may have more than one meaning, and that they may need to look for clues in the sentences around a word to figure out its meaning. Write the following sentences on the board.

- **The Pueblos use screens to sift lumps out of clay.**
- **My mother doesn't want me to sit too close to the television screen.**

Ask students which sentence uses the same meaning for *screens* as the one shown in the poster. Repeat with *figures* and *polish*.

I'm Thinking Of . . .

Write the selection vocabulary words on the board. Then play "I'm Thinking Of . . ." Tell students:

- **I'm thinking of something that keeps the mosquitoes out of my house. What is it?**
- **I'm thinking of something I can do to my fingernails. What is it?**

Encourage students to use the vocabulary words to answer.

RESOURCES

Use *Scott Foresman ESL,* Grade 4, for additional instruction and activities.

- Chapter 5, "The First Americans"
- Video, Unit 3, "Early People in North America"

Questions	Answers
1. How is a clay figure made? 2. What materials do we need?	

Transparency 24

ADD ENGLISH WORDS

Through listening and watching, assess students' knowledge of selection vocabulary.

pottery **figures**
screens **polish**
symbols

Guide students as they read "Crafty Clay," Scott Foresman Reading, *page 632. Ask them what they will do when they come across a word with more than one meaning.*

Students can participate in the Write About It activity that follows. When possible, have English language learners work in groups with students whose home language is English to make a list of art supplies.

Present the Reading Selection

Use these activities with *Children of Clay,* Teacher's Edition, *Scott Foresman Reading,* pages 632–644.

Preview Illustrations and Captions

Explain the strategy: *Before I begin to read, I look at the pictures and captions in the story to get an idea of what it will be about.* Invite students to look at the pictures on pages 635, 636, and 637. Ask them what they see being made and what it is being made of. Continue previewing the pictures.

Develop Concepts

Have two volunteers dramatize a common classroom event, such as getting ready for lunch. Ask another volunteer to tell, or narrate, what the students are doing. Then explain to students that if they wrote this event down it would be in a style called narrative nonfiction, a true story being told by a person outside the action. Ask students to think of examples of narrative nonfiction.

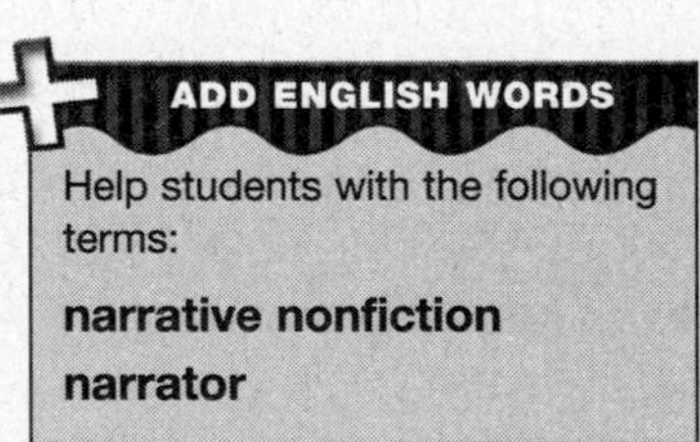

Set Purposes

Students can participate in Set Purposes, Teacher's Edition, *Scott Foresman Reading,* page 633. Ask students to think about how clay pots and figures are made. Encourage students to fill in their T-charts with more questions and answers as they read the story. Remind them that they are using a strategy called Asking Questions.

Guide students as they read Children of Clay, Scott Foresman Reading, *pages 632–644. To support comprehension, use the suggestions in Meeting Individual Needs, ESL, in the Teacher's Edition.*

Selection Audio CD 11/Tape 32

Response Log

- Ask students to review the steps for making clay pots and figures. Have them write about which step is the hardest and tell why.
- Ask students to draw a picture of a figure they would like to make out of clay. They can refer to the Adding English Poster for support.

Practice Selection Concepts

To help students tell what they learned, choose from these activities.

- Have students finish their T-charts by filling in answers to the questions they wrote earlier. If students have posed questions that are not anwswered in the selection, help them consult other sources to find the answers.
- Cut the ten important sentences into strips and have students work in pairs to put them in sequential order.

Strategy: Self-Assess

Ask: *Did the strategy Asking Questions help you understand how the Pueblo Indians make figures out of clay? How?*

Questions	Answers
1. How is a clay figure made?	1. we follow many steps.
2. What materials do we need?	2. We need clay, water, sand, screws, sandpaper, polishing stones, brushes, and a fire.

Transparency 24

Ten Important Sentences
Page 39

Language Awareness

Provide supported practice by using the Adding English Grammar and Phonics Practice Masters, pages 231–232, with the suggestions below.

Grammar: Capitalization

Write some students' names on the board without capitalization. Elicit that the names are written incorrectly because they are not capitalized. Go over the capitalization rules presented in this lesson (first word in a sentence, proper nouns, important words in titles, first letter of abbreviation, titles before people's names).

Students can complete the Practice Master individually or with a partner.

Adding English
Grammar Practice Master
Page 231

Phonics: Irregular Plurals

Review that when we make a noun plural, we usually add *-s* or *-es*. Write some examples on the board. Then distribute the Practice Master. Have students listen, read, and repeat as you say the words in Exercise A. Explain that some nouns in English don't follow the regular plural rule. We have to memorize their plurals. Prompt students to use the words in sentences.

For Exercise B, have students read the sentences aloud before they choose an answer.

Adding English
Phonics Practice Master
Page 232

PART 3

Connect Selection Concepts

Use these activities with Reader Response, Teacher's Edition, *Scott Foresman Reading,* page 644.

Literature Discussion Groups

When possible, have English language learners work in groups with students whose home language is English. Together they can discuss what they learned from reading *Children of Clay.* In what ways does the Pueblo culture seem like their own? In what ways does it seem different?

We Are Artists

Ask students to bring in a sample of artwork that they have made. Have students work in groups to compare and contrast their artwork with the pottery of the Pueblo Indians.

Reading Across Texts: "Clay Old Woman and Clay Old Man," pages 645–647

To support students as they learn about and read a myth:

- Activate prior knowledge by asking students if they know what a myth is. Help them understand that it is a story that explains something in nature.
- Use the Adding English Poster to build background about the myth.
- Ask students: *How is "Clay Old Woman and Clay Old Man" like* Children of Clay*? How is it different?* Record their responses in a Venn diagram, Graphic Organizer Transparency 21.

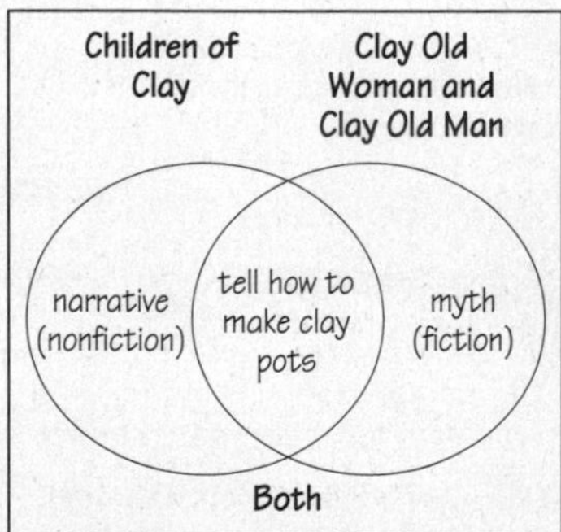

Transparency 21

Assess

Refer to the list below to assess students' progress.

Reading

- ☐ Uses words related to making pottery.
- ☐ Identifies steps in a process.
- ☐ Recognizes narrative nonfiction.
- ☐ Recognizes myths.

Language Awareness

Grammar

- ☐ Identifies and uses correct capitalization.

Phonics

- ☐ Identifies and decodes irregular plural nouns.

Learning Strategies

- ☐ Asks questions to learn new information.
- ☐ Uses context clues to understand multiple-meaning words.

Name ____________________

Capitalization

A. Circle the capital letters.

1. *Sees Behind Trees* is a good book about a Native American boy.
2. New Mexico is in the United States.
3. The people of Santa Clara sell their pottery.
4. Ms. Rina Swentzell lives in Santa Fe, New Mexico.

B. Rewrite each sentence. Add capital letters.

5. aunt tessie likes the shiny polish on her pot.

____

6. i made a clay frog for mr. jackson.

____

7. the art store is on main street.

____

____

C. Talk with a partner about something you made. Then write about it and draw a picture.

Once, I made a/an ____________________

____

____

____

Name ____________________________________

Phonics

Irregular Plurals

A. Listen to the words. Read each word. Then say each word.

child/children

woman/women

goose/geese

B. Choose the correct plural to complete each sentence.

1. A group of ____________ drew pictures of animals. (children/childs)

2. There were pictures of ____________. (deer/deers)

3. There were also pictures of ____________. (gooses/geese)

4. Did anyone draw pictures of ____________? (mice/mouses)

5. Some ____________ made the pictures into animals on a carousel. (people/peoples)

C. Say the underlined words. Read the paragraph to a partner. Then listen as your partner reads it to you.

Look at those clay pots and bowls. There are clay animals and <u>people</u> too. The <u>men</u>, <u>women</u>, and <u>children</u> in Gia Rose's family helped make them. To prepare the clay, these artists used their bare <u>feet</u> to work sand into the clay. When it was ready, everyone had fun making beautiful things out of the clay.

Coming Home

Pages 648–665

Crossing Cultures • In this lesson, students read about a famous American poet's childhood and his search for a place called home. What does "home" mean to English language learners? Is it their house? Is it their family? Is it a city or country?

PART 1

Preview the Skill Lesson

Use these activities with the Skill Lesson: "Naomi's Geese," Teacher's Edition, *Scott Foresman Reading,* pages 648–649.

Activate Prior Knowledge

Display Adding English Poster 28 and ask students to talk about birds they see and other birds they know about. What kinds of birds are they? Where do they live? Have students describe their favorite bird and draw a picture of it. Allow them to use their home language as needed.

Poster Tips
Page 16

Use Context Clues

Use the vocabulary words at right to preview the Skill Lesson literature. Write them on the board. Explain the strategy: *When I hear a word I don't know, I listen for other words around it to help me understand its meaning.*

Have students listen for the vocabulary words as you read the following passage. Encourage them to use what they know about birds to help them understand unfamiliar words. Model the strategy by pointing out examples of context clues, such as "fly back to their homes."

> Geese and loons are some of the birds that migrate from north to south every fall. When spring comes, they fly back to their homes in the north. Some people also migrate to avoid cold winters. People move for many reasons. Sometimes they go from the country to the city. Other people move from one part of the world to another. At these times people may be worried about where they will live. Birds aren't concerned about migrating, though; they move by instinct.

Ask students to use the vocabulary words to describe what they see on the poster. Ask volunteers to choose a word and use context clues to explain it.

ADD ENGLISH WORDS

Listen for students' understanding of these words:

geese	country
migrate	city
loons	worried

Present the Comprehension Strategy

Comprehension: Fact and Opinion

Use Comprehension Strategies, *Adding English Guide,* page 10, to introduce Fact and Opinion.

GO TO Comprehension Strategies
Page 10

Relate to Personal Experience

Ask students to talk about soccer and to say *soccer* in their home language. What do they think about the game? Do they enjoy it? Do they like to play or watch soccer? Then ask what kind of ball is used to play the game. What is one rule? Point out to students that when they were describing their feelings, they were expressing their *opinions*. When they talked about a rule, they were stating a *fact*. Make sure students understand that a fact can be checked, but an opinion tells how someone feels or what someone thinks. It can't be right or wrong. This activity may be helpful for all students in the class.

Guide students as they read "Naomi's Geese," Scott Foresman Reading, *pages 648–649. Remind students to look for facts and opinions.*

Selection Audio CD 11/Tape 33

Practice

Ask students what facts and opinions they noticed in the book review? How could each fact be proved true or false? What clue words showed that a sentence was an opinion? Students can use the Adding English Poster and vocabulary words as support.

Assess

If... students are not able to distinguish between facts and opinions,

then... write the following sentences on the board. Ask students to decide which are fact and which are opinion, and to explain why.

- **Naomi becomes friends with the two geese.**
- **Naomi likes the geese right away.**
- **Most people who like nature will like this book.**

Help students see that the first two sentences are facts. Even though the second sentence is not correct, it can be proved true or false.

ADD ENGLISH WORDS

Review these clue words related to fact and opinion:

fact	**opinion**	**prove**
true	**false**	**think**
believe	**feel**	

PART 2

Preview the Reading Selection

Use these activities before reading *Coming Home,* Teacher's Edition, *Scott Foresman Reading,* pages 650–663.

Activate Prior Knowledge

Point to the calendar and have students identify the current date. Then ask them to find dates in the future. Explain that the future is any time from today on. Then have them talk about their dreams for the future. What kind of work would they like to do? Where would they like to live? Have students refer to the Adding English Poster and record their ideas in a web, Graphic Organizer Transparency 4.

Build Background

Write the words at the right on the board. Then draw a simple picture of person in a house, holding two coins but dreaming (in a bubble) of a big pile of money. Ask students which vocabulary words are shown in the picture. (*home, alone, dream, poor*) Help students use the Adding English Poster as a context for using the words in sentences.

Vocabulary: Synonyms

Use these activities with the Vocabulary Lesson and paragraph "Books and Bravery," Teacher's Edition, *Scott Foresman Reading,* page 650.

Write the vocabulary words on the board. Write these synonyms in random order next to the words: *shake, imagination, managers, floated, idols.* Explain that words that have the same meaning or nearly the same meaning are called synonyms. Use *start* and *begin* as examples. Challenge students to match the synonyms to the correct vocabulary words. They can refer to a dictionary or thesaurus and the Adding English Poster for support.

Find Base Words

Write the vocabulary words on the board. Tell students that they can look for a base word within a word to help them understand its meaning. Have students use a T-chart, Graphic Organizer Transparency 24.

Guide students as they read "Books and Bravery," Scott Foresman Reading, *page 650. Ask how they can use synonyms to find the meanings of unfamiliar words.*

Students can participate in the Write About It activity that follows. When possible, have English language learners talk in groups with students whose home language is English about books they have read in English or in their home languages.

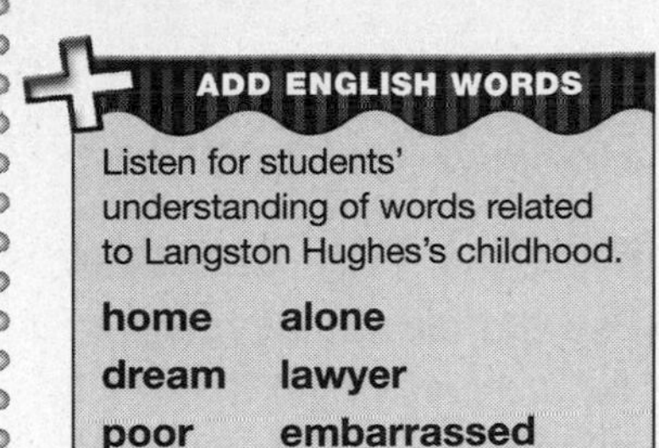

ADD ENGLISH WORDS

Listen for students' understanding of words related to Langston Hughes's childhood.

home **alone**
dream **lawyer**
poor **embarrassed**

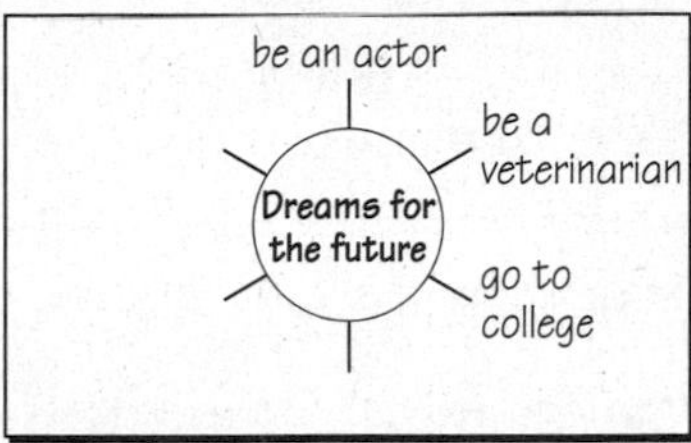

Transparency 4

RESOURCES

Use *Scott Foresman ESL,* Grade 3, for additional instruction and activities.

- Chapter 5, "Life in the City"
- Video, Unit 1, "The Farm and the City"

ADD ENGLISH WORDS

Through listening and watching, assess students' knowledge of selection vocabulary.

tremble **librarians**
dreamer **drifted**
heroes **rusty**

Vocabulary words	Base Words
librarians	library
dreamer	dream
rusty	rust

Transparency 24

Present the Reading Selection

Use these activities with *Coming Home,* Teacher's Edition, *Scott Foresman Reading,* pages 650–663.

Preview Title and Illustrations

Explain the strategy: *Before I begin to read, I look at the title and the pictures to get an idea of what the story will be about.* Invite students to read page 651. Ask: *What is the title of the story? Who is Langston Hughes?* Point out the poem on page 651 as a clue. Then look at the picture on pages 650–651. Is the boy at home in this picture? Have students turn to page 652. What is the boy doing? Next, talk about what is happening on page 656. Finally, have students turn to pages 660 and 661. What is the boy doing, and where is he when he is a man? Have students begin a story sequence chart, Graphic Organizer Transparency 12.

Strategy: Using a Story Sequence Chart

Explain the strategy: *When I want to understand the events in a story, I can use a chart. It is a strategy called Using a Story Sequence Chart.* Be sure students understand that sequencing is putting story events in order. Model filling out the first part of the chart based on the title and the illustrations. Then have students begin their own story sequence charts.

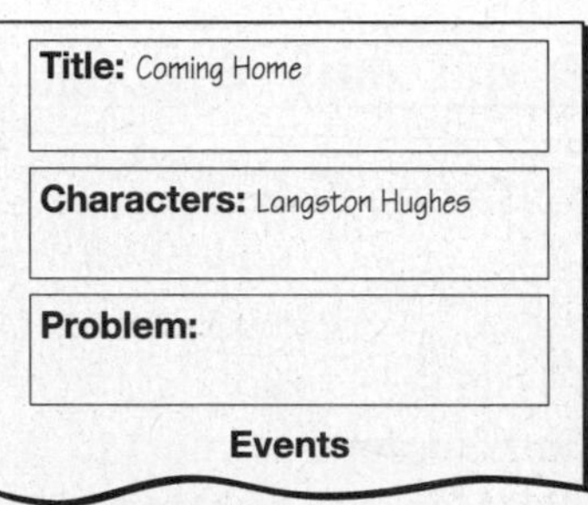

Transparency 12

Develop Concepts

For this selection, students may need help in understanding imagery. Explain that writers use imagery to help readers see, feel, taste, smell, and hear details of their stories. To do this, writers describe unknown things by comparing them with something familiar. On the board, write: *Auntie spoke in a voice as sweet as dessert.* Can students hear her voice? What does it sound like? Write: *His eyes were as dark as the night.* What color are the eyes? Can students see them? Pair students and have them think of two sentences using imagery to share with the rest of the class.

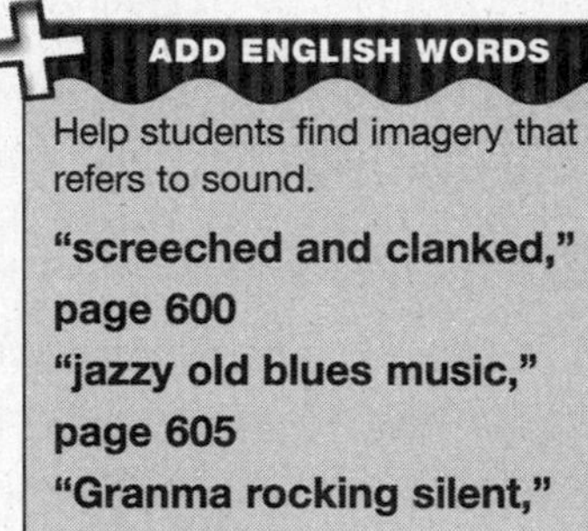

ADD ENGLISH WORDS

Help students find imagery that refers to sound.

"screeched and clanked," page 600
"jazzy old blues music," page 605
"Granma rocking silent," page 606

Set Purposes

Students can participate in Set Purposes, Teacher's Edition, *Scott Foresman Reading,* page 651. Encourage students to look for a problem and to notice the order of events as they read. Remind them that they are using a strategy called using a story sequence chart. They may want to keep their charts handy while they read.

Guide students as they read Coming Home, Scott Foresman Reading, *pages 650–663. To support comprehension, use the suggestions in Meeting Individual Needs, ESL, in the Teacher's Edition.*

Selection Audio CD 11/Tape 33

Response Log

- Ask students them to write about a hero they look up to and tell why. Students can use the Adding English Poster for ideas.
- Invite students to draw a picture of their home and write a description of it underneath.

Practice Selection Concepts

To help students tell what they learned, choose from these activities.

- Help students complete their story sequence charts by adding other characters and the problem, events, and solution.
- Distribute the ten important sentences, cut into strips. Have partners put them in order.

Strategy: Self-Assess

Ask: *Did the strategy Using a Story Sequence Chart help you understand the events in Langston Hughes's life? How?*

Language Awareness

Provide supported practice by using the Adding English Grammar and Phonics Practice Masters, pages 239–240, with the suggestions below.

Grammar: Commas

Invite volunteers to pick up three ordinary objects. On the board write: *I have* _____. Ask students to complete the sentences and circle the commas. Sample sentences: *I have a book, a pencil, and a ruler. I have a coat, scissors, and an audio tape.* Explain that commas are used to separate items in a series. Then explain that commas also are used to separate names when someone is spoken to directly and to separate the exact words of a person from parts of the sentence, such as: *He said* and *They said.* Write the following examples on the board. Have students circle the commas. *Marco, did your brother go home? She said, "It is time to eat now."*

Students can complete the Practice Master individually or with a partner.

Phonics: Consonant Sounds /k/ and /f/

Distribute the Practice Master. Have students listen, read, and repeat as you say the words in Exercise A. Point out the various spellings of /k/ and /f/. Ask students to use the words in sentences.

For Exercise B, have students read each word aloud before they answer.

Title: Coming Home

Characters: Langston Hughes, Granma Mary Langston, James Nathaniel Hughes, Carrie Hughes, Auntie and Uncle Reed

Problem: Langston wants a home with his ma and pa.

Events

Langston lives with Granma. She tells stories of heroes.

He visits his parents in Mexico and in Kansas City.

He goes to live with Auntie and Uncle Reed.

Langston travels the world and writes poetry.

Solution: He finds his home with Auntie and Uncle Reed and inside himself.

Transparency 12

Ten Important Sentences
Page 40

Adding English
Grammar Practice Master
Page 239

Adding English
Phonics Practice Master
Page 240

ADD ENGLISH WORDS

Students may have trouble pronouncing /k/ and /f/. Provide practice in distinguishing these sounds from similar sounds using contrasting examples such as:

fan van came game

PART 3

Connect Selection Concepts

Use these activities with Reader Response, Teacher's Edition, *Scott Foresman Reading,* page 663.

Dramatize

When possible, have English language learners work in groups with students whose home language is English. Ask them to review the characters described in *Coming Home.* Each student should then choose a character to act out for the group. Group members must guess which character is being portrayed.

At Home

Have students reread the paragraph on page 608 that tells about where and what home was for Langston Hughes. Invite students to think of an activity or a place they really enjoy. Then have them draw a picture of the place or activity and write a sentence telling why it makes them feel at home.

READING ACROSS TEXTS

Reading Across Texts: "The Dream Keeper" and "Dreamer," pages 664–665

Guide students as they read these poems. To support comprehension and make connections to Coming Home, *see the suggestions in the Teacher's Edition,* Scott Foresman Reading.

Assess

Refer to the list below to assess students' progress.

Reading

- ☐ Uses words related to migrating birds.
- ☐ Uses words related to homes and families.
- ☐ Knows the difference between fact and opinion.
- ☐ Identifies imagery.

Language Awareness

Grammar

- ☐ Recognizes and uses commas in direct address and in a series.

Phonics

- ☐ Pronounces and decodes words with /k/ and /f/.

Learning Strategies

- ☐ Uses a story sequence chart to understand the events in a story.
- ☐ Uses synonyms to understand the meanings of unfamiliar words.

Name ______________________________

Commas

A. Circle the commas in these sentences.

1. We're going to the country, Naomi.
2. "This house is dirty and ugly," Naomi said sadly.
3. Naomi began to watch, feed, and care for the geese.

B. Add commas where they belong.

4. He grew up hungry lonely and poor.
5. Langston I have a surprise for you!
6. "You're going to be a star" his ma said.
7. Langston crossed his eyes stretched his mouth and imitated her.
8. Are you lonely Langston?
9. Neighbors gave Granma their used dresses shirts and shoes.
10. This is your new home Langston.

C. If you could live anywhere in the world, where would you live? Why? Talk with a partner. Then write about it.

I would live in ______________________________

because ______________________________

____

____

____

____

Name ______________________________________

Consonant Sounds /k/ and /f/

A. Listen to the words. Read each word. Then say each word.

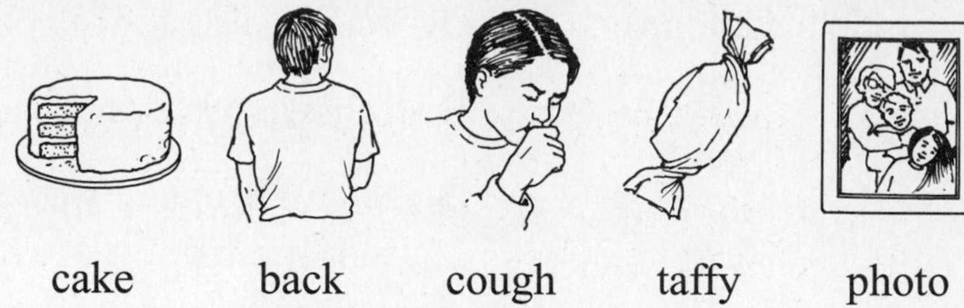

cake back cough taffy photo

B. Circle the letters that sound like /k/. Underline the letters that sound like /f/.

bake phone black offer

funny graph laugh

C. Say the underlined words. Read the paragraph to your partner. Then listen to your partner read it.

Langston Hughes lived down the block from a jazz music hall. Audiences laughed when Langston made faces. Langston moved to Harlem, where many other black artists and photographers lived.

Out of the Blue

Pages 666–683

Crossing Cultures • Throughout the lesson, encourage English language learners to ask questions. Engage them by having them vote on the value of one of Franklin's inventions, or let them use yes and no answers. Convey high expectations of English language learners and show confidence that they can express themselves.

PART 1

Preview the Skill Lesson

Use these activities with the Skill Lesson: "Working on the Railroad," Teacher's Edition, *Scott Foresman Reading,* pages 666–667.

Poster Tips
Page 16

Activate Prior Knowledge

Have students tell what they know about trains and about railroad workers. Display Adding English Poster 29. Ask: *Where would railroad workers be on this train? What might they do?* Record their responses on a web, Graphic Organizer Transparency 5.

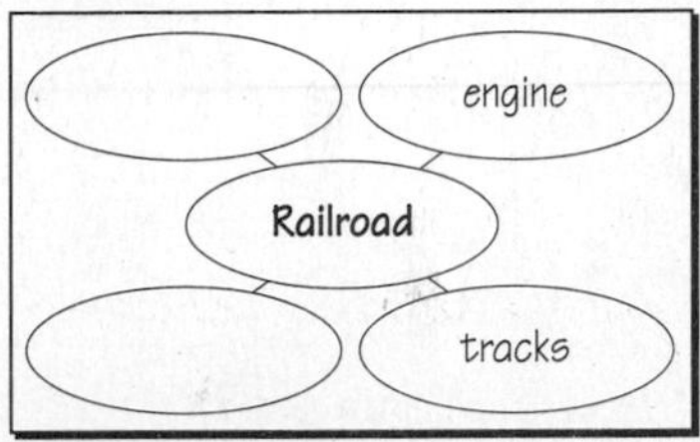

Transparency 5

Use Context Clues

Introduce the Skill Lesson literature by previewing vocabulary at the right. List the vocabulary words on the board. Explain the strategy: *When I hear a word I don't know, I listen to the sentences around it. They help me to figure out the word's meaning.*

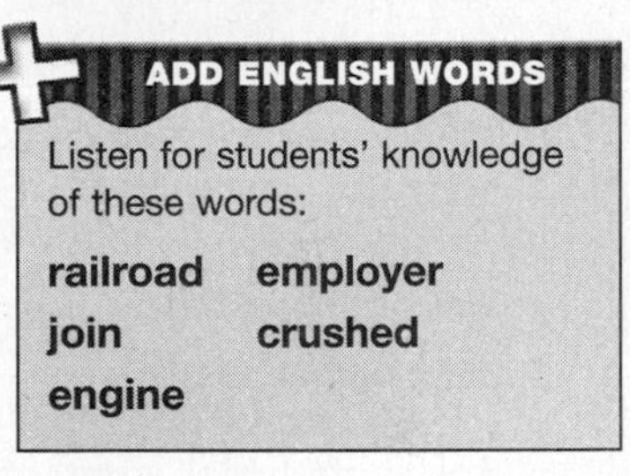

As you read the following paragraph, have students either point to parts of the Adding English Poster that relate to the vocabulary words or dramatize the words. Model using context clues for identifying word meanings.

> My grandfather works on trains. His employer is the Union Pacific Railway Company. He has worked as a train conductor and as an engine mechanic. That railroad job is important because the engine makes the train move. He tells us to be careful at train stations. If a train hit something on the tracks, it would be crushed. I like to watch the railroad cars. Grandpa and other workers join many cars together to make a long train.

Assign pairs of students one vocabulary word. Have them write and illustrate a sentence using the word. Ask volunteers to share their sentences and illustrations with the class.

Present the Comprehension Strategy

Comprehension: Main Idea and Supporting Details

Use Comprehension Strategies, *Adding English Guide,* page 10, to introduce Main Idea and Supporting Details.

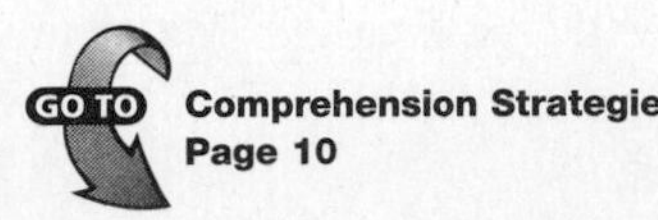

Comprehension Strategies
Page 10

Relate to Personal Experience

Have students suggest a movie or television show that most students know. Point out that the central thing it is about is the *main idea* and ask students to state the main idea. Ask: *What is one detail, or smaller piece of information, that tells more about the main idea?* Tell students that thinking about the main idea and supporting details will help them understand what they read.

Guide students as they read "Working on the Railroad," Scott Foresman Reading, *pages 666–667. Remind them to look for the main idea and details.*

Selection Audio CD 12/Tape 34

Practice

Have students identify the main idea and supporting details from "Working on the Railroad".

ADD ENGLISH WORDS

Review these clue words related to main idea and supporting details:

main idea
supporting details
most important pieces of information

Assess

If... students are not able to find the main idea and supporting details,

then... write the following sentences on the chalkboard:

- *Oiling the engine was a hot, dirty, and dangerous job.*
- *Most railroad jobs were hard and dangerous, so workers sometimes made inventions to make their work easier and safer.*

Ask students which sentence tells the main idea. Copy it onto a main idea chart, Graphic Organizer Transparency 15. Have groups find supporting details in the selection and add them to the chart.

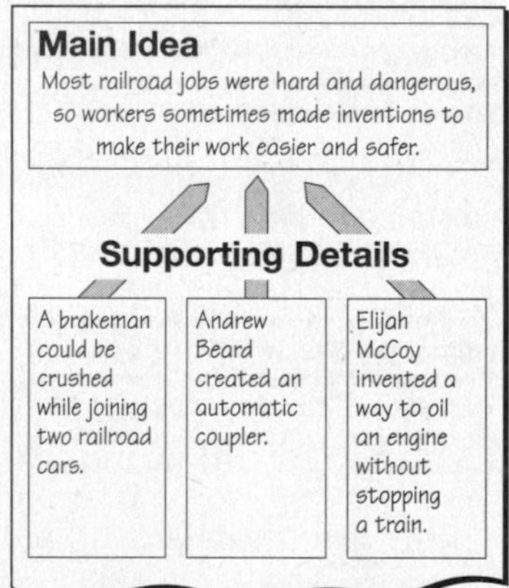

Transparency 15

PART 2

Preview the Reading Selection

Use these activities before reading "Out of the Blue," Teacher's Edition, *Scott Foresman Reading,* pages 668–680.

Activate Prior Knowledge

Turn the lights in the classroom on and off. Tell students that the electric lightbulb is an invention. Have them think of other inventions, such as the automobile, the computer, and TV. Display the Adding English Poster and have students brainstorm how an inventor thinks.

ADD ENGLISH WORDS

Listen for students' knowledge of words related to electricity.

argue	**ideas**
sparks	**lightning**
kite	**key**

Build Background

Tell students that they will read about Benjamin Franklin, a famous American inventor, who lived about three hundred years ago. Write 1506, 1706, and 1906 on the board and have students guess the year Franklin was born. (1706) Then ask students whether the following inventions would have existed in Franklin's time: printing press (✓), TV, ladders (✓), clocks(✓) automobile, airplane, telephone.

Strategy: Using a K-W-L Chart

Explain the strategy: *When I want to learn new things that are facts, I can use a chart. It is a strategy called Using a K-W-L Chart.* Be sure students recall that *K* means what they know, *W* refers to what they want to know, and *L* refers to what they have learned. Begin a K-W-L chart, Graphic Organizer Transparency 7, about Benjamin Franklin. Model filling out the K column. Have students fill in the K column of their own charts.

Vocabulary: Context for Unfamiliar Words

Use these activities with the Vocabulary Lesson and paragraph, "Franklin: Man with Many Jobs!," Teacher's Edition, *Scott Foresman Reading,* page 668.

Use a Cloze Paragraph

Help students identify the vocabulary words on the Adding English Poster. Then read the following sentences, pausing when a word is missing. Emphasize the context clues as you read. Reread the sentences and have students choose one of the Words to Know on page 614 for the missing words.

> Inventors like to try out an idea because they believe in a (theory). They try over and over again to create new (inventions). Each time they try, they learn something from the (experiment). In their experiments they may use special equipment or wires for (electricity). Some people think inventions are strange or (mysterious), but inventors think they are fun!

Have students do research to find biographies of inventors, or people who had important theories, from their home cultures. Encourage them to display books, pictures, and printouts of what they find.

Word Building

Write *mysterious, circulating, inventions,* and *electricity* on the board. Ask students to look for a base word within each word. Write the base words on the board. Pair students to think of other words related to each word (for example, *inventor, invented* for *inventions*). They can refer to the dictionary for support. Have students share their lists with the class.

RESOURCES

Use *Scott Foresman ESL,* Grade 3, for additional instruction and activities.

- Chapter 4, "What Light Can Do"
- Video, Unit 2, "Light"

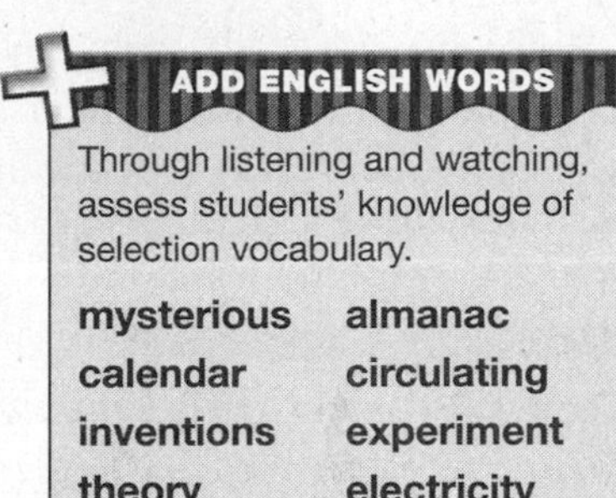

K What I Know	W What I Want to Know	L What I Learned
Benjamin Franklin discovered that lightning is electricity. He was an American. He was an inventor.		

Transparency 7

ADD ENGLISH WORDS

Through listening and watching, assess students' knowledge of selection vocabulary.

mysterious	**almanac**
calendar	**circulating**
inventions	**experiment**
theory	**electricity**

Guide students as they read "Franklin: Man with Many Jobs!," Scott Foresman Reading, *page 668. Ask students what they will do if they find an unfamiliar word.*

Students can participate in the Write About It activity that follows. If possible, first have English language learners work in groups with students whose home language is English to discuss what they learned about Benjamin Franklin from the paragraph.

Present the Reading Selection

Use these activities with "Out of the Blue," Teacher's Edition, *Scott Foresman Reading,* pages 668–680.

Preview Illustrations

Explain the strategy: *Before I begin to read, I look at the pictures in the story to get an idea of what it will be about.* Invite students to look at all the pictures. Then discuss the picture on page 670. How does Benjamin Franklin look compared to the others in the picture? What's his mood? Is he happy? Have students turn to page 673 and read the captions about the inventions. Next have them look at pages 678 and 679. Talk about what Franklin is doing. Would students try this kind of experiment? Why or why not?

Develop Concepts

Remind students that *Coming Home,* in the previous lesson was a biography of Langston Hughes; now they will read a biography of Benjamin Franklin. Explain that a biography:

- is a story about a real person
- is written by another person and based on real events
- can be about a person who is dead or alive

Set Purposes

Students can participate in Set Purposes, Teacher's Edition, *Scott Foresman Reading,* page 669. Then help students fill in the W column of their K-W-L charts with things they want to find out about Ben Franklin. Remind students that they are using the strategy called using a K-W-L chart.

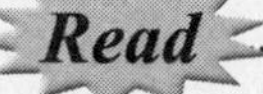

Guide students as they read "Out of the Blue," Scott Foresman Reading, *pages 668–680. To support comprehension, use the suggestions in Meeting Individual Needs, ESL, in the Teacher's Edition.*

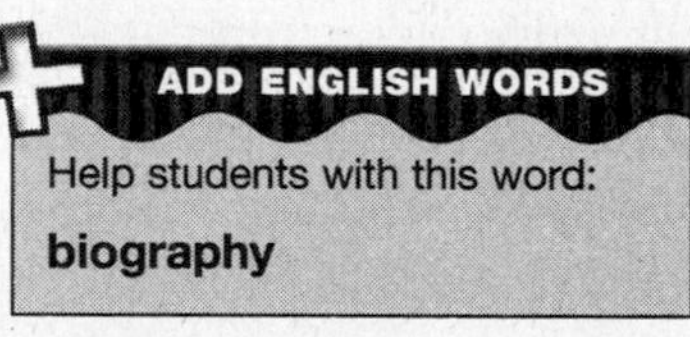

K What I Know	W What I Want to Know	L What I Learned
Benjamin Franklin discovered that lightning is electricity. He was an American. He was an inventor.	When did he live? Where did he live? What did he invent? What else did he do?	

Transparency 7

Selection Audio CD 12/Tape 34

Response Log

- Have students write about which of Ben Franklin's ideas is most exciting or interesting to them and why.
- Invite students to draw a captioned picture of Benjamin Franklin trying his kite experiment. They can use the Adding English Poster or the book illustrations for help.

K What I Know	W What I Want to Know	L What I Learned
Benjamin Franklin discovered that lightning is electricity. He was an American. He was an inventor.	When did he live? Where did he live? What did he invent? What else did he do?	He lived from 1706 to 1790. He lived in Boston and Philadelphia. He invented a special stove and a stepladder chair. He was a printer and a writer. He published an almanac and helped write the Declaration of Independence.

Transparency 7

Practice Selection Concepts

To help students tell what they learned, choose from these activities.

- Help students complete their K-W-L charts by filling in the L column with facts they learned about Benjamin Franklin.
- Distribute the ten important sentences. Have partners read the sentences and think of them as supporting details for the main idea of the selection. Have each pair write the main idea.

Ten Important Sentences
Page 41

Strategy: Self-Assess

Ask: *Did the strategy Using a K-W-L Chart help you learn new information about Benjamin Franklin? How?*

Language Awareness

Provide supported practice by using the Adding English Grammar and Phonics Practice Masters, pages 247–248, with the suggestions below.

Grammar: Quotations and Quotation Marks

Have students look at page 673 and read the sentences in quotation marks. Explain that quotation marks show the exact words someone said. Tell students that quotation marks are also used with titles of songs and stories, but not book titles.

Students can complete the Practice Master alone or with a partner.

Adding English
Grammar Practice Master
Page 247

Phonics: Suffixes

Distribute the Practice Master. Have students listen, read, and repeat as you say the words in Exercise A. Explain that new words can be made by adding endings or suffixes to base words. Write *protect* and *-ion* on the board. Ask students if they can make a new word using the suffix. Write the suffixes *-en, -ity, -ive, -some, -ion, -tion,* and *-sion* on the board and say words with these endings.

For Exercise B, have students say the base word and suffix aloud before writing the new word.

Adding English
Phonics Practice Master
Page 248

PART 3

Connect Selection Concepts

Use these activities with Reader Response, Teacher's Edition, *Scott Foresman Reading,* page 680.

Dramatize

If possible, have English language learners work in groups with students whose home language is English. Ask students to act out scenes from Ben Franklin's life, such as the following:

- Ben and his wife running a store
- Ben running the first library
- Ben proving that lightning is electricity

Proverbs We Know

Remind students that Benjamin Franklin wrote many sayings or proverbs in *Poor Richard's Almanack.* Explain that these sayings entertained readers as well as helped them in everyday situations. Have students ask someone at home to tell them proverbs or sayings from their home cultures and to write them on construction paper in both languages, if possible. Students can make a bulletin board display.

Reading Across Texts: "A Really Bright Idea," pages 681–683

To support students as they read an informational article:

- Have students preview the article. Activate prior knowledge by asking what students already know about Thomas Edison. Have students talk about other inventors they know of. Which of their inventions are part of our everyday lives?
- Ask students to compare the inventions of Thomas Edison to those of Benjamin Franklin. Use a T Chart to record student responses.

Assess

Refer to the list below to assess students' progress.

Reading

- ☐ Uses words related to Ben Franklin and his inventions.
- ☐ Identifies main idea and supporting details.
- ☐ Understands biography.

Language Awareness

Grammar

- ☐ Recognizes and uses quotation marks correctly.

Phonics

- ☐ Makes new words from base words and suffixes.

Learning Strategies

- ☐ Uses a K-W-L chart to learn and organize facts.
- ☐ Uses context clues to find the meanings of unfamiliar words.

Name ______________________________

Quotations and Quotation Marks

A. Circle the quotation marks in each sentence.

1. Buffalo Bill's favorite song was "Home on the Range."

2. "Turn off the TV and finish your homework!" my father said.

3. "A penny saved is a penny earned" is a famous saying from *Poor Richard's Almanack.*

B. Add quotation marks where they are needed.

4. Ben Franklin's neighbor asked, What's all the noise coming from your house?

5. Ben replied, I am making a stove.

6. I enjoyed reading Out of the Blue.

7. *Poor Richard's Almanack* is full of advice, such as Eat to live, not live to eat.

C. Talk with a partner about Ben Franklin's inventions. Which one do you think is the most important? Write about it.

Franklin's most important invention was ________________

____

because ______________________________________

____

____

Name ______________________________

Suffixes

Phonics

A. Listen to the words. Read each word. Then say each word.

creative electricity circulation deepen extension troublesome invention

B. Add the suffix to make a new word.

1. act + -ive = ______________

2. awe + -some = ______________

3. strength + -en = ______________

4. author + -ity = ______________

5. exhibit + -ion = ______________

C. Say the underlined words. Read the paragraph to a partner. Then listen as your partner reads it to you.

There is an old saying "<u>Necessity</u> is the mother of <u>invention</u>." What does it mean? Think about keeping warm. If you were cold, you might make an <u>invention</u> so you would have heat. Heat is a <u>necessity</u>. Ben Franklin was very <u>creative</u>. He wondered what would happen if he used <u>electricity</u>. Some of his <u>investigations</u> were <u>troublesome</u>. Others were <u>awesome</u>!

Chocolate Is Missing

Pages 684–709

Crossing Cultures • In this lesson, students read a mystery. Before reading, find out if students have similar ideas about what makes a good story. Should a good story make the reader scared or happy or something else? Should it be told aloud? What stories would students like to hear again?

PART 1

Preview the Skill Lesson

Use these activities with the Skill Lesson: "Breakfast with Brede," Teacher's Edition, *Scott Foresman Reading,* pages 684–685.

Activate Prior Knowledge

Show students Adding English Poster 30 and ask them to describe what they see. Ask volunteers to talk about parties or special meals they've attended. Have them focus on what they wore, what they ate, how they ate, and so on. Discuss good table manners, and have students give examples. (Students' comments may reflect their cultural background.) Ask students if they behave differently when they eat at home and when they are at a special meal. Use a T-chart, Graphic Organizer 24, to record their responses.

Poster Tips
Page 16

At Home	At a Special Meal
wear jeans	wear nice clothes

Transparency 24

Use Total Physical Response

Introduce the Skill Lesson literature by previewing the vocabulary at right. Write the words on the board. As you read the passage that follows, act out the motions and have students follow the directions. Remind students to listen for the vocabulary words.

Listen for students' knowledge of these words:

scones **horrible**
nibbled **frowned**
hard

> Let's imagine we're at a tea party. Here we are sitting at a table. First, I'll pour us each some tea. Have a sip. Mmmm. Now try some scones I baked. Take a bite. Did you hear that crunch? They're hard to chew. Here's some butter to make them softer. Try it again. My scone is just as hard as the first time I nibbled it. It tastes horrible! How is your scone? Show me the face you make when something tastes horrible. I think a lot of you frowned.

Have students talk about what they would taste, hear, smell, feel, and see at a tea party like the one described. Remind them to use the vocabulary words and to point out pictures on the poster.

Present the Comprehension Strategy

Comprehension: Author's Purpose

Use Comprehension Strategies, *Adding English Guide,* page 10, to introduce Author's Purpose.

Comprehension Strategies
Page 10

Relate to Personal Experience

Put out a selection of written materials students are likely to be familiar with, including the Sunday comics, advertisements, short stories, newspaper articles, and newsletters. Discuss why the authors might have written each example—to entertain, inform, express, or persuade. Have students look for the author's purpose in each piece and write this information on a four column chart, Graphic Organizer Transparency 26. All students in the class might benefit from this activity.

Entertain	Inform	Express	Persuade
comics	newspaper article	editorial	advertise-ment

Guide students as they read "Breakfast with Brede," Scott Foresman Reading, *pages 684–685. Ask them to think about the author's purpose.*

Selection Audio CD 12/Tape 35

Practice

Have students retell the story and state the author's purpose. Encourage them to refer to their charts for ideas.

Assess

If... students are not able to state the author's purpose,

then... have them tell what they liked about "Breakfast with Brede" and what they learned. Based on students' responses, have them decide whether the author's purpose was to entertain or to inform. Help students see that the author's purpose was to entertain.

ADD ENGLISH WORDS

Review these words related to author's purpose:

entertain **inform**
express **persuade**
purpose

PART 2

Preview the Reading Selection

Use these activities before reading *Chocolate Is Missing,* Teacher's Edition, *Scott Foresman Reading,* pages 686–707.

Activate Prior Knowledge

Display the Adding English Poster and discuss the pictures that depict the words at the right. Ask students if they can identify the guinea pig. Is it a wild animal or a pet? Do any students have pets? Where do they keep their pets? Do they have guinea pigs? Have each student write a sentence relating one of the vocabulary words to the poster. Then have volunteers read their sentences, omitting the vocabulary word. Challenge the class to say the missing word.

ADD ENGLISH WORDS

Listen for students' understanding of words related to pets:

guinea pig **pet**
cage **stolen**
escaped **drawer**

Build Background

Show an announcement for an animal or object that is lost or missing. Talk with students about the missing item and why they think it might be lost. Could it have escaped or been stolen? How would students try to find it?

Use Steps in a Process

Encourage students to think about a time a favorite toy or other item disappeared. Ask volunteers to tell what they did to try to find the missing item. Did they ask anybody about it? Did they advertise? Did they offer a reward? Where did they look for it? Have students use a steps in a process chart, Graphic Organizer Transparency 22, to organize their thoughts. They can refer to the Adding English Poster for support.

Vocabulary: Multiple Meaning Words

Use these activities with the Vocabulary Lesson and paragraph "Sniffing Out Clues!," Teacher's Edition, *Scott Foresman Reading,* page 686.

Write the vocabulary words on the board. Provide an example of *brag,* such as: *I'm very smart and beautiful.* Then have students write the word on a self-stick note and attach it to an appropriate part of the Adding English Poster. Have volunteers use the word as they talk about the scene.

Point out that some words have more than one meaning. Demonstrate *approach* by walking near a student, saying: *I approach you.* Then direct students to approach you. Tell students that *approach* also means "a way of doing something." Have students answer these questions in complete sentences.

What approach will you use to solve the math problem?

Will you approach the principal today?

Vocabulary Tick-Tack-Toe

Write the vocabulary words on the board and draw a tick-tack-toe grid. Organize students into two teams, O and X. Tell the teams they are required to say the meaning of a word you choose. The first team to say the correct meaning puts an O or an X in a space on the grid. The winner is the first team to get three in a row. Then reverse the game: erase the words and write the definitions on the board. Teams say the correct words to match the definitions you indicate.

Guide students as they read "Sniffing Out Clues!," Scott Foresman Reading, *page 686. Ask students what they will do if they find a word with more than one meaning.*

RESOURCES

Use *Scott Foresman ESL,* Grade 5, for additional instruction and activities.

- Chapter 9, "What Do You Read"
- Video, Unit 5, "Reading Fun"

Transparency 22

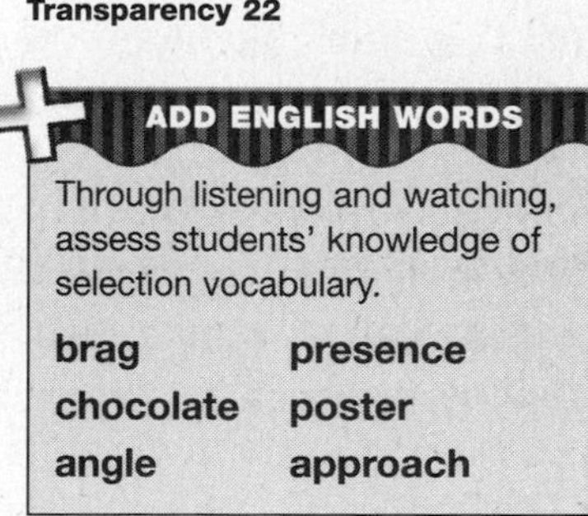

Students can participate in the Talk About It activity that follows. When possible, have English language learners work in groups with students whose home language is English to make up sentences using the vocabulary words.

Present the Reading Selection

Use these activities with "Chocolate Is Missing," Teacher's Edition, *Scott Foresman Reading,* pages 686–707.

Preview Title and Illustrations

Explain the strategy: *Before I begin to read, I look at the pictures and title to get an idea of what the story will be about.* Invite students to look at the title and ask: *What clue word hints that there may be a problem in the story?* Now ask them to look at the picture on pages 686 and 687 and focus on the faces of the kids and the empty cage. Can they guess what has happened? Continue previewing the illustrations. Have students begin a problem and solution chart, Graphic Organizer Transparency 20.

Strategy: Using a Problem and Solution Chart

Explain the strategy: *When I want to understand how a problem is solved in a story, I can use a chart. It is a strategy called Using a Problem and Solution Chart.* Be sure that students understand that a problem is something that needs to be answered, and the solution is the answer to the problem. Model filling out the first part of the chart with the title and a possible problem based on the title and illustrations. Have students begin their own charts.

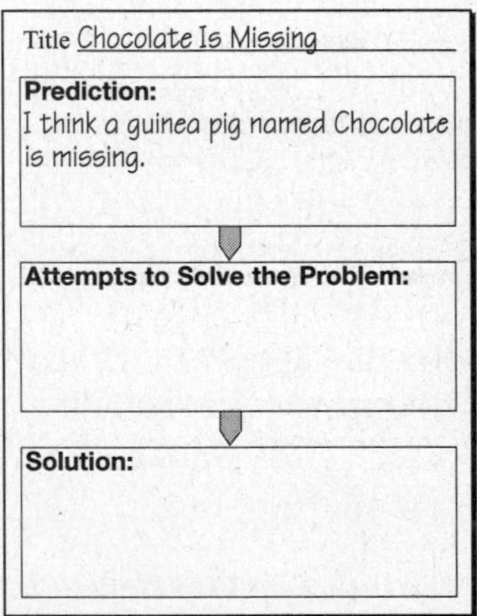

Transparency 20

Develop Concepts

Students may need help understanding the use of humor in this selection. Tell them that authors use humor to entertain and to make the reader laugh. The characters may be shown in funny situations, or the author can make comparisons that cause us to laugh. Have students read aloud parts of "Breakfast with Brede" that they think are humorous.

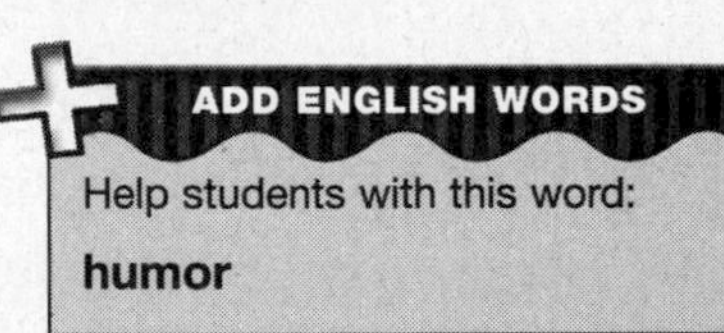

Set Purposes

Students can participate in Set Purposes, Teacher's Edition, *Scott Foresman Reading,* page 687. Remind them that they are using a strategy called using a problem and solution chart. Encourage students to watch for the problem and its solution as they read.

Guide students as they read "Chocolate Is Missing," Scott Foresman Reading, *pages 686–707. To support comprehension, use the suggestions in Meeting Individual Needs, ESL, in the Teacher's Edition.*

Selection Audio CD 12/Tape 35

Response Log

- Have students stop reading the story after paragraph six on page 690. Ask them to write about how they would go about finding chocolate. Then they can finish reading the story.
- Ask students to draw a picture of the empty cage and of Chocolate and her babies. Have them write a label under each picture.

Title Chocolate Is Missing

Prediction:
I think a guinea pig named Chocolate is missing. After reading I was right!

Attempts to Solve the Problem:
Lila and Gayle make posters to put up; the girls interrogate suspects; Lila searches the classroom.

Solution:
Lila finds Chocolate—and three babies—hiding in a drawer.

Transparency 20

Practice Selection Concepts

To help students tell what they learned, choose from these activities.

- Help students finish their problem and solution charts by noting whether their predicted problem happened—and filling in a real problem if it did not. Have students complete the chart.
- Distribute the ten important sentences. Have partners read the sentences and underline examples of humor.

Ten Important Sentences Page 42

Strategy: Self-Assess

Ask: *Did the strategy Using a Problem and Solution Chart help you understand the story? How?*

Language Awareness

Provide supported practice by using the Adding English Grammar and Phonics Practice Masters, pages 255–256, with the suggestions below.

Grammar: Review of Compound and Complex Sentences

Write the following sentence on the board: *Oral reports were Gayle's specialty.* This is a simple sentence because it expresses a single and complete thought. Then write: *I don't like to brag, but lots of times I get ideas.* A compound sentence contains two simple sentences usually joined by a comma and a conjunction (*and, but, or, nor, for, so, yet*). Write this sentence on the board: *When I'm at school, I'm famous for my great ideas.* Explain that this is a complex sentence, a simple sentence and a group of words that can't stand alone.

Students can complete the Practice Master individually or with a partner.

Adding English Grammar Practice Master Page 255

Phonics: Word Building and Sound Changes

Distribute the Practice Master. Have students listen, read, and repeat as you say the words in Exercise A. Point out that when a suffix is added to a base word, the spelling and pronunciation can change.

For Exercise B, have students read the words aloud before matching them.

Adding English Phonics Practice Master Page 256

Base Words, Endings

PART 3

Connect Selection Concepts

Use these activities with Reader Response, Teacher's Edition, *Scott Foresman Reading,* page 707.

Literature Discussion Groups

When possible, have English language learners work in groups with students whose home language is English. Ask them to talk about what clues in the story helped them solve the mystery. Did they solve it in their minds before Lila did? Would they have tried a different approach from Lila's?

Make Posters

Have students look at Lila's poster on page 688. Ask them to design posters for other missing pets or items, such as a watch, a ring, a book, or a toy. Display the posters in the classroom.

Reading Across Texts: "The Zoo Crew," pages 708–709

To support students as they read an informational article:

- Have students preview the article. What will they read about?
- Students can compare the job of taking care of zoo animals with the job of taking care of animals in a classroom. How are the jobs different? How are they the same?

Assess

Refer to the list below to assess students' progress.

Reading

- ☐ Uses words related to solving a mystery.
- ☐ Uses words related to pets.
- ☐ Uses words related to table manners.
- ☐ Identifies the author's purpose.
- ☐ Recognizes humor.

Language Awareness

Grammar

- ☐ Recognizes and uses compound and complex sentences.

Phonics

- ☐ Pronounces and recognizes sound changes and shifts in stress due to word building.

Learning Strategies

- ☐ Uses a problem and solution chart.
- ☐ Recognizes words with multiple meanings and uses context clues to determine the correct meaning.

Name ______________________________

Review of Compound and Complex Sentences

A. Listen to the sentences. Say the sentences. Underline the compound sentence. Circle the complex sentence.

1. When we got our class pet, we decided to get a guinea pig.
2. The guinea pig's fur was brown, and we named him Chocolate.

B. Circle the words in parentheses that best complete each sentence.

3. Chocolate was missing, ________________.

   (the cage door was open/and we needed to find him)

4. Did he get out by himself, ________________?

   (or did someone take him/how could he)?

5. When Lila found Chocolate, ________________.

   (but she had babies/everyone was happy)

C. What is the best pet for the classroom? Talk with a partner. Draw a picture of the animal. Write why this is a good pet.

The best pet for the classroom is ________________

____

____

____

Name ________________________________

Phonics

Word Building and Sound Changes

A. Listen to the words. Then say the words.

educate/education   direct/direction

B. Match each word on the left to its base word on the right.

1. nomination	**a.** investigate
2. organization	**b.** interrogate
3. interrogation	**c.** nominate
4. investigation	**d.** inform
5. protection	**e.** organize
6. information	**f.** protect

C. Say the underlined words. Read the paragraph to a partner. Then listen as your partner reads it to you.

Chocolate was missing, and there was no explanation. With her best friend, Gayle, Lila began an investigation. They made posters that had information about the guinea pig, including a description. They also asked many questions during an interrogation of a classmate. However, it was because of Lila's poor organization of a report that they found the missing class pet.

Name ____________________

A Visit with Grandpa

Sentences

Grammar

A. Listen to the words. Underline the complete sentence.

1. Grandpa made biscuits for lunch.
2. Ate the biscuits.

B. Make each sentence complete by adding the word or words in parentheses.

3. The cowboys running. (are)
The cowboys are running.
4. The pasture big. (is)
The pasture is big.
5. was going very fast. (The cowboy)
The cowboy was going very fast.
6. cook biscuits with raisins. (I)
I cook biscuits with raisins.
7. Who the fence? (will fix)
Who will fix the fence?

C. What would you do on a vacation? Talk to a partner. Then write about the vacation.

Answers will vary.

On my vacation I would like to ____________________

A Visit with Grandpa 23

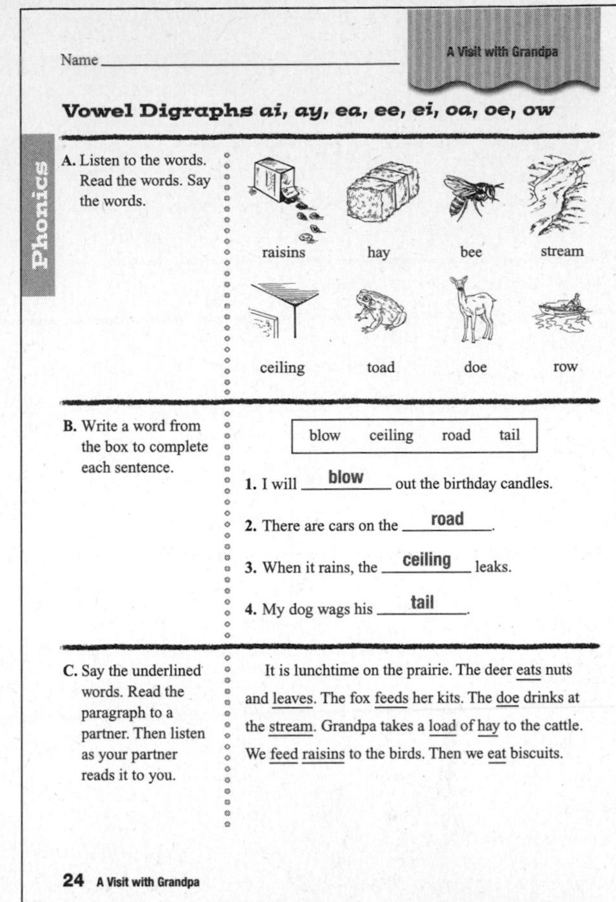

Name ____________________

A Visit with Grandpa

Vowel Digraphs *ai, ay, ea, ee, ei, oa, oe, ow*

Phonics

A. Listen to the words. Read the words. Say the words.

raisins hay bee stream
ceiling toad doe row

B. Write a word from the box to complete each sentence.

blow	ceiling	road	tail

1. I will **blow** out the birthday candles.
2. There are cars on the **road**.
3. When it rains, the **ceiling** leaks.
4. My dog wags his **tail**.

C. Say the underlined words. Read the paragraph to a partner. Then listen as your partner reads it to you.

It is lunchtime on the prairie. The deer eats nuts and leaves. The fox feeds her kits. The doe drinks at the stream. Grandpa takes a load of hay to the cattle. We feed raisins to the birds. Then we eat biscuits.

24 A Visit with Grandpa

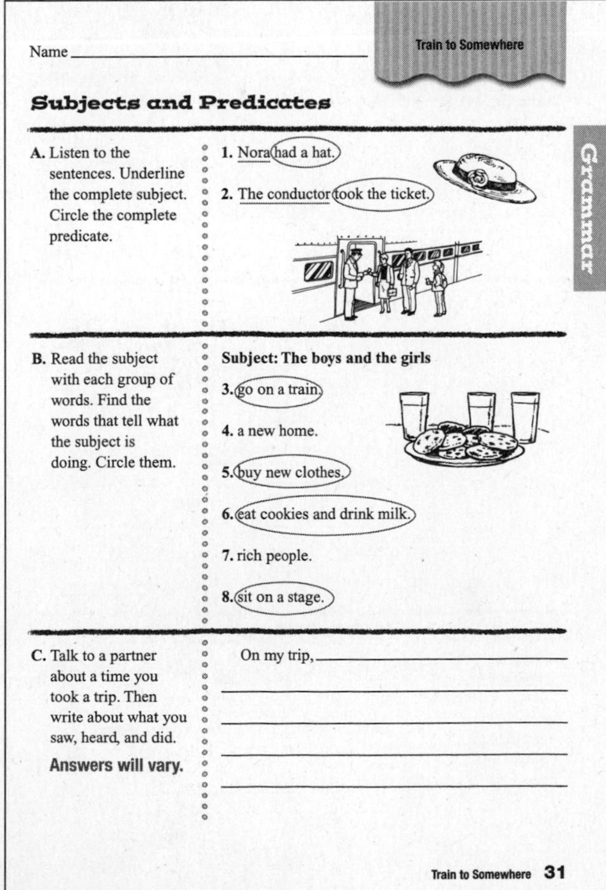

Name ____________________

Train to Somewhere

Subjects and Predicates

Grammar

A. Listen to the sentences. Underline the complete subject. Circle the complete predicate.

1. Nora had a hat.
2. The conductor took the ticket.

B. Read the subject with each group of words. Find the words that tell what the subject is doing. Circle them.

Subject: The boys and the girls

3. go on a train.
4. a new home.
5. buy new clothes.
6. eat cookies and drink milk.
7. rich people.
8. sit on a stage.

C. Talk to a partner about a time you took a trip. Then write about what you saw, heard, and did.

Answers will vary.

On my trip, ____________________

Train to Somewhere 31

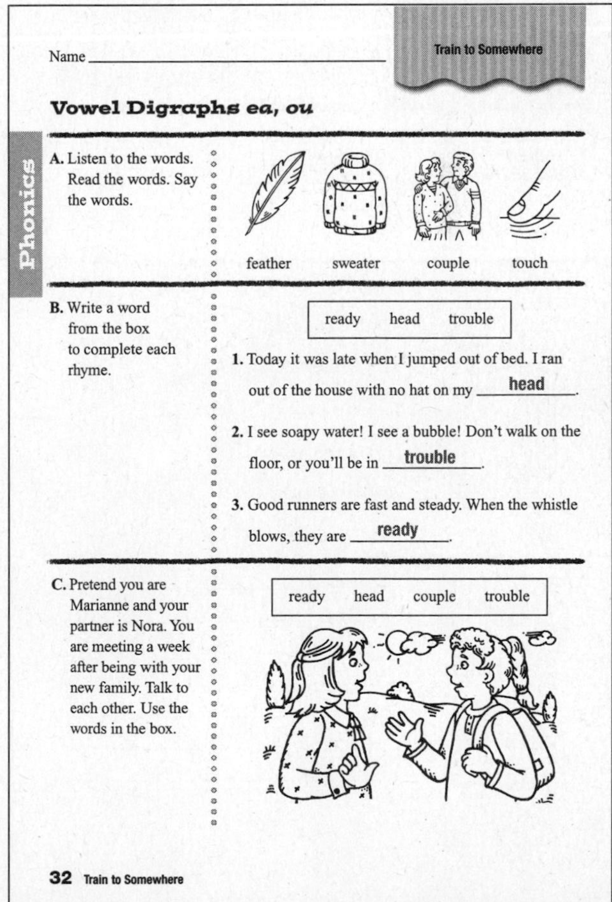

Name ____________________

Train to Somewhere

Vowel Digraphs *ea, ou*

Phonics

A. Listen to the words. Read the words. Say the words.

feather sweater couple touch

B. Write a word from the box to complete each rhyme.

ready	head	trouble

1. Today it was late when I jumped out of bed. I ran out of the house with no hat on my **head**.
2. I see soapy water! I see a bubble! Don't walk on the floor, or you'll be in **trouble**.
3. Good runners are fast and steady. When the whistle blows, they are **ready**.

C. Pretend you are Marianne and your partner is Nora. You are meeting a week after being with your new family. Talk to each other. Use the words in the box.

ready	head	couple	trouble

32 Train to Somewhere

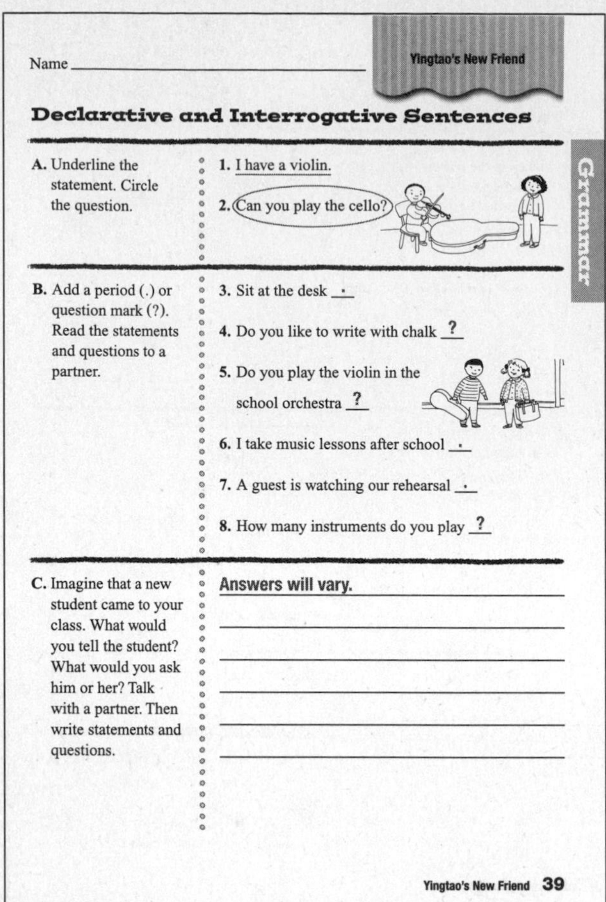

Name ______________________ Yingtao's New Friend

Declarative and Interrogative Sentences

Grammar

A. Underline the statement. Circle the question.

1. I have a violin.
2. Can you play the cello?

B. Add a period (.) or question mark (?). Read the statements and questions to a partner.

3. Sit at the desk **.**
4. Do you like to write with chalk **?**
5. Do you play the violin in the school orchestra **?**
6. I take music lessons after school **.**
7. A guest is watching our rehearsal **.**
8. How many instruments do you play **?**

C. Imagine that a new student came to your class. What would you tell the student? What would you ask him or her? Talk with a partner. Then write statements and questions.

Answers will vary.

Yingtao's New Friend 39

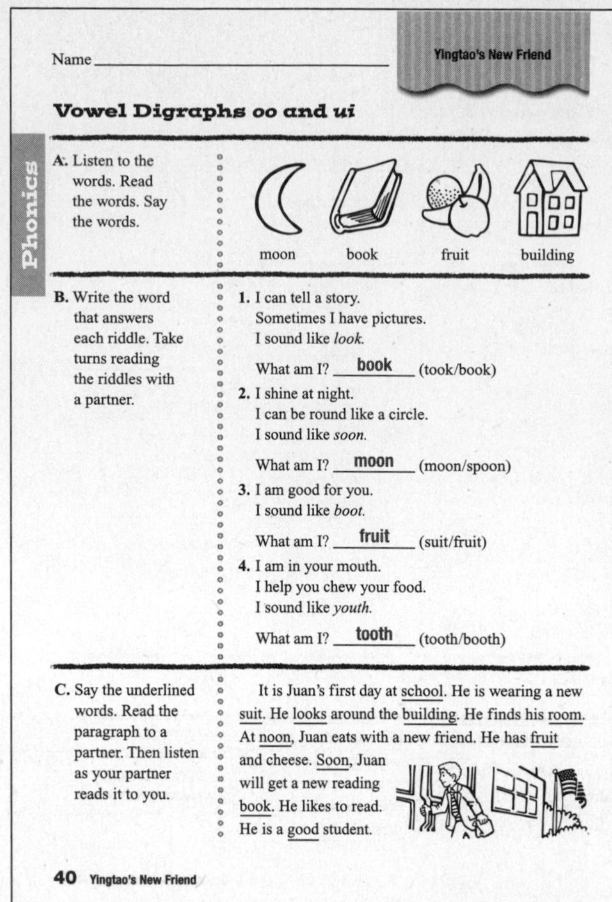

Name ______________________ Yingtao's New Friend

Vowel Digraphs *oo* and *ui*

Phonics

A. Listen to the words. Read the words. Say the words.

moon book fruit building

B. Write the word that answers each riddle. Take turns reading the riddles with a partner.

1. I can tell a story.
Sometimes I have pictures.
I sound like *look.*
What am I? **book** (took/book)
2. I shine at night.
I can be round like a circle.
I sound like *soon.*
What am I? **moon** (moon/spoon)
3. I am good for you.
I sound like *boot.*
What am I? **fruit** (suit/fruit)
4. I am in your mouth.
I help you chew your food.
I sound like *youth.*
What am I? **tooth** (tooth/booth)

C. Say the underlined words. Read the paragraph to a partner. Then listen as your partner reads it to you.

It is Juan's first day at school. He is wearing a new suit. He looks around the building. He finds his room. At noon, Juan eats with a new friend. He has fruit and cheese. Soon, Juan will get a new reading book. He likes to read. He is a good student.

40 Yingtao's New Friend

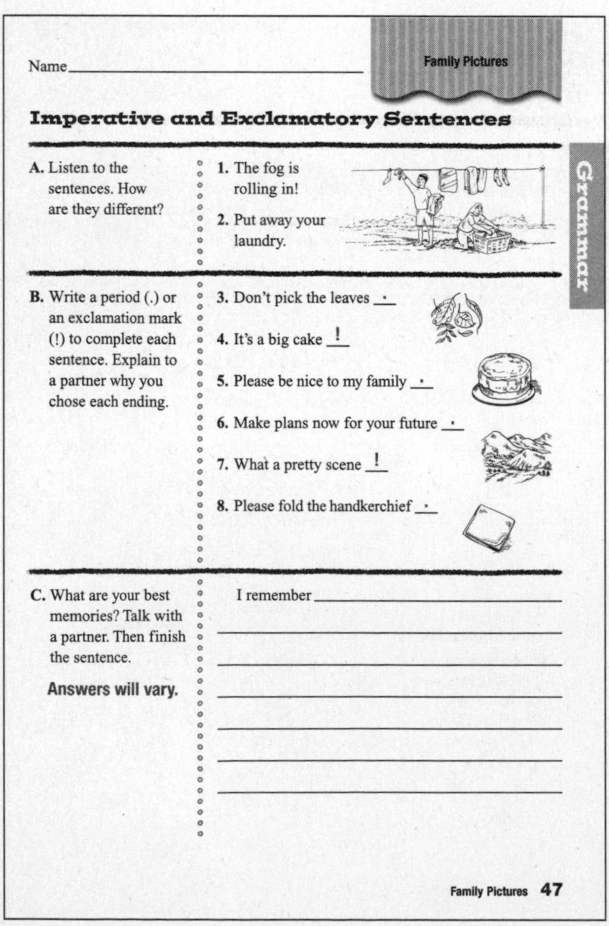

Name ______________________ Family Pictures

Imperative and Exclamatory Sentences

Grammar

A. Listen to the sentences. How are they different?

1. The fog is rolling in!
2. Put away your laundry.

B. Write a period (.) or an exclamation mark (!) to complete each sentence. Explain to a partner why you chose each ending.

3. Don't pick the leaves **.**
4. It's a big cake **!**
5. Please be nice to my family **.**
6. Make plans now for your future **.**
7. What a pretty scene **!**
8. Please fold the handkerchief **.**

C. What are your best memories? Talk with a partner. Then finish the sentence.

Answers will vary.

I remember ______________________

Family Pictures 47

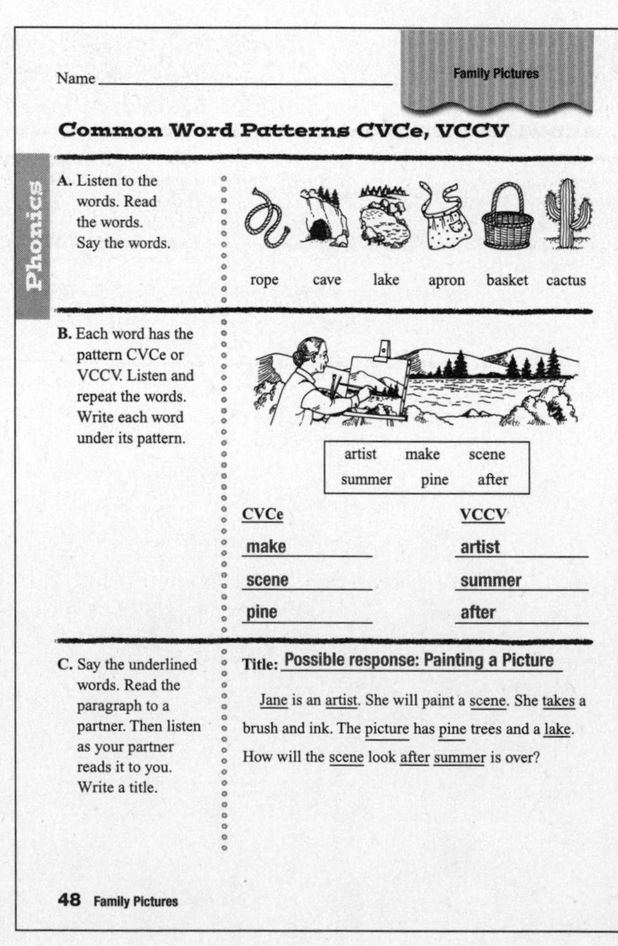

Name ______________________ Family Pictures

Common Word Patterns CVCe, VCCV

Phonics

A. Listen to the words. Read the words. Say the words.

rope cave lake apron basket cactus

B. Each word has the pattern CVCe or VCCV. Listen and repeat the words. Write each word under its pattern.

artist make scene
summer pine after

CVCe	VCCV
make	**artist**
scene	**summer**
pine	**after**

C. Say the underlined words. Read the paragraph to a partner. Then listen as your partner reads it to you. Write a title.

Title: **Possible response: Painting a Picture**

Jane is an artist. She will paint a scene. She takes a brush and ink. The picture has pine trees and a lake. How will the scene look after summer is over?

48 Family Pictures

Name ______________ Addie in Charge

Compound and Complex Sentences

Grammar

A. Underline the sentence with the connecting word. Circle the connecting word.

1. The fire was hot, but we were safe.
2. Although the fire was hot, we were safe.

B. Add the punctuation and words from the parentheses to make one sentence.

3. When the wind blows. Ma stays inside. (,)
   When the wind blows, Ma stays inside.
4. While Burt napped. Addie worked on her sampler. (,)
   While Burt napped, Addie worked on her sampler.
5. Addie's legs shook. Her legs hurt. (, and)
   Addie's legs shook, and her legs hurt.
6. Addie was afraid. She did something brave. (, but)
   Addie was afraid, but she did something brave.

C. Imagine that you saw a house on fire. Talk with a partner. Then write what you would do.

Answers will vary.

If I saw a fire, ______________

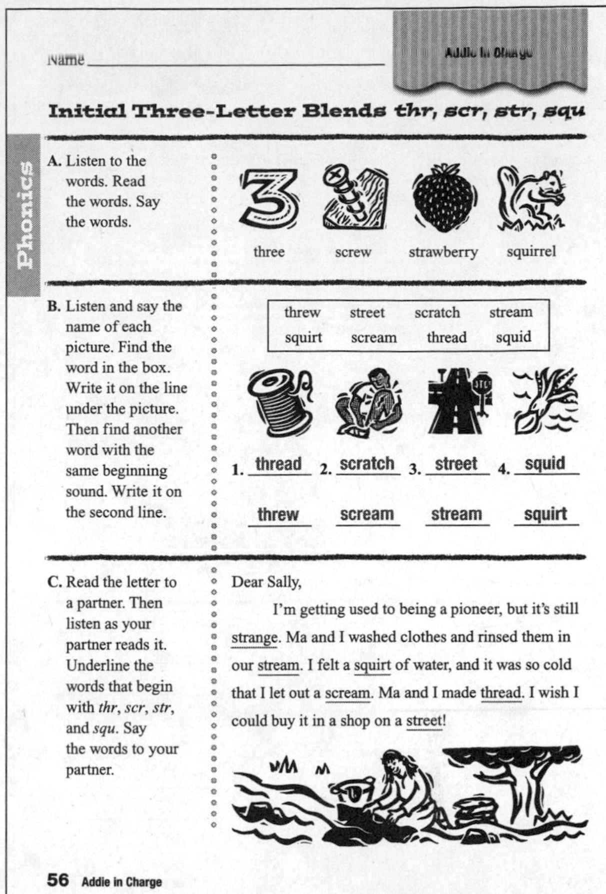
Name ______________ Addie in Charge

Initial Three-Letter Blends *thr, scr, str, squ*

Phonics

A. Listen to the words. Read the words. Say the words.

three screw strawberry squirrel

B. Listen and say the name of each picture. Find the word in the box. Write it on the line under the picture. Then find another word with the same beginning sound. Write it on the second line.

threw	street	scratch	stream
squirt	scream	thread	squid

1. **thread** 2. **scratch** 3. **street** 4. **squid**

threw **scream** **stream** **squirt**

C. Read the letter to a partner. Then listen as your partner reads it. Underline the words that begin with *thr, scr, str,* and *squ*. Say the words to your partner.

Dear Sally,

I'm getting used to being a pioneer, but it's still strange. Ma and I washed clothes and rinsed them in our stream. I felt a squirt of water, and it was so cold that I let out a scream. Ma and I made thread. I wish I could buy it in a shop on a street!

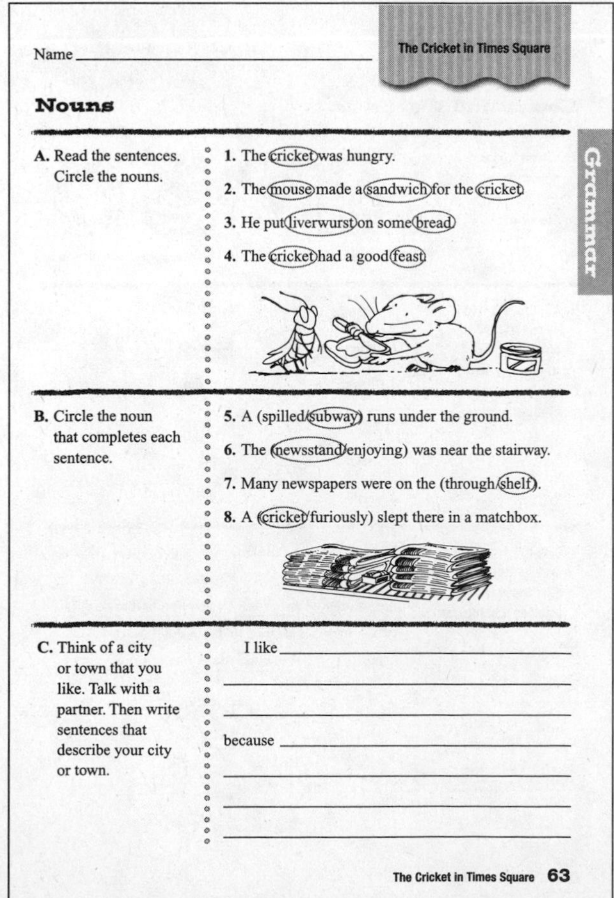
Name ______________ The Cricket in Times Square

Nouns

Grammar

A. Read the sentences. Circle the nouns.

1. The cricket was hungry.
2. The mouse made a sandwich for the cricket.
3. He put liverwurst on some bread.
4. The cricket had a good feast.

B. Circle the noun that completes each sentence.

5. A (spilled/subway) runs under the ground.
6. The (newsstand/enjoying) was near the stairway.
7. Many newspapers were on the (through/shelf).
8. A (cricket/furiously) slept there in a matchbox.

C. Think of a city or town that you like. Talk with a partner. Then write sentences that describe your city or town.

I like ______________

because ______________

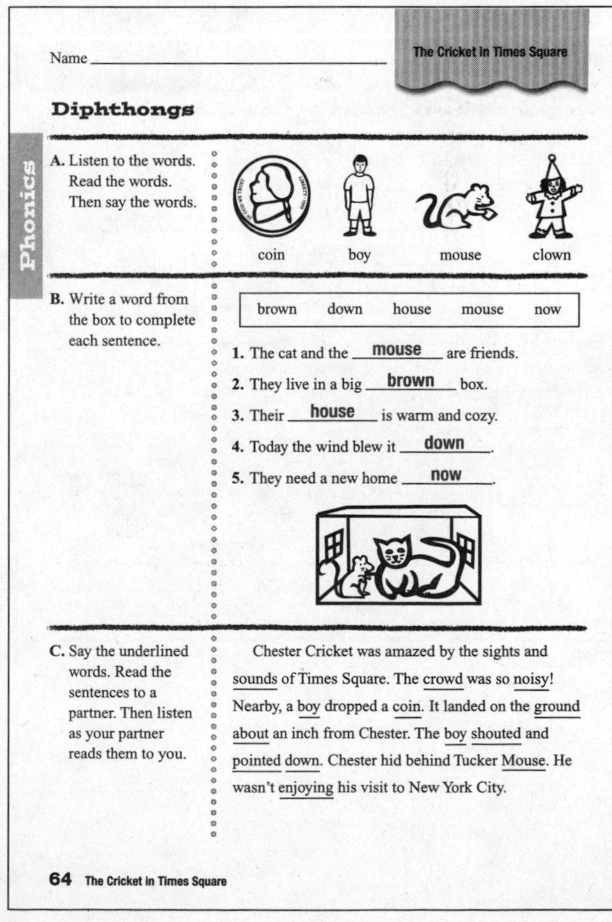
Name ______________ The Cricket in Times Square

Diphthongs

Phonics

A. Listen to the words. Read the words. Then say the words.

coin boy mouse clown

B. Write a word from the box to complete each sentence.

brown	down	house	mouse	now

1. The cat and the **mouse** are friends.
2. They live in a big **brown** box.
3. Their **house** is warm and cozy.
4. Today the wind blew it **down**.
5. They need a new home **now**.

C. Say the underlined words. Read the sentences to a partner. Then listen as your partner reads them to you.

Chester Cricket was amazed by the sights and sounds of Times Square. The crowd was so noisy! Nearby, a boy dropped a coin. It landed on the ground about an inch from Chester. The boy shouted and pointed down. Chester hid behind Tucker Mouse. He wasn't enjoying his visit to New York City.

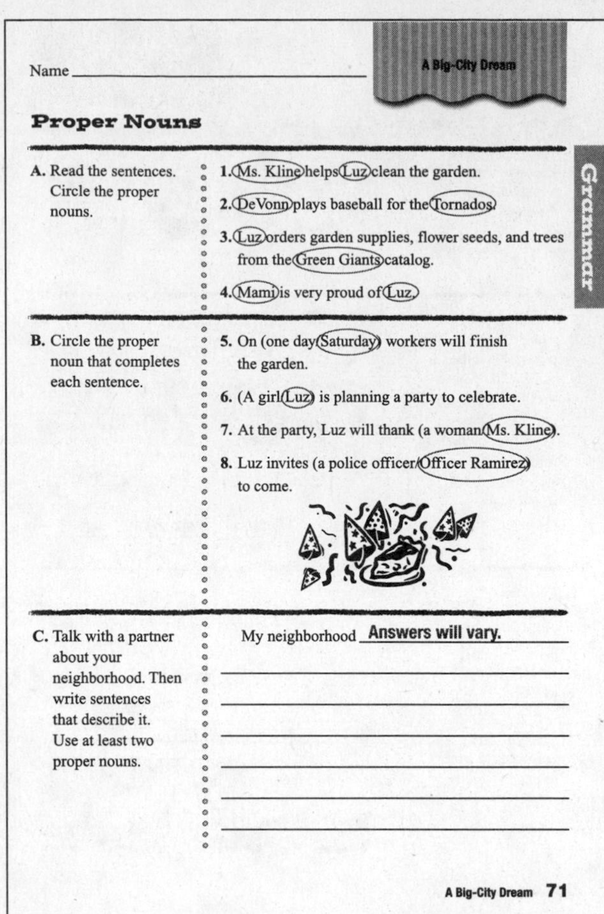

Name ______________ A Big-City Dream

Proper Nouns

Grammar

A. Read the sentences. Circle the proper nouns.

1. Ms. Kline helps Luz clean the garden.
2. DeVonn plays baseball for the Tornados.
3. Luz orders garden supplies, flower seeds, and trees from the Green Giants catalog.
4. Mami is very proud of Luz.

B. Circle the proper noun that completes each sentence.

5. On (one day/Saturday) workers will finish the garden.
6. (A girl/Luz) is planning a party to celebrate.
7. At the party, Luz will thank (a woman/Ms. Kline).
8. Luz invites (a police officer/Officer Ramirez) to come.

C. Talk with a partner about your neighborhood. Then write sentences that describe it. Use at least two proper nouns.

My neighborhood **Answers will vary.**

A Big-City Dream 71

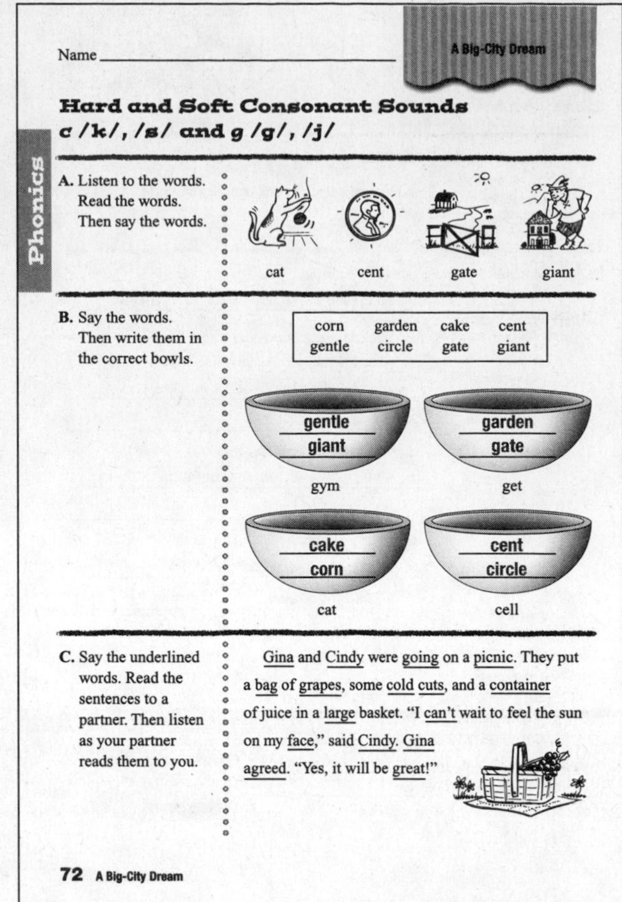

Name ______________ A Big-City Dream

Hard and Soft Consonant Sounds c /k/, /s/ and g /g/, /j/

Phonics

A. Listen to the words. Read the words. Then say the words.

cat cent gate giant

B. Say the words. Then write them in the correct bowls.

corn	garden	cake	cent
gentle	circle	gate	giant

gym: **gentle**, **giant**

get: **garden**, **gate**

cat: **cake**, **corn**

cell: **cent**, **circle**

C. Say the underlined words. Read the sentences to a partner. Then listen as your partner reads them to you.

Gina and Cindy were going on a picnic. They put a bag of grapes, some cold cuts, and a container of juice in a large basket. "I can't wait to feel the sun on my face," said Cindy. Gina agreed. "Yes, it will be great!"

72 A Big-City Dream

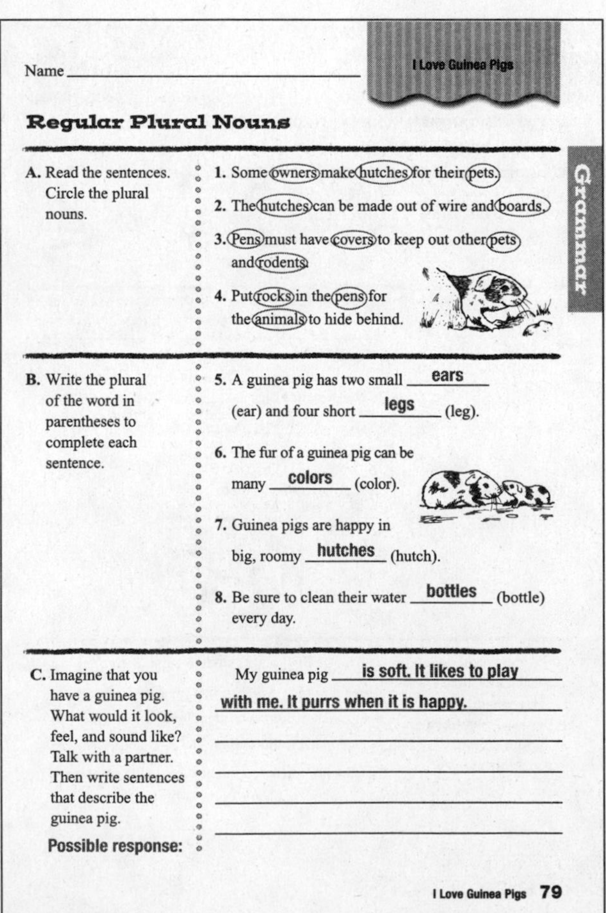

Name ______________ I Love Guinea Pigs

Regular Plural Nouns

Grammar

A. Read the sentences. Circle the plural nouns.

1. Some owners make hutches for their pets.
2. The hutches can be made out of wire and boards.
3. Pens must have covers to keep out other pets and rodents.
4. Put rocks in the pens for the animals to hide behind.

B. Write the plural of the word in parentheses to complete each sentence.

5. A guinea pig has two small **ears** (ear) and four short **legs** (leg).
6. The fur of a guinea pig can be many **colors** (color).
7. Guinea pigs are happy in big, roomy **hutches** (hutch).
8. Be sure to clean their water **bottles** (bottle) every day.

C. Imagine that you have a guinea pig. What would it look, feel, and sound like? Talk with a partner. Then write sentences that describe the guinea pig.

Possible response:

My guinea pig **is soft. It likes to play with me. It purrs when it is happy.**

I Love Guinea Pigs 79

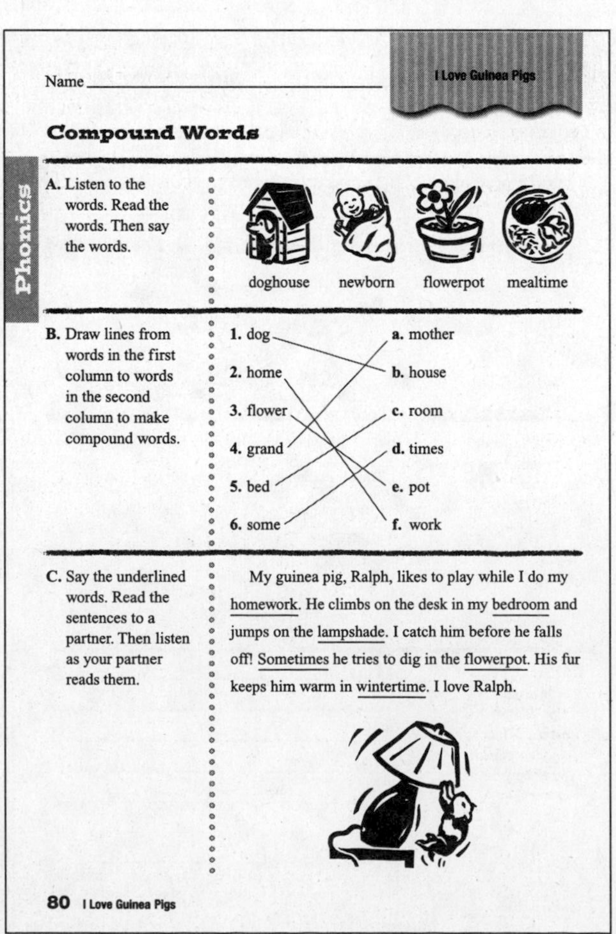

Name ______________ I Love Guinea Pigs

Compound Words

Phonics

A. Listen to the words. Read the words. Then say the words.

doghouse newborn flowerpot mealtime

B. Draw lines from words in the first column to words in the second column to make compound words.

1. dog	a. mother
2. home	b. house
3. flower	c. room
4. grand	d. times
5. bed	e. pot
6. some	f. work

C. Say the underlined words. Read the sentences to a partner. Then listen as your partner reads them.

My guinea pig, Ralph, likes to play while I do my homework. He climbs on the desk in my bedroom and jumps on the lampshade. I catch him before he falls off! Sometimes he tries to dig in the flowerpot. His fur keeps him warm in wintertime. I love Ralph.

80 I Love Guinea Pigs

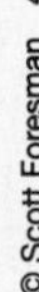

Name ____________________

The Swimming Hole

Irregular Plural Nouns

Grammar

A. Read the sentences. Circle the plural noun in each sentence.

1. The **leaves** had turned a beautiful golden color.
2. Some **bunnies** scampered around a stump.
3. Two **deer** disappeared behind a large tree.
4. Three tiny field **mice** ran toward the creek.

B. Circle the word that completes each sentence.

5. Both (child/**children**) helped Ma with the work.
6. Laura put straw down for the two (**calves**/calf).
7. Mary helped her mother bake four (**loaves**/loaf) of bread.
8. The girls filled their pails with (berry/**berries**).

C. Imagine that you live on a prairie in pioneer times. Talk with a partner. Then write sentences that describe your home.

Possible response:

My home on the prairie **is made of wood. There is tall grass all around. I run and play outdoors.**

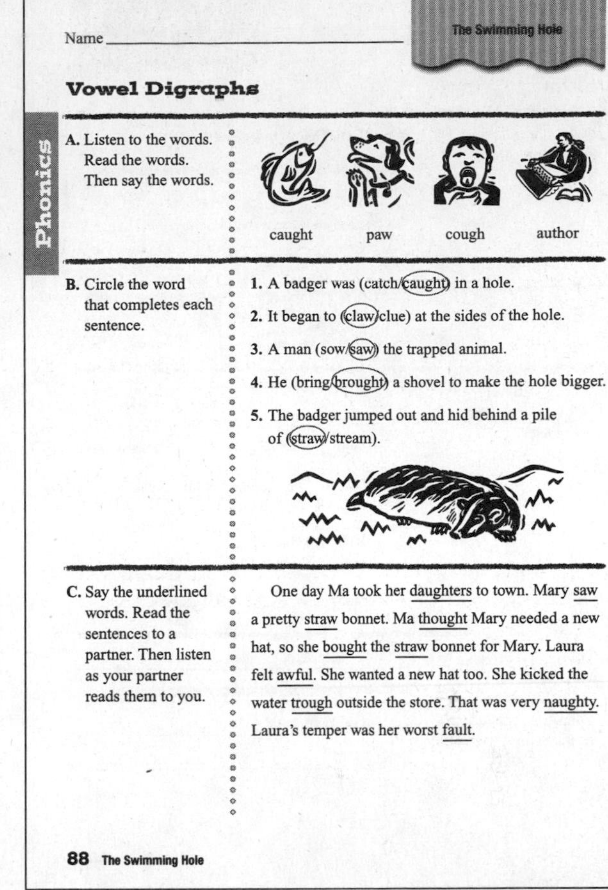
Name ____________________

The Swimming Hole

Vowel Digraphs

Phonics

A. Listen to the words. Read the words. Then say the words.

caught paw cough author

B. Circle the word that completes each sentence.

1. A badger was (catch/**caught**) in a hole.
2. It began to (**claw**/clue) at the sides of the hole.
3. A man (sow/**saw**) the trapped animal.
4. He (bring/**brought**) a shovel to make the hole bigger.
5. The badger jumped out and hid behind a pile of (**straw**/stream).

C. Say the underlined words. Read the sentences to a partner. Then listen as your partner reads them to you.

One day Ma took her daughters to town. Mary saw a pretty straw bonnet. Ma thought Mary needed a new hat, so she bought the straw bonnet for Mary. Laura felt awful. She wanted a new hat too. She kicked the water trough outside the store. That was very naughty. Laura's temper was her worst fault.

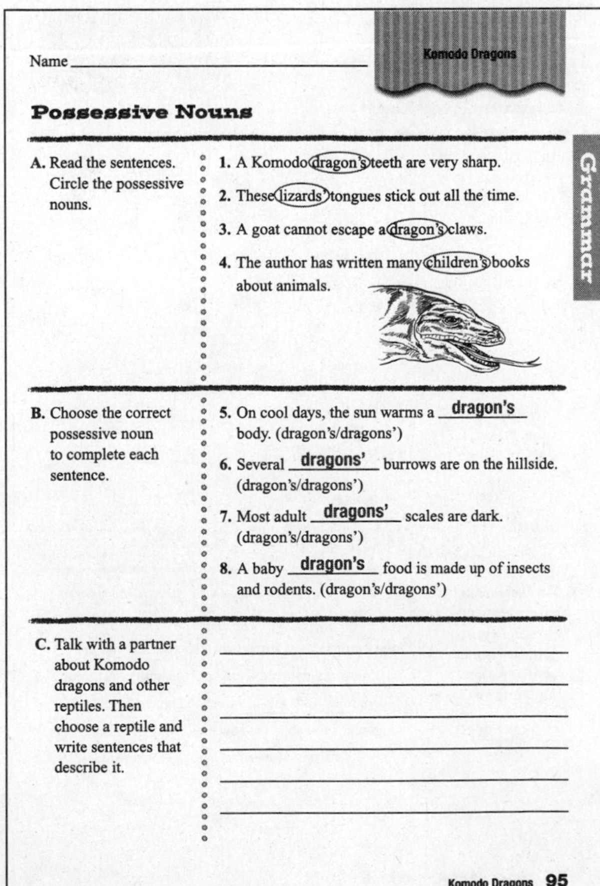
Name ____________________

Komodo Dragons

Possessive Nouns

Grammar

A. Read the sentences. Circle the possessive nouns.

1. A Komodo **dragon's** teeth are very sharp.
2. These **lizards'** tongues stick out all the time.
3. A goat cannot escape a **dragon's** claws.
4. The author has written many **children's** books about animals.

B. Choose the correct possessive noun to complete each sentence.

5. On cool days, the sun warms a **dragon's** body. (dragon's/dragons')
6. Several **dragons'** burrows are on the hillside. (dragon's/dragons')
7. Most adult **dragons'** scales are dark. (dragon's/dragons')
8. A baby **dragon's** food is made up of insects and rodents. (dragon's/dragons')

C. Talk with a partner about Komodo dragons and other reptiles. Then choose a reptile and write sentences that describe it.

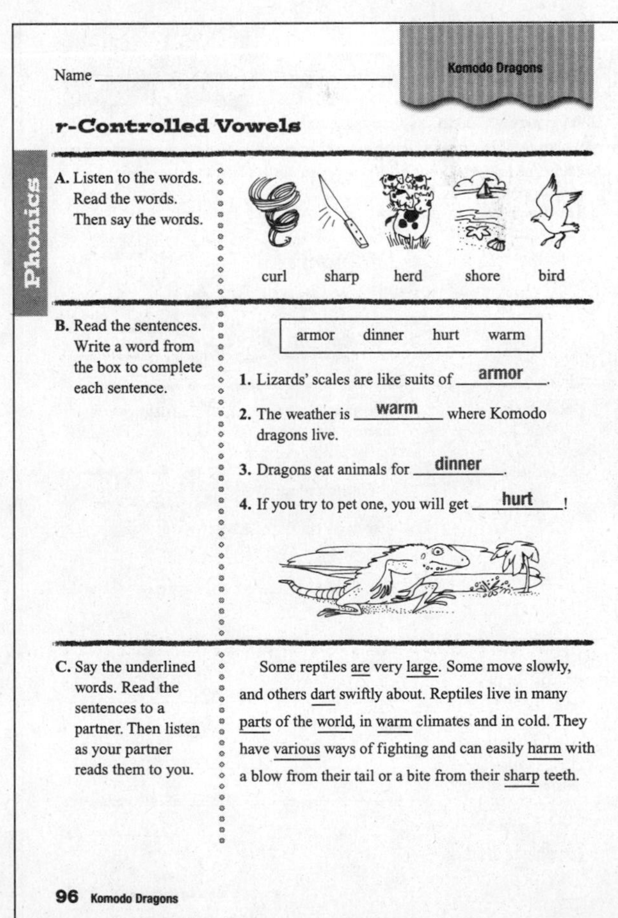
Name ____________________

Komodo Dragons

r-Controlled Vowels

Phonics

A. Listen to the words. Read the words. Then say the words.

curl sharp herd shore bird

B. Read the sentences. Write a word from the box to complete each sentence.

armor dinner hurt warm

1. Lizards' scales are like suits of **armor**.
2. The weather is **warm** where Komodo dragons live.
3. Dragons eat animals for **dinner**.
4. If you try to pet one, you will get **hurt**!

C. Say the underlined words. Read the sentences to a partner. Then listen as your partner reads them to you.

Some reptiles are very large. Some move slowly, and others dart swiftly about. Reptiles live in many parts of the world, in warm climates and in cold. They have various ways of fighting and can easily harm with a blow from their tail or a bite from their sharp teeth.

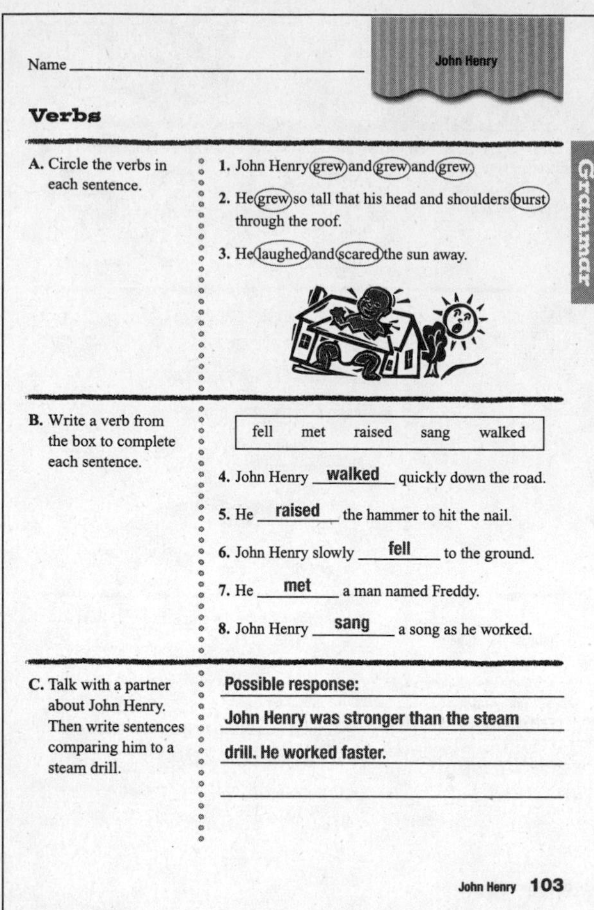

Name ______________________ John Henry

Verbs

A. Circle the verbs in each sentence.

1. John Henry (grew) and (grew) and (grew).
2. He (grew) so tall that his head and shoulders (burst) through the roof.
3. He (laughed) and (scared) the sun away.

B. Write a verb from the box to complete each sentence.

fell	met	raised	sang	walked

4. John Henry **walked** quickly down the road.
5. He **raised** the hammer to hit the nail.
6. John Henry slowly **fell** to the ground.
7. He **met** a man named Freddy.
8. John Henry **sang** a song as he worked.

C. Talk with a partner about John Henry. Then write sentences comparing him to a steam drill.

Possible response:
John Henry was stronger than the steam drill. He worked faster.

Grammar

John Henry 103

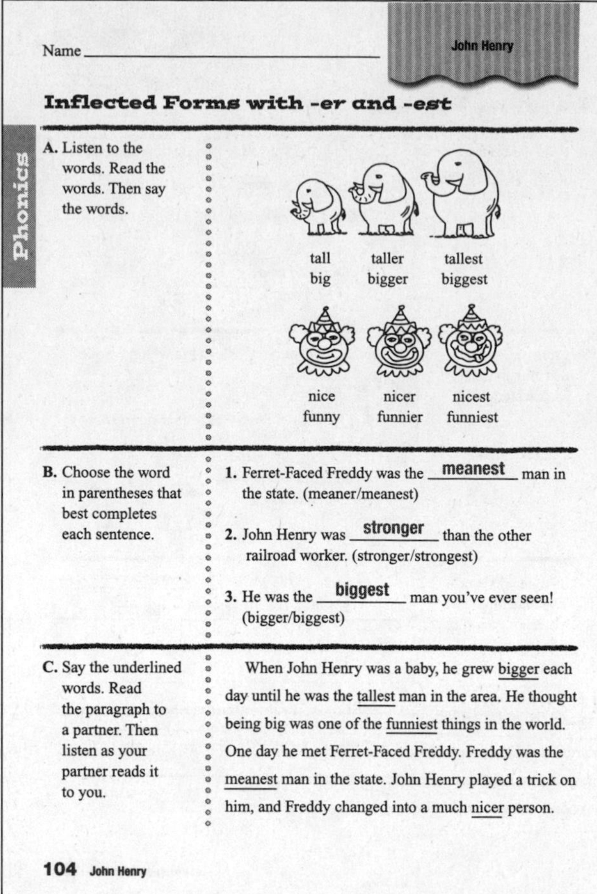

Name ______________________ John Henry

Inflected Forms with -er and -est

A. Listen to the words. Read the words. Then say the words.

tall	taller	tallest
big	bigger	biggest
nice	nicer	nicest
funny	funnier	funniest

B. Choose the word in parentheses that best completes each sentence.

1. Ferret-Faced Freddy was the **meanest** man in the state. (meaner/meanest)
2. John Henry was **stronger** than the other railroad worker. (stronger/strongest)
3. He was the **biggest** man you've ever seen! (bigger/biggest)

C. Say the underlined words. Read the paragraph to a partner. Then listen as your partner reads it to you.

When John Henry was a baby, he grew bigger each day until he was the tallest man in the area. He thought being big was one of the funniest things in the world. One day he met Ferret-Faced Freddy. Freddy was the meanest man in the state. John Henry played a trick on him, and Freddy changed into a much nicer person.

Phonics

104 John Henry

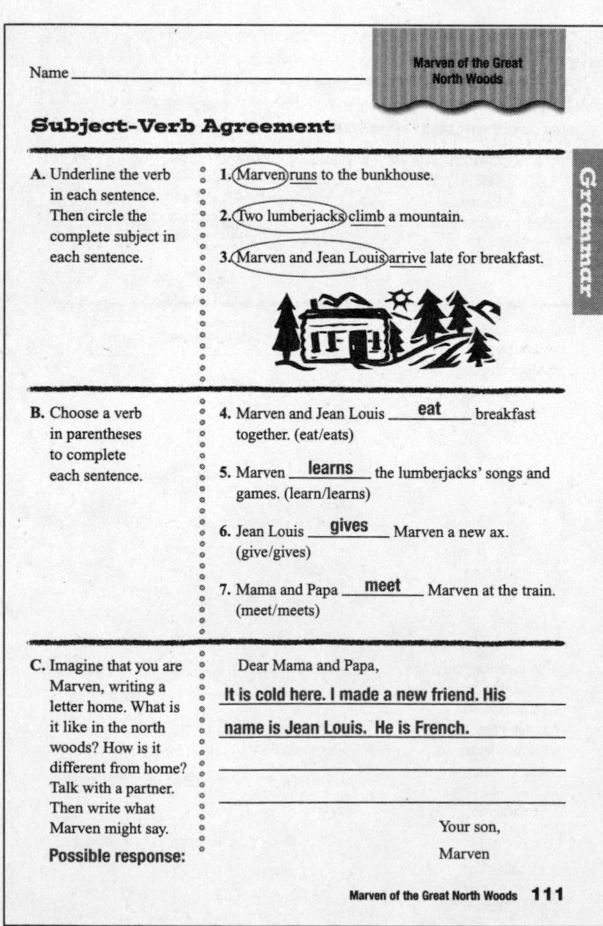

Name ______________________ Marven of the Great North Woods

Subject-Verb Agreement

A. Underline the verb in each sentence. Then circle the complete subject in each sentence.

1. (Marven) runs to the bunkhouse.
2. (Two lumberjacks) climb a mountain.
3. (Marven and Jean Louis) arrive late for breakfast.

B. Choose a verb in parentheses to complete each sentence.

4. Marven and Jean Louis **eat** breakfast together. (eat/eats)
5. Marven **learns** the lumberjacks' songs and games. (learn/learns)
6. Jean Louis **gives** Marven a new ax. (give/gives)
7. Mama and Papa **meet** Marven at the train. (meet/meets)

C. Imagine that you are Marven, writing a letter home. What is it like in the north woods? How is it different from home? Talk with a partner. Then write what Marven might say.

Possible response:

Dear Mama and Papa,

It is cold here. I made a new friend. His name is Jean Louis. He is French.

Your son,
Marven

Grammar

Marven of the Great North Woods 111

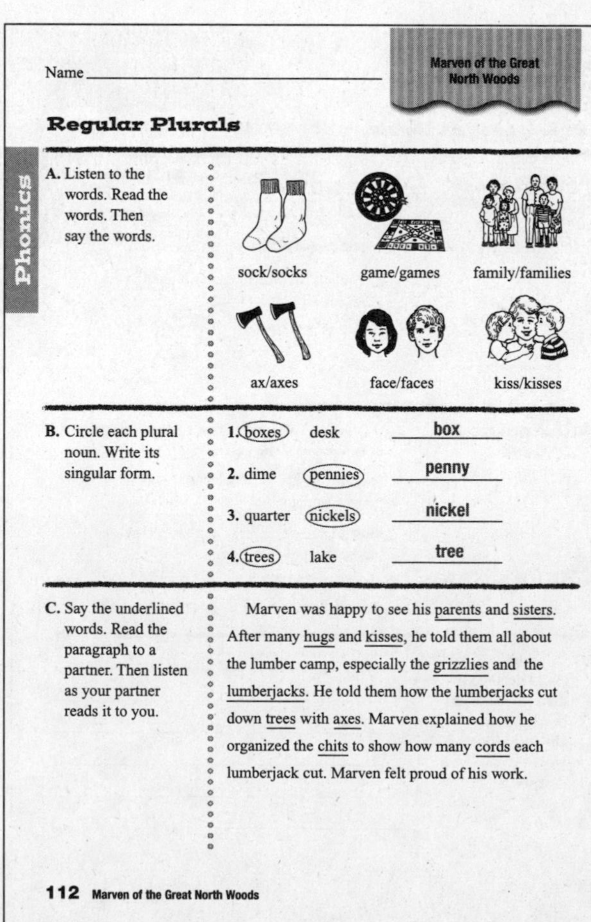

Name ______________________ Marven of the Great North Woods

Regular Plurals

A. Listen to the words. Read the words. Then say the words.

sock/socks game/games family/families
ax/axes face/faces kiss/kisses

B. Circle each plural noun. Write its singular form.

1. (boxes) desk **box**
2. dime (pennies) **penny**
3. quarter (nickels) **nickel**
4. (trees) lake **tree**

C. Say the underlined words. Read the paragraph to a partner. Then listen as your partner reads it to you.

Marven was happy to see his parents and sisters. After many hugs and kisses, he told them all about the lumber camp, especially the grizzlies and the lumberjacks. He told them how the lumberjacks cut down trees with axes. Marven explained how he organized the chits to show how many cords each lumberjack cut. Marven felt proud of his work.

Phonics

112 Marven of the Great North Woods

Name ______________________ **On the Pampas**

Present, Past, and Future Verb Tenses

Grammar

A. Underline the verb in each sentence.

1. I lived with my family in Buenos Aires.
2. Susanita lives at the estancia all year round.
3. Next summer I will live on the ranch again.

B. Circle the verb in parentheses that best completes each sentence.

4. Next summer I (visited, visit, will visit) La Carlota again.
5. Last year we (admired, admire, will admire) the belts at the general store.
6. I (wanted, want, will want) to visit the ranch every summer.
7. I hope that I (was, am, will be) a good gaucho someday!

C. Imagine that you will go to a ranch. Talk with a partner. Then write what you will do.

Possible response:

At a ranch, I will **ride horses and learn about other animals. I will play with foals. I will take siestas.**

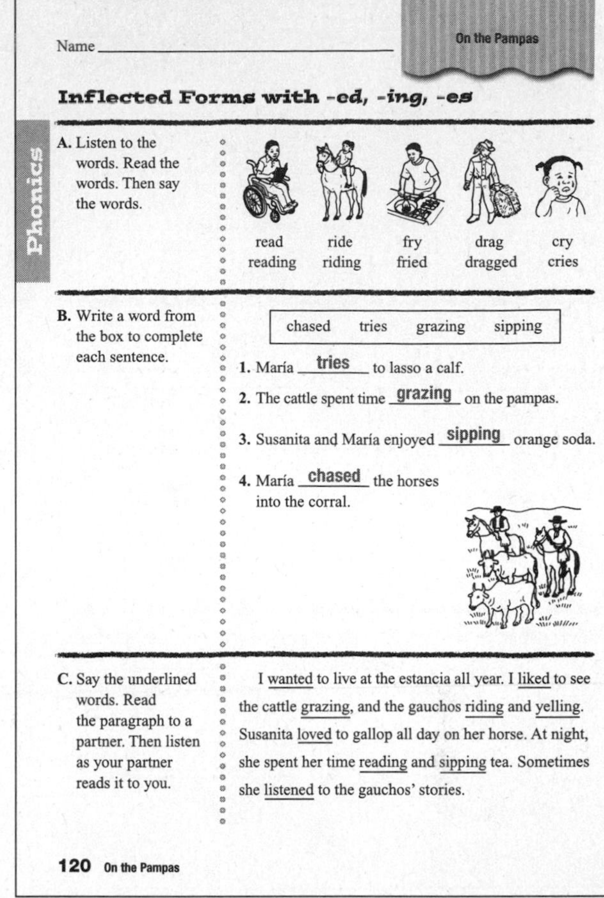

Name ______________________ **On the Pampas**

Inflected Forms with -ed, -ing, -es

Phonics

A. Listen to the words. Read the words. Then say the words.

read reading | ride riding | fry fried | drag dragged | cry cries

B. Write a word from the box to complete each sentence.

chased tries grazing sipping

1. María **tries** to lasso a calf.
2. The cattle spent time **grazing** on the pampas.
3. Susanita and María enjoyed **sipping** orange soda.
4. María **chased** the horses into the corral.

C. Say the underlined words. Read the paragraph to a partner. Then listen as your partner reads it to you.

I wanted to live at the estancia all year. I liked to see the cattle grazing, and the gauchos riding and yelling. Susanita loved to gallop all day on her horse. At night, she spent her time reading and sipping tea. Sometimes she listened to the gauchos' stories.

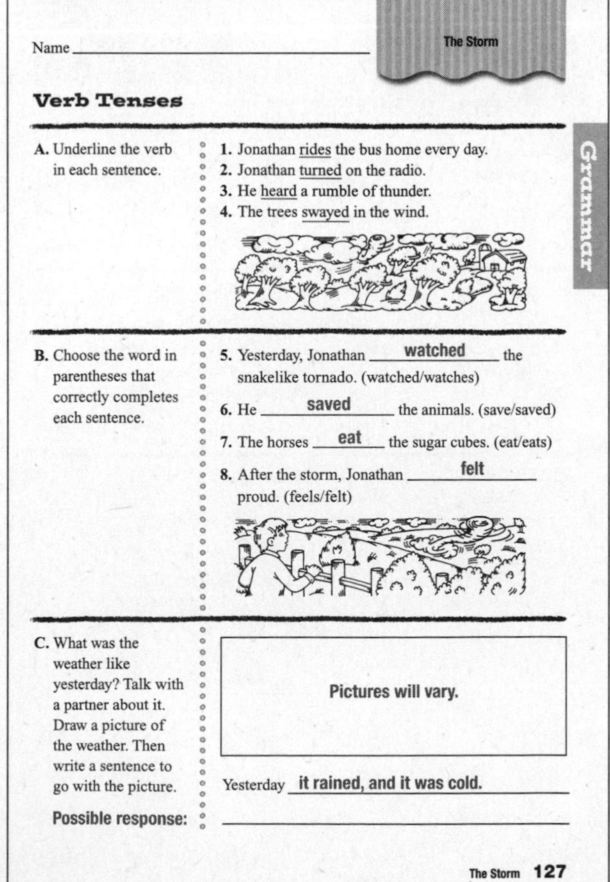

Name ______________________ **The Storm**

Verb Tenses

Grammar

A. Underline the verb in each sentence.

1. Jonathan rides the bus home every day.
2. Jonathan turned on the radio.
3. He heard a rumble of thunder.
4. The trees swayed in the wind.

B. Choose the word in parentheses that correctly completes each sentence.

5. Yesterday, Jonathan **watched** the snakelike tornado. (watched/watches)
6. He **saved** the animals. (save/saved)
7. The horses **eat** the sugar cubes. (eat/eats)
8. After the storm, Jonathan **felt** proud. (feels/felt)

C. What was the weather like yesterday? Talk with a partner about it. Draw a picture of the weather. Then write a sentence to go with the picture.

Possible response:

Pictures will vary.

Yesterday **it rained, and it was cold.**

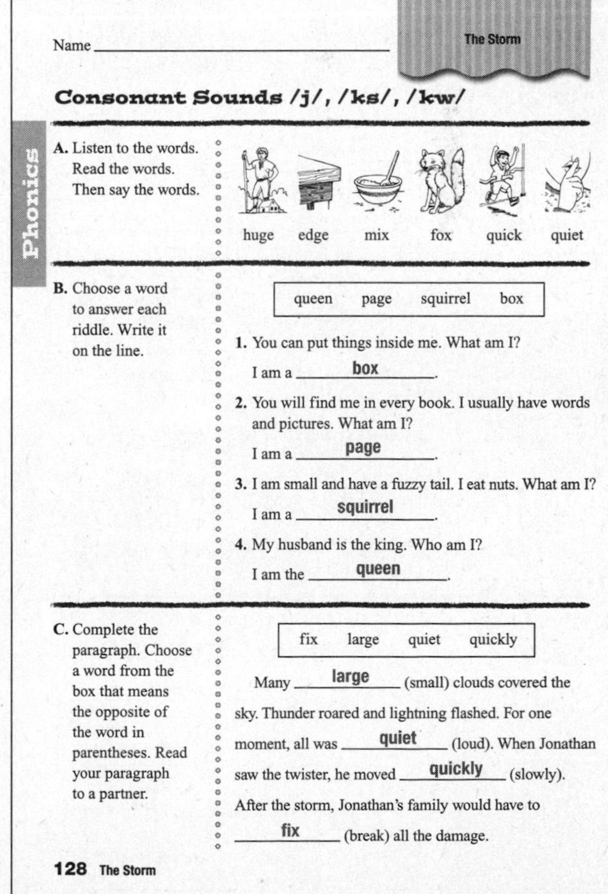

Name ______________________ **The Storm**

Consonant Sounds /j/, /ks/, /kw/

Phonics

A. Listen to the words. Read the words. Then say the words.

huge edge mix fox quick quiet

B. Choose a word to answer each riddle. Write it on the line.

queen page squirrel box

1. You can put things inside me. What am I?
   I am a **box**.
2. You will find me in every book. I usually have words and pictures. What am I?
   I am a **page**.
3. I am small and have a fuzzy tail. I eat nuts. What am I?
   I am a **squirrel**.
4. My husband is the king. Who am I?
   I am the **queen**.

C. Complete the paragraph. Choose a word from the box that means the opposite of the word in parentheses. Read your paragraph to a partner.

fix large quiet quickly

Many **large** (small) clouds covered the sky. Thunder roared and lightning flashed. For one moment, all was **quiet** (loud). When Jonathan saw the twister, he moved **quickly** (slowly). After the storm, Jonathan's family would have to **fix** (break) all the damage.

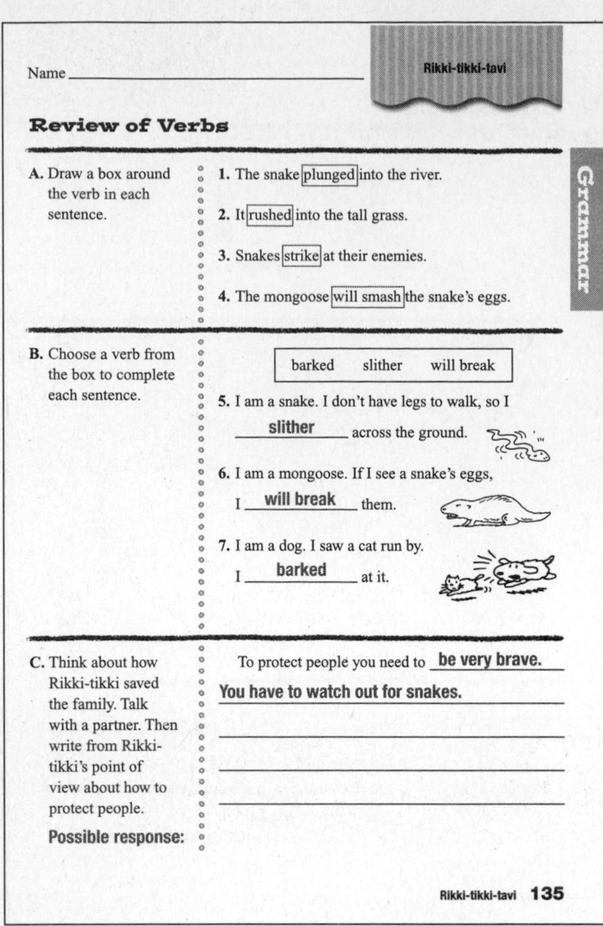

Name ______________________ Rikki-tikki-tavi

Review of Verbs

Grammar

A. Draw a box around the verb in each sentence.

1. The snake [plunged] into the river.
2. It [rushed] into the tall grass.
3. Snakes [strike] at their enemies.
4. The mongoose [will smash] the snake's eggs.

B. Choose a verb from the box to complete each sentence.

barked slither will break

5. I am a snake. I don't have legs to walk, so I **slither** across the ground.
6. I am a mongoose. If I see a snake's eggs, I **will break** them.
7. I am a dog. I saw a cat run by. I **barked** at it.

C. Think about how Rikki-tikki saved the family. Talk with a partner. Then write from Rikki-tikki's point of view about how to protect people.

Possible response:

To protect people you need to **be very brave. You have to watch out for snakes.**

Rikki-tikki-tavi 135

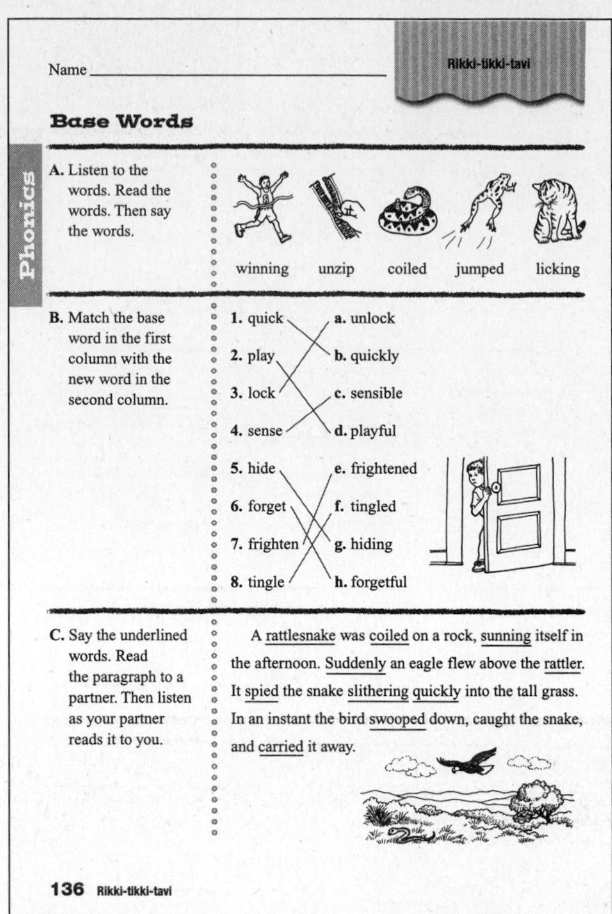

Name ______________________ Rikki-tikki-tavi

Base Words

Phonics

A. Listen to the words. Read the words. Then say the words.

winning unzip coiled jumped licking

B. Match the base word in the first column with the new word in the second column.

1. quick	a. unlock
2. play	b. quickly
3. lock	c. sensible
4. sense	d. playful
5. hide	e. frightened
6. forget	f. tingled
7. frighten	g. hiding
8. tingle	h. forgetful

C. Say the underlined words. Read the paragraph to a partner. Then listen as your partner reads it to you.

A rattlesnake was coiled on a rock, sunning itself in the afternoon. Suddenly an eagle flew above the rattler. It spied the snake slithering quickly into the tall grass. In an instant the bird swooped down, caught the snake, and carried it away.

136 Rikki-tikki-tavi

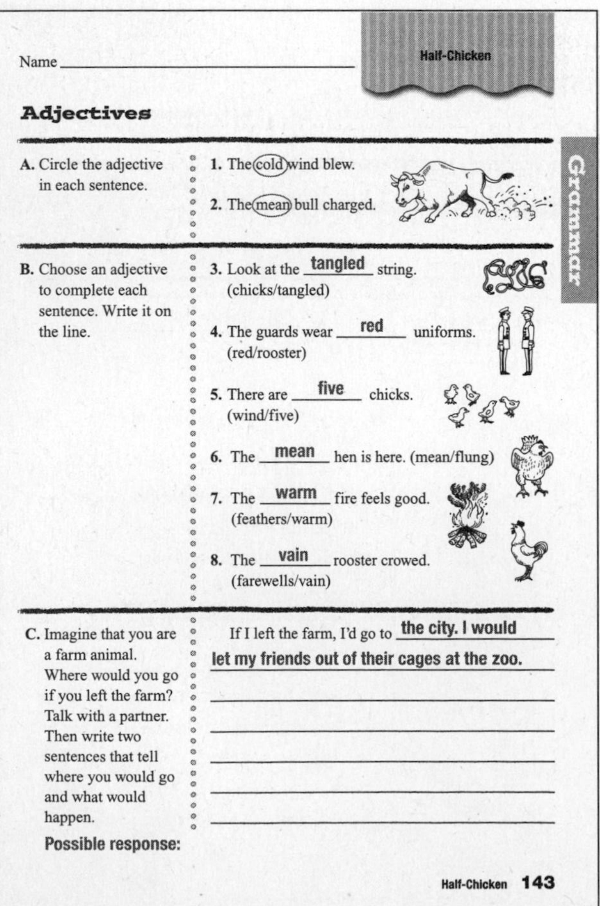

Name ______________________ Half-Chicken

Adjectives

Grammar

A. Circle the adjective in each sentence.

1. The (cold) wind blew.
2. The (mean) bull charged.

B. Choose an adjective to complete each sentence. Write it on the line.

3. Look at the **tangled** string. (chicks/tangled)
4. The guards wear **red** uniforms. (red/rooster)
5. There are **five** chicks. (wind/five)
6. The **mean** hen is here. (mean/flung)
7. The **warm** fire feels good. (feathers/warm)
8. The **vain** rooster crowed. (farewells/vain)

C. Imagine that you are a farm animal. Where would you go if you left the farm? Talk with a partner. Then write two sentences that tell where you would go and what would happen.

Possible response:

If I left the farm, I'd go to **the city. I would let my friends out of their cages at the zoo.**

Half-Chicken 143

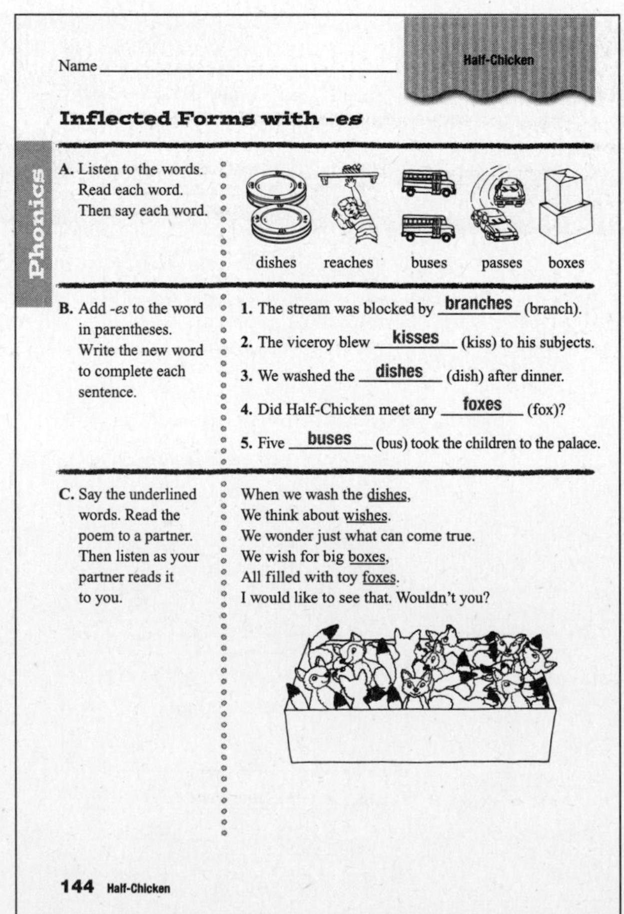

Name ______________________ Half-Chicken

Inflected Forms with *-es*

Phonics

A. Listen to the words. Read each word. Then say each word.

dishes reaches buses passes boxes

B. Add *-es* to the word in parentheses. Write the new word to complete each sentence.

1. The stream was blocked by **branches** (branch).
2. The viceroy blew **kisses** (kiss) to his subjects.
3. We washed the **dishes** (dish) after dinner.
4. Did Half-Chicken meet any **foxes** (fox)?
5. Five **buses** (bus) took the children to the palace.

C. Say the underlined words. Read the poem to a partner. Then listen as your partner reads it to you.

When we wash the dishes,
We think about wishes.
We wonder just what can come true.
We wish for big boxes,
All filled with toy foxes.
I would like to see that. Wouldn't you?

144 Half-Chicken

Name ______________________ **Blame It on the Wolf**

Using Adjectives to Improve Sentences

Grammar

A. Underline the adjective in each sentence.

1. The wolves walked on the snowy trail.
2. The gray wolves played in the snow.

B. Choose an adjective to complete each sentence.

3. The **gray** wolf was the color of storm clouds. (gray/brick)
4. The **red** sky looked like fire. (slender/red)
5. The **thick** snow covered the house. (green/thick)
6. The pigs lived in a **brick** house. (brick/bread)
7. Three **little** pigs gave evidence. (stage/little)

C. Choose an adjective from the box to describe each character or pair of characters.

afraid evil hungry innocent

Hansel and Gretel: **hungry**

Chicken Little: **afraid**

Auntie Pot Pie: **evil**

Wolf: **innocent**

Blame It on the Wolf 151

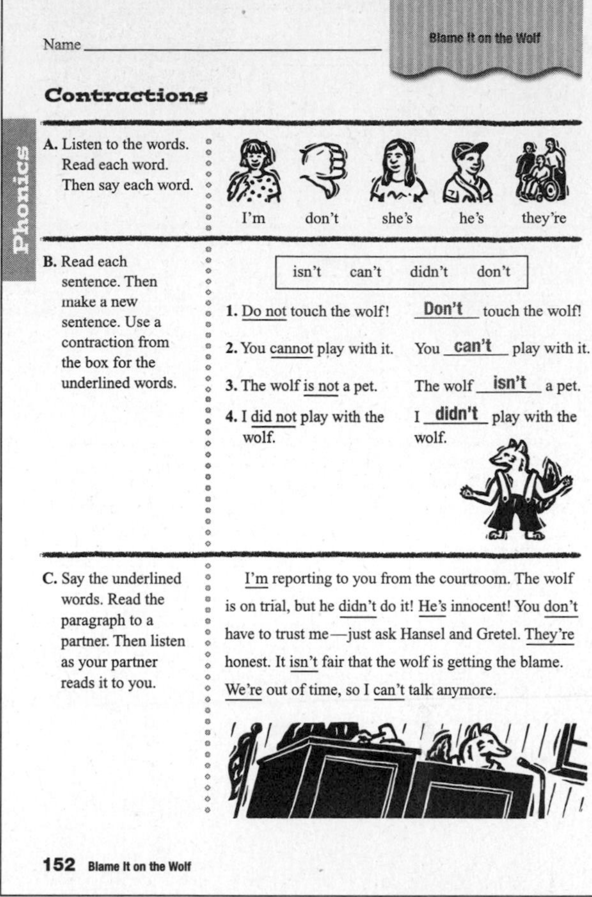

Name ______________________ **Blame It on the Wolf**

Contractions

Phonics

A. Listen to the words. Read each word. Then say each word.

I'm don't she's he's they're

B. Read each sentence. Then make a new sentence. Use a contraction from the box for the underlined words.

isn't can't didn't don't

1. Do not touch the wolf! — **Don't** touch the wolf!
2. You cannot play with it. — You **can't** play with it.
3. The wolf is not a pet. — The wolf **isn't** a pet.
4. I did not play with the wolf. — I **didn't** play with the wolf.

C. Say the underlined words. Read the paragraph to a partner. Then listen as your partner reads it to you.

I'm reporting to you from the courtroom. The wolf is on trial, but he didn't do it! He's innocent! You don't have to trust me—just ask Hansel and Gretel. They're honest. It isn't fair that the wolf is getting the blame. We're out of time, so I can't talk anymore.

152 Blame It on the Wolf

Name ______________________ **Lou Gehrig: The Luckiest Man**

Comparative and Superlative Adjectives

Grammar

A. Underline the comparative adjective. Circle the superlative adjective.

1. Babe Ruth was luckier than Ty Cobb.
2. Lou Gehrig was the luckiest man of all.

B. Choose the comparative or superlative adjective to complete each sentence.

3. Amy is **taller** than Max. (taller/tallest)
4. Miguel is the **tallest** player of all. (taller/tallest)
5. My hair is **longer** than yours. (longest/longer)
6. T'Aysha's hair is the **longest** on the team. (longest/longer)
7. Yohei is a **stronger** player than John. (stronger/strongest)
8. Lisa is the **strongest** player on the team. (stronger/strongest)

C. Choose one sport you like. Talk with a partner about it. Then write sentences telling how to play it well.

My favorite sport is **Answers will vary.**

Lou Gehrig: The Luckiest Man 159

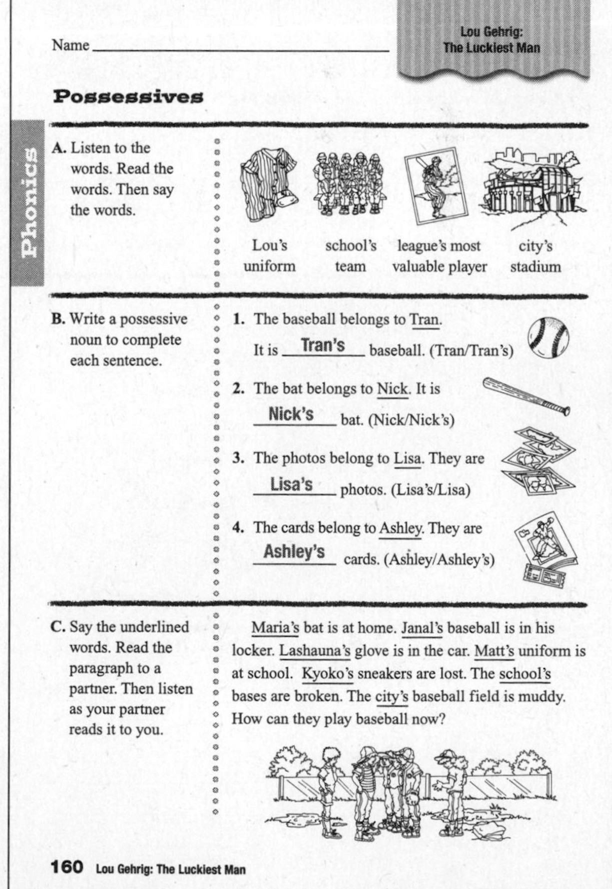

Name ______________________ **Lou Gehrig: The Luckiest Man**

Possessives

Phonics

A. Listen to the words. Read the words. Then say the words.

Lou's uniform — school's team — league's most valuable player — city's stadium

B. Write a possessive noun to complete each sentence.

1. The baseball belongs to Tran. It is **Tran's** baseball. (Tran/Tran's)
2. The bat belongs to Nick. It is **Nick's** bat. (Nick/Nick's)
3. The photos belong to Lisa. They are **Lisa's** photos. (Lisa's/Lisa)
4. The cards belong to Ashley. They are **Ashley's** cards. (Ashley/Ashley's)

C. Say the underlined words. Read the paragraph to a partner. Then listen as your partner reads it to you.

Maria's bat is at home. Janal's baseball is in his locker. Lashauna's glove is in the car. Matt's uniform is at school. Kyoko's sneakers are lost. The school's bases are broken. The city's baseball field is muddy. How can they play baseball now?

160 Lou Gehrig: The Luckiest Man

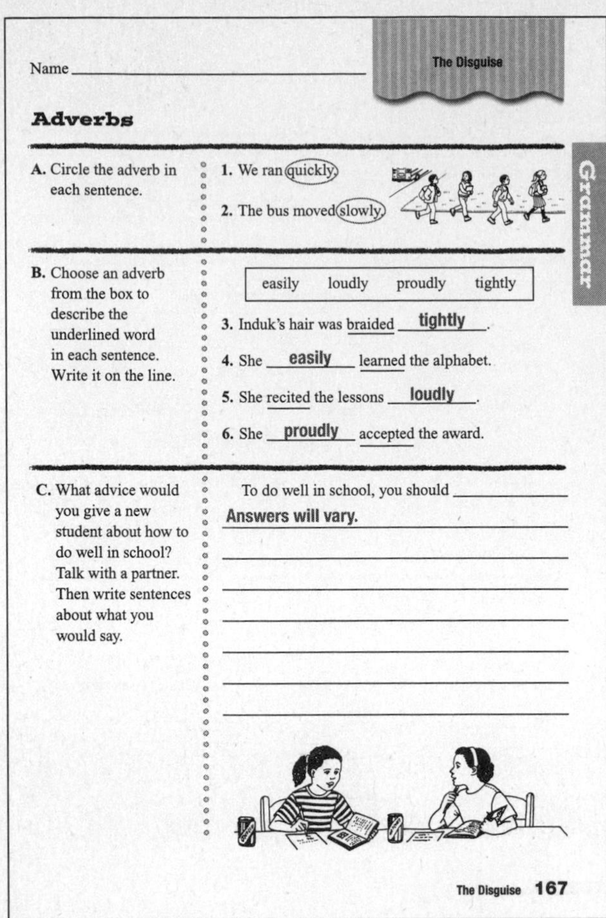

Name ____________________ The Disguise

Adverbs

Grammar

A. Circle the adverb in each sentence.

1. We ran (quickly).
2. The bus moved (slowly).

B. Choose an adverb from the box to describe the underlined word in each sentence. Write it on the line.

easily	loudly	proudly	tightly

3. Induk's hair was braided **tightly**.
4. She **easily** learned the alphabet.
5. She recited the lessons **loudly**.
6. She **proudly** accepted the award.

C. What advice would you give a new student about how to do well in school? Talk with a partner. Then write sentences about what you would say.

To do well in school, you should **Answers will vary.**

The Disguise 167

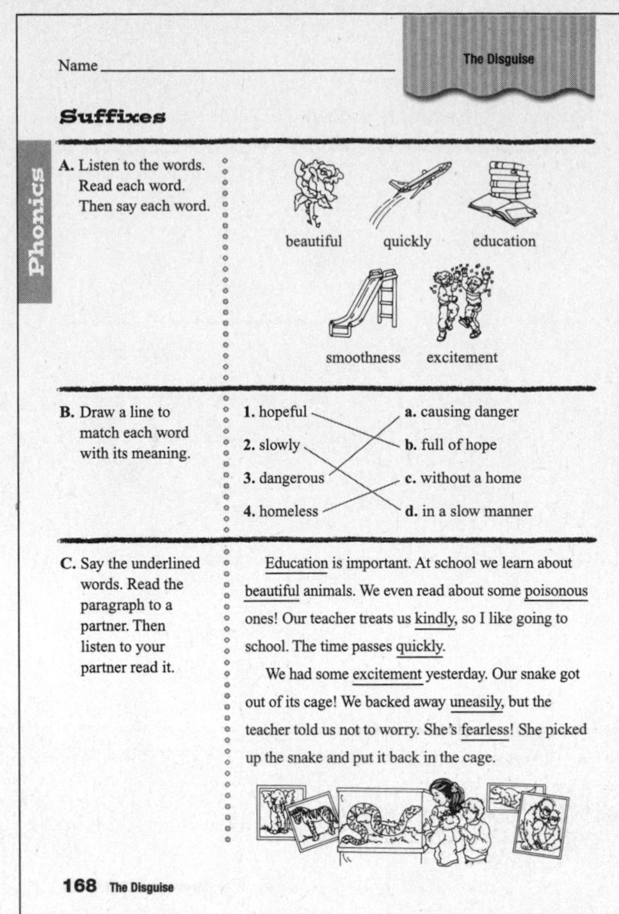

Name ____________________ The Disguise

Suffixes

Phonics

A. Listen to the words. Read each word. Then say each word.

beautiful quickly education

smoothness excitement

B. Draw a line to match each word with its meaning.

1. hopeful — b. full of hope
2. slowly — d. in a slow manner
3. dangerous — a. causing danger
4. homeless — c. without a home

C. Say the underlined words. Read the paragraph to a partner. Then listen to your partner read it.

Education is important. At school we learn about beautiful animals. We even read about some poisonous ones! Our teacher treats us kindly, so I like going to school. The time passes quickly.

We had some excitement yesterday. Our snake got out of its cage! We backed away uneasily, but the teacher told us not to worry. She's fearless! She picked up the snake and put it back in the cage.

168 The Disguise

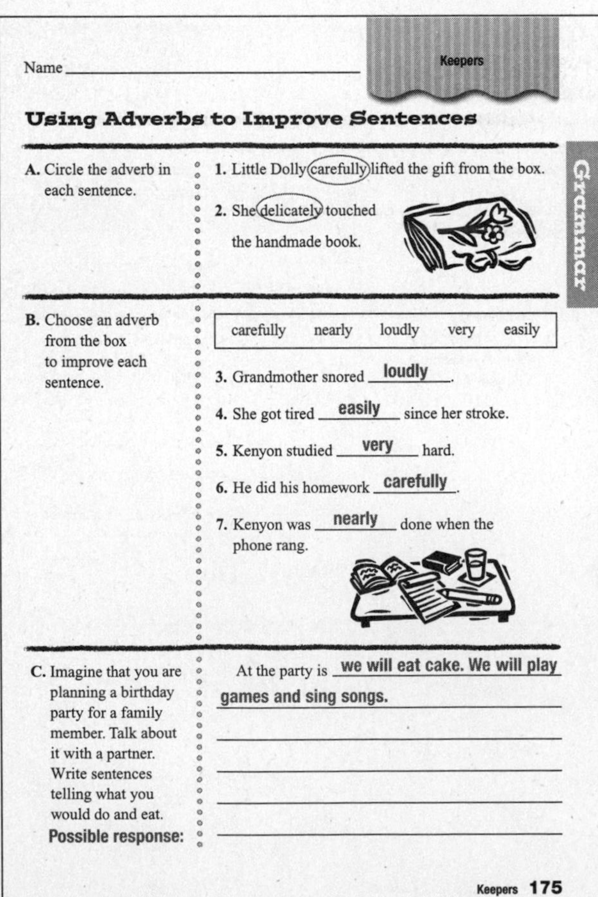

Name ____________________ Keepers

Using Adverbs to Improve Sentences

Grammar

A. Circle the adverb in each sentence.

1. Little Dolly (carefully) lifted the gift from the box.
2. She (delicately) touched the handmade book.

B. Choose an adverb from the box to improve each sentence.

carefully	nearly	loudly	very	easily

3. Grandmother snored **loudly**.
4. She got tired **easily** since her stroke.
5. Kenyon studied **very** hard.
6. He did his homework **carefully**.
7. Kenyon was **nearly** done when the phone rang.

C. Imagine that you are planning a birthday party for a family member. Talk about it with a partner. Write sentences telling what you would do and eat. **Possible response:**

At the party is **we will eat cake. We will play games and sing songs.**

Keepers 175

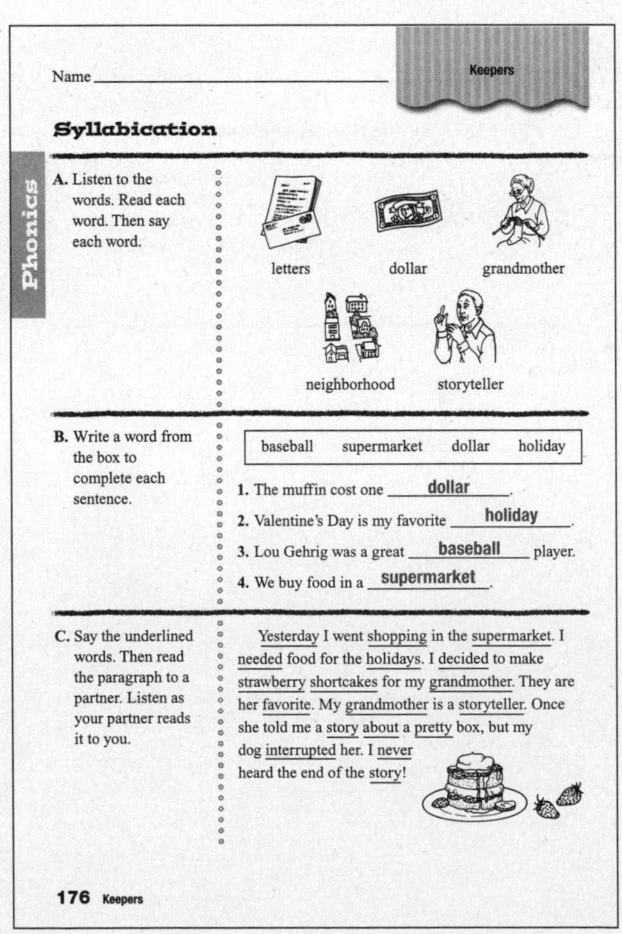

Name ____________________ Keepers

Syllabication

Phonics

A. Listen to the words. Read each word. Then say each word.

letters dollar grandmother

neighborhood storyteller

B. Write a word from the box to complete each sentence.

baseball	supermarket	dollar	holiday

1. The muffin cost one **dollar**.
2. Valentine's Day is my favorite **holiday**.
3. Lou Gehrig was a great **baseball** player.
4. We buy food in a **supermarket**.

C. Say the underlined words. Then read the paragraph to a partner. Listen as your partner reads it to you.

Yesterday I went shopping in the supermarket. I needed food for the holidays. I decided to make strawberry shortcakes for my grandmother. They are her favorite. My grandmother is a storyteller. Once she told me a story about a pretty box, but my dog interrupted her. I never heard the end of the story!

176 Keepers

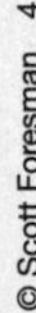

Name ____________________ **Amazing Alice!**

Pronouns

Grammar

A. Read the sentences. Circle the pronouns.

1. Hermine was young when she went on the trip.
2. Hermine said, "Alice, I want to go on the trip with you."
3. "We will go in the motorcar to California if it will take us that far," Alice said.
4. Alice said, "Minna, I want you to ride with me."

B. Read the sentences. Circle the correct pronouns to complete the sentences.

5. Mr. Kelsey told Alice that (him/she) was a good driver.
6. Alice told Hermine, "(We/I) am glad (you/her) are going."
7. The motorcar was stuck, and (it/them) would not move.
8. People cheered when (me/they) saw Alice.

C. Think about traffic signs and what they mean. Talk with a partner. Draw a picture of the traffic sign and write about it.

Possible response:

One traffic sign is **a picture of a deer.**

It means **to be careful of deer that cross the road.**

Pictures will vary.

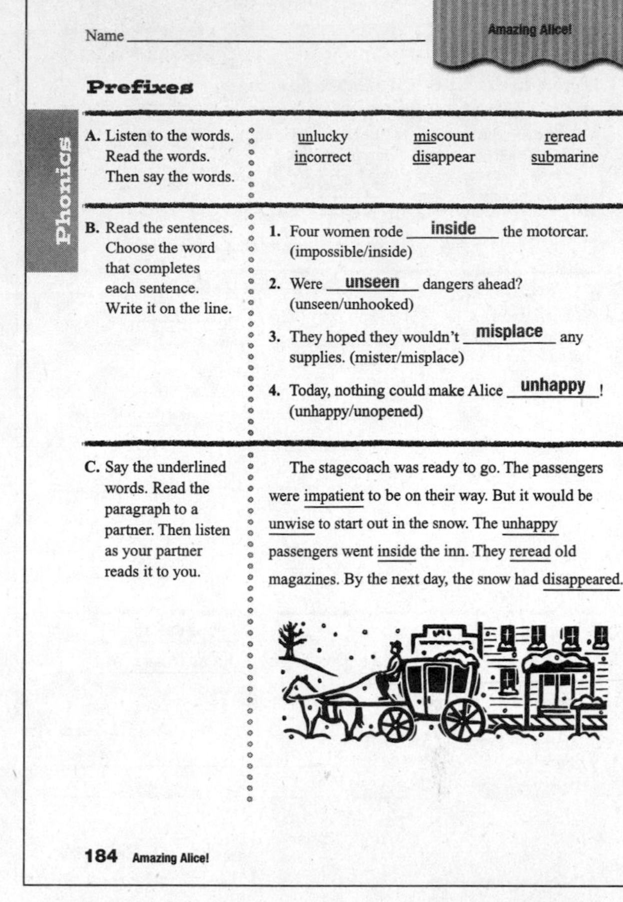

Name ____________________ **Amazing Alice!**

Prefixes

Phonics

A. Listen to the words. Read the words. Then say the words.

unlucky miscount reread
incorrect disappear submarine

B. Read the sentences. Choose the word that completes each sentence. Write it on the line.

1. Four women rode **inside** the motorcar. (impossible/inside)
2. Were **unseen** dangers ahead? (unseen/unhooked)
3. They hoped they wouldn't **misplace** any supplies. (mister/misplace)
4. Today, nothing could make Alice **unhappy**! (unhappy/unopened)

C. Say the underlined words. Read the paragraph to a partner. Then listen as your partner reads it to you.

The stagecoach was ready to go. The passengers were impatient to be on their way. But it would be unwise to start out in the snow. The unhappy passengers went inside the inn. They reread old magazines. By the next day, the snow had disappeared.

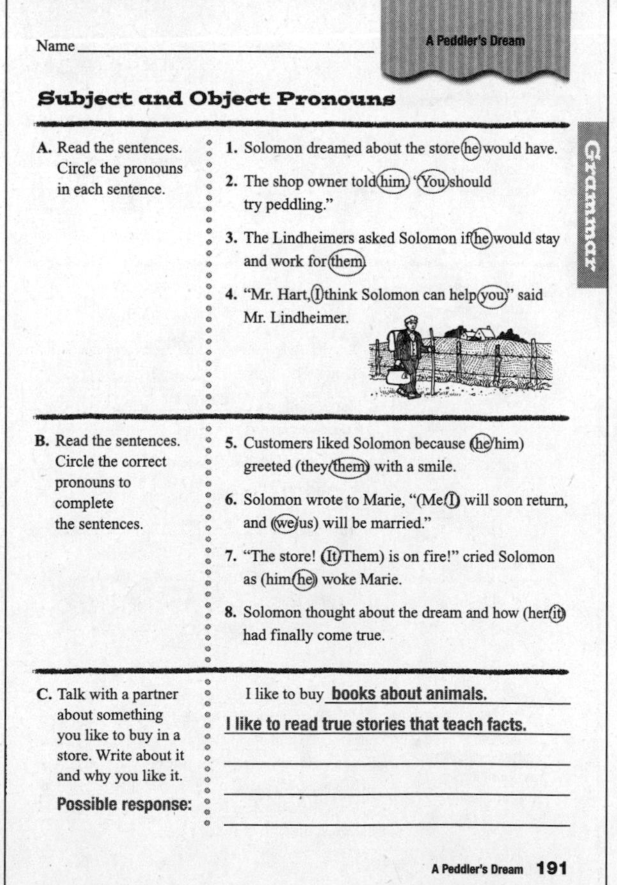

Name ____________________ **A Peddler's Dream**

Subject and Object Pronouns

Grammar

A. Read the sentences. Circle the pronouns in each sentence.

1. Solomon dreamed about the store he would have.
2. The shop owner told him, "You should try peddling."
3. The Lindheimers asked Solomon if he would stay and work for them.
4. "Mr. Hart, I think Solomon can help you," said Mr. Lindheimer.

B. Read the sentences. Circle the correct pronouns to complete the sentences.

5. Customers liked Solomon because (he/him) greeted (they/them) with a smile.
6. Solomon wrote to Marie, "(Me/I) will soon return, and (we/us) will be married."
7. "The store! (It/Them) is on fire!" cried Solomon as (him/he) woke Marie.
8. Solomon thought about the dream and how (her/it) had finally come true.

C. Talk with a partner about something you like to buy in a store. Write about it and why you like it.

Possible response:

I like to buy **books about animals.**

I like to read true stories that teach facts.

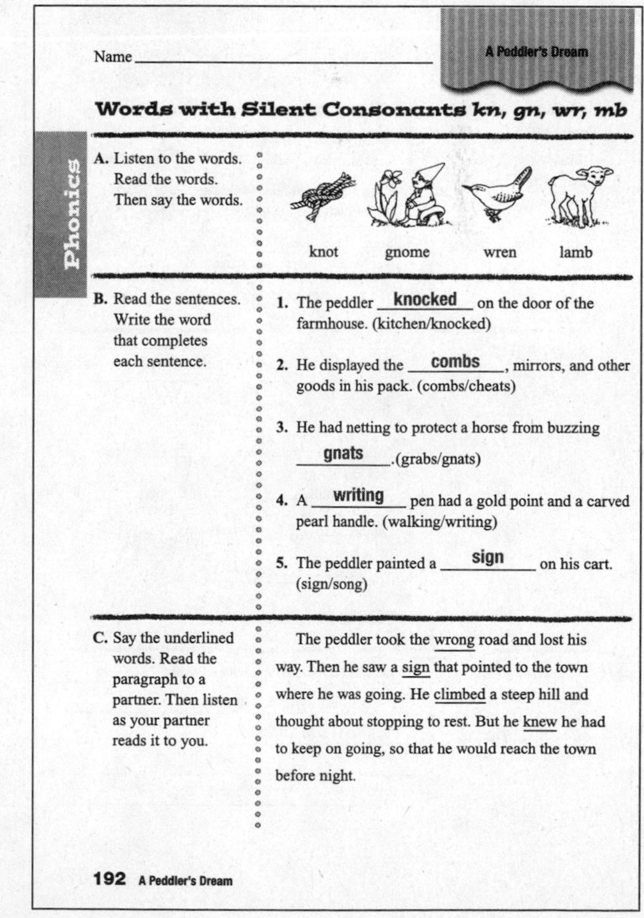

Name ____________________ **A Peddler's Dream**

Words with Silent Consonants *kn, gn, wr, mb*

Phonics

A. Listen to the words. Read the words. Then say the words.

knot gnome wren lamb

B. Read the sentences. Write the word that completes each sentence.

1. The peddler **knocked** on the door of the farmhouse. (kitchen/knocked)
2. He displayed the **combs**, mirrors, and other goods in his pack. (combs/cheats)
3. He had netting to protect a horse from buzzing **gnats**. (grabs/gnats)
4. A **writing** pen had a gold point and a carved pearl handle. (walking/writing)
5. The peddler painted a **sign** on his cart. (sign/song)

C. Say the underlined words. Read the paragraph to a partner. Then listen as your partner reads it to you.

The peddler took the wrong road and lost his way. Then he saw a sign that pointed to the town where he was going. He climbed a steep hill and thought about stopping to rest. But he knew he had to keep on going, so that he would reach the town before night.

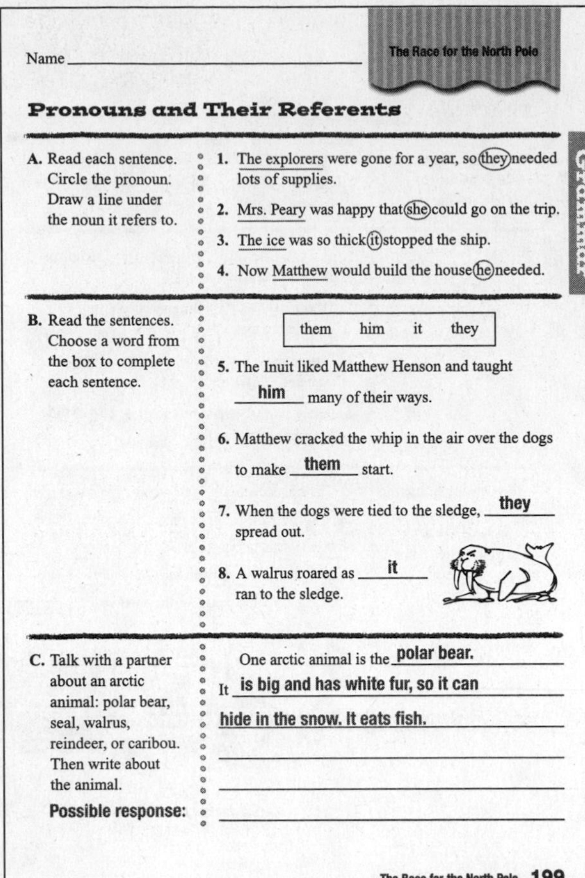

Name____________________ The Race for the North Pole

Pronouns and Their Referents

Grammar

A. Read each sentence. Circle the pronoun. Draw a line under the noun it refers to.

1. The explorers were gone for a year, so (they) needed lots of supplies.
2. Mrs. Peary was happy that (she) could go on the trip.
3. The ice was so thick (it) stopped the ship.
4. Now Matthew would build the house (he) needed.

B. Read the sentences. Choose a word from the box to complete each sentence.

them	him	it	they

5. The Inuit liked Matthew Henson and taught **him** many of their ways.
6. Matthew cracked the whip in the air over the dogs to make **them** start.
7. When the dogs were tied to the sledge, **they** spread out.
8. A walrus roared as **it** ran to the sledge.

C. Talk with a partner about an arctic animal: polar bear, seal, walrus, reindeer, or caribou. Then write about the animal.

Possible response:

One arctic animal is the **polar bear.** It **is big and has white fur, so it can hide in the snow. It eats fish.**

The Race for the North Pole 199

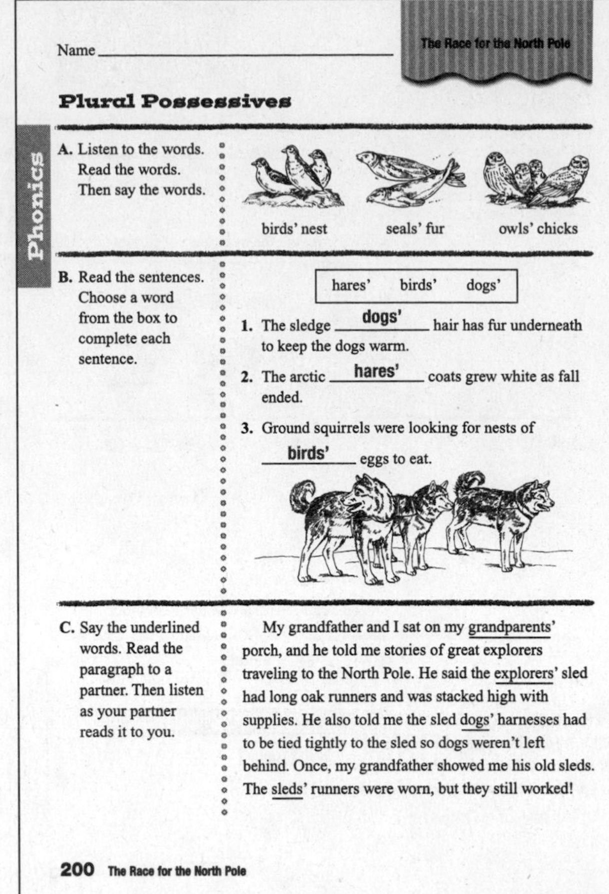

Name____________________ The Race for the North Pole

Plural Possessives

Phonics

A. Listen to the words. Read the words. Then say the words.

birds' nest — seals' fur — owls' chicks

B. Read the sentences. Choose a word from the box to complete each sentence.

hares'	birds'	dogs'

1. The sledge **dogs'** hair has fur underneath to keep the dogs warm.
2. The arctic **hares'** coats grew white as fall ended.
3. Ground squirrels were looking for nests of **birds'** eggs to eat.

C. Say the underlined words. Read the paragraph to a partner. Then listen as your partner reads it to you.

My grandfather and I sat on my grandparents' porch, and he told me stories of great explorers traveling to the North Pole. He said the explorers' sled had long oak runners and was stacked high with supplies. He also told me the sled dogs' harnesses had to be tied tightly to the sled so dogs weren't left behind. Once, my grandfather showed me his old sleds. The sleds' runners were worn, but they still worked!

200 The Race for the North Pole

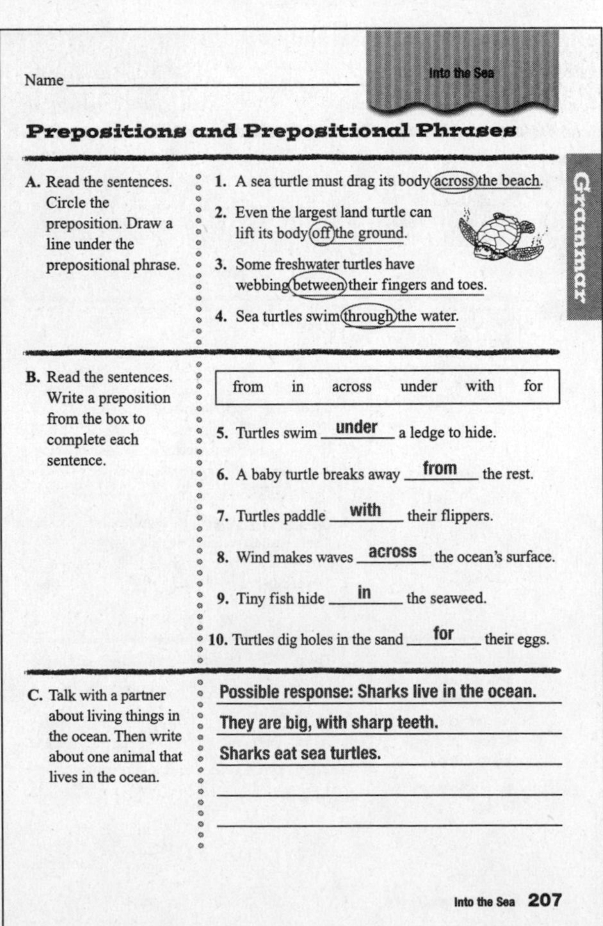

Name____________________ Into the Sea

Prepositions and Prepositional Phrases

Grammar

A. Read the sentences. Circle the preposition. Draw a line under the prepositional phrase.

1. A sea turtle must drag its body (across) the beach.
2. Even the largest land turtle can lift its body (off) the ground.
3. Some freshwater turtles have webbing (between) their fingers and toes.
4. Sea turtles swim (through) the water.

B. Read the sentences. Write a preposition from the box to complete each sentence.

from	in	across	under	with	for

5. Turtles swim **under** a ledge to hide.
6. A baby turtle breaks away **from** the rest.
7. Turtles paddle **with** their flippers.
8. Wind makes waves **across** the ocean's surface.
9. Tiny fish hide **in** the seaweed.
10. Turtles dig holes in the sand **for** their eggs.

C. Talk with a partner about living things in the ocean. Then write about one animal that lives in the ocean.

Possible response: Sharks live in the ocean. They are big, with sharp teeth. Sharks eat sea turtles.

Into the Sea 207

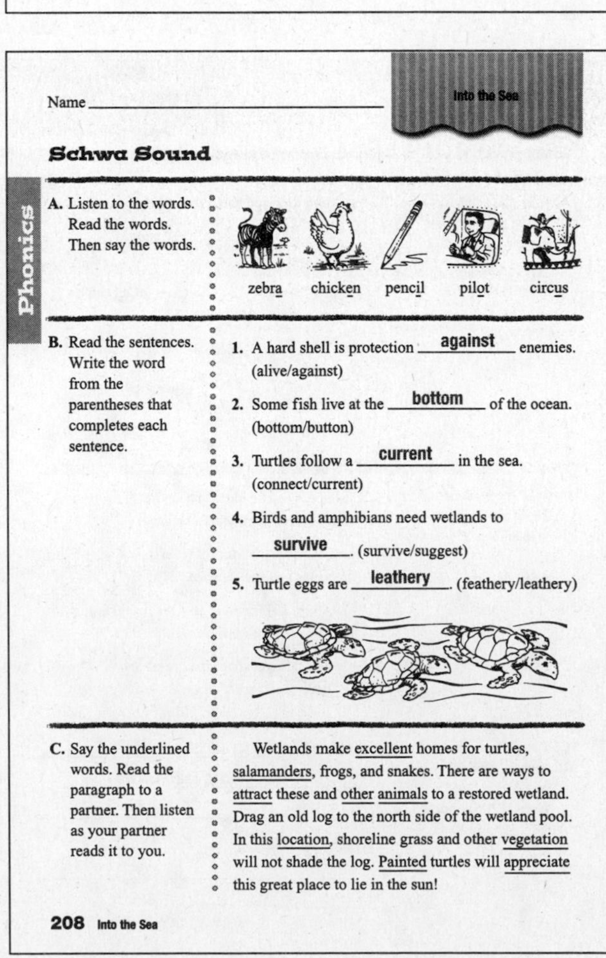

Name____________________ Into the Sea

Schwa Sound

Phonics

A. Listen to the words. Read the words. Then say the words.

zebra — chicken — pencil — pilot — circus

B. Read the sentences. Write the word from the parentheses that completes each sentence.

1. A hard shell is protection **against** enemies. (alive/against)
2. Some fish live at the **bottom** of the ocean. (bottom/button)
3. Turtles follow a **current** in the sea. (connect/current)
4. Birds and amphibians need wetlands to **survive**. (survive/suggest)
5. Turtle eggs are **leathery**. (feathery/leathery)

C. Say the underlined words. Read the paragraph to a partner. Then listen as your partner reads it to you.

Wetlands make excellent homes for turtles, salamanders, frogs, and snakes. There are ways to attract these and other animals to a restored wetland. Drag an old log to the north side of the wetland pool. In this location, shoreline grass and other vegetation will not shade the log. Painted turtles will appreciate this great place to lie in the sun!

208 Into the Sea

Name ____________________

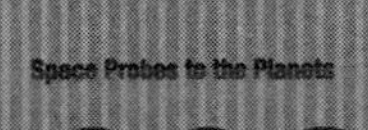

Conjunctions

Grammar

A. Read the sentences. Circle the conjunction in each sentence.

1. Mercury is the closest planet to the sun, (and) it is covered with craters.
2. Venus is the hottest planet, (but) it is not the closest planet to the sun.
3. People can live on Earth, (but) they cannot live on the sun.
4. There may have been life on Mars once, (but) scientists are not sure.

B. Read the sentences. Circle the conjunction that completes each sentence.

5. Jupiter is the fifth planet from the sun, ((and)/because) it is also the largest planet.
6. All the planets spin, (so/(but)) Jupiter spins faster than the others.
7. Three other planets have rings, (because/(yet)) no planet has as many as Saturn.
8. You could read more about one planet, ((or)/for) you could find out more about the entire solar system.

C. Talk with a partner about which planet you would most like to learn more about. Write some questions about this planet.

Possible response:

I would like to learn more about **Mercury**.

Questions: **What are meteorites, and why did they crash into Mercury?**

Name ____________________

Space Probes to the Planets

Syllabication

Phonics

A. Listen to the words. Then say the words. Count the number of syllables that you hear.

unexplored wonderful disappear useless

un•ex•plored **won•der•ful** **dis•ap•pear** **use•less**

B. Read the sentences. Say the underlined words. Count the syllables. Write the number on the line.

1. Space probes have sent back beautiful pictures of Mars. **3**
2. Is it impossible for life to exist on any planet but Earth? **4**
3. Scientists make sure there are no unsafe conditions when launching probes. **2**
4. There is no plan to discontinue launching space probes. **4**

C. Work with a partner. Make new words by adding a syllable from the box. Use one new word in a sentence and write it below.

im	ful	un

wonder **wonderful**

possible **impossible**

care **careful**

safe **unsafe**

broken **unbroken**

Answers will vary.

Name ____________________

Koya's Cousin Del

Review of Sentences and Sentence Punctuation

Grammar

A. Read the sentences. Write a period (.), a question mark (?), or an exclamation point (!) to end each sentence.

1. Koya and her family were at the airport **.**
2. Isn't that somebody famous **?**
3. You forgot to say good evening **.**
4. Your album is great, Del **!**

B. Draw a line to make a sentence.

Subject	Predicate
5. Koya and Loritha	a. missed his family.
6. Del	b. ran over to hug Delbert.
7. A teenage boy	c. were proud of their cousin.
8. Koya	d. wanted his mother to take a picture.

C. Talk with a partner about a special concert you would like to see. Write about it.

I would like to see **Answers will vary.**

Name ____________________

Koya's Cousin Del

Complex Spelling Patterns

Phonics

A. Listen to the words. Read the words. Then say the words.

light

caught

thought

B. Say the underlined words. Then make new words. Follow the spelling patterns.

night	bought	caught
1. f**ight**	4. f**ought**	7. t**aught**
2. t**ight**	5. br**ought**	8. n**aught**y
3. s**ight**	6. th**ought**	9. d**aught**er

C. Write a rhyming word to complete each pair of lines. Read the sentences to your partner.

10. At 7:21, one exciting night, Koya went to meet Del's fl**ight**.
11. The gift that Cousin Del brought was wonderful, Koya th**ought**.
12. Seeing his hometown felt just right. To Del it was a happy s**ight**.

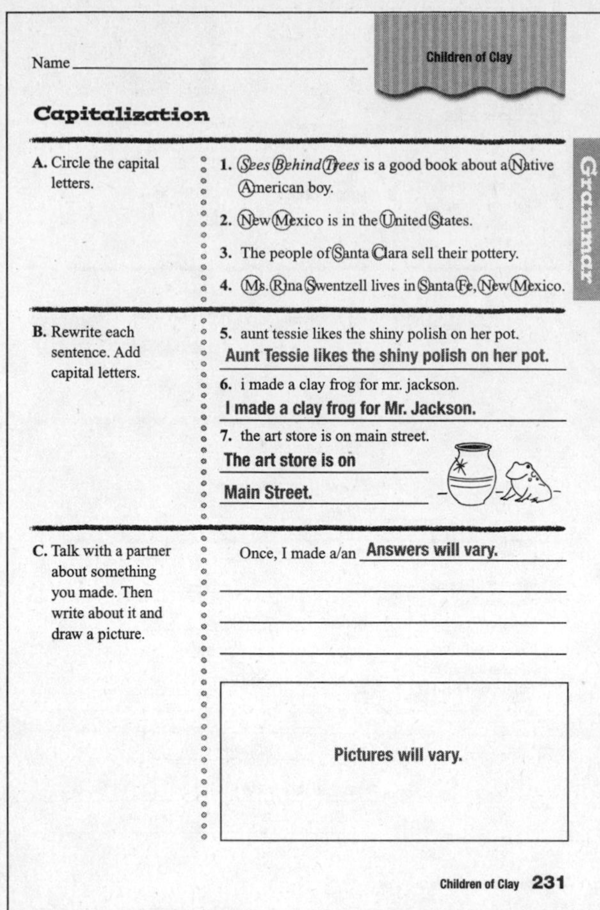
Name ______________________ Children of Clay

Capitalization

Grammar

A. Circle the capital letters.

1. *Sees Behind Trees* is a good book about a Native American boy.
2. New Mexico is in the United States.
3. The people of Santa Clara sell their pottery.
4. Ms. Rina Swentzell lives in Santa Fe, New Mexico.

B. Rewrite each sentence. Add capital letters.

5. aunt tessie likes the shiny polish on her pot.
Aunt Tessie likes the shiny polish on her pot.
6. i made a clay frog for mr. jackson.
I made a clay frog for Mr. Jackson.
7. the art store is on main street.
The art store is on Main Street.

C. Talk with a partner about something you made. Then write about it and draw a picture.

Once, I made a/an **Answers will vary.**

Pictures will vary.

Children of Clay 231

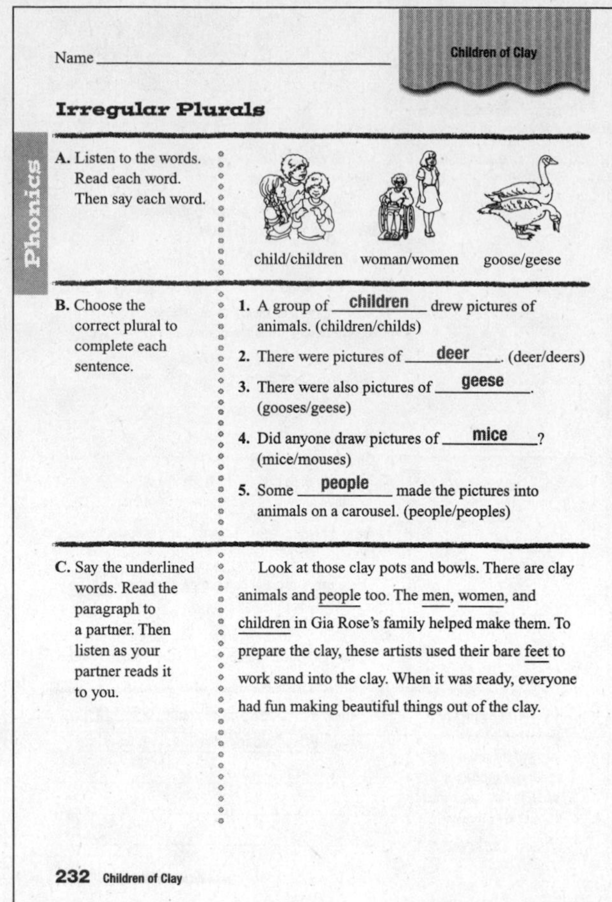
Name ______________________ Children of Clay

Irregular Plurals

Phonics

A. Listen to the words. Read each word. Then say each word.

child/children woman/women goose/geese

B. Choose the correct plural to complete each sentence.

1. A group of **children** drew pictures of animals. (children/childs)
2. There were pictures of **deer**. (deer/deers)
3. There were also pictures of **geese**. (gooses/geese)
4. Did anyone draw pictures of **mice**? (mice/mouses)
5. Some **people** made the pictures into animals on a carousel. (people/peoples)

C. Say the underlined words. Read the paragraph to a partner. Then listen as your partner reads it to you.

Look at those clay pots and bowls. There are clay animals and people too. The men, women, and children in Gia Rose's family helped make them. To prepare the clay, these artists used their bare feet to work sand into the clay. When it was ready, everyone had fun making beautiful things out of the clay.

232 Children of Clay

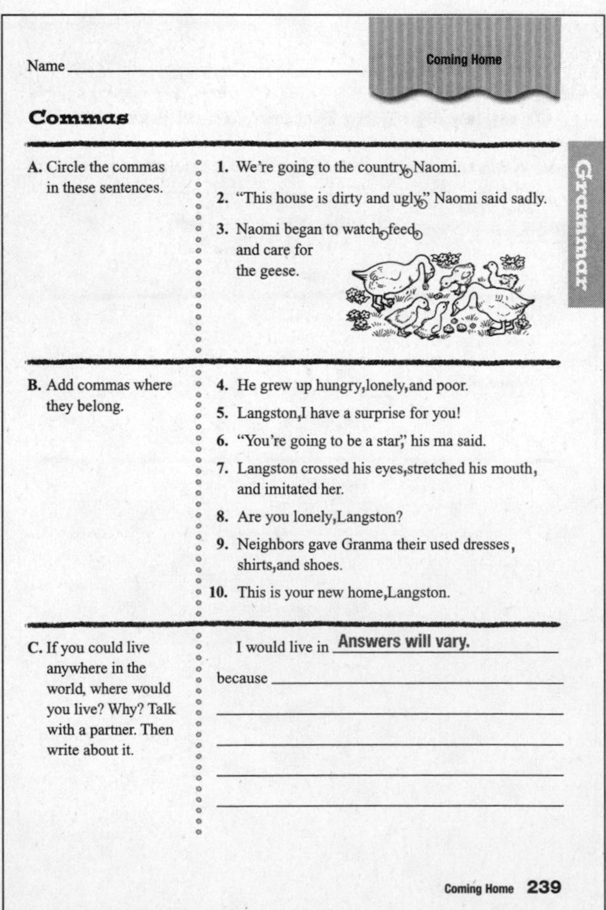
Name ______________________ Coming Home

Commas

Grammar

A. Circle the commas in these sentences.

1. We're going to the country, Naomi.
2. "This house is dirty and ugly," Naomi said sadly.
3. Naomi began to watch, feed, and care for the geese.

B. Add commas where they belong.

4. He grew up hungry, lonely, and poor.
5. Langston, I have a surprise for you!
6. "You're going to be a star," his ma said.
7. Langston crossed his eyes, stretched his mouth, and imitated her.
8. Are you lonely, Langston?
9. Neighbors gave Granma their used dresses, shirts, and shoes.
10. This is your new home, Langston.

C. If you could live anywhere in the world, where would you live? Why? Talk with a partner. Then write about it.

I would live in **Answers will vary.**
because

Coming Home 239

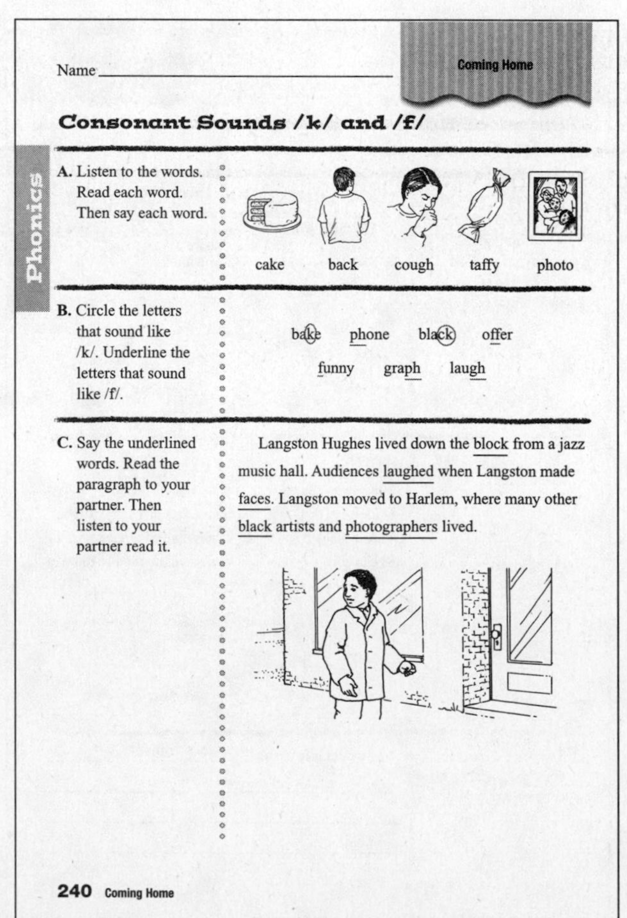
Name ______________________ Coming Home

Consonant Sounds /k/ and /f/

Phonics

A. Listen to the words. Read each word. Then say each word.

cake back cough taffy photo

B. Circle the letters that sound like /k/. Underline the letters that sound like /f/.

bake phone black offer
funny graph laugh

C. Say the underlined words. Read the paragraph to your partner. Then listen to your partner read it.

Langston Hughes lived down the block from a jazz music hall. Audiences laughed when Langston made faces. Langston moved to Harlem, where many other black artists and photographers lived.

240 Coming Home

Name ______________________ Out of the Blue

Quotations and Quotation Marks

Grammar

A. Circle the quotation marks in each sentence.

1. Buffalo Bill's favorite song was "Home on the Range."
2. "Turn off the TV and finish your homework!" my father said.
3. "A penny saved is a penny earned" is a famous saying from *Poor Richard's Almanack*.

B. Add quotation marks where they are needed.

4. Ben Franklin's neighbor asked, "What's all the noise coming from your house?"
5. Ben replied, "I am making a stove."
6. I enjoyed reading "Out of the Blue."
7. *Poor Richard's Almanack* is full of advice, such as "Eat to live, not live to eat."

C. Talk with a partner about Ben Franklin's inventions. Which one do you think is the most important? Write about it.

Possible response:

Franklin's most important invention was **the chair with a fan**

because **I don't like bugs.**

Out of the Blue 247

Name ______________________ Out of the Blue

Suffixes

Phonics

A. Listen to the words. Read each word. Then say each word.

creative electricity circulation deepen extension troublesome invention

B. Add the suffix to make a new word.

1. act + -ive = **active**
2. awe + -some = **awesome**
3. strength + -en = **strengthen**
4. author + -ity = **authority**
5. exhibit + -ion = **exhibition**

C. Say the underlined words. Read the paragraph to a partner. Then listen as your partner reads it to you.

There is an old saying "Necessity is the mother of invention." What does it mean? Think about keeping warm. If you were cold, you might make an invention so you would have heat. Heat is a necessity. Ben Franklin was very creative. He wondered what would happen if he used electricity. Some of his investigations were troublesome. Others were awesome!

248 Out of the Blue

Name ______________________ Chocolate Is Missing

Review of Compound and Complex Sentences

Grammar

A. Listen to the sentences. Say the sentences. Underline the compound sentence. Circle the complex sentence.

1. When we got our class pet, we decided to get a guinea pig.
2. The guinea pig's fur was brown, and we named him Chocolate.

B. Circle the words in parentheses that best complete each sentence.

3. Chocolate was missing, ______________.
   (the cage door was open/and we needed to find him)
4. Did he get out by himself, ______________?
   (or did someone take him/how could he)?
5. When Lila found Chocolate, ______________.
   (but she had babies/everyone was happy)

C. What is the best pet for the classroom? Talk with a partner. Draw a picture of the animal. Write why this is a good pet.

The best pet for the classroom is **Answers will vary.**

Pictures will vary.

Chocolate Is Missing 255

Name ______________________ Chocolate Is Missing

Word Building and Sound Changes

Phonics

A. Listen to the words. Then say the words.

educate/education direct/direction

B. Match each word on the left to its base word on the right.

1. nomination	a. investigate
2. organization	b. interrogate
3. interrogation	c. nominate
4. investigation	d. inform
5. protection	e. organize
6. information	f. protect

C. Say the underlined words. Read the paragraph to a partner. Then listen as your partner reads it to you.

Chocolate was missing, and there was no explanation. With her best friend, Gayle, Lila began an investigation. They made posters that had information about the guinea pig, including a description. They also asked many questions during an interrogation of a classmate. However, it was because of Lila's poor organization of a report that they found the missing class pet.

256 Chocolate Is Missing

Poster 1

A Visit with Grandpa

page 17

List A: The Red Fox
fox, litter, kits, predators, den, danger

List B: A Visit with Grandpa
housework, easy, fence, cook, cry

List C: Words to Know
rumpled, prairie, wrinkled, biscuits, teasing, raisins, dough

Poster 2

Train to Somewhere

page 25

List A: Will Sarah Return?
porch, wagon, sweep, lemonade, sheep

List B: Train to Somewhere
families, conductor, orphans, pretty, feather, ready

List C: Words to Know
misery, couple, adopt, atlas, carriage, platform

Poster 3

Yingtao's New Friend

page 33

<u>List A</u>: Anna's New School
cry, desk, different, blackboards, chalk, glasses

<u>List B</u>: Yingtao's New Friend
conductor, audition, cello, violin, lessons, guest

<u>List C</u>: Words to Know
rehearsal, orchestra, instruments, triangle, measures

Poster 4

Family Pictures

page 41

<u>List A</u>: Painting Mist and Fog
mist, fog, wet, brush, ink, line

<u>List B</u>: Family Pictures
family, artist, grandparents, pick, birthday party, leaves

<u>List C</u>: Words to Know
handkerchief, laundry, inspired, scene, involved, memories, border, future

Poster 5

Addie in Charge

page 49

List A: **Ma on the Prairie**
prairie, letters, relatives, lonesome, trees, smile

List B: **Addie in Charge**
grass, fire, hide, burn, well, ladder

List C: **Words to Know**
billows, tufts, bellows, smarted, crouched

List D: **Merle Builds a Sod House**
sod, plow, blocks, heavy, build, dirt

Poster 6

from The Cricket in Times Square

page 57

List A: **Caught in the Kitchen**
bowl, cream, mice, sugar, spilled, picnic basket

List B: ***from* The Cricket in Times Square**
cricket, country, newsstand, stump, train, city

List C: **Words to Know**
subway, traffic, railroad, venturing, occasion, chirp, melody, furiously

List D: **The Country Mouse and the City Mouse**
travel, crust, feast, cakes, fear, peace

Poster 7

A Big-City Dream

page 65

List A: Super Cooper Scoopers
creek, fish, cleanup, garbage, shovels, trash

List B: A Big-City Dream
lot, neighborhood, garden, corner, fence, soil, proud

List C: Words to Know
padlock, catalog, blisters, celebrate, impressed

Poster 8

I Love Guinea Pigs

page 73

List A: Your Best Friend
feed, groom, owner, relative, wolf, pet

List B: I Love Guinea Pigs
guinea pigs, teeth, hutch, pen, handle

List C: Words to Know
varieties, fond, gnawing, sow, boars

Poster 9

The Swimming Hole

page 81

<u>List A</u>: Ant and Dove
thirsty, pool, danger, bank, barefoot

<u>List B</u>: The Swimming Hole
swimming hole, splashed, path, badger, watch

<u>List C</u>: Words to Know
bristled, shallow, rushes, jointed, naughty, dugout, punish

Poster 10

Komodo Dragons

page 89

<u>List A</u>: Crocodilians
scales, sun, themselves, hiding, nostrils, ripple

<u>List B</u>: Komodo Dragons
komodo dragons, islands, burrows, claws, tongues, eggs

<u>List C</u>: Words to Know
lizards, reptiles, roam, harshest, armor, fierce, prey

<u>List D</u>: Two Uncommon Lizards
uncommon, shape, insects, defense, smooth, length

Poster 11

John Henry

page 97

List A: Welcome to McBroom's Farm
seeds, ground, paint, barn, nearsighted

List B: John Henry
jumped, race, rainbow, buried

List C: Words to Know
shivered, tunnel, boulder, hollered, rhythm, glimpse, horizon

Poster 12

Marven of the Great North Woods

page 105

List A: Winter of the Snowshoe Hare
raced, flying, whistle, hare, chest

List B: Marven of the Great North Woods
bookkeeper, lumberjacks (jacks), beards, in the sack, skis, flu

List C: Words to Know
flapjacks, snowshoes, depot, grizzly, cord

List D: Counting Money
bills, coins, digits, dollar, quarter, penny, dime, nickel

Poster 13

On the Pampas

page 113

List A: Salmon for All
salmon, fox, den, tracks

List B: On the Pampas
cattle, mare, belt, buckle, saddles, nest, foal

List C: Words to Know
corral, manes, bridles, reins, herd, calves, brand, initials

Poster 14

The Storm

page 121

List A: Summer Surfers
surfers, seal, wave, board, pushed, shore

List B: The Storm
thunderstorm, barn, wind, funnel, saved

List C: Words to Know
wail, tornado, accident, coaxed, soothing, nuzzled

List D: Tornado Tales
strange, carried, dropped, frogs, scary

Poster 15

Rikki-Tikki-Tavi

page 129

List A: Another Death on the Ranch
ranch, chicken, pack, snarl, squawk

List B: Rikki-Tikki-Tavi
mongoose, eggs, saved, hole

List C: Words to Know
cobra, coiled, plunged, lame, triumph

Poster 16

Half-Chicken

page 137

List A: Blue Jay Takes the Heat
fire, warm, mean, cold, feathers, pay

List B: Half-Chicken
vane, rooster, wind, hen, chicks

List C: Words to Know
farewells, tangled, uniforms, vain, suggested, flung

Poster 17

Blame It on the Wolf

page 145

List A: Wolves
wolf, wolves, gray, fur, red, slender

List B: Blame It on the Wolf
jury, stage, judge, verdict, trail, twin

List C: Words to Know
character, courtroom, guilty, evidence, rescued

Poster 18

Lou Gehrig: The Luckiest Man

page 153

List A: Cal Ripken, Jr.
stadium, baseball, catcher, team, coach, pitching

List B: Lou Gehrig: The Luckiest Man
citizenship, bat, teammate, umpire, signed, lucky

List C: Words to Know
courageous, immigrants, engineer, convinced, gradually

List D: The Baseball Hall of Fame
display, statues, computer, photo, bases, uniforms

Poster 19

The Disguise

page 161

List A: Korean Food
vegetables, spices, rice, grains, fruits, eggs

List B: The Disguise
alphabet, soldier, jacket, son, secret, swim

List C: Words to Know
cautious, disguise, dangerous, chanting, principal, suspected, recite

Poster 20

Keepers

page 169

List A: One Particular Small, Smart Boy
egg, salt, pocket, giant, squeeze, mud

List B: Keepers
glove, present, birthday, storyteller, antique, chocolates

List C: Words to Know
stroke, reminder, considering, taunted, diamond, grounders, definitely

Poster 21

Amazing Alice!

page 177

<u>List A</u>: Stagecoaches, Then . . . and Now
Westerns, roads, passengers, stagecoach, mail

<u>List B</u>: Amazing Alice!
motorcar, driver, seat, road map, axle, steers

<u>List C</u>: Words to Know
forge, blacksmith, crank, dependable, ravines, telegraph

Poster 22

A Peddler's Dream

page 185

<u>List A</u>: Atlanta's Race
race, marry, challenge, golden, apple, won, lost

<u>List B</u>: A Peddler's Dream
dream, store, clerk, stories, customers, peddler

<u>List C</u>: Words to Know
bound, fortune, trudged, quarters, mission, peddling, purchased

<u>List D</u>: Welcome to the United States
welcome, years, immigrants, Ellis Island, ports of entry, arrived

Poster 23

The Race for the North Pole

page 193

List A: Polar Lands
north, south, pole, ice-covered, frozen, surround

List B: The Race for the North Pole
expedition, Inuit, sledge, survive, supplies, explorer

List C: Words to Know
region, navigate, glaciers, walruses, adventure

Poster 24

Into the Sea

page 201

List A: Saving Our Wetlands
saving, wetlands, swamps, marshes, nursery, migrating

List B: Into the Sea
sea turtle, paddle, dive, floats, underwater, nest, hatch

List C: Words to Know
protection, awkward, flippers, muscles, current, ridges, coral, underside

List D: I Work in the Ocean
photograph, environment, sharks, dolphins, scuba diving, pollution

Poster 29

Out of the Blue

page 241

<u>List A</u>: **Working on the Railroad**
railroad, employer, join, crushed, engine

<u>List B</u>: **Out of the Blue**
argue, ideas, sparks, lightning, kite, key

<u>List C</u>: **Words to Know**
mysterious, almanac, calendar, circulating, inventions, experiment, theory, electricity

Poster 30

Chocolate Is Missing

page 249

<u>List A</u>: **Breakfast with Brede**
scones, horrible, nibbled, frowned, hard

<u>List B</u>: **Chocolate Is Missing**
guinea pig, pet, cage, stolen, escaped, drawer

<u>List C</u>: **Words to Know**
brag, presence, chocolate, poster, angle, approach

Poster 25

Space Probes to the Planets

page 209

List A: Out-of-This-World Rocks
meteorites, comets, planets, space rocks, glassy, solar system

List B: Space Probes to the Planets
circle, moons, clouds, spacesuits, spin, orbit

List C: Words to Know
incredible, atmosphere, probes, spacecraft, craters

Poster 26

Koya's Cousin Del

page 217

List A: Seeds
curb, wedge, watermelon, gripping, dribbles

List B: Koya's Cousin Del
cousin, famous, album, parents, crowd

List C: Words to Know
imitation, performers, auditorium, impatient, applause, microphones, autographs

Poster 27

Children of Clay

page 225

List A: From Drawing to Carousel Critter
drawing, carousel, critter, wizard, deer, foam

List B: Children of Clay
artists, clay, create, designs, shiny, piece

List C: Words to Know
pottery, figures, screens, polish, symbols

List D: Clay Old Woman and Clay Old Man
pots, coils, broken, departed

Poster 28

Coming Home

page 233

List A: Naomi's Geese
geese, country, migrate, city, loons, worried

List B: Coming Home
home, alone, dreams, lawyer, poor, embarrassed

List C: Words to Know
tremble, librarians, dreamer, drifted, heroes, rusty